AF819088

Long March of Islam

The Future Imperfect

Long March of Islam

The Future Imperfect

R.K. Ohri, IPS (Retd.)

Manas Publications
New Delhi - 110002

Manas Publications
(Publishers, Distributors, Importers & Exporters)
4858, Prahlad Street,
24, Ansari Road, Darya Ganj,
New Delhi-110002 (INDIA)
Ph.: 23260783, 23265523
Fax: 011-23272766
E-mail: manaspublications@vsnl.com

©RK Ohri, IPS (Retd.)

2004

ISBN 81-7049-186-X
Rs 695/-

No part of this book can be reproduced, stored in a retrieval system, or transmitted in any form, by any means, including mechanical, electronic, photocopying, recording, or otherwise, without prior written permission of the publisher.

The views expressed in this book are those of the author and not necessarily of the publisher. The publisher is not responsible for the views of the author and authenticity of the data, in any way whatsoever.

Typeset at
Manas Publications

Printed in India at
Nice Printing Press
and Published by Mrs Suman Lata for
Manas Publications, 4858, Prahlad Street,
24, Ansari Road, Darya Ganj,
New Delhi - 110 002 (INDIA)

Dedicated to

My Sweet Grand Daughters,

Saloni and Jaisal

and

My Soulmate, Pushpa.

Foreword

Political Islam has gone broadly unchallenged, mainly as a consequence of the tyranny of political correctness that has tended to prohibit critical discourse on the less savoury aspects of all religions, and particularly of Islam, virtually through the last century. The disastrous consequences of this neglect are now manifested in the increasing radicalisation of this ideology, and its assertion through an assortment of Islamist terrorist movements projected by their principals as *jihad*.

The events of September 11, 2001 have, in some measure, brought focus on the dangers of this ideology and its physical manifestations in terrorism worldwide. The global response has, however, centred overwhelmingly on neutralizing these manifestations alone–the terrorist groups that constitute immediate and direct threats to individual and state security. An ideological response to the rising tide of Islamist terrorism is yet to emerge in significant measure.

Nevertheless, a discourse that was entirely stagnant has at least begun to produce new ripples, though most of these are the result of pebbles thrown into the pool from the outside. In the absence of a vigorous intellectual movement within Islam which could confront the violent dogma of extremist political Islam, it has increasingly become incumbent upon voices within the victim societies that have been targeted by the terrorist *jihad*, to question the ideological underpinnings of this vast and violent movement.

This alone cannot suffice. Eventually, the ideology of extremist Islam will have to be challenged and neutralized from within the community of Islam, for its roots lie in a particular interpretation of the Faith and cannot effectively be challenged from the outside. Nevertheless, commentaries and critiques from those who do not share the Faith can be expected to catalyse a defence of its core, and provoke a greater critical effort within the Muslim community.

India has been one of the prime victims of Islamist terrorism, harnessed by Pakistan to mobilize a steady supply of violent cadres from as many as 18 countries, who were seduced by this vaunting ideology of world domination. Much has been written about this 'proxy war', unleashed by Pakistan against India, and sustained for nearly a decade and a half now. Little attention has, however, been paid to the centrality of the ideology of extremist political Islamism in mobilizing and maintaining the continuous flow of the Pakistan sponsored '*mujahideen*', who have brought death to thousands on the Indian soil.

Any effort to understand the dynamics that has led to this immense ideological mobilization necessarily takes us back to the very birth of Pakistan. Indeed, they go back to the birth of the *idea* of Pakistan that led to India's violent Partition, and beyond, to the sub-continent's turbulent history, which shaped the structure of communities and communal mindsets in the region over the centuries. An exclusive focus on contemporary Islamist terrorism in the sub-continent would fail to explain the deep and unrelenting animus against the idea of India that has established itself at the very core of the Pakistani identity. It would fail, equally, to provide realistic solutions to ongoing conflicts, since all efforts at resolution would ignore the essential causal mechanisms that sustain these.

R.K. Ohri's *Long March of Islam* is an effort at such an analysis. It provides a particular perspective on the ongoing campaigns of Islamist terrorism, locating these in history, and particularly the history of the subcontinent, and, crucially, in particular trends of demography which have been decisive in the past, and threaten to be critical in determining the course of its future as well.

Ohri has served in the Indian Police Service, and his career has given him wide opportunities to observe closely both the positive and negative character of relations between communities in this country. His perspectives challenge the deafening silence that has long been established by the tyranny of the politically correct, and will variously provoke interest, antagonism, curiosity, resentment, agreement and violent disagreement. They will, hopefully, also trigger some systematic responses and elaborations, which will take the debate further, towards the rationalisation of a discourse that has long remained mired in unshakable dogma, on the one hand, and in Panglossian neglect, on the other.

K.P.S Gill

Acknowledgments

This book has now been in writing for more than sixteen months. It would have been virtually impossible to complete this manuscript without the help of many well wishers and friends to whom I owe a debt of gratitude.

The inspiration for writing on the subject came from my daughter, Shivani, a great book lover who always tries to keep abreast of all that goes on across the globe. Occasionally during our frequent exchange of ideas on topical subjects, especially certain aspects of the dynamics of demography and Huntington's thesis of clash of civilizations, we held different opinions. It was, however, Shivani who encouraged me most to undertake this difficult venture. She plied me with books, magazines, more books, more ideas and that made me take the plunge.

But Shivani is a Mumbaikar, while I am based in Delhi. Therefore, once in a while communication would become a problem. And that is where my dear friend, Krishan Diesh, a very well read wisecrack, stepped in to help me out. Frankly, I used Krishan far too often, almost for one year, as a sounding board for testing and cross checking many concepts and some of my ideas. We discussed and talked about the long term implications of Islamist terror in the context of demographic changes, especially for India, over dozens of cups of cappuccino. Krishan's critical comments on certain historical aspects of Islam's long march have been of great help.

My special thanks are due to T.J. Sriraman for editing the manuscript and making invaluable suggestions for adding another chapter and updating some others. I was truly impressed by his deep knowledge of the subject and am grateful to him for sparing so much time for my book.

I must also thank Neeraj Kumar, Joint Commissioner of Police, and his deputy Ashok Chand, both of Delhi Police, for furnishing useful information and promptly responding to my short notice requests. They have helped me in updating the details of the horrendous attack on the Indian Parliament on December 13, 2001, and putting together the two Appendices.

Lastly I must thank my wife, Pushpa, for bravely putting up with my disorganized work schedule, late hours and the mess in which she often found my room while I worked on the manuscript. She gracefully tolerated all that with a smile and always encouraged me to meet the difficult deadlines. But for her committed support I could not have progressed thus far.

RK Ohri

Introduction

Terrorism has been playing havoc with the civilized world now for several years. It has already taken a heavy toll of life and property in dozens of countries and threatens to undermine and destroy all civilizational norms, democratic institutions and pluralistic societies. Islamist terror derives sustenance from the controversial doctrine of jihad enunciated by Prophet Muhammad in the medieval times. The Jihadi fervour, especially among the young educated Muslims, has now been on a roll for several decades across the globe. What is more disturbing is that the malaise of Islamist terror is growing phenomenally. Unfortunately most of us have become helpless spectators to the frequent bouts of suicide bombings and senseless raw violence committed day in and day out by the purveyors of terror. Perhaps the civil society was never so helpless as it has been during the last ten years.

There were many imperatives for undertaking this study, but the major provocations were two. First, the September 11, 2001 attack on the twin towers of New York which took a heavy toll of human life and shocked the civilized world. And second, the audacious attack on the Indian Parliament, barely three months later, on December 13, 2001, which had the potential of wiping out almost the entire political leadership of India. These two events, frozen till date in my memory, awakened me to the rising sound of the footfalls of Islam's long march. In writing this tract I have made use of certain empirical conclusions arrived at by the well known author, Samuel Huntington, whose research on the clash of civilizations in early 1990s gave a wake up call to the civil society about the growing menace of Islamist terror. An earlier alert sounded by Sir Vidia Naipaul in early 1980s through his celebrated tome, *Among the Believers : An Islamic Journey*, somehow did not register much with the world community.

This book, though formally rooted in the present, is essentially about tomorrow and the day after. The intention is to forewarn the civil society about the long march of Islam which is turbo-driven by the increasing percentage of Muslim population in many countries and regions and their growing numbers worldwide. As explained in the two chapters on demographic developments, the population of Muslims is increasing at a fast pace, almost exponentially, both in the Islamic and the non-Islamic countries. Our past experience shows that any far-reaching changes in the religious composition of a country have the potential of triggering major faultline conflicts, especially where the Muslims happen to be the community gaining in population. Because of Islam's divisive postulates of Dar-ul Islam (the land of peace where Islam rules) and the Dar-ul Harb (the land of conflict where Islamic rule needs to be established), all such demographic changes have the potential of destabilizing the concerned nation-states due to the likely clamour by Muslims for secession from the parent country. Another important factor promoting the secessionist trait in the Muslim societies is the concept of 'ummah' which transcends the ideal of nation-state and coalesces the entire fraternity of Muslims worldwide into one single entity, "the Nation of Islam", as opposed to "the Nation of Kufr" which comprises the rest of the world, i.e., the infidels. It has been experienced that as soon as the percentage of Muslims in any country reaches the benchmark of 30-40 per cent of the total population, frequent faultline conflicts start erupting which often culminate in violent secessionist wars. Some classical examples of this phenomenon are the partition of India in 1947, the Greco-Turkish stand off over Cyprus, the civil war in Lebanon, the separatist terrorism in Chechenya, Jammu & Kashmir and the Philippines and the ugly bloodbath in Kosovo and Bosnia. Historically Islam has always been a clash and conquest oriented religion, though the word 'Islam' does mean 'peace'. The concept of jihad which forms core of the Islamic faith lies at the root of the hostility of Muslim societies towards neighbouring civilizations. The importance of jihad for Muslims has been succinctly summed up by the well known journalist and author, M.J. Akbar, who calls it "the signature tune" of Islamic history. As claimed somewhat proudly by a Pakistani scholar, Akbar S. Ahmed, in his book *Islam under Siege*, even today Muslims are at war with every civilization, every religion of the world. Possibly in the coming decades the Indian sub-continent and many other regions of the world could become major theatres of religion-based faultline conflicts.

The growing threat of Islamist terror has acquired a massive reach starting with the U.S.A. through the Europe (notably the Balkans), Chechenya (Russia), countries of the Maghreb and North Africa, Iraq, Syria, Iran, Afghanistan, Pakistan, India (especially the state of Jammu and Kashmir), Bangladesh and Indonesia, extending right upto the Philippines. During the Afghan campaign of 2001 the U.S. forces had captured more than 760 jihadi warriors belonging to 42 countries of whom 600 are still held for interrogation at the Guantonamo Bay Naval Base camp. Evidently the contagion of Islamist terror has already spread to at least fortytwo countries, if not more.

Radical Islam has been on a long march since the creation of Pakistan in 1947. Allama Iqbal, a celebrated Urdu poet and author of the popular song, "*Saare jahan se accha Hindustan hamara*", was the idealogue of Pakistan. He also played a major role in promoting the pan-Islamic movement in a bid to restore the lost grandeur of Islam through his soul-stirring *magnum opus* "Shikwa" (the Lament) and another poetic composition *"Tarana",* which is a jingoistic one, laying claim to China and India on behalf of Islam. Iqbal's *Tarana* has been very popular with the hordes of jihadis being trained in the Pakistan-occupied Kashmir and terror-training camps of Pakistan. It is also a compulsory 'must-read' gospel prescribed for the students of government schools upto class V in Pakistan who are also expected to give talks on the importance of "jihad" and understand the differences between the Muslims and the Hindus. Thus the government of Pakistan has been indoctrinating the young minds during the very first five years of schooling in the idealogy of jihad against the infidels. This devious mode of poisoning the young minds of Pakistani children, though widely known to well informed Indians, was finally confirmed in June 2003 in an article by the well known columnist of Pakistan, Ardeshir Cowasjee. That clearly shows the highest level of official priority accorded by the Pakistani rulers to the jihadist campaign against the infidels, especially the Hindus.

Iqbal's 'Shikwa' was translated into Arabic by Effendi and then into several other languages, including the Indonesian Bhasa, to spread the message of militant Islam. It has been winning converts to the Islamist cause now for almost fifty years. The state of Pakistan was born through enormous bloodletting in the sub-continent, virtually by a gory caesarean, resulting from the rabid call for 'jihad' given by the Muslim League in August 1946 through a printed proclamation, first circulated in Calcutta (now Kolkata, in West Bengal), a few days before the Direct Action Day.

The Pakistani army and the ISI have played a pivotal role in promoting radical Islam by training thousands of jihadis whom they started infiltrating into Kashmir as early as 1965. The general impression, created by the repetitive chants of political analysts, that Islamic terrorism is a post-Laden phenomenon, is altogether incorrect. The strategy to destabilise Kashmir for debilitating the Indian nation through terror tactics by training ten thousand jihadis had been discussed in a high level meeting of the Pakistani establishment in August 1953. A suggestion to this effect had been made by Chaudhri Ghulam Abbas, a former President of the so-called Azad Kashmir. After skilful fine-tuning, the strategy was deftly implemented in the state of Jammu & Kashmir in mid 1960s, i.e., several years before bin Laden appeared on the Islamic screen. When Russia occupied Afghanistan in 1979, the same strategy was successfully sold by Pakistan to the Saudis and the CIA for winning the Afghan war. Several billion dollars were extracted from the CIA and the Saudi government for waging jihad against the Russians. And the strategy succeeded superbly, thanks to the massive funding by the CIA and the Saudis.

Osama bin Laden was essentially an occasion-produced leader, though he certainly possesses tremendous courage, charisma and organising ability. Yet without the total support of the ISI and

Pakistani army he could not have achieved much – certainly not the kind of success and the name which he now has. The terror tactics being used by the Islamist outfits bear the unmistakable stamp of the ISI and the Pakistani army who indoctrinated and trained jihadi hordes in hundreds of thousands. Charisma and the enormous zeal for waging holy war to spread the faith of Prophet Muhammad were bin Laden's main contribution to the long march of jihadist Islam.

The consequences of Islamic militancy for the civil society, especially the future generations, could be very damaging. It is infinitely more dangerous and deeply rooted than the Nazi idealogy or communism neither of which had the support of a religion-based one billion strong following across the globe, nor could they promote the cult of mass murders and suicide bombings. The Nazis, even in their heydays, just could not promote the fanatical zeal of the kind displayed by the jihadist storm troopers.

Interestingly the two nation theory about which endless columns have been written by the Indian litterati and which is incessantly talked about in the drawing rooms of India's capital, New Delhi, was neither the invention of Mohammed Ali Jinnah nor Veer Savarkar. The concept of two separate nations has its roots in the rigid orthopraxy of Islam which bifurcates the world into two compartments: Dar-ul Islam (the land of peace) and Dar-ul Harb (the land of conflict) which are in perpetual conflict. Even Louis Farrakhan, that fiery leader of America's Black Muslim movement, calls it the 'Nation of Islam' – an entity altogether different from the American nation. As pointed out by Pendrel Moon in his book, *Divide and Quit*, Sir Syed Ahmed Khan, the founder of the Aligarh Muslim University, was the first Indian to propound the thesis that the Hindus and the Muslims were two different nations due to which reason, after the departure of the British, India will have to be partitioned into two countries. Obviously for arriving at that conclusion Sir Syed Ahmed had taken inspiration from the divisive idealogy of Islamic scriptures wherein the concepts of Dar-ul Islam and Dar-ul Harb have been expounded with considerable clarity and finality. It has been the refrain of Muslim leadership worldwide now for over eighty years, right from Sir Syed Ahmed to Allama Iqbal to Rehmat Ali and onwards to Alija Izetbegovitch (the idealogue of the Muslim nation of Bosnia), that Muslims are a separate nation with a different cultural identity. Therefore they cannot live peaceably with other religious groups. This doctrinaire belief, widely prevalent among the Muslims of both Islamic and non-Islamic countries, is the single most important cause of the present civilizational conflict.

One of the most important events of the twentieth century was the stupendous increase in the population of Muslims worldwide, almost unprecedented in the history of mankind. And the increase is still continuing. Muslims are likely to constitute 30 percent or more of the total world population by the year 2025 A.D. A huge worldwide flow of youthful Muslims is likely to burst across the globe during the next 2 to 5 decades. In all probability, this massive increase in Muslim numbers will continue into the next millenium. That could spell a defining increase in the population of Muslims worldwide. If this trend of sharp growth of Muslims continues into the next millenium, it will have the potential of changing the course of human history. The reasons for the exceptionally high fertility rates of Muslim societies are three: non-acceptance of the small family norm on religious grounds; non-emancipation of the Muslim women; and the scriptural sanction for multiple wives, though not more than four at one time. Intensive proselytizing activities of the Tablighi Jamaat are another important reason. Some examples of high Muslim fertility rates are : Yemen multiplying on a fertility rate of 7 children per woman, Saudi Arabia 6.15, Afghanistan 5.6, Nigeria 5.4, Pakistan 4.1 and so on. In sharp contrast, the fertility rates of European countries are very low, ranging between 1.20 and 1.50. Most of the European countries have a trend of declining populations. Russia is already trapped in a depopulation crisis – comically dubbed as the "do it yourself genocide". The last thirty years have seen large scale influx of Muslims into a number of countries and regions, e.g., the U.S.A., the Europe and India (from Bangladesh) due to their sharply growing population. The situation has been compounded by the appalling indifference of many soft states, including India, to the growing avalanche of illegal Muslim immigrants.

Several regions of the world like the Middle East, the Europe, the Indian sub-continent and Russia are likely to face growing religion-based faultline conflicts because of the sharp upswing in Muslim populations and their influx into the neighbouring countries and regions in search of pastures greener. The population of almost every European country is in a declining mode resulting in rapidly declining numbers of indigenous Christian citizens. Even India has a declining fertility rate of 2.91, while Pakistan and Bangladesh have fertility rates of 4.1 and 3.2 respectively. The population growth rate of India is 1.47 percent as against 2.1 per cent of Pakistan and Bangladesh. Within the Indian Union the growth rate of Muslims is nearly one-and-a-half times higher than that of the Hindus, Sikhs and Buddhists, counted together. There has been a silent invasion of Muslim migrants from the Islamic-majority countries and regions into non-Muslim countries during the last thirty years. With the increasing pressure of the sharp growth in the Muslim numbers, the population profiles of many countries, including India, are bound to undergo radical changes in the coming decades. For that reason India and many other countries are likely to face more religion-based conflicts.

The Muslim societies and their radical leaders have become highly conscious of their higher population growth. The Islamists are jubilant on this score because they hope to overwhelm the world through sheer force of growing numbers in due course of time, may be within the next few decades. The massive growth in Muslim numbers in the Middle East and North African nations like Egypt, Syria, Iraq, Sudan and countries of the Maghreb is already impacting Europe. It is visibly reflected in the growing presence of large numbers of Muslims in the Balkans, France, Italy, Germany, Netherlands and the U.K. Their dramatic growth can be seen all over the Europe. India, too, is being flooded by the growing influx of Bangla Muslims who have overwhelmed many districts of Assam, Meghalaya and West Bengal and whose growing presence in large clusters is visible in scores of Indian cities.

Due to this unprecedented increase in the population of Muslims, both in the Muslim and non-Muslim countries, four regions of the world are under acute Islamist pressure: the West Asia where Israel has remained in constant embattlement with Palestinian terror groups, aided by neighbouring Muslim countries ; the Balkans and the Western

Europe where Christian population is in a tailspin and the heavy out-migration from North Africa and the Middle East towards Europe threatens to overwhelm the Christian Europe; the Indian sub-continent where the aggregate Muslim population of Pakistan, Bangladesh, and India is likely to outgrow the total non-Muslim population of the Indian Republic by the year 2061, or even earlier; and the depopulating Russia which has a vulnerable soft underbelly dotted with a number of Muslim countries having higher population growth and where the militant Islam is in an ascendant mode.

In percentage terms the population of Hindus in India has been declining now continuously for the last 110 years. After partition of the country in 1947 this trend has gathered more speed. In percentage terms, during 1981-91 the Muslims grew at a rate nearly one-and-a half times compared to that of the Hindus, Sikhs and Buddhists, counted together.

The growing population invariably needs extra space, additional economic opportunities for earning livelihood, greater say in the affairs of the concerned country and also in the world affairs. It generates religion-based tensions and creates new cultural schisms. The changed religious profile of a country's population has often led to eruption of civil strifes of the kind experienced in Lebanon in the Middle East, Kosovo and Bosnia in the Europe and Chechenya in Russia. The Muslim majority province of Chechenya has been causing serious concern to the Russian people because of its high population growth, while the rest of Russia is trapped in a freefall of population.

Within the Indian Republic the rising percentage of the Muslim population and a corresponding percentage decline in the aggregate population of the Hindus, Sikhs and Buddhists has the potential of escalating the religion-based faultline conflicts. The dice of demography is heavily loaded against the Hindus, the Sikhs and the Buddhists. At this rate, the Indian civilization could ultimately head for a Lebanon-like situation where Muslims outpaced Christian numbers within six to seven decades and Lebanon became a Muslim majority nation by 1970-75, amidst a raging civil war. A repeat of that kind of tragic scenario in India could take a little longer, but the contours of a latent threat are already visible. In Lebanon, the

Christians who formed a whopping 77 percent of Lebanon's population in the year 1900, were reduced to 35 percent by 1975. Similarly in the Balkans, Kosovo and Bosnia were converted into Muslim majority territories within a few decades. A fate similar to that of Bosnia might overtake Macedonia during the next three to four decades, or even earlier.

India, too, might face major religion-based faultline conflicts or civil war like conditions, triggered by demographic changes, say in another 30 to 40 years – just as Lebanon and Bosnia had. Ultimately after one hundred years or so, even certain parts of India could follow the trend set by Lebanon, Kosovo and Bosnia. What should cause greater concern is that a massive upheaval resulting from the drastic demographic changes, could plunge the Indian nation in a civil strife of the kind witnessed in the Balkans where roughly 15 percent of the total population was displaced and forced to move out to save their lives. Pushed to the wall by climactic demographic changes, India could even break up into a number of States in accordance with the changed religious configuration of different areas. We have seen how the Muslim state of Bosnia was born in the Balkans after a massive bloodbath. In India the presence of three crore Bangla Muslims and their progeny could act as a trigger for the balkanization of the country, perhaps starting with certain districts of Assam and West Bengal.

Historically, Muslim populations have a high propensity to secede from their parent countries. It springs from the concept of 'ummah' which transcends the ideal of nation-state. As soon as the percentage of Muslims reaches the benchmark of 30 to 40 percent in any country, large scale faultline conflicts start erupting and the battle cry of jihad is raised which often results in violent secessionist wars. Some classic examples of this phenomenon are the partition of India in 1947, the Greco-Turkish dispute over Cyprus, the civil war in Lebanon, the separatist insurgency in Chechenya and the Philippines, and the bloody civil strife in Kosovo and Bosnia.

Within the next few decades there could be a further increase in faultline conflicts between the Hindus and the Muslims in India. The intensity of such religion-based clashes could be very high because of the persecution suffered by the Hindus during the Muslim rule. As and when the Muslim percentage in certain regions or States of India approaches the benchmark of 30-40 percent, the problem could become more acute. Again, say around 2040 or 2050 A.D., when combined population of the Hindus and Muslims in the sub-continent could be more than 2.5 billions, the sheer size of the absolute numbers of the two communities getting involved in a civil strife could spell a human disaster of unimagineable magnitude. That grim possibility should be a cause for concern at least to the saner leadership of the two communities.

Islamists have already declared jihad against the U.S.A., Israel and India since 1998 and these three nations are on their hit list. Powered by the concept of 'ummah', today Islam is the biggest union of nearly 60 countries comprising almost 1.2 billion Muslims worldwide. Islam being a religion demanding transnational loyalty, even beyond allegiance to the motherland, the Islamists are able to enlist support for their cause across the globe. The Islamic 'ummah' is like a multinational corporation, flush with petro funds, 57 member countries and more than 1.2 billion members – call them shareholders if you will. The Muslims are not bound by the concept of loyalty to their motherland. Their only loyalty is to their religion and 'ummah', i.e., to their co-religionists anywhere in the world. That being the reality no single country can face the Islamist terror effectively. In medieval times only a coalition of Christian kings could prevent the jihadi warriors of Islam from overrunning the Europe. The Islamic armies were routed convincingly in 732 A.D. in the battle of Tours-Poitiers (France) and in 1683 at Vienna (Austria), the latter being the seat of the rich and powerful Hapsburg rulers. In sharp contrast, the Persian civilization was decimated and Hinduism badly battered and bruised because neither the Persians nor Hindus could understand the unique bonding of ummah and the resolve of jihadi warriors to destroy all neighbouring civilizations.

By undertaking this study I have tried to project the hidden threat which is likely to confront the Indian people tomorrow and the day after. It is time for the national leadership to wake up to the twin threats of the violent terrorism of radical Islam reflected in its long march and the likely adverse consequences of the dynamics of demography on the future of Indian nation. There is a prima facie need for evolving a pragmatic population policy which should be reviewed every five years by taking into account the manpower needs of the defence services, the national targets of economic growth and the need to meet any adverse geopolitical developments. The Indian people must avoid getting trapped in the Russian-style "do it yourself genocide" crisis.

Unlike dictatorships, democracies are governed by the numbers game called elections, based on universal franchise – the principle of one-person-one-vote. If the present demographic trends continue, there might be large scale religion-based faultline conflicts in India, and perhaps in the entire sub-continent within the next three to four decades. The hostility between the two major communities is already growing at a fast clip and communal clashes are increasing.

As spelt out by Bernard Lewis, once Islam becomes a majority religion in any country that nation is likely to be taken over by the radical Islamists. Votes may be cast and counted only once. Thereafter democracy might just disappear and an Islamic caliphate or dictatorship established, just like most other Islamic countries. There is no tradition of democracy in Muslim majority countries – perhaps there could never be unless Islam sheds its dogmas and intolerance. Thus the danger to the future of Indian democracy and our pluralistic secular order could be both immense and imminent.

The Author

Contents

1

Challenge of Terror

"It is the day of the bad boys running wild."
— A line from the Rockers Scorpion.

The world is in turmoil. After America's two successive high voltage military campaigns against Afghanistan and Iraq, both Muslim countries, in a bold bid to stem the rising tide of Islamic militancy, there is rampant rage across the Islamic street. The October 2001 war against the Taliban-ruled Afghanistan, code named 'Operation Enduring Freedom' was a direct consequence of the Al Qaeda's attack on the World Trade Centre and the Pentagon headquarters in the U.S.A. on September 11, 2001. However, the attack on Iraq was believed to have been occasioned by the widespread fear that Iraq's Baathist ruler, Saddam Hussein, was producing and stockpiling weapons of mass destruction. But the attack on Iraq, if seen in the backdrop of the U.S. decision to withdraw its troops from Saudi Arabia, may be viewed as part of a grand strategy evolved by the ascendant policy-making group of neo-conservatives to protect America's global interests. And if we add to these millitary campaigns of considerable geo-political significance, the recent warnings given by the U.S. establishment to Iran to desist from following its nuclear programme, we might be able to assess the high degree of angst among Islamic nations against America and the world coalition against terror. Should the spat between the U.S.A. and the fundamentalist Shia regime in Iran result in another armed conflict in future, it will cause a huge groundswell of hostility against the West in the Islamic world. Post September 11, 2001, the famously controversial analysis of the ongoing faultline conflicts by the Harvard Professor Samuel Huntington, in his acclaimed book *Clash Of Civilizations and the Remaking of World Order* has drawn compelling attention of political scientists, intellectuals and scholars across the world to the growing threat of Islamist terrorism. Like a catastrophe foretold, slowly but surely, the prophesy made by Huntington appears to be coming true. Huntington has classified the conflicts facing the mankind broadly under four categories, namely

(i) the conflicts between monarchs and rulers which occurred in the past, largely occasioned either by the territorial ambitions of the kings, or motivated by economic gains;

(ii) the conflicts between nation-states which started occurring after the French Revolution, when the concept of nation-state became universally popular;

(iii) conflicts between competing idealogies like communism, fascism, democratic liberalism, etc., which were caused by desire of the respective protagonists to improve their ideological base, as happened during the times of cold war; and

(iv) the conflicts between civilizations which are likely to increase in frequency and would continue to dominate the geo-political scene in the coming years.

According to Huntington, during the cold war era nations or countries were described largely in terms of their political, economic, and technological progress. The standard terminology used for classification was the developed or developing countries or the first, second and third world countries. He feels that in today's world, nations should be classified in terms of their culture and civilization because these two components of our social milieu have always played an important role in the history and progress of mankind. Huntington argues that the western civilization, which has been dominating the modern world, has been losing its prime position after the end of the cold war era and lately the centre of gravity has been shifting in favour of non-Western civilizations. This change has altered the political equations due to which non-western civilizations, which had earlier been subjugated by the western regimes, have become more active and might even become dominant players in the foreseeable future. Every civilization is based on certain cultural values, religion, language, history, customs, social institutions plus certain objective factors, e.g., the manner in which the people belonging to that civilization define themselves, or relate to their reference group. Civilization and culture both refer to the overall way of life of a people, and a civilization is a culture writ large.[1] Throughout the history of mankind, religion has been a defining characteristic of all civilizations. It has always been an important component of every culture. In a nutshell, every civilization is like a broad stream of homogenous cultural entity with which a group of people identify themselves. Virtually all the major civilizations in the world in the twentieth century either have existed for a millenium or, as with Latin America, are the immediate offspring of another long-lived civilization. Huntington emphasizes that while civilizations endure, they also evolve. By virtue of being dynamic, they rise and fall and merge and divide. Civilizations also disappear and get buried in the sands of time. At present, broadly speaking, there are eight major civilizations in the world. Huntington has listed these as the Western, the Slavic, the Sinic (i.e., the Sino-Confucian), the Japanese, the Hindu, the Latin American, the Islamic, and the African. He does not include the Jewish civilization in this list, because in terms of numbers, Judaism is not a major civilzation although with the creation of Israel, Jews have acquired all necessary features of a civilization: religion, language, customs, literature, institutions, and a territorial and political home.[2] But Huntington's premise to overlook the Jewish civilization because of their small numbers is somewhat flawed and unacceptable. It would be most unfair to exclude Judaism from the list of contemporary civilizations if we consider the excellence achieved by the Jews in the fields of science, arts and culture throughout history and their enormous contribution to the world civilization. In terms of antiquity, Judaism is older both to Christianity and Islam and looking at the dour manner in which Israel has defended itself against terror attacks of Palestinian groups, backed by radical Islam, shows that it cannot be ignored or written off. Despite long spells of persecution, the Jewish civilization has displayed high visibility and a strong survival instinct throughout history. It is well known that Jews have bagged a very large number of Nobel prizes in science, arts and literature and achieved many other intellectual distinctions – quite disproportionately in excess of the percentage of their population numbers.

On the basis of the recent world history of wars and violent clashes, which he calls 'faultline conflicts', Huntington zeroes on the Islam as the most militant and clash-prone civilization. In reaching this conclusion he has cited the examples of the Afghan and Gulf wars, the recent Bosnian war between the Serbs and the Muslims, the long festering conflict between Turkey and Greece over Cyprus and several religious clashes between the sub-nation states of the former U.S.S.R. many of which are now independent countries. If one looks at the long list of the current 'faultline conflicts', a new terminology used by Huntington, starting from the Balkans in the Europe and then running through North Africa, the Middle East, Central Asia, South East Asia and thence to the South Pacific, one does realize that a number of Islamic nations are caught in the throes of violent clashes and are engaged in wars with their neighbouring civilizations. And that scenario reinforces Huntington's analysis. The historical evolution of the faultline conflicts between the Islamic and the Christian civilizations could be traced to the attempts of Islam in the eighth century to conquer Europe. That made the European kings close their ranks and culminated in the launching of a series of crusades by the Christian Europe in the eleventh century to wrest back the holy city of Jerusalem. It was the beginning of the centuries-old faultline wars between the two civilizations.

On the basis of several empirical studies, Huntington has identified Islamic civilization to be the most violence-prone. He concludes that as a rule, Islamic societies have a relatively higher propensity to take recourse to violence for solving the crisis and conflict situations facing them. Between 1928 and 1979, Muslim countries used violence to resolve their problems in 76 instances of crises out of a total of 142 in which they were involved. In almost fifty percent cases violence was the primary method of dealing with the crises, and in 41 percent instances they resorted to full scale war.[3]

As a rule Muslim societies are more militarized, both in terms of hardware and manpower, than other societies. Muslim bellicosity and violence are facts of late twentieth century which neither Muslims nor non-Muslims can deny[4].

In support of his conclusions, Huntington has cited six examples where Islamic countries have been involved in civilizational clashes, referred to by him as faultline wars, with their neighbours. These were the Afghan war, the Gulf war, the war between the Serbs and the Albanians, the confrontation between Turkey and Greece, religion-based wars and clashes in the former U.S.S.R. and the war between Azerbaijan and Armenia. Islam has been at war in each one of these conflicts. No other societal group or civilization has a comparable record of being involved in so many faultline clashes. Interestingly, a well known Pakistani scholar, Akbar S.Ahmed, now based in America, has referred to the fact of Islam being in simultaneous confrontation with all major religions of the world as a unique event. He has alluded to this all round confrontation as if it were a matter of great pride.[5]

One might find fault with Huntington's thesis. Yet there is lot of truth in his assertions. This is also an incontrovertible that today worldwide ninety-five per cent of the gun-totting terrorists and almost ninety-nine per cent of the suicide bombers are Muslims. Several political analysts and columnists have been arguing that Muslims are angry because they have some genuine grievances which need to be addressed, especially the demand for a Palestinian state. The Pakistani President, General Musharraf, was also parroting the same line when he said that the real causes of terrorism like the Palestinian and Kashmir issues should be resolved in order to redress the grievances of Muslims; only then terrorism can be countered. That is a lame excuse. There are some very pertinent questions which need to be answered by those holding brief for terrorism. Are Muslims the only community in this wicked, wide, world who have grievances that need immediate redressal? What about the long lists of grievances of the people belonging to other faiths? Is it that Muslims have an *a priori* claim for grievance redressal over similar claims of other groups? Many communities have long standing grievances about the atrocities committed by Muslim countries and

Islamist groups, too. How about redressal of the grievances of the Christian minority in Indonesia where thousands were killed in Mulukus and Sulawesi islands by Laskar Jihad and other radical outfits of Muslims? Why not address the grievances of the Christians of Pakistan? Just look at the squeeze on the hapless Maronite Christians of Lebanon who in the year 1900 formed approximately 77 per cent of Lebanon's population but now stand reduced to less than 30 percent, after remaining under seige by the Islamists for decades. They were in a state of incessant embattlement from 1970 to 1990 during which period they suffered heavily. Just now the Christians have practically no say in the governance of Lebanon. Again no one has been able to prevent the ongoing decades old ethnic cleansing of Hindus from Jammu & Kashmir or redress their grievances. Similar ethnic cleansing of Hindus in Pakistan went on for several years till most Hindus were thrown out of that country or forced to convert to Islam. And spare a thought for the hapless Hindus and Buddhist Chakmas of Bangladesh who have been repetitively subjected to gross atrocities by militant Muslim outfits with open connivance of the Islamic government and on whose womenfolk unspeakable indignities were heaped, as vividly described by that brave Muslim woman writer, Taslima Nasreen, in her famous book *Lajja* (i.e., 'Shame'). She was declared an apostate and faces death on return to her motherland. Hundreds of thousands of Hindus and Chakmas have been driven out from Bangladesh, but no one cares for them. How is the plight of Bangladeshi Hindus less worthy of attention than that of the Palestinians or Chechens? Then there is a littany of ghastly profanities committed by the Taliban and the Al Qaeda against innocent men and women, including the repulsive manner in which they destroyed the Bamiyan Buddhas which hurt the religious susceptibilities of more than one billion Buddhists and Hindus across the globe. One more question, an important one : are the grievances of the Muslims of Palestine, Bosnia, Chechenya, Kashmir and Philippines really so huge as the length and breadth of the entire earth and so overwhelming as to warrant the unleashing of multiple terrorist attacks from New York to New Delhi and onwards to Indonesia and the Philippines? Many communities and groups have much bigger and more serious problems. Perhaps the real problem is not about redressal of the grievances of the Muslims, e.g. in Palestine or Chechenya. It is with the mindset of radical Islamists who want to overrun the globe by undermining and overturning the soft states by recourse to bombings and killings, while raising the battle cry of jihad at the drop of a hat in a bid to hold the civil society to ransom. Huntington has referred to it as the 'bellicosity' of Islam. Every community has its long list of woes and grievances. But Muslims seem to be the only group which takes recourse to violent means for redressal of theirs. This attitude has given rise to serious security concerns about the safety of the civil society in several countries. Radical Islam is now an international phenomenon for which reason it ought to be called "international Islamist terrorism" – a comprehensive expression which connotes its global dimensions. Although most world leaders, ranging from George Bush, Tony Blair and Vladimir Putin to our own Prime Minister, Atal Behari Vajpayee, have been proclaiming that the war against "terror" has nothing to do with Islam, the truth is that militant Islamists worldwide have become the torch bearers of jihadi terrorism largely due to the machinations of the Inter Services Intelligence of Pakistan (ISI) and Osama bin Laden. For obvious reasons the denials of non-Muslim political leaders, mostly members of the world coalition against terror, about complicity of Islamists in terrorist activities have to be taken with a pinch of salt. Their soft pedalling of the issue of association of Islam with the terror trail across the world is nothing more than mere posturing, some kind of half hearted attempts at staying on a politically correct course. Perhaps such denials are quite necessary, nay eminently desirable, to prevent the possibility of racist reprisals against innocent Muslim residents of several western countries as well as those living under the democratic and secular political dispensations of Asia. More importantly, it is equally desirable for the secular nations not to alienate their innocent peace-loving Muslim populations from the mainstream. These two important considerations appear to have weighed heavily with the Indian political leadership too, because Muslims constitute a sizeable proportion of India's population. But credit must be given to Salman Rushdie, that fiery literatteur, for speaking out truth, when he questioned: "This isn't about Islam."

He criticised the world's leaders for repeating this mantra for weeks, partly in the virtuous hope of deterring attacks on innocent Muslims living in the West and partly to ensure that the efforts of America to maintain its coalition against terror was not impaired by linking Islam with terrorism in any way.[6] Rushdie candidly pointed out that the trouble with this necessary disclaimer is that it isn't true. "If this isn't about Islam, why the worldwide Muslim demonstrations in support of Osama bin Laden and the Al Qaeda? Why did those 10,000 men armed with swords and axes mass on the Pakistan-Afghanistan frontier answering some mullah's call for jihad?" He further asked that how was it that the war's first British casualties were three Muslims who died fighting on the Taliban side? He even questioned the bonafides of the Pakistani cricketer Imran Khan who wanted that the evidence of Al Qaeda's guilt should be shown while turning a deaf ear to the self-incriminating warning of Al Qaeda's spokesman to Muslims in the West not to live or work in tall buildings because there will be "a rain of aircraft from the skies".[7] Rushdie had no hesitation in admitting that this paranoid Islam which blames outsiders as, "infidels," for all the ills of Islamic societies and whose proposed remedy is to close all Muslim societies to modernity, is presently the fastest growing version of Islam in the world. Rushdie, being an intellectual, was only being honest. The ground reality is that today's international terrorism, grandly proclaimed as jihad, or "holy war", launched in 1998 against 'infidels' by bin Laden and his followers, and adroitly engineered by the Pakistani establishment, has become the turbo engine of the fast expanding Islamic militancy. Lately the 'universal civilization', the more appropriate term used by Sir Vidia Naipaul to describe the western civilisation, has been shaken by the daring and determination of Islamist terrorist groups to launch attacks of vicious intensity across the globe, ranging from the destruction of twin towers of New York to the terrible attack on the Indian Parliament in New Delhi and from bloody mayhem in a Moscow theatre and killings in Grozny in Chechenya to Kuta beach in Bali in October 2002 and on the J.W. Marriott Hotel in Jakarta in August 2003-plus the frequent bombings in the far away Philippines. The August 2003 attack on J.W. Marriot, Jakarta, a prestigious hotel run by Americans, appeared to be directly aimed at the U.S. tourists and western clientele who prefer staying there. This attack came barely one month after the U.S. embassy held its July 4 Independence Day bash in this very hotel. On August 13, 2003, just eight days after the attack on Hotel Marriott, the American Ambassador summoned a meeting of American residents in Jakarta to caution them about the possibility of future terrorist attacks. "The unprecedented decision to hold this town meeting at the embassy is based on our assesment that it is currently the most secure environment in Jakarta to hold a large gathering of American citizens," Ambassador Ralph L.Boyce said in his message announcing the Meeting.[8] He told the Americans that if they left the meeting a little more concerned, even more frightened, then it meant that they got the message which he wanted to convey. There was a determined group in Indonesia with access to bomb-making material. Therefore it was safe to presume that there will probably be more terrorist attempts.[9] It was no pure coincidence that the bombing was staged when the high-profile criminal trial of Islamic militants involved in the October 2002 Bali bomb blast came up for hearing, including that of Abu Bakr Bashir, a powerful leader of Jemmah Islamiah. Perhaps the blast was organised by design on that specific day. The Marriott Hotel terrorist attack was a sort of defiance, or call it a challenge to the U.S. by the Islamist warriors – a grim reminder that they were alive and kicking. Interestingly just a week earlier Washington had issued an alert saying that the terrorists were planning a new hijacking or suicide bombing in America or somewhere abroad. After Pakistan, Indonesia seems to be emerging as another hotspot of terror proliferation.One reason could be that like Pakistan, Indonesia too has an abnormally large number of Islamic seminaries, called madarasas, where hatred against infidels is preached and the Islamic doctrine of jihad openly propagated among Muslim youth. The phenomenon of indoctrinating the youth in jihadi ideology was first started in Pakistan in the fifties of the last century primarily to target the so-called Hindu India by means of jihadist campaigns, but soon it spread worldwide, both in Muslim and non-Muslim countries, due to the enormous funds provided by the petro-dollar rich Saudi Sheikhdom to advance the cause of pan-Islamism. According to the

Indonesian Defence Minister the perpetrators of the deadly car bombing at Jakarta's Marriott Hotel had been trained with the Al Qaeda in Afghanistan and Pakistan; he felt that there were many more terrorists in the country. "Each one of them has special abilities received from training in Afghanistan and Pakistan," Matori Abdul Djalil claimed. He said that the bombers were linked to a group of people arrested last month in Semarang and alleged to be members of the Al Qaida linked terror group Jemaah Islamiyah.[10] Surely most of the pan-Islamic terrorist groups operating worldwide have strong links with radical Islamic outfits of Pakistan. It is well known that the ISI of Pakistan, acting in close collaboration with the Al Qaeda, was the major sponsor of Islamic militancy and terror in different parts of the world. The recent testimony of John S. Pistole, Deputy Assistant Director of the Federal Bureau of Investigation (FBI), before a Senate panel in the last week of July 2003 confirming the eventual tracing of the 9/11 terror attacks to Al Qaeda accounts in Pakistan has further reinforced the mounting evidence of Pakistan's complicity in promoting the cause of radical Islam. Presently America, Israel and the 'Hindu India' are the three main countries on the hit list of the Islamist oufits. Unfortunately it took the western nations quite some time, almost three decades, plus the shocking experience of the Black Tuesday, to comprehend that all terrorist organisations operating against India, more specifically in Jammu & Kashmir, had been openly nurtured, trained and armed by Pakistan. For instance, the Muttahida (United) Jihad Council, a conglomerate of 17 Pakistan-based terrorist outfits has been operating with impunity in Kashmir and some other parts of India from its bases in Pakistan, and Pak-occupied Kashmir. Ever since the partition of the sub-continent in 1947, Pakistan has been targeting India primarily due to their visceral hatred of the Hindus. After the emergence of bin Laden as a role model for Muslims, the virulent virus of Islamist terror, spawned by the Pakistani establishment and the Saudis, captured the imagination of Muslim youths in a number of countries. No wonder today the world stands at the cross-roads of mankind's history – although not many nations, nor world leaders were able to comprehend what civilizational values were at stake at this critical juncture, till Samuel Huntington gave a wake up call to the world. Earlier in 1979-80, V. S. Naipaul had sounded an alert when he wrote about the growing virus of Islamic fundamentalism. Unfortunately that did not register with the world community and intellegentsia – certainly not in India. The vast geographical span and the increasing frequency of the depredations of Islamist militants, actively backed by more than one hundred thirty five organisations of radical Islam across the globe, and covertly supported by Pakistani and Saudi regimes, have recorded an exponential growth in recent years. Just now at least 135 radical Islamic outfits, enumerated in Appendix-I, straddle dozens of countries across the globe.The menace is no longer limited to any specific country or geographical region. The jihadi movement has won wide support in dozens of Muslim countries, and on a conservative count, the killer contagion has already struck roots in at least forty-two countries or perhaps more. Some analysts place the figure as high as eighty, including both Muslim and non-Muslim countries.

Systematic use of violence to create a climate of fear among civilian population has been a regular feature of mankind's history, especially in the twentieth century which saw the rise of several terrorist ideologies in various parts of world. The rise in terror activities has been facilitated by rapid advancements in science and technology and sophistication of modern weapons. But there is a qualitative difference in the objectives, methodology and reach of the terrorist activities of Islamists and those of the country-specific radical groups whose activities are limited in terms of their goals, ambitions and geographical reach. For instance, the Irish Republican Army, which is confined to Northern Ireland, or the Basque insurgency limited to Spain, or the leftists groups like Revolutionary Armed Forces (FARC) in Columbia, the Lankan Tamil Tiger Elam (LTTE) in Sri Lanka, or the Maoists in Nepal. They are all localised terrorist groups with no global ambitions or extended reach. The ambition of Islamist terrorists, who have acquired global reach, belongs to an altogether different genre. They have displayed tremendous organisational skills, rare unity, enormous raw courage and have set before themselves the ideal of restoring through jihad the old grandeur of Islam, reminiscent of the medieval times. In terms of sophisticated operational network, trans-continental geographical spread, financial clout and availability of committed manpower imbued with ruthless militancy, the radical Islam is miles ahead of all other terrorists groups put together, or any other comparable radical international movement in modern times. The threat posed by its long reach and proven capacity for unremitting violence through organised terrorism is far greater than that posed in the last century by the Nazis under Hitler or for that matter, even by the erstwhile communist movement which had led to major upheavals in several parts of the world during the cold war. Today, thanks to the vast network of Jihadi manufactories in Pakistan there are hundreds of thousand jihadi warriors spread all over the world, across many continents. It is no surprise that the West perceives Islamic terrorism to be as great a threat as communism was 50 years ago. No political analyst can differ with the former North Atlantic Treaty Organization (NATO) Secretary-General Willy Claes and the former chief of British MI 5, Stella Remington, who had "called radical Islam as the geopolitical menace of the future."[11] The fascist doctrine of Nazi ideology, though dangerously ruthless, remained mostly confined to Germany, Italy and a major part of the Europe which Hitler was able to overrun. Although German and Italian troops did make massive forays into North Africa, their reach could never extend to Asia or America. Hitler launched a massive attack on the Soviet Russia in a bold bid to enslave that huge country but got bogged down at Stalingrad and was unable to subjugate the Russian people. Undoubtedly the Nazi storm troopers of Hitler were as determined and ruthless as today's Islamists are but the geographical reach of the Nazi campaign was only a fraction of the sweep of today's Islamists. Though Hitler's army did manage to cross the Mediterranean and fought savage wars in the desert of North Africa, they were not allowed by the Allies to overrun Egypt, nor seize the Suez canal. The ideology of Nazis could not grow across the world in the manner in which the radical Islam has. The creed of communism was much more widespread and popular especially in poverty-stricken societies, but relied heavily on the trade union movement in most countries, and peasant struggle in China. Neither the Nazi ideology, nor the communist campaigns in different countries, were able to take the dangerous route of serial terror attacks on innocent civilians for achieving their goals in the manner in which the Islam's soldiers are doing today. There is, however, an uncanny resemblance between the beliefs and the thought process of Nazis and the warriors of Islam. Both professed and preached that they were a superior people, a group which was a cut above the rest and had a right to impose their ideology on lesser mortals, the *hoi polloi* of the world. The Nazis unabashedly claimed that the blue-eyed Aryan race was the fountain-head of all knowledge and power owing to which they were destined to rule the world. The Islamic theologians go one step further and proclaim that the faith of Prophet Muhammad is the only genuine religion which could provide salvation to mankind. They believe that Muslims have both the divine right and a holy obligation to convert the entire world to Islam.The Islamists have a world view of re-ordering the entire world into Dar-ul-Islam. According to their philosophy the goal of converting every 'kafir' to Islam must be achieved, if necessary by violence, through jihad. It may be recalled that neither the Nazis nor communists were able to develop the kind of global culture of Klashnikov, RDX and suicide bombings which the Islamist terrorists have successfully promoted. To that extent the Islamist terror is much more deep rooted and widespread and far more deadly and dangerous than the Nazi threat or the communist movement of the twentieth century. Perhaps the combined threat of the Nazis and the communist movement could not have matched the ferocity and determination of today's terror.The rapid advance of the pan-Islamic movement after the creation of Pakistan provided a strong motivation to growth of militant Islam, while the ISI and the Pakistani establishment managed to put together a solid infrastructure and trained committed manpower for carrying out terror attacks. At the right moment Osama bin Laden appeared on the scene to provide the necessary leadership.That is how the menace of international Islamist terror was born. This international terrorism is sustained by a vast network of jihadi cells and action stations functioning in scores of countries. Thanks to the nefarious gameplan of the ISI, funded by the Saudis, the radical Islam has been on a roll for several decades and is now well entrenched worldwide.

The civil society had never witnessed the ugly spectacle of daily bombings and senseless killings on such large scale. We have become accustomed to brutal killings, including those of children, and mass destruction on day to day basis, whether it is in the West Asia, Chechenya, Indonesia or Kashmir. The extremist ideology has poisoned the minds of young Muslims with such intense hostility against the so-called infidels that even moderate Muslim regimes find it difficult to rein them. The Islamist terrorists are already using all kinds of deadly strategies against the target-civilizations and countries. There is little doubt that they will not hesitate to use deadly non-conventional weapons like the nuclear devices and other Weapons of Mass Destruction (WMDs), whenever they come to possess them. Not long ago a number of anthrax-laden letters were sent through the American postal system but the origin of that mischief could not be traced. It is believed that at least one or two of those anthrax letters were mailed from the area where Mohammed Atta, the key suicide bomber of September 11, 2001, had resided. The very fact that Islamist terrorists like Mohammed Atta, who are new role models for many Muslim youths, had a religious belief that by killing innocent non-Muslims he was carrying out the command of Allah, places them in a category altogether different from the Nazis or the communists. Apparently moderate Muslims appear to have lost both their voice and initiative, perhaps they never had either. It looks as though they never counted for anything in Islamic societies. A moderate Muslim remains a non-entity. This impression is reinforced by the recent events in France which showed how in a liberal socialist country the leadership of the Muslim community has passed into the hands of radicals. The French society has a tradition of treating every community and ethnic group in a just and fair manner. A strong belief in democracy, human rights, respect of individual freedom, gender equality, freedom of speech, expression and worship and equality of opportunity are inviolable aspects of the French political system. But the precipitate growth in Muslim population, estimated to be between 3 to 5 million, in recent times has stirred a major debate on whether or not Muslims can be integrated into the liberal republican mainstream of France.[12] Many French thinkers believe that Islam is intrinsically hostile to democracy, human rights, women, to freedom of expression and is intolerant of non-believers and dissidents within its own ranks. The deep commitment of Muslims to the ummah or the unique indivisible community of believers is also considered to be incompatible with the modern idea of a nation state. "With more and more young, educated, French speaking Muslims lending a sympathetic ear to radical Islamic preachers, fears have been expressed that France's republican tradition can no longer be sustained."[13] Another school of thought, however, contends that Muslims can and do come to terms with these traditions as is evident from the example of Tunisia's Muslim community. They assert that while Quran cannot be tampered with, the sharia and other theological texts should be seen in their historical contexts. These can be interpreted in a manner which should enable Muslims to fully adhere to the humanitarian demands of the modern world. But the reformists were soon proved wrong. In April 2003 the first ever elections were held for the general assembly and the central committee of the French Council for the Muslim Religion, set up on the lines of similar bodies for the Catholic, Protestant, and Jewish communities. It was hoped that the representative body of French Muslims will be persuaded to function in accordance with the country's liberal republican ethos. That turned out to be wishful thinking because soon, much to the chagrin of the secularists, it was seen that the hardliners, some of them affiliated to the fanatic Muslim Brotherhood, won the elections in the new body hands down.[14] Our own experience in India has been quite similar to the French episode. Post-independence leadership of the Muslim community in India has always remained in the hands of the fundamentalist radical elements – just as it was during the pre-partition days! The radical Muslim groups of India saw to it that Rushdie's book, *Satanic Verses*, was banned. In another case, that of famous Shah Bano, they launched a campaign to ensure that the verdict of the Supreme Court was overturned through a new legislation. The Muslims of India have been opposing the singing in schools of Vande Matram, a vintage patriotic song, which was the heartbeat of the independence movement. They had opposed it during pre-partition days and continue to do so even in independent India. These facts add another complex dimension to the divisive politics of India and the threat of Islamist terror. We see almost every day, in the visual and print media, the daily toll of killings and bombings staged by terrorists either in Jammu & Kashmir or Maharashtra or Gujarat or in and around Delhi itself. A regular dose of terror-laden news is now a regular feature of every Indian's humdrum existence. The communal politics and frequent terror strikes have provided a quantum jump to communal tensions and accelerated polarisation between Hindus and Muslims.

As mentioned earlier, India has been a major target of terrorist outfits, launched at the behest of the Inter Services Intelligence of Pakistan, which played a leadership role in promoting pan-Islamic movement in most parts of the world. As a direct result of their recourse to terror tactics, there has been a complete ethnic cleansing in the Kashmir valley by terrorising Hindu minority in flagrant violation of human rights supposed to be upheld by the United Nations. More than three hundred thousand Kashmiri Hindus have been driven out of the valley by now. On a rough estimate during the last three decades, the ISI and Pakistani army have recruited, trained and equipped approximately three to four hundred thousand militant youths, mostly Pakistanis, Arabs and Afghans, albeit with a liberal sprinkling of thousands of volunteers belonging to more than two dozen countries including the U.K. and Bosnia in Europe, Algeria, Somalia and Sudan in Africa and half a dozen countries of Asia, going right up to Sulu and Mindnao islands in the far away Philippines. Initially, quite a few thousand jihadis had been trained by the ISI in early 1960s to fight in Kashmir. On the basis of that experience massive numbers were trained in 1970s and 1980s for waging holy war against Russian occupation of Afghanistan with the financial and tactical support provided by the Central Intelligence Agency (CIA) and the Saudis. Later on many of them were used by the ISI for supplementing the insurgents and terror groups already infiltrated into the State of Jammu & Kashmir since 1960s. But due to sheer over-production of militants in the terror camps of Pakistan and Afghanistan, and their burgeoning zeal for jihad, from 1990s onwards a large number of these battle-hardened 'holy warriors' were directed to participate in the campaigns launched in various parts of the globe. As explained by a Pakistani political analyst, Mohammed Amir Rana, in his investigative treatise '*Jihad-e-Kashmir and Afghanistan*' (published in Urdu by Masha'l Books, Lahore), the jihadi culture in Pakistan was inspired by the Iranian Revolution spearheaded by Ayatollah Khomeini. Soon it struck deep roots mainly due to the collaboration between the ISI and the CIA. America invested huge resources in the Islamic war against Russian occupation of Afghanistan.[15] In the summer of 1979, the U.S. President Carter's National Security Adviser, Zbigniew Brzerzinski, made Carter sign a secret directive for extending covert aid of $500 million to fund the activities of Muslim mujahideens for throwing out the Russians from Afghanistan for freeing the Middle East of all communist influence. With this money a secret operation code-named "Operation Cyclone" was planned entailing an expense of $4 billion,a part of which was used by the ISI for establishing a chain of madarasas in Pakistan. Before 1980 the big madarasas in Pakistan numbered 700 which increased at the rate of 3 per cent per year. "This rate galloped to a whopping 136 per cent in 1986. And now the number of big madarasas (i.e. madarasas that give degrees of M.A. & Ph.D) is 7,000."[16] According to Rana, the zealots of the Islamic groups from Pakistan were also sent to the training camps of the CIA in Virginia where they learnt the first lessons in terrorism. That is how the future members of Al Qaeda were born. Some youths were imparted training in terrorism in the Brooklyn Islamic School. In Pakistan they were trained by the officers of the British MI6 and the ISI. Osama bin Laden's personal wealth and his charismatic leadership provided greater extremist orientation to the jihadi movement and the Talibans added their fundamentalist muscle to it. The ISI was remodelled to meet the goals of Operation Cyclone, and the war against Russia was directed and controlled by the CIA and the ISI jointly. Incidentally, the American establishment has denied that groups of mujahideen were trained in America, or by the CIA. But such routine denials appear to be a mere formality. The American interest came to an end with the exit of the Soviet army from the area, but the war had far reaching implications for Pakistan. One obvious manifestation of this was the growth of jihadi culture that has taken roots there. Another was the increase in the sectarian clashes between the Shias and the Sunnis. Subsequently in 1987 Pakistan decided to organize a militant movement in the Kashmir Valley (the reference here is to Indian Kashmir).[17] For this purpose leaders of Jamat-e-Islami and Jammu & Kashmir Liberation Front (JKLF) kept meeting Zia-ul-Haq, Pakistan's President, and in 1989 the militancy was intensified and jihadi organisations of Pakistan took advantage of this and reached Indian Kashmir, ostensibly to help the local people for stepping up insurgency and terrorism. Amir Rana estimates that during the last twenty years nearly 30,000 Pakistani youths died in Afghanistan and Kashmir, 2000 sectarian clashes occurred in Pakistan and about 12 lakh youth took part in the activities of jihadi and religious organisations.[18] The very fact that during the last ten years more than thirty thousand Pakistanis have laid down their lives in the cause of jihad and that another 1.2 million youth have at one point or another actively participated in jihadi and radical Islamist activities clearly points to the direction in which the sub-continent is likely to move in the decades ahead. These are formidable statistics depicting the massive growth of the philosophy of terror among the people of Pakistan, and bodes ill not only for India and Pakistan but for the entire world community.

Apparently neither the ubiquitous Central Intelligence Agency (CIA) nor the strategic think tanks of U.S.A., could fathom the intensity of hatred and hostility which Muslim militants had developed towards America and the western civilization or assess their enormous capacity for hitting the so-called 'kafir America' across the Atlantic, though the U.S. establishment had been aware for at least eight years, more specifically since 1993, of the threat of radical Islam looming large on their horizon. The 9/11 stunning bombing of the World Trade Centre (WTC) woke up the Americans from their deep slumber. It was a mindboggling experience not only for the U.S.A. but for the entire civil society when in a spectacular suicide mission 19 Muslim terrorists, 14 of them Saudis, hijacked 4 commercial planes from U.S. airports and crashed two of them into the twin towers of World Trade Centre in New York and one into the Pentagon office in Washington D.C., while the fourth plane crashed near Pittsburgh. The crashes resulted in the total destruction of the twin towers, demolition of a part of the southern wing of the Pentagon office, took a toll of 266 persons aboard the hijacked planes and caused almost three thousand deaths in the WTC buildings and nearby areas. These attacks had been master-minded and deftly executed by a handpicked group of Osama bin Laden's Al Qaeda militants, trained, financed and supported by the good offices of the ISI of Pakistan. It was only then that the grim consequences of playing poker with the radical Islam dawned on the U.S.A. They learnt at a very heavy cost, both in terms of life and property, that experience is a harsh teacher; she gives test first, lesson afterwards. In one go, the Black Tuesday announced with a bold hard knock the arrival of Islamist terror at the gates of the western civilization and awakened them to the likely shape of things to come. Incidentally subsequent investigations by the Federal Bureau of Investigation led to filing a criminal charge in the Federal Distict Court in Alexandria, against one Zacarias Moussaoui, a French national, said to be the twentieth bomber. He had been assigned the mission of bombing the White House on the fateful Black Tuesday but could not. Though part of the plot, he was arrested earlier in August 2001 on unlawful immigration charges, having aroused the suspicion of his instructors at a flight school in Eagan, Minnesota. The prosecution alleged that Mr Moussaoui "was keenly aware of why he was here: it was to fly a plane into White House."[19] Though the role played by the Pakistani establishment and their intelligence outfit, ISI, in training hundreds of thousands jihadi warriors and sending them across dozens of countries for waging jihad is well known, the biggest surprise has been the use by the Muslim terror groups of a number of European countries as sanctuaries as well as training centres. They took full advantage of the Europe's commitment to democracy and freedom. Add to this scenario the highly controversial and fundamentalist activities and fiery preachings of Abu Hamza-al Misri, a naturalised British citizen and supporter of jihad, who formerly preached from London's Finsbury Park mosque and took the risk of losing his British passport for acts seriously prejudicial to the vital interests of Britain. And then came the shocking news of the involvment of two Pakistanis, holding British citizenship, Omar Khan Sharif, 27, and his accomplice Asif Mohammed Hanif, 21, who blew himself up while kiling three others during a suicide attack on a café in Tel Aviv on the night of April 29, 2003. Grim British pundits recalled the earlier example of a British passport bearing Pakistani terrorist Omar Ahmad Sheikh who was engaged in fighting a "jihad for Kashmir" and was awarded the death penalty in Pakistan for the murder of U.S. journalist Daniel Pearl.[20] These incidents caused considerable dismay amid rising fears that soon the U.K. might be perceived as the world's western capital of terrorism. Meanwhile, in the customary inflammatory tirade the extremist Britain-based Islamist group, Al-Muhajiroun, applauded the suicide attacks on Israel. The group's general secretary Anjem Choudhary insisted that the two British bombers were engaged on "a jihad that can be rightly fought in Kashmir or Chechenya too".[21] That shows the extent of open support by the U.K-based radical Islamists to the current Islamist terrorism. To rub salt into the wounds of the chatterati of the liberal Europe, recently on the occasion of the second anniversary of 9/11, Al Muhajiroun brought out colourful posters openly eulogising the martyrdom of the "magnificient 19", the notorious suicide bombers and also announced plans for organising a meeting of the Muslim groups in their memory. These developments clearly show that the seeds of Islamist militancy have been sown quite deep in the U.K. and the unmistakable imprint of Pakistani connection runs through all such events, because a large number of Pakistani diaspora are known to be ardent supporters of Al Muhajiroun. Perhaps more such instances will come to notice in the years ahead. But then U.K. is not the only European country to be afflicted by the lethal virus of jihadi terror. There are many more countries across the Europe suffering from the same malaise. The Pakistani diaspora has spread it far and wide, all over Europe and America. Investigations have revealed that over the years many European nations, including the U.K., the Netherlands, Germany and France have served as training ground for Muslim terrorists operating in different countries, including the state of Jammu & Kashmir in India. Two militants who received training and attended sermons in Eindhoven, the Netherlands, were killed by the Indian troops in the Jammu & Kashmir last year i.e. in 2002.[22] The notorious Al Qaeda terrorists linked to the September 11 attacks on WTC had also received indoctrination in radical Islam in Eindhoven, Netherlands. There are indications that similar training centres preaching radical Islam also exist in Germany and France. The fresh evidence of global links of J&K militants has only vindicated New Delhi's claims that "the violence in Kashmir is not a freedom struggle" but sheer terrorism being practised in the name of jihad.[23] One of the most active Islamic groups providing training to militants in Europe is the extremist Al-Waqf-al-Islami Foundation which arranges sermons in the Al-Furqan mosque in Eindhoven and is reportedly funded by wealthy Saudis and other fatcats of oil-rich Sheikhdoms of the Middle East. Even some of the Al Qaeda militants suspected to be behind September 11 violence had attended sermons in the Al-Furqan mosque in Eindhoven.[24] Ever since 1980s the radical sermons at the Al-Waqf have been drilling extremism into the heads of thousands of Muslim youth coming from all over the Europe. The most infamous attendees of these Islamist sermons were the six terrorists from Hamburg, Germany, who had allegedly plotted the notorious Black Tuesday attacks. Similarly in France intelligence officials have expressed concern about the goings on at the L'institut European des Sciences Humanies at the Chateau-Chinon in the Burgundy region. At least one member of the Hamburg terrorist cell had taken a correspondence course provided in the institute. In Germany, an Islamic seminary, the Hans des Islam, in the small town of Lutzelbach near Frankfurt is under observation of German intelligence. This organisation had been established sometime in 1980s, perhaps with the help of cash smuggled from the Middle East. It is believed that many radical Islamists who fled Afghanistan are currently safely ensconsed in many cities of Pakistan, especially Karachi and Lahore. It may be recalled that during the operations in Afghanistan an American Taliban, John Walker Lindh, had been arrested. His interrogation had revealed that he had been trained and indoctrinated in a camp in the Himalayas, across the road from a Pakistani military base and that Pakistani intelligence officers regularly came to the training camp to impart instructions. Apparently he had been trained by the Hizb-ul Mujahideen, under the tutelage of the ISI, to fight in Jammu & Kashmir before he was shifted to a base in Afghanistan for jihad against the Russians. In a nutshell Pakistan, proudly proclaimed as the fortress of Islam by Musharraf, has become the nucleus of the Jihadi Highway to Dar-ul Islam, charted by Islamists, which meanders through the U.K. Netherlands, France, Spain, Germany, Italy, Albania, Kosovo, Bosnia, Serbia, Algeria, Libya, Tunisia, Egypt, Palestine, Syria, Lebanon, Saudi Arabia, Iraq, Chechenya, Dagestan, Azerbaijan,

Turkmenistan, Uzbekistan, Afghanistan, Iran, India (Kashmir), Bangladesh, Malayasia, Indonesia and right into the Philippines. All these countries, thirty in all, have witnessed grand revival of jihadist movement and scores of radical outfits have come up in each one of them to wage holy war in the cause of Allah.

Any assessment of the geo-political implications of the long reach of radical Islam and the consequences of their global designs for the civil society of "tomorrow and the day after" should take into account three important aspects. First, at present there are 135 militant Islamic organisations involved in jihadi campaigns worldwide which is a mind-boggling figure.[25] They are playing havoc with the law and order and security apparatus of dozens of countries from America to the Philippines, by keeping them in a state of constant embattlement. In the process, over a period of time many nation states, certainly the soft variety, are likely to disintegrate and disappear, while the remaining ones will be considerably debilitated. That will make the task of jihadi groups much easier, say after a decade or two, whenever they decide to go for the kill. Second, during the Operation Enduring Freedom, i.e., the war against Al Qaeda waged by the U.S.-led coalition in Afghanistan, more than 760 Muslim militants belonging to a whopping forty-two countries were captured and taken to the U.S. Naval Base at Guantonamo Bay for interrogation by the CIA. Since these forty two countries have already been sucked into the vortex of terrorism, they will transmit the contagion to their neighbouring nations which could have a major destabilizing effect on several regions of the world. But the third aspect is the most important one. During the twentieth century there has been a phenomenal increase in the world population of Muslims who are likely to comprise something like thirty per cent of the global population by the year 2025 A.D., perhaps even earlier. The increasing Muslim numbers will have the potential to cause serious major upheavals in several parts of Asia, Europe and Africa due to eruption of multiple intra-civilization faultline conflicts on large scale. More importantly, those pushing for the jihadi culture are very much conscious of the fact that the numbers of Muslims are growing fast and that is what makes them gung-ho about the future of radical Islam. In specific terms, the cult of Islamist terror has already won hundreds of thousand ready recruits in many countries, willing to wage holy war and ready to die. Just now the majority of these holy warriors happen to be concentrated in Pakistan, Afghanistan, Palestine, Iraq, Syria and most countries of the Middle East and in Indonesia and the Philippines. But their ranks are growing rapidly, as the contagion spreads far and wide in Asia, Africa and Europe. The widespread commitment of Muslims to jihad was demonstrated by the sympathetic reactions to the death of a notorious Saudi militant, Khallad al-Madani, killed in Chechenya in February 2000 while fighting the Russians. In the course of one day, messages of support for al-Madani's family poured in from South Africa, the United States, Lebanon, Malaysia, Canada, New Zealand, Saudi Arabia, Turkey, Sri Lanka, and India.[26] Apart from Kashmir, the global character of radical Islam's "mission jihad" is also reflected in the Chechen holy war which is being waged against Russia since 1991. The foremost leader of the Chechen war has been a notorious Saudi militant named Khattab who had earlier fought in Afghanistan under the banner of bin Laden. Chechens honed their battle skills in Afghan training camps and graduates of Pakistan's religious schools fight alongside the rebels in Chechenya.[27] It is well known that many Chechen Islamists have fought alongside Pakistanis and Afghans in Kashmir. Barcelona in Spain is reported to have already become the point of passage for Jihadists moving between Europe and Chechenya.[28] Recently on the occasion of the second anniversary of 9/11 there was a spontaneous show of sympathy by a group of Muslims in the United Kingdom for the so-called 'Magnificent 19", the Islamist suicide bombers who had attacked the WTC and Pentagon.The rising tide of militant Islam in many parts of Europe, including the U.K. and the Balkans, across the African nations of Sudan, Algeria, Egypt, several West Asian countries and Indonesia underline the visible contours of the coming faultline conflicts of varying dimensions in several parts of world. As a sequel to 9/11 and the consequential military build up ordered by the U.S. establishment, there was a huge groundswell of rage in many Islamic countries. Sinister threats were held out to American tourists and citizens in parts of Indonesia, mostly Central Java, and it was reported that hotels were being 'searched' for them. These are ominous signs. Indonesia has the largest Muslim population and has seen a dramatic resurgence of radical Islam during the last two decades. A number of Indonesian Islamists and the Moro Islamic Liberation Front (MILF) secessionists of Philippines have received training in the camps in Afghanistan and Pakistan, run by the ISI and the Al Qaeda, and were initiated into terror tactics and suicide bomb attacks during the Afghan jihad against Soviet troops. The clerics of Indonesia have been highly critical of the U.S.A. The Secretary General of the Indonesian Ulemas Council (MUI), Din Syamusddin, gave a call on September 26, 2001, to Muslims the world over to wage a jihad should the U.S. and its allies go ahead with their planned aggression against Afghanistan. The U.S.A. was not deterred and rightly so. But such 'fatwas', regularly issued by Muslim clerics, point to the turbulent times ahead for the civil society. That the Islamist contagion has spread far and wide is evident from the broad spectrum of the nationalities of detainees at Guantanamo Bay Naval Base. According to New York Times roughly 660 detainees are suspected of links to the terrorist network of Al Qaeda or the ousted Afghan Taliban regime.[29] Originally more than 760 Muslim terrorists had been arrested in Afghanistan, out of which 600 are still under interrogation. Prima facie the ideology of jihadi terrorism has already struck roots among Muslims of dozens of countries and there may be many more nations whose Islamist volunteers could not be captured in Afghanistan by the coalition forces. In this age of easy access to the new frontiers of science and technology the possibility of Islamist terrorists seizing nuclear assets of Pakistan, or using chemical and biological weapons of mass destruction, for achieving their pan-Islamic terror objectives, cannot be ruled out. To meet this threat it is necessary for the strategists of the world coalition to monitor both the overt and covert operations of innumerable terorists, cells planted in a number of countries, perhaps anything between fifty to eighty nations, both Islamic and non-Islamic. That is a huge task. It is equally important to devise and execute effective strategies to counter this rapidly growing threat. The concern expressed by the U.S. President, George Bush, about the attempts by the Iranian government to develop nuclear weapons, and the strategic thinking of the neo-conservatives to confront the Islamists on their home turf in the Middle East have to be viewed in the context of these global threat perceptions.

2

The Five Pillars of Islam

"All of us belong to one God, one father,
one religion". – Prophet Muhammad

To comprehend the phenomenal growth of radical Islam during the last five decades, it is necessary to understand the theological structure of Islam, its societal ethos, cultural implications and the chequered history of Muslim conquests during the medieval times with special reference to the controversial doctrine of jihad.

Basic Tenets of Islam

Islam is a vigorously intense religion, totally monotheistic in character and wholly uncompromising. As expounded in the Quran, it has five important constituents. First, the 'Shahada' which is a declaration of faith entailing the recitation of 'Kalma' thereby affirming belief in a single God, that is Allah, of whom Muhammad was the messenger. Second, the saying of prayers (i.e., Namaz) five times, every day. Third, 'Zakat' which means giving charity which should be equal to 2.5% of one's income. Fourth, fasting in the month of Ramadan, which in India is also called 'Roza'. And fifth, the 'Haj' which means going for pilgrimage to Kaaba, at least once in lifetime, provided the faithful can afford it. It may be clarified that the combined body of Revelations from Allah which constitute the Quran (the Holy Book of Islam) appeared to the Prophet without a logical sequence over a period of twenty-three years of his prophetic career (609 to 632).[1] Therefore it does not discuss the religious tenets of Islam systematically or in accordance with its chapters due to which many theological concepts have been discussed at different places in different chapters. The Quran has 114 chapters and some six thousand verses. It is believed to have been revealed by Archangel Gabriel to Prophet Muhammad for the first time when he was praying in the cave of Hira, near Mecca.

Prof. Akbar Muhammad of Binghamton University in New York explains that the fundamentals of Islam, populary known as the "five pillars of Islam", are the "Shahada" which is an affirmation that there is no deity, except Allah, and that Muhammad is his prophet, his messenger. That constitutes the first pillar, or fundamental. The second pillar is prayer, i.e., salat; the third is the fasting, which is "sawm", or the fast of Ramadan; and the fourth pillar is the payment of a social tax called zakat by every Muslim. It is charity which is equal to 2.5 percent of what one has had, what one owned of certain kinds of wealth for a period of one year. The fifth pillar is the pilgrimage, the hajj. The pilgrimage has to be to the Kaaba - not to Mecca *per se* - but to the Kaaba, which is in Mecca. These are the five pillars or the five fundamentals of Islam.[2] According to Imam Feisal Abdul Rauf, an Islamic scholar and Imam of Masjid al-Farah, New York, the fundamental idea which defines a human being as a Muslim is the declaration of faith that there is a creator, God, whom Muslims call Allah, in Arabic - and that the creator is one and single. And this is reiterated by the declaration of faith, the shahada, whereby the faithful bear witness to the truth that there is no God but Allah, and that all Muslims are accountable to Allah for their actions.[3] Then there are other things, secondary things like the rules of dress and the rules of behaviour and rules about what may be considered right or wrong. Most of these come from Islam's cultural norms and from secondary sources of Islamic jurisprudence. Unlike Christianity, Islam does not have a church, nor an ordained priesthood. However, in addition to the aforesaid five pillars, there are certain important theological concepts, intricately interwoven with the Islamic faith, without understanding which it would be difficult to comprehend the deep commitment of Muslims to their religion, and the causes of the current faultline conflicts in several countries.

The Hadith, the Sunna and the Sharia

In addition to the five pillars of Islam, there are three important components of Islamic theology. These are the Hadith; the Sunna and the Sharia. Strict observance of these is mandatory for every follower of the Prophet. Islam places on its followers the onus of conforming totally to Prophet Muhammad's ideal in their day to day lives. Every Muslim is required to follow what is known as the example of the Prophet, or the "sunna" of Muhammad. The word 'hadith' means any report of something the Prophet either said, or did. That is hadith with a small "h". Hadith with a capital 'H' is a collection of all these reports.[4] Thus Hadith is a first hand record of the Prophet's doings and sayings which came to be known through His companions who were called "Sahabah" in Arabic. Total commitment to Hadith is mandatory for all Muslims because it consists of what the Prophet's companions had heard from His own mouth or what they had found the Prophet doing at a certain time. Among those companions the most important and well known was the Prophet's favourite wife, Ayesha, while the others were Abu Hurairah, Jabir, Anas bin Malik, Abu Sayeed and Abu Musa. The term "Sunna" refers to the normative practices of the prophet. Literally the word 'sunna' means the practice. In Islamic parlance it means the practice of the Prophet which is regarded as canonical and has the value of being equal to the injunctions ordained in the Quran. Islamic jurists have defined the general sunna of the Prophet Muhammad to mean every thing that he did or said. The source of the Sunna is the Hadith. In other words, Hadith is a kind of report of the Sunna. All that Muhammad did, that is the practice of the prophet, namely certain class of His actions constitute the norms to be followed by the faithful. The Ahadith (plural of Hadith), which are regarded by the Sunnis (orthdox Muslims) to have canonical value, have been collected in six works which are called 'Sihah Sittah', which means "the six authentics". The Ahadith by Imam Bukhari and Imam Muslim are believed to be the most authentic. The study of Ahadith is actually quite a fascinating and educative experience, because through the hadith one can become familiar with the nuances of Islamic history. While the Quran has a canonical value and is common to all Muslims, the Ahadith of the

Shias are not the same as those of the Sunnis.The "Sharia" is the term given to define the collectivity of laws that govern the lives of Muslims. The Sharia has been derived both from the Quran and the Ahadith. Thus, Sharia is the Quranic law; it constitutes the foundation of the Islamic faith. For instance, the Prophet prayed in a certain way - always facing the Kaaba. This has a Sharia value which is compulsory for all Muslims to follow wherever they be. Islam is regarded by its followers as a system which covers every aspect of their lives. There is a belief that the Sharia embodies all the specific laws mentioned in the Quran and those which were practised by the Prophet. In that sense the Sharia may be regarded as the jurisprudence of the Islamic school of thought. So any law, anything said in the Quran or Hadith, is definitely Sharia. It is considered as divinely legislated and everyone must follow it. Muslims believe that the Creator has laid down certain rules or legislated certain laws through the Quran and Ahadith for Muslims to follow under all circumstances. Yet if there are some issues about which a doubt arises, those should be decided preferably by the analogy of the Prophet's life, or resolved by the Islamic theologians through consensus. But as long as they do not conflict with the Quran and the Hadith of the Prophet, these are to be considered "Sharia".

The Ummah and Unique Bonding of Muslims

'Ummah', also pronounced as Umma, is the grand idea that binds Muslims all over the world into a common brotherhood or one single fraternity. Now, if we consider the concept of Ummah, that is that all Muslims belong to one community, a nation, called the Ummah - and this nation is extra-territorial in modern terminology, i.e., a Muslim could be in any country, say Finland or Greenland, and still belong to Ummah, because he or she is a Muslim. From the point of view of Sharia, if a part of that Ummah is attacked, then the entire Ummah is responsible for the defence of that area and the Muslims living there. In other words, if the Palestinians are attacked, if the Iranians are attacked, if the Iraqis are attacked, indeed, if Muslims in the USA, are attacked, then Muslims elsewhere should come to the aid of those Muslims.[5] Imam Feisal further elaborates the concept: "So long as Muslims continue to be attacked —and they have been attacked throughout, for centuries, et cetra—

then the fight continues." The struggle continues. That could be a justification for those who say, "wherever I attacked you and whatever Western interests I attack, are covered. I'm doing this with the blessings of Sharia."[6] Thus the concept of ummah has empowered Muslims with a unique system of bonding with their co-religionists even in the farthest corners of globe, across the oceans. That explains why nearly 600 Afghans led by Abu Sayyaf, all jihadis, left Pakistan almost ten years ago and have been fighting against the Christian government of Philippines, in the forests and swamps of southern islands of Mindnao and Sulu, shoulder to shoulder with the local Moro insurgents, i.e., the warriors of the MILF (Moro Islamic Liberation Front). That also explains how and why thousands of Pakistanis, Saudis, Egyptians, Algerians, Sudanese, Somalis, Chechens, Uzbeks and Indonesians and volunteers from many more countries, promptly responded to bin Laden's call to join the Afghan jihad and thousands remain holed up in Pak-occupied Kashmir to fight the so-called Hindu India. There is no parallel example anywhere in the world of such unique and intense bonding between people speaking different languages and coming from far away diverse regions to constitute one single legion of militant soldiers as Muslims have. It is like a transnational corporation. For comprehending the phenomenon of unique bonding between Muslims, wherever they be, and the strong motivation for joining the holy war, which rules their hearts and heads, it is important to know the implications of being part of the ummah. The concept of ummah connotes that all Muslims across the world are united, have a common identity and are one single people belonging to the Nation of Islam, that is 'Ummah'. It is perhaps for this reason that Louis Farrakhan calls the Black Muslims of America as 'the Nation of Islam". And this nation is an extra-territorial entity, namely the Islamic identity; it ignores national and transnational borders and places the Islamic fraternity above every other identity, including one's motherland. And Sharia enjoins on all Muslims the duty to join the battle and wage holy war or jihad, whenever any part of ummah is persecuted or attacked. "The west must understand", says Ahmed Suhelmi, an Islamic scholar at the University of Indonesia, "that the Ummah is a unity that cannot be divided. It is like human body – if you hurt even the little finger the whole body feels the pain... That certainly makes a potent crying".[7] The concept of Ummah constitutes the bedrock of the Pan-Islamic movement, because Islam does not recognize territorial affinities. Its affinities are social and religious and therefore extra-territorial.[8] In other words, a Muslim need not have any commitment to his motherland because he has another commitment, a higher commitment, that is his allegiance to the global Muslim fraternity called 'Ummah'. A strange and disquieting aspect of this extra-territorial commitment is that, in preference to a call to defend their motherland, Muslims are entitled to seek the aid of a foreign Muslim power to make jihad a success, or if the foreign Muslim power intends to proclaim a jihad, help that foreign nation in making the jihadist mission successful. Dr. Ambedkar has explained this aspect very lucidly by quoting from the deposition of Maulana Mahomed Ali, a well known Indian Khilafat activist having deep knowledge of Islamic law, when the latter was facing trial in a Sessions Court on charges of conspiracy and preaching sedition on the basis of a resolution passed by the Khilafat Conference on July 8, 1921, at Karachi in relation to a war waged by the Amir of Afghanistan against the British in 1919. The Maulana had exhorted the Muslims, including soldiers in the Indian army, not to join the fight against the Muslim Amir of Afghanistan. In his address to the jury in the Sessions Court Mahomed Ali had defended his stand by pointing out that the British government were apparently uninformed about the manner in which Islam guided all actions of Muslims including those which were considered as mundane. He asserted that Islam does not permit the believer to pronounce an adverse judgment against another believer without seeing a convincing proof that the latter had not taken up arms "in defence of their faith." Therefore, without adequate proof of the Amir's malice or madness, he did not want Indian soldiers, especially the Muslims, to join the war and attack Afghanistan. On the contrary, if the Amir of Afghanistan had no quarrel with India and her people and if he was motivated by the unrest which existed in Muslim countries to wage jihad in defence of the Khilafat and against wrongful occupation of the Jazirut-ul-Arab and the holy places, Islam does not permit them to take up arms against the Amir. In the event of jihad, the law of Islam requires that in the first place, no Muslim should render anyone any assistance against the Mujahideen; and in the second place if the Jihad approached the region where Muslims were living, every Mussalman in that region *must* join the Mujahideen and assist them to the best of his or her power. That was the clear and undisputed law of Islam, as amplified by Maulana Mahomed Ali in his court testimony about the call given by the Khilafat Committee to Muslim soldiers of the Indian army in relation to the 1919 war between the British and the Afghans.[9]

This is the basis of Pan-Islamism. It is this religious commitment which leads every Mussalman in India to say that he is a Muslim first and an Indian afterwards, as pointed out by Ambedkar.[10] The same extra-territorial philosophy of Ummah was justified by Sir Aga Khan when he wrote : "This is a right and legitimate Pan-Islamism to which every sincere and believing Mahomedan belongs – that is, the theory of the spiritual brotherhood and unity of the children of the Prophet."[11]

A classic example of the unique bonding between Muslims, based on the concept of Ummah, was witnessed during the recent Iraq war, "Operation Iraqi Freedom", when in an army camp in Kuwait on March 23, 2003, one U.S. soldier was killed and 15 were wounded because a Muslim American serviceman apparently angered by the war against Iraq rolled hand-grenades into their tents.[12] "He is a Muslim, and it seems he was just against war," said one U.S. military source, who did not wish to be identified. Another U.S. military source said that the assault appeared to be well-planned with the suspect first knocking out a generator that supplied electricity to the tents and then lobbing grenades.[13] Obviously that Muslim soldier of the U.S. army was gravely offended by the American attack on Iraq.This incident underlines the average Muslim's strong commitment to the concept of Ummah, which for all practical purposes, is the life-blood of Islamic unity.

Apart from being strongly enshrined in the sharia, the theological commitment to ummah has been regularly preached and propagated by clerics from the pulpits of mosques and stoutly supported by Islamic scholars. The core idea of Ummah is to rally all Muslims across the world to rush to the succour of their co-religionists when they are under threat due to any reason and take up arms to defend them. Thus when the U.S.A. attacked Afghanistan, it was a religious imperative in terms of the duty cast on all Muslims, members of the ummah, to rush to Afghanistan and help the Taliban. That was why 10,000 armed Pakistani militants rushed to Afghanistan to join the war against the U.S. in Kabul and Kunduz, and how several Muslims living in the U.K. decided to proceed to Afghanistan and Pakistan to join the ranks of jihadi warriors. It was the commitment to ummah which led hundreds and thousands of militant Muslim, fired by fundamentalist zeal, to join the fight against Russians in Afghanistan, and later on made them land in Chechenya and Bosnia – thousands came from distant Algeria and Tunisia in the west to Indonesia and Phillipines in the east, while some came even from the communist China. It is the same story in Jammu & Kashmir. Inspired by the religious bonding, terrorists from more than twenty countries have been participating in the so-called jihad in Kashmir which has taken a toll of more than 60,000 human lives during the last fifteen years. This unique bonding of Islamic fraternity has led to massive ethnic cleansing of Kashmir valley from where more than three hundred thousand Hindus (Kashmiri Pandits) have been driven out on pain of death. To cite another instance of ethnic cleansing by jihadis we have just to recall the chain of bloody events in the Indonesian island of Sulawesi where the soldiers of Laskar-Jihad ravaged the countryside and killed thousands of Christians some three years ago. Similarly in the faraway Malaku islands of Indonesia, another battle ground between Muslims and Christians, "some 10,000 have died in the past four years, including thousands of women and children, some of them tortured and mutilated."[14] A similar call to defend ummah by waging jihad, this time against the America and the U.K. was repeated during the recent Iraq war and in response therto quite a few thousand self-styled Islamic warriors from a number of countries, mostly neighbouring Muslim states like Syria, Jordan and Yemen, and some even from far away European countries like France, started moving into Iraq,while many more queued up for enlistment as volunteers for joining jihad, even in countries far removed from Iraq, like Bangladesh and Indonesia.

Prof. Riaz Hassan, an Australia based Islamic scholar, in an article on the subject, has expressed the hope that in the years to come the globalisation may lead to a reformulation of the concept of a single ummah. That could result in the emergence of multiple centres of Islam rather than the current one, based in Saudi Arabia, thereby leading to the recognition of a number of regional ummahs. The impact of colonialism and the emergence of nationalist movements which spearheaded the struggle against it, have also served to fragment the Islamic world into over 45 Muslim countries with competing economic and political interests.[15] He expressed the view that a decentred Muslim ummah would confer a kind of legitimacy on the regional ummahs and thus could cause them to chart their own social, political, economic and cultural goals for development along distinctive lines suitable to the regional history and temperament of their people. He further argues that "in a globalising world diversity and cultural crossovers will become a matter of routine."[16] While admitting that a survey of the evolution of Islam in recent decades shows that ummah - a universal community based on shared Islamic faith and implementation of its law – has indeed become a greater reality in an ever-shrinking world, he is hopeful that globalisation may transform different Islamic countries and regions into autonomous cultural systems. But Prof. Hassan's wishful thinking is far removed from reality. Till date the overall impact of globalisation and rapid advancement of science and technology on the 'faithful' has been in the opposite direction. Globalisation has, in effect, brought the Muslims living in far away regions closer to each other, thereby making the ummah a more closely knit and better bonded entity. Most Muslim countries and their population have always been suspicious of the process of globalization and Muslim clerics and scholars everywhere have been decrying and deriding it vehemently. They view globalization as a strategem for westernizing and corrupting the Islamic culture and enslaving the Muslim masses. Surprisingly Prof. Hassan has missed the important fact that the very idea of 'decentred' regional ummahs is antithetical to the basic precepts of Islam and any move in that uncharted direction will send alarm bells ringing across the Muslim world, especially among the clergy and the die-hard theologians. Islam as a religious faith has always been a grand monolith and globalization has already promoted greater unity and cohesion among various groups of Islamist terrorists and given fillip to the culture of Klashnikov and suicide bombing. Frankly, today the unity of the followers of Prophet Muhammed has reached a stage where no attempt to divide the ummah on the basis of cultural diversity or economic interests can succeed. In fact, by virtue of the sheer size of the Muslim population and the vast stretch of the geographical land mass over which they are spread the concept of ummah appears to be far more organised and better bonded than the so-called unity of the western nations (mostly Christian countries practising secularism) or for that matter more closely knit than the mighty North Atlantic Treaty Organization (NATO) – both of which almost fell apart during the recent Operation Iraqi Freedom. Some Islamic scholars feel that Imam Gazzali, a renowned scholar of the eleventh century, was responsible for making Islam a highly rigid and exclusivist religion, impervious to discourse and deliberations based on rationalism and philosophy. It may be mentioned that, at one time, a rationalist school of thought called 'Mutzalah' did come up in the Islamic society through the process of evolution. They were votaries of *'Ijtehad'* which meant arriving at a consensus through discussions and deliberations. They believed in rationalism and logic and tried to confront the external challenges to Islamic beliefs from various religions and cultures by trying to answer their doubts and queries. The Mutzalah scholars had a solid faith in the rationalist approach to Islamic faith and societal needs, in a way to make them complementary to each other. They believed in explaining and defining Islamic beliefs, ethos and basic fundamentals by using logic and philosophy. But they happened to be in a hopeless minority and were over-ruled by the Ulema who resented the Mutzalah approach. Ultimately the fundamentalist school (known as 'Isharah') managed to establish its supremacy. Their leitmotif was to accept the Quran and Sunnah as it is. They gave utmost importance to words and the construction of verses, totally neglecting the recondite aspects of the Quranic message. "Isharah deemed that the first group of Islam - that is Prophet Muhammad's companions' method, their strategy and way of living - must be followed *in toto*, by rejecting the scope for any changes to meet the needs of the society. They ruled out *Ijtehad*.[17] Ever since Imam Gazzali consolidated and standardised the Islamic beliefs and teachings of the Prophet in the eleventh century, no voice of dissent has been raised. Imam Gazzali brought together the whole gamut of the teachings of various schools and gave Muslim society a consolidated and standardized Islamic 'Fiqh' (that is, Islamic thought and philosophy). This led to unity amongst Muslims and ended the prevailing obfuscation. "Unfortunately, this consolidation and standardisation of Islamic teaching ended the dynamism and growth of Islamic thoughts and led to the phase of blind imitation and stagnation."[18]

3

Jihad in the Way of Allah

"The main goal of the future is to stop violence.
The world is addicted to it." – Bill Cosby

Apart from the five well known fundamentals, the conceptual framework of Islam enjoins on its followers a sixth condition as well – and a controversial one at that. It is the obligation placed on all Muslims to wage a holy war called 'jihad' against non-believers and infidels for spreading the message of Prophet Muhammad to four corners of the world. The literal meaning of the word 'jihad' is "to strive or to make an effort". But in the context of the doctrine of jihad propounded in the Quran and further exemplified in Hadith, it means to fight or strive in the cause of Islam, as ordained by Allah. Therefore the technical expression used in the Quran is *Jihad fi Sabilillah*, that is to strive or fight in the way of Allah. The concept of jihad has been enunciated quite lucidly in the eighth *surah* (chapter) of the Quran, i.e., the *Surah Anfal*, and the ninth *surah* titled *Taubah*, although jihad has been enjoined on the faithful in many other chapters as well. The most significant verse on the subject is 8.39 the meaning of which is similar to verse 2.193. Both these verses exhort the faithful to "fight them (the infidels) until persecution is no more and religion is all for Allah." These verses exhort the faithful to carry out perpetual jihad for the abolition of all non-Islamic religions the world over. N.J. Dawood's rendering of the same verse, "Make war on them until idolatory is no more and Allah's religion reigns supreme", brings out the meaning more explicitly.[1] The Quran chides those Muslims who shy away from jihad and exhorts them to fight in way of Allah. Ever since the birth of Islam, throughout history the Muslim warriors have remained busy battling with their neighbours and even with people living far away. As explained in the Publisher's note of the widely read commentary captioned "Jihad in the Quran and Sunnah" authored by Sheikh Abdullah bin Muhammad bin Humaid (ex Chief Justice of Saudi Arabia), Jihad is regarded as the best thing one can offer voluntarily. It is considered superior to non-obligatory prayers, fasting, Zakat, Umra and Hajj, as mentioned in the Quran and the Ahadith. The benefits of Jihad are deemed to be of great value to Muslims, while its effects are widespread and far reaching for the cause of Islam. For an individual Muslim, Jihad includes all acts of worship and all aspects of belief, thus bringing him greatest reward and vast blessings. And for the Muslim nation, Jihad provides all kinds of success in respect of prosperity and dignity, victory and glory—thus bringing magnificence and splendour.[2] In the aforesaid exposition, the Islamic scholar has emphasized that Allah has ordained Al-jihad (the holy fighting in Allah's Cause) to be carried out by the following three means:

1. With the heart (intentions or feelings),
2. With the hand (weapons, etc.),
3. With the tongue (speeches, etc., in the Cause of Allah).

It has been ordained that Allah will reward all those who perform jihad with lofty dwellings in the Gardens of Paradise.

Waging holy war or jihad against the infidels as ordained by the Quran has been the time-honoured tradition of most Muslim rulers as well as the commoners. Verses 47:4, 47.5 and 47.6 of the Quran say "So when you meet (in fight .... Jihad in Allah's Cause) those who disbelieve smite at their necks till when you have killed and wounded many of them, then bind a bond firmly (on them, i.e. take them as captives). Thereafter (is the time) either for generosity (i.e., free them without ransom) or ransom according to what benefits Islam), until the war lays down its burden. Thus you are ordered by Allah to continue in carrying out Jihad against the disbelievers till they embrace Islam (i.e. are saved from the punishment in the Hell fire) or at least come under your protection] but if it had been Allah's Will He Himself could certainly have punished them (without you). But (He lets you fight) in order to test you, some with others. But those who are killed in the Way of Allah, He will never let their deeds be lost. He will guide them and set right their state. And admit them to Paradise which He has made known to them.[3] The foregoing text underlines the importance of jihad in the Islamic scheme of world order and shows that it is an integral part of the Islamic theology, having been ordained by the Prophet himself. That jihad is the greatest duty of a Muslim has been described in the Hadith without any scope for ambiguity. As stated in Imam Muslim, it has been confirmed in Sahih Muslim on the authority of Abu Hurairah, an important companion of the Messenger of Allah, the prophet had said that a Muslim who died but did not fight in the way of Allah, nor did express any desire or determination for *Jihad* died the death of a hypocrite.[4] Further it has been reiterated on the authority of Abu Said Khudri that the Messenger of Allah had told him that whoever cheerfully accepts Allah as his Lord, Islam as his religion and Muhammad as his Apostle, is necessarily entitled to enter Paradise. But there is another act which elevates the position of a man in Paradise to a grade one hundred times higher and the elevation between one grade and the other is equal to the height of the heaven from the earth. Abu Said asked: "What is that act? He replied: *Jihad* in the way of Allah! *Jihad* in the way of Allah".[5]

Every Muslim while receiving lessons in the Quran during his childhood years is taught to swear by *jihad*, and knows that it is obligatory for him to fight in the way of Allah. Osama bin Laden while referring to the Afghan war in an interview on television (CNN), aired on May 10, 1997, had grandly proclaimed, "the acme of this religion is Jihad". Osama bin Laden has been a great admirer of Taqi al Din Ibn Taymiyah, a well known Islamic scholar and famed mujahid of Sham, i.e., the present Syria, who was responsible for training several mujahideen groups to wage holy war against heathen Tartars in the medieval times. Ibn Taymiyah eulogised the mujahideen and extolled the virtues of jihad waged for Allah's sake. He explained that jihad will continue till the day of judgment, by using the following authentic Hadith as proof:

"There will always remain a group of people from my nation who will establish the truth. They will never be agonised by those who let them down nor by those who disagree with them till the day of judgment".[6]

Thus for Muslims '*jihad*' is continuum; it is a holy war to be waged throughout the ages till the Day of Judgment. Prophet Muhammad himself had undertaken nearly twenty six jihads which were called Ghazwahs. In Arabic tradition, a jihad to destroy the infidels, personally led by the prophet was called 'Ghazwah' —a word etymologically related to the title 'Ghazi' which means a victorious "kafir slaying soldier" of Islam. To be a 'ghazi' is therefore the religious ambition of every devout Muslim because it bestows on him prestige in this world and assures his entry into heaven in the after-life. After Akbar's victory in the second battle of Panipat in November 1556, when Hemu was brought before him in an injured condition, Bairam Khan prompted Akbar to earn the covetted title of Ghazi by killing Hemu. Referring to the slaying of Hemu by Akbar, Will Durant writes: "Like a good Turk, he had no effeminate distaste of human blood; when at the age of fourteen, he was invited to win the title of Ghazi—Slayer of the Infidel - by killing Hindu prisoner, he cut off the man's head at once with his scimitar."[7] That was how, Akbar, one of the most illustrious and cultured Mughal kings began his royal career. The commonly accepted story that young Akbar had exhibited a chivalrous unwillingness to strike a wounded prisoner is not true; it is a subsequent courtly invention.[8]

The same centuries old Islamic tradition of holy war and commitment of the faithful to jihad is now being emulated and carried forward into the twentyfirst century by the Islamists. The importance of jihad has also been highlighted by the well known journalist and author, M.J. Akbar, in his book "The Shade of Swords" where he has reiterated in the Introduction itself that *jihad* is "the signature tune of Islamic history". Elaborating the concept he points out that although the Prophet insisted that a greater jihad was the struggle to cleanse impurity within, that does not detract from the fact that it was the lesser jihad which had inspired the spirit that once powered the armies of Islam and made them all conquering.[9] For Muslims, jihad is not merely a question of cleansing the inner spirit; it is also a call for holy war regularly heard since the beginning of Islam. There is a saying by the Prophet: "Paradise comes under the shade of swords."[10] A call for jihad has always evoked prompt response from Muslims across the world. The Quranic doctrine of 'paradise comes under the shade of swords' has been exemplified by Abu Musa, another prominent companion of the Prophet, in Hadith No. 4549 of Mishkat. According to Abu Musa, Allah's Messenger had said that the portals of heaven lie under the shadow of the swords. On hearing this a lean and emaciated man stood up and asked Abu Musa whether the latter had heard this hadith with his own ears? As soon as Abu Musa replied in the affirmative, the emaciated man went to his companions and bid them salaam. Soon the man broke the sheath of his sword and proceeded towards the enemies. He killed many enemies and ultimately attained martyrdom.[11]

Another important aspect of Jihad is the justification flowing from Verse 8:67 of the Quran for "slaughter in the land" meaning thereby that during jihad the infidels are to be put to slaughter. A typical example of "slaughter in the land' was the treatment meted out by the Prophet himself to the Jews of Banu Kuraizah, a tribe of Medina, after the battle of Ditch in 627 A.D. Although the Jews of Banu Kuraizah did not participate in the battle of Ditch, they were supposed to be hostile to the Prophet and suspected to be conspiring against him. After victory in the battle of Ditch, the Prophet's army laid seige to the stronghold of Banu Kuraizah till they were starved into submission. The Jews offered to go into exile, but were not allowed. They appealed for mediation by the Arab tribe of Aus, of which they were clients, which request was granted by the Prophet. The Ausite chief, Sa'd bin Mua'z, pronounced his judgement in the name of Allah whereby all male members of the Kuraizah, barring children, were to be put to death, while their women and children were to be sold into slavery. The Prophet praised Sa'd for having adjudged the case with the judgment of God, the Exalted and Glorified one.[12] Then a big pit was dug in the market of Medina, and 800 Jews (as estimated by William Muir) were brought down, chained and manacled, and were beheaded. The slaughter was presided over by the Prophet himself. A woman whose husband had just been beheaded, admitted to having killed a Muslim by throwing a big stone during the Kuraizah seige, but refused the gift of life being granted to the enslaved womenfolk, was promptly executed at her own request. Her smiling face, as she stepped forward for execution was said to have haunted the Prophet's favourite wife, Ayesha, to the end of her days.[13]

In recent years the concept of jihad has gained enormous popularity among Muslim youth and the clergy. As pointed out by Afsir Karim, the last two decades of the twentieth century have witnessed the emergence of a most dangerous form of international terrorism. It has been led by the self-styled Islamic mullahs whose aim is to target Christian, Jewish and Hindu communities and non-conformist Muslims around the globe. The political agenda of this violent jihadi movement is to establish an Islamic order in various parts of the world (Nizam-e-Mustafa - an order propagated by the Prophet during his time - as interpreted by the fundamentalists and their mentors).[14] The Islamic fundamentalists believe that Jihad by force (*bil saif*) is justified to annihilate enemies of Islam. Many fundamentalist leaders advocated violent jihad against all unbelievers and called it the suppressed sixth pillar of Islam.[15] Palestinian Jihadi leader, Abdullah Azzam (1941-1989) who joined the Afghan resistance against the Soviet army and was also considered Bin Laden's mentor, claimed that Jihad is a forgotten obligation of every Muslim, as infidels today occupy Muslim lands in Palestine, Afghanistan (1980s) and Kashmir.[16] It is remarkable that a large number of Muslim scholars and intellectuals, ranging from Maulvis to authors and journalists, are in broad agreement with bin Laden's views about the importance of *jihad* in Islamic theology, as spelt out during his interview to the television channel CNN in May 1997. No wonder the idealogue of Pakistan, Allama Iqbal, too, in one of his widely read pan-Islamic poem, captioned *'Tarana'* which is a favourite song of Pakistan-based Islamic terrorists operating in Kashmir, had referred to the Muslim warriors being brought up under the shade of swords and claimed that 'halali dagger', i.e. the butcher's knife, was the representative symbol of Islam when he sang "Teghon ke saye mein ham pal kar jawan huey hain, khanjar halal ka hai qaumi nishan hamara". Translated in English it means that we, Muslims, have been brought up under "the shade of swords" and Iqbal further announced that the 'killer dagger' was the symbol of the Nation of Islam. Clearly there is much more to the concept of jihad and the consequential militancy which it has spawned than what some of the present day Muslim theologians have been trying to explain. It must be understood that so long as the twin ideals of jihad and the lure of paradise under the shade of swords continue to fire the imagination of young Muslims, it would be well nigh impossible to avoid the impending clash of civilizations prophesied by Samuel Huntington. The so-called superiority of jihad-e-akbar (i.e.,the higher jihad aimed at spiritual improvement of one's self) over the so-called jihad-e-asghar (i.e., the lesser jihad involving taking up arms in the cause of Islam) is being presented largely as an excuse, just to pacify the angry millions outraged all across the globe by the bombings of the WTC and Pentagon in America which resulted in the death of thousands of innocent men and women and the subsequent relentless terror strikes, both prior to and after 9/11. It is interesting to note that lately it is being increasingly argued that jihad is a struggle within one's soul to become a better human being. Perhaps this hair splitting is being done by some Muslim scholars and intellectuals to mollify the indignant public opinion alarmed by the prospects of Islamists taking up arms to wage a holy war—as indeed is being done presently in a number of countries, including those where Muslims are in minority. Frankly, the term "*jihad*" as expounded in the Quran and the Hadith and more importantly as practised by Muslims rulers and clergy for centuries and as commonly understood both by Muslims and non-Muslims stands for waging war against the so-called infidels (read non-Muslims) to convert them and spread the message of Prophet Muhammad worldwide. Jihads personally waged by Prophet Muhammad were called "Ghazwahs". It has been recorded by some historians that in his lifetime Prophet Muhammad himself had approved more than 82 jihads, or holy wars against the infidels and in at least 26 jihads (called Ghazawahs) he himself led the warriors, while the remaining jihads were waged by his lieutenants. Some of the important Ghazawahs personally led by the Prophet were the battle of Nakhla in 623 A.D., the battle of Badr in 624 A.D., the battle against Banu Kainuka in 624 A.D. (Banu Kainukas were the first tribe of Jews to be banished from Medina), the battle of Uhud in 625 A.D. against the Koreish tribe of Mecca, the battle against Banu Nazir in 625 A.D. who were the second Jewish tribe to be expelled from Medina, the battle against Banu Mustalik in 626-627 A.D. (the Mustalik were a non-Muslim Arabic tribe hostile to the

Prophet), the battle of the Ditch in 627 A.D. which is also called the battle of Ahzab in which the beseiging Koreish army was repulsed from Medina, the jihad against the Jewish tribe of Banu Kuraizah in 627 A.D. (which resulted in the slaughter of all menfolk of Kuraizah Jewish clan), the expedition of Hudaibiyah in 628 A.D. against the Koreish ruler who did not allow the Prophet and his army to enter Mecca, the battle of Khaibar in 628 A.D. in which the non-Medinese Jews of Khaibar were reduced to the status of 'kharajguzars' and jiziya was imposed on them (the Jews of Khaibar were the first non-Muslim group to be subjected to Jiziya), the battle of Mecca in 630 A.D. in which the Koreish clan was defeated, the battle of Hunain in 630 A.D. which led to the seige of Taif, and the battle of Tabuk which was the last Ghazwah led by the Prophet.

Although historically innumerable jihads were waged in India by Muslim invaders against Hindus, labelled as the infidels, in modern times too there have been at least three well known instances of jihads in India. The first jihad was launched in 1824 by one Said Ahmed, a Wahabi leader, who regularly preached holy war or jihad against infidels. Said Ahmed had begun his life as a Sawar, or horseman, under Ameer Khan Pindary. Originally Pindaries were thugs and highway robbers who used to waylay and loot the common travellers. He had accompanied Ameer Khan Pindary in many freebooting raids in Malwa, but after quitting his service Said Ahmed became a disciple of Shah Abdul Aziz, a fundamentalist Sunni cleric of Delhi, who believed in the puritan Wahabi Islam of Saudi Arabia. Soon thereafter, Said Ahmed became an exponent of the Wahabi doctrine and launched the Wahabi movement in northern India. His first disciples were two close relations of Shah Abdul Aziz, one his nephew Maulvi Mahomed Ismael, and the other his son-in-law, Maulvi Abdul Haye. Accompanied by them Said Ahmed proceeded to Calcutta (now Kolkata) but took up a circuitous route first northwards to Saharanpur, and then westward to Rampur - the seat of a large and turbulent body of Pathans.[17] In this journey he successfully preached Islam and won new followers among the Muslims of Bengal by spreading his Wahabi doctrine. Soon he acquired a large number of followers or 'murids' in Kolkota, then called Calcutta, and certain parts of Bengal, Bihar and U.P., at that time known as the Western Provinces. Originally the Wahabi sect had been created by one Muhammad, son of Abdul Wahab who was born at Najad in Arabia in 1691.The basic Wahabi doctrine rests on the principle that there is only one God, that is Allah, and that Muhammad was his Messenger. Wahabis repudiate all those rituals and ceremonies which are not sanctioned by the Quran and Hadith, and strictly forbid any belief in holy men, i.e., *pirs, walis* and *saints*. They denounced illumination of the shrines of *pirs* and maintained that visits to such places and paying obesience to *pirs* was forbidden by Islam. Wahabis strongly support the duty of jihad or holy war, against the infidels. They repose absolute faith in the Quran and Hadith and felt that lessons taught by Hadith were being neglected by the Muslims in general and for this reason they also came to be addressed as 'Ahl-e-Hadith'. In 1824 Said Ahmed travelled through Kandhar and Kabul, which at that time happened to be under the suzerainty of the famous Sikh ruler Maharaja Ranjit Singh of Punjab and reached among the Yusufzai tribes on the Peshawar border. He made an alliance with the Barakzai Sardars and proclaimed a religious war against the Sikhs.[18] The call for jihad against Sikhs was issued by Said Ahmed through a proclamation titled "Targhib-ul Jihad" which stated that the Sikhs had been in power for a long time in Lahore and other adjoining places, and that during their oppressive rule thousands of Muslims were killed and disgraced, so much so that even the Azan, or summons to their prayer, and the slaughter of cows had been banned. As their tyranny could no longer be tolerated, Said Ahmed accompanied by thousands of believers, proceeded in the direction of Kabul, and asked the faithful to tread the path of God's service and on 20th Jumadi-ul-Sani 1242 'Hijree (21st December 1826) declared Jihad against the 'Kafir' Sikhs.[19]

The progress of this jihad launched by Said Ahmed was watched with interest by the Muslims of North India. Many Muslim residents of the Western Provinces (U.P.) proceeded in groups to join the holy war under the banner of the self-styled "Ameer-ul-Momineen", or leader of the faithful, a title which he had now assumed.[20] Ultimately Said Ahmed and his mujahideen, known as the "Hindustanis", were defeated by the Sikh army and he fled to Surat. He again returned to the area north of Kabul in 1828 and succeeded in extending his influence over the area north of the Kabul river and in 1929 he managed to seize the Peshawar valley. Soon he started taking strong measures for enforcing the Islamic law as interpreted by Wahabis and abolished many local customary laws which were in conflict with the spirit of Islam. The local population neither liked the rigid Wahabi doctrine nor did they approve of the high-handed manner in which they were being treated by Said Ahmed. Discontent spread all over the tribal area rapidly and soon Pathans came to the conclusion that no useful purpose would be served by replacing the Sikhs with Said Ahmed and his followers. They decided to kill Said Ahmed and his Wahabi soldiers, known as 'Hindustani Fanatics'. On the appointed night they murdered all followers of Said Ahmed. Luckily Said Ahmed was away to Panj Tar on that fateful night, along with a band of his devoted soldiers. He decided to turn back with his soldiers and while crossing the river Indus, he was met by a Sikh force under the renowned Sikh general, Hari Singh Nalwa. He joined the battle against Sikhs but his mujahideen warriors were defeated by the Sikh force under Hari Singh Nalwa near Phulera on the right bank of Siran river, west of Mansehra. In 1830 he again tried to confront the Sikhs in Hazara district and paid for his folly with his life in the battle of Balakot.[21] Thus the first jihad proclaimed by the Wahabi leader Said Ahmed against Sikh rulers of Punjab and North Western Frontier Province ended on a tragic note.

After death of Maharaja Ranjit Singh and annexation of Punjab by the British, Wahabi *jihad* came to be directed against the British rulers. The struggle was kept up by a handful of Said Ahmed's followers known as mujahideen who believed that soon the former will reappear as *Imam Mahdi* and off and on they continued to fight the British rulers. The Government of India had to send a number of punitive expeditions to the Frontier Province and Afghanistan to crush the Wahabi movement. The Wahabis or mujahideen, also known as Hindustani Fanatics, lied low from 1898 to 1914 and did not give much trouble to the British. But in 1914 when Britain declared war on Turkey, they became active once again and renewed the call for *jihad* against the British. In the year 1915 at the instance of Maulana Mahmud-ul-Hasan of Deoband, one Fazl-e-Walid, son of Faiz Ahmad Haji Khel Mohammed, Pirzada of Turangzai (popularly known as the Haji of Turangzai) in North Western Frontier Province raised the standard of "*jihad*" against the British but failed to achieve any success.[22] At that time there was a feeling of outrage against the British governement among the Muslims of India. Several attempts were made by some disaffected Muslim leaders of Punjab and North Western Frontier Province, like Maulvi Fazal Elahi and Maulvi Abdul Rahim of Chiniyawala mosque in Lahore, who went to Kabul, accompanied by some students of the Medical and Law Colleges of Lahore, to seek help of the Amir of Afghanistan. The latter did start a war in the year 1919 against the British but nothing much happened and finally the challenge of the Wahabi jihad petered out.

The second declaration of jihad was made by the Khilafat Committee and several Muslim groups in 1920s when the Ottoman Caliphate was abolished, consequent upon the defeat of Turkey in 1918 by the British and French armies resulting in the seizure of Constantinople, the capital of Turkey. This call for jihad was given by the Khilafat Committee comprising the Ali brothers, Mohammed Ali and Shaukat Ali, who were joined by Hasrat Mohani, and even Maulana Abul Kalam Azad. Beginning with the year 1920 there occurred in that year in Malabar, now in Kerala, what is notoriously known as the Moplah rebellion. It resulted from the agitation carried out by two Muslim organizations, the Khuddam-i-Kaaba (servants of the Mecca Shrine) and the Central Khilafat Committee. Agitators preached the doctrine that India under the British rule was Dar-ul-Harab and therefore the Muslims must fight against it and if they could not, they must carry out the alternative principle of *Hijrat*.[23] The latter alternative (i.e. *Hijrat*) meant that Muslims should migrate *en masse* out of British India. The idea was mooted that, if the British failed to do justice to Sultan of Turkey, the Khalifah, all Muslims should migrate to the nearest Dar-ul-Islam, Afghanistan. This fantastic suggestion was taken up.[24] About 18,000 Muslims sold whatever they had with the resolve to migrate and many more might have joined the *Hijrat* if the Afghan government had not imposed restrictions on the entry of immigrants. This campaign of *Hijrat* was nothing short of ruin for the 18,000 families. Later on although the protagonists of Khilafat did try to mitigate the sufferings of those who survived and returned to their homes, the *faux pas* did not serve as a reminder that religious ardour should be tempered with sober thought.[25] Needless to mention that the second option of '*Hijrat* ', or migration from India, exercised by 18,000 families was quite absurd and failed miserably.

The Khilafat movement was a disaster in more than one way. The Moplahs of Malabar were suddenly carried off their feet by this proclamation of jihad by the Khilafat Committee. They resorted to large scale violence which was supposed to be a rebellion against the British Government who were considered responsible for the abolition of the Caliphate. The aim of the so-called jihad was to establish the kingdom of Islam in Malabar by overthrowing the British Government. Swords and spears were secretly manufactured, and bands of desperadoes collected for an attack on the British authorities. On August 20,1920, an encounter took place between the Moplah jihadis and the British forces at Pirunangadi. Roads were blocked, telegraph lines cut, and the railway tracks destroyed in a number of places. As soon as the administration collapsed, the Moplahs declared that they had become independent. One Ali Musaliar was made the ruler and the flag of Khilafat was unfurled. Ernad and Wallurnad districts were declared Khilafat kingdoms. As a rebellion against the British Government the jihad could be understandable but what shocked most people was the horrid treatment meted out by the Moplahs to the Hindus of Malabar. Many of them were massacred, their homes plundered and womenfolk subjected to foul outrages and brutal indignities. Many temples were desecrated and there were instances of forcible conversions to Islam. The brutalities continued till the troops could reach the interior of Malabar to restore law and order. The exact number of Hindus killed, wounded or converted to Islam could not be known. But the number must have been enormous.[26] Although this so-called *jihad* was finally put down by the British Government, its consequences were very ugly and far reaching. It further widened the growing chasm between the Muslims and the Hindus and the latter started questioning the bonafides of Muslims for their senseless targeting of Hindus and their religious places. While the anger of Muslims against the British was somewhat understandable, no one could explain the rationale of their fiery hostility towards Hindus. In this infamous *jihad* the worst victims of the atrocities of Moplah jihadis were not the British but the hapless Hindus of Malabar who were in no way responsible for the defeat of Turkey and abolition of the Ottoman caliphate. But then, reason has never been a strong point of the religious bigots.

The third jihad was declared by the All India Muslim League in 1946 for creation of Pakistan as an independent homeland for Muslims of the sub-continent when the separatist movement was at its peak. At that time the Muslim League was in power in Bengal and as Minister in charge of Law and Order, H.S. Suhrawardy, cleverly managed to transfer most of the Hindu police officers from key posts. Muslim League declared 16th August 1946 as 'the Direct Action Day' to press forward the demand for Pakistan. Although Calcutta (now Kolkata) was a Hindu majority city, on the day of 'Direct Action', August 16 1946, Muslim police officers were in charge of twenty-two police stations out of a total of twenty-four, and the remaining two were controlled by Anglo-Indians.[27] A detailed programme for direct action on the fateful day was drawn up by the Muslim League which was given wide publicity in the Muslim Press. The programme called for a total hartal, i.e. strike, and cessation of all business in the city. A mass rally and meeting were to be held at the foot of the Ochterlony Monument from 3 p.m. onwards over which Suhrawardy was to preside. The Mayor of Calcutta, Mohammed Usman, wanted a million Muslims to congregate in the maidan as a demonstration of their strength. A leaflet was issued bearing the title "Manifesto" which exhorted the Muslims to reach out to the people of their "Illaqa, mohalla, in mosques, in schools, colleges, clubs, tea-stalls and hotels" and asking them to "awake, arise, and unite under the banner of Muslim League and make the hartal a success". They were directed to reach the Ochterlony Monument in processions with the accompaniment of bands at 3 p.m., and "lead the procession with such strength and enthusiasm that even the blind, deaf and dumb can appreciate their strength and determination".[28] Another leaflet issued by the Calcutta Mayor, Mohammed Usman, captioned "Munajat for Jihad", containing the proclamation of jihad and a prayer for its success is worth quoting in full:

"Munajat for the Jihad"

(To be said at every mosque after the Jumma prayer)

"It was in this month of Ramzan that the Holy Quran was revealed! It was in this month of Ramzan that 313 Muslims were victorious through the grace of God over the *Kafers* in the battle of Badr and the *Jehad* of the Muslims commenced ! It was in this month that ten thousand Muslims marched to Mecca and were conquerors and thus there was the establishment of the Kingdom of Islam. By the grace of God we are ten crores in India but through bad luck we have become slaves of the Hindus and the British. We are starting a *Jehad* in Your Name in this very month of Ramzan. We promise You that we entirely depend on You. Pray make us strong in body and mind - give Your helping hand in all our actions - make us victorious over the *Kafers* - enable us to establish the Kingdom of Islam in India and make proper sacrifices for this *Jehad* - by the grace of God may we build up in India the greatest Islamic Kingdom in the world. The Muslims in China, Manchuria, Mongolia, Malaya, Java and Sumatra are all fighting for their freedom - pray Your Grace they may succeed. May You bring freedom to the Muslims of Turkey, Iran, Iraq, Albania, Arabia, Egypt and the Sudan and also to the Muslims of Tunis, Algiers, Morocco, Africa. May God help us so that Muslims of the world may be able to build up a very strong Islamic Kingdom in this world."[29]

And then followed some Arabic quotations from the Quran and Hadis. Below the above proclamation of jihad was a footnote saying that this prayer should be kept with care - must not be touched with foot or dishonoured in any way.

It is believed that before the Direct Action Day, hundreds of bad characters who were in detention during the World War II had been released by the Bengal Government. A large number of Muslims armed themselves with lathis, spears and daggers which created enormous panic among the Hindus - it may be recalled that at that time Calcutta was a Hindu majority city. In the morning of August 16, 1946, several groups of storm troopers of the Muslim League, armed with spears, daggers and lathis, and some allegedly carrying guns roamed the streets of Calcutta, forcing the Hindus to close their shops and business establishments. By the afternoon all hell broke loose and there was large scale rioting and arson all around, aimed at the Hindus. Hundreds were being killed but the Army was not called out to control the rampaging mobs and extensive rioting. For a day and a half Muslim rioters held their own. On the third day the tide began to turn and the Hindus and the Sikhs began to retaliate and hit back in anger. Only when this change began to spell disaster for the marauders did the government requisition services of the army for assistance in riot control.[30] Hundreds of dead bodies rotted in the streets of Calcutta and their disposal by cremation and burying became a huge problem. Finally by August 27, 1946, (i.e. 13 days after the butchery had started on the Direct Action Day) all dead bodies could be disposed of. According to a rough assessment given by Gopal Das Khosla, in 'Stern Reckoning', a total of 3,173 dead bodies were collected and disposed of by different organisations.[31] The actual number of persons killed was much larger. Many had been burnt alive in their houses, while many more bodies were thrown into the river and went down into the sea. The Hindus suffered grievously both in life and property – their loss of property was colossal and much more than that of the Muslims. If the hospital figures were accepted as a basis for determining the ratio of Muslims and Hindu casualties, it appeared that the Muslims fared almost as badly as the Hindus. But Calcutta killings set the tone for outbreak of large scale rioting and communal clashes all over the country from August 1946 onwards till August 1947 when the partition of India was announced – riots continued for several months even thereafter. After seeing what had happened in Calcutta on the Direct Action Day it was crystal clear that the division of the sub-continent would lead to a massive bloodbath and butchery because of the call for jihad. Unfortunately nothing was done to devise a mechanism for preventing that foreseeable mammoth holocaust. Only if the British and the Congress leadership had cared to read the history of various jihads waged in the past in India and glanced at the colossal loss of life and property during the previous years of communal rioting which had ravaged the sub-continent, they would have been wiser and could have saved lakhs of lives. But alas, they neither had the vision nor the wisdom to prevent the impending holocaust in which lakhs of innocent lives were lost.

An analysis of the Calcutta Killings organised by the Muslim League, with the tacit support of the British bureaucracy, showed that once again the centuries old time-tested battle cry of *jihad* was used as the medium for mobilizing the Muslim masses to take recourse to violence. But the British Government remained an indifferent silent spectator to the *jihad* launched by the Muslim League which resulted in large scale killings.

The most important futuristic underpinning of the proclamation of jihad made by Muslim League on the eve of the Direct Action Day was the reference to the miserable plight of Muslims of China, Mongolia, Malaya, Java, Sumatra and several Arab and African countries who were fighting for freedom and establishment of a "very strong Islamic kingdom in this world". With the benefit of hindsight, now one can say that these words turned out to be almost prophetic at the end of the twentieth century. The unequivocal pronouncements made by the Muslim League for the establishment of a very strong Islamic kingdom in this world could not have left anyone in doubt about the futuristic ambitions of the protagonists of Pakistan - even as early as the year 1947 ! And the creation of Pakistan was surely the first step forward in that direction, as later developments eventually proved. For the students of Indian history the call for jihad made in 1947 was not something new because there had been many jihads earlier. In the history of medieval India, starting with Mohammed bin Qasim and Mahmud of Ghazni, throughout the Muslim rule there were innumerable *jihads* - the aim of every successive *jihad* being to convert the Hindu infidels to Islam. One of these was by the notorious Taimur, who claimed to have killed more than one hundred thousand idolater Hindus, and who, in his memoirs, explained that his object in the invasion of India was to lead a campaign against the infidels,"to convert them to the true faith according to the command of Muhammad ……. ……. to purify the land from the defilement of misbelief and polytheism, and overthrow the temples and idols, whereby we shall be Ghazis and Mujahids, companions and soldiers of the faith before God".[32] While referring to the Muslim invasions of India, Dr. Ambedkar has pointed out that these were not undertaken merely out of lust for loot or conquest. There was another objective behind them. For instance, the expedition against Sind by Mohammed bin

Qasim was apparently of a punitive character mainly undertaken to punish Raja Dahir of Sind who refused to make restitution for the seizure of an Arab ship at Debal, a seaport town of Sind. There is, however, no doubt that striking a blow at the idolatory of Hindus and establishing Islam in India were also the aims of that expedition.[33] According to Dr. Titus, in a despatch to the Hajjaj, the Caliph of Islam, Mahommad bin Qasim had said that the nephew of Raja Dahir, his warriors and principal officers had been dispatched and the infidels converted to Islam. In place of temples, mosques had been built, the Khutbah was read, the call to prayers raised, so that devotions are performed at stated hours. "The Takbir and praise to the Almighty God are offered every morning and evening."[34] In reply the Hajjaj reminded Mohammed bin Qasim of God's commandment : "Give no quarter to infidels but cut their throats. Then know that this is the command of the great God. You shall not be too ready to grant protection, because it will prolong your work".[35] Thus the ongoing jihad in Jammu & Kashmir, sponsored by Pakistan and backed by thousands of holy warriors from more than twenty countries, is by no stretch of imagination the first *jihad* launched against the Indian civilization. There have been a series of such *jihads* earlier, too; three of which, stated above, having taken place in the modern times. And at least one of these modern day jihads, namely the one waged for the creation of Pakistan, was a thumping success. Perhaps that is what makes the Pakistan Army and the ISI consider the annexation of Kashmir as part of their left over agenda of partition—a task, they feel, left unfulfilled since 1947.

Closely associated with Islamic jihad are two more concepts. First, the practice of 'Ghanima' or plunder, undertaken after vanquishing the enemy in the holy war, and second the imposition of 'Jiziya' on the infidels, i.e., the Kafirs, as enunciated in the Quran and elaborated in the Hadith. When a mujahid attains martyrdom in *jihad*, he earns a place in the paradise and is rewarded with a number of virgin maidens, called houris—as many as seventy of them. But if he succeeds in the holy war and comes out victorious, what reward does he get? Well, that reward is ghanima, the 'war booty', or the spoils of war, i.e., everything which belonged to the vanquished infidel - his land, gold and silver, other goods, and even his wife and children. Etymologically the word 'ghanima' is derived from the Arabic word 'ghanim" which means the enemy. In other words, the term ghanima means the property which has been seized from the enemy. The concept is explained in the eighth chapter of the Quran, captioned *Anfil* which means the "surplus earning" or 'bonus'. This chapter provides the justification for ghanima or plunder, after victory, and lays down some modalities for distribution of the booty obtained in jihad. For instance, verse 41 of Surah Anfal (i.e. Verse 8.41) says: "And know that whatever ye take spoils of war, lo! A fifth thereof is for Allah and His Messenger and for the kinsmen and orphans and the needy and the wayfarer." It empowers the mujahids to collect spoils of war as a right and further enjoins that one-fifth of the booty shall be earmarked for Allah and His Messenger. This one-fifth of the plunder is called the 'holy one-fifth' by Islamic scholars because this one-fifth share of plunder used to be sent to the Muslim king's treasury, when the Prophet was no more. Indirectly this verse provides some share for the mujahids also, perhaps the remaining four-fifths of the booty. The concept of enjoying the booty captured from the vanquished is clarified in Surah Anfal, through verse 8.69, which proclaims, "Eat ye the spoils of war. They are lawful and pure".[36] In other words, there is nothing improper about plunder and enjoying the spoils of war; it is a mujahid's prerogative. Similarly verse 4.24 asserts that "All married women are forbidden (to you) save those (captives) whom your right hands possess."[37] The expression 'right hands possess' means those women who have been captured in jihad. In brief, the property of the infidel - his wealth, his women and children are lawful plunder for the mujahid.[38] Possibly the practice of ghanima is a continuation of the tribal Bedouin tradition of plunder.

The next question is, after attaining victory in jihad, what should the faithful do with the vanquished Kafirs? The options are three: first, their forcible conversion to Islam; second, their mass slaughter (referred to as "slaughter in the land") followed by plunder (i.e. ghanima); or the third option, namely the imposition of "jiziya" or poll tax. The ultimate aim of jihad is to conquer the whole world and make the people everywhere conform to the Islamic doctrine, enunciated by the Prophet. Verse 9.29 of the Quran says : "Fight against such of those who have been given the Scripture as believe not in Allah nor the Last Day, and forbid not that which Allah hath forbidden by His Messenger, and follow not the religion of truth, until they pay the tribute readily, being brought low".[39] The actual requirement about the mode of payment of jiziya is that it should be paid by the Zimmi (also called 'dhimmi') in person, in a low abject posture of submission.The imposition of jiziya, or poll tax, is meant to make life more difficult for the infidels by subjecting them to grave financial strain. Interestingly the levy of jiziya appears to be the only bloodless activity associated with jihad. Originally the option of being allowed to survive under Muslim rulers, by paying a poll tax, was meant only for the Jews and the Christians, i.e.,the people of the Scriptures (Ahl-e-Kitab or the People of the Book whose prophets are mentioned in the Quran). All others namely the idolaters and polytheists were supposed to face 'slaughter in the land'. The extension of this facility of surviving by paying a tax to idolaters outside Arabia appears to be a latter day development. In essence the payment of jiziya is a mark of degradation for non-Muslims, and they are referred to as '*kharajgujars*' that is the humble payers of poll tax who had to do so as a token of subjugation. The quantum or the scale of the levy has not been mentioned anywhere in Islamic laws. The Jews of Khaibar were the first non-Muslims subjected to jiziya, and the tax imposed on them resulted in making them tenants in their own lands. The rate of tax, if Sir William Muir is to be believed, was half the produce of the land. But the Christian subjects of the Governor of Alia, whom the Prophet had defeated during his Tabuk campaign in 630 A.D., were called upon to pay a gold piece (dinar) per head per annum.[40] According to the Hidayah the capitation tax is a species of punishment inflicted upon the kafirs on account of their infidelity which means Jizyat. Therefore etymologically Jiziya means a tax imposed by way of retribution. Lane Pool in his treatise, *Medieval India*, has stated that the Hindus were taxed to the extent of half the produce of their land, and had to pay jiziya on all their buffaloes, goats and milch cattle. The tax was levied equally on the rich and the poor, at so much per bigha, so much per animal. Any collectors or officers taking bribes were summarily dismissed and heavily punished. The rules for the collection of jiziya were strictly carried out so that one revenue officer would string together 20 Hindu notables and enforce payment by blows.[41] As explained by Sir Jadunath Sarkar in the *History of Aurangzeb*, the jiziya hit the poorest sections of the population the hardest. It could never be less than Rs 31/3 on a man, which was the money for nine maunds of wheat flour at the average market price at the end of the 16th century. The ruler, therefore, at the lowest incidence of the tax, annually took away from the poorest man the full value of one year's food as the price of allowing him to practise his own religion.[42] In India, as surely as in many other countries, the ultimate objective of the imposition of jiziya by Muslim rulers was to speed up the pace of conversion to Islam, especially among the poor and the financially marginalised classes. And thus in most such countries very often the poor, and sometime the rich too, became converts to Islam – just to escape the clutches of the impost called 'Jiziya'.

Islam divides the world into two separate entities: one, the Dar-ul Islam ('the abode of peace') which is a pure Islamic state and where every citizen follows the tenets of Islam; and the second, the Dar-ul-Harb ('the land of conflict or war') where Islam is not the state religion and Muslims have to perforce live under adverse or hostile conditions. It is the religious duty of Muslims living in Dar-ul-Harb to continue their struggle for the supremacy of Islam and wherever necessary take recourse to *jihad*, as indeed was done by Prophet Muhammad himself after his flight to Medina and by his followers on several subsequent occasions. It is incumbent on Muslims living in the countries labelled as Dar-ul-Harb to overcome adversity and reshape Dar-ul-Harb into Dar-ul-Islam, if necessary, by taking up arms. The ultimate objective is to convert the entire world into 'the abode of peace', that is to remake it into an Islamic society. If that can be achieved by peaceful means, no violence may be necessary. But if there is a resistance to the advancement of Islam, the goal must be reached by taking up arms and waging jihad. That is precisely what the present day Islamic terrorists are trying to do. They have been launching successive suicide attacks against the civil society (read Dar-ul-Harb) ferociously and relentlessly. Hence the emphasis by the Islamic clerics and the scholars alike on finding paradise under the shade of swords. For centuries holy war or Jihad has been the battle cry of Muslims ever since the small army of Muslims, about 313 strong, under the inspiring leadership of Prophet Muhammad, defeated the 1000 strong army of the Qureish in the famous battle of Badr on the 17th day of Ramdan. After victory, Muslim soldiers claimed that angels, in white turbans, came to help them in a battle in which they were heavily outnumbered. The believers to this day are convinced that they will receive Allah's help in the midst of battles. Stories of Badr are part of Islamic inspiration.[43] M. J. Akbar believes that the resonance of jihad comes from the nature of its strife. According to him "jihad is the holy war, the war of righteousness, the struggle against tyranny." It is a passion indifferent to the fate of battle because the jihadis will win either way: in the long run, the war will be won; and in the short run, death will bring martyrdom and paradise.[44]

While Akbar's advocacy tries to philosophically rationalize the faith and the commitment of Muslims of all shades and opinions to jihad, it leaves certain uncomfortable questions totally unanswered. If jihad is a war waged in the cause of righteousness, then what is the moral justification for the concept of "slaughter in the land" which ordains killing of innocent men and women simply because they refuse to embrace Islam. By what logic can a war waged for promoting a certain religious belief be proclaimed as "righteous". The word "righteous" has a deep moral, almost sacred, connotation. It has an ethical dimension. Who is to adjudge what is right and moral and what is wrong and immoral? Is it expected that whatever Islamic scriptures, or Muslim theologians, say has to be accepted as the acid test of righteousness? Further, how can the Islamic claim to purity of the spoils of war, called 'ghanima', flowing from victory in jihad, be considered as righteous? Similarly by what logic can the imposition of 'jiziya' sanctioned in the Quran, be considered as an act of righteousness? During Muslim rule, many saintly people, almost godly people, were subjected to jiziya simply because they professed another faith - the faith of their forefathers. How could the imposition of a poll tax on a righteous god-fearing man be deemed as an act of righteousness? Let us not forget that in imposing jiziya no distinction was ever made between the rich and the poor, nor was the capacity to pay of the 'zimmy' ever taken into account. Nor is any assessment made about the unfortunate infidel's capacity to pay the poll tax ordained by the Islamic scriptures. In the circumstances, to call jihad as a war waged in the cause righteousness is a highly questionable proposition. To put the seal of righteousness on the manner in which the jihadi warriors of Islam have conducted themsleves for almost one thousand years and are acting even today would be an affront to the very concept of righteousness and morality. On a rational analysis one finds that the doctrine of jihad is somewhat akin to the dreaded nihilist philosophy of destroying and overturning all prevalent societal institutions for inventing an altogether different world order of questionable civilizational values. Many of the orthodox Islamic values, flaunted by Jihadis, may not be acceptable to the majority of the population of a country or a continent - or even to the educated Muslim women of a fundamentalist country like Pakistan which is choc-a-bloc with Jihadis and prospective Ghazis! Suffice it to say that the concept of jihad is a total misfit in the context of today's politico-economic world order. It negates all modern civilizational values which lay special emphasis on humane, tolerant and pluralistic societal ethos. It is unfortunate that that even the professedly modern Islamic scholars refuse to accept this simple truth. For them jihad is an article of faith—a holy war ordained by their prophet. When such is their purblind, *albeit* religious, commitment to the necessity and infallibility of jihad, how can the civilizational conflict be prevented from further escalation? So shall we presume that the ongoing civilizational war will carry on merrily for decades—perhaps more sadly than merrily?

4

In Search of Lost Grandeur

"Everyone is trying to accomplish something big, not realising that life is made up of little things" – Frank A. Clark

Islam is a powerful religion, deeply dogmatic and clash and conquest-oriented. It is essentially a warrior's religion and does not allow any separation of the spiritual from the temporal. Over the centuries it has evolved a system of "unique bonding" among its followers, assiduously nurtured and promoted by fundamentalist clerics through the concept of 'ummah' which imparts tremendous resilience to the pan-Islamic movement. History of Islam shows that for almost 500 years, from seventh to twelfth centuries, Muslim armies carried out a series of armed campaigns resulting in spectacular conquests across the continents of Asia, Africa and Europe. That was the golden era of Islam resplendant with grandeur when it swept across Asia and Africa and made inroads into Europe where it met fierce resistance from the Christian kings. Islam advanced rapidly through the medium of holy wars or jihads against the so-called infidels and the process of conquest of their lands and property was started by the Prophet himself.

The first blood in the cause of Islam was drawn by mujahideen late in the year 623 A.D. when Prophet's troops captured the settlement of Nakhla, inhabited by the infidel Koreish tribe, in which one Koreish was killed and two made captives and a meagre booty was obtained. According to Ibn Ishaq, one of the earliest biographers of Prophet Muhammad, this "was the first booty which the Muslims obtained, the first captives they seized and the first life they took".

The amount of ransom money charged was 40 ounces of silver for cash for each of the two captured Koreishites.[1] During the initial years of Islam's ascendancy, jihads could be waged only against immediate neighbours most of whom were idolaters and therefore dubbed kafirs or infidels. Among them was the powerful Koreish tribe of Mecca. The Koreish army was defeated in the famous battle of Badr in 624 A.D. resulting in the slaughter of a large body of Koreishites many of whom were taken captives. The leader of the Kureish army, Abu Hakim (i.e., the father of wisdom), nicknamed by the Prophet as Abu Jahl (the father of ignorance), was killed on the battlefield and his famous sword 'Zulfiqar' presented to the Prophet. The battle of Badr brought to the victors a huge booty including 70 Koreishite captives, 114 camels, 10 horses and a vast quantity of garments and leather goods. According to an estimate made by Sir William Muir, the amount of ransom extracted was approximately 100,000 dirhams. It was a historic battle which turned the tide in favour of the Prophet and the faithful. The victory of Badr was followed up by a number of holy wars launched mostly against several Jewish tribes living in the immediate neighbourhood. A prominent Jewish tribe, the Banu Kainuka, was defeated in 624 A.D. and made to flee Medina. Then another jihad was waged against the second Jewish tribe, Banu Nadir, also called Banu Nazir, which was defeated and expelled from Medina in 625 A.D. That campaign was followed by the defeat and total destruction of another Jewish tribe, the third one, the Banu Kuraizah of Medina in 627 A.D. Although the leaders of Banu Kuraizah did not join the battle against the Prophet and his army, their motives were suspect. Therefore the entire clan of Banu Kuraizah was put to slaughter, as explained in a previous chapter. In the year 628 A.D. Prophet's army made a surprise attack on another Jewish tribe, this time a non-Medinese group of Jews and seized their stronghold Khaibar after which the Jews of Khaibar were reduced to the status of kharajguzars of Islam and made to pay a poll tax, called jiziya, for being allowed to live humbly under the supremacy of Islam. That was the first instance of the Islamic impost called 'jiziya', a poll tax, being levied by the mujahideen on the infidels, i.e., non-Muslims. Jihads were also waged in the years 626-627 A.D. by the Prophet against Banu Mustalik, an Arab tribe, but not Jewish, which had refused to submit to Islam till they were defeated in 627 A.D. The capture of Mecca in 630 A.D. from the powerful Kureish tribe brought the entire region effectively under the control of Islam, although two more important jihads were waged by the Prophet against the infidels namely the battle of Hunain in 630 A.D., after the conquest of Mecca, which was followed by the seige of Taif in 630 A.D. The battle of Taif was the last ghazwah led by the Prophet.

Thus, Jewish tribes being some of the oldest inhabitants of Arab lands and immediate next door neighbours of the Muslims of Arabia, were the first to face the onslaught of jihads launched by the Prophet. According to an English version, authored by Abdul Hamid Saddiqi (a Pakistani scholar) of the famous Hadith, *Sahih Muslim,* the Jews of Banu Nadir and Banu Quraiza fought against the Prophet who expelled Banu Nadir but allowed the Quraiza to stay on and granted favour to them until they too fought against him. Then he killed their men and distributed their women, children and properties among the Muslims. The Prophet turned out all the Jews of Medina—Banu Qainuqa and the Jews of Banu Haritha and every other Jew who was in Medina.[2] Thus the roots of the present sixty years old conflict between the Israelis, i.e., the Jewish civilization and the Muslim Palestinians, who are Arabs, lie in the 1400 years old bloody history of clashes between the two sister Semetic faiths, both original natives of the same arid lands. The Jews had been attacked and plundered earlier by the Romans. Later on they were persecuted by the Christians. With the rise of Islam, once again they came under pressure and lost their ancestral land to the Muslims and were forced to flee Arabia and other parts of the Middle East. That happened 1400 years ago and in the interregnum they continued to be harassed and persecuted both in Europe and Russia. They suffered heavily at the hands of the Nazis during Hitler's reign when millions were killed mercilessly in gas chambers. After facing centuries of persecution in the Europe, Jews were able to regain their holy land when the state of Israel came into existence in the year 1948 as a late and recalcitrant follow-up of the Balfour Declaration made in 1919. Interestingly, the *Sahih Muslim* refers to another hadith according to which the Prophet is believed to have declared, "I will expel the Jews and Christians from the Arabian Peninsula and will not leave any but Muslims".[3] This proclamation of the Prophet constitutes the bedrock of the edict issued by Osama bin Laden and other militant Islamist groups in February 1998, calling upon the Muslims worldwide to wage jihad for the expulsion of Amercian troops and all Christians and other infidels from Arab lands, more specifically from Saudi Arabia.

The history of Islam's growth is replete with instances of numerous clashes and incessant wars with the extant civilizations of the Middle East, North Africa, Europe and Indian sub-continent. After the death of Prophet Muhammad in 632 A.D., within five years the Arabs over-ran the Zoroastrian Sassanid kingdom of Persia thereby destroying one of the most splendid and ancient civilizations of the Middle East. In the year 637 A.D. at the Battle of Al-Qadisiyyah a determined Arab army under Saad Ibn Waqqas, a cousin of Prophet Muhammad, battled for three days with a numerically superior Sassanid army led by their Zoroastrian commander Rustam and finally emerged victorious on the fourth day when the Arabs succeeded in slaying Rustam, after a fierce battle. That defeat led to the total rout of the Sassanid army and the consequential annihilation of Zoroastrian faith in the land of its birth. Persia was a prosperous land and the people had a rich tradition of learning and architecture. Persians were a handsome and cultured people. Their nobles lived in beautiful homes and had luxuriant gardens. They were fond of stylish furnishings and furniture - tables plated or inlaid with silver or gold, couches spread with exotic coverlets, floors carpeted with rugs resilient in texture and rich in all the colours of earth and sky.[4] They drank wines from goblets of gold and silver and adorned their tables and shelves with vases moulded by foreign hands. Persians loved song and dance and were fond of musical instruments like the harp, the flute, the drum and the tambourine. Jewellery was plentiful, ranging from tiaras and ear-rings to golden anklets. Men too flaunted jewels on necks and ears and arms.[5] After tasting victory, the Arabs raced ahead, capturing and plundering many rich and flourishing cities and towns. No quarter was given to Zoroastrians and thousands were put to sword, and their Aatish-Kadas ('fire-temples') were razed to ground. The process of converting the Zoroastrians to Islam and destruction of their fire-temples continued unabated for almost two hundred years. In ninth and tenth centuries hundreds of Zoroastrian nobles and clergy sailed out through Persian Gulf and many of them, mainly the nobles and the clergy, landed on India's west coast and took shelter in Sindh and Gujarat, under Hindu rulers. According to recorded history around 928 A.D. a large group of Zoroastrians landed on the Gujarat coast near Sanjan and sought shelter in the kingdom of Jadi Raja saying that they would live among the local people in a self-effacing manner and become like sugar in a pot of milk- a promise which they have always lived upto. The Zoroastrians, known as Parsis in India, have truly adopted India as their motherland and have contributed to the nation building in a significant manner through their talent and enterprise.

The Arabs turned their attention to Sind sometime between 634 and 644 A.D., during the reign of the second caliph or successor to the Prophet and in the next sixty or seventy years made ten attempts at conquest.[6] Towards the end of the seventh century Hajjaj became governor of Iraq. After taking permission of the Caliph, he sent an army to conquer Sind which was ruled by Raja Dahir. In one of the first campaigns, Hajjaj's army was defeated by Dahir's son and the Arab commander was killed and many Arabs taken prisoner. But that setback did not deter Hajjaj. Between 711 and 713 A.D. a number of campaigns were launched to capture the vast kingdom of Sindh which stretched across the north western coast of the sub-continent, far beyond the present province of Sindh in Pakistan. The country was called Sindhu, because of the great river that flows through that region, referred to as Indus by the Greeks and other Europeans. Finally in the year 713 A.D. Hajjaj decided to take another chance. He selected 6,000 experienced soldiers from Syria, appointed his seventeen year old son-in-law Mohammed bin Qasim as commander and supervised every detail of the campaign. The army was sent by land, while the supplies, including naphtha arrows, coats of mail, battering rams and a special catapult which required hundreds of men to operate, were sent by sea. Hajjaj continued to send copious military instructions along with religious exhortations from his headquarters at Kufa to bin Qasim by letters delivered through runners. The attack was to be focussed at the port town of Debal where Mohammed bin Qasim arrived by land, as per schedule. The supplies came by sea. After detailed preparations the battle was joined on the eighth day under orders of Hajjaj. According to a legend, at the end of the first day of the battle a Brahmin came out of the town who was apparently bribed. He confided in the Arabs that Raja Dahir's army and the towns people had a strong belief that the fort of Debal was guarded by a magic charm the core of which were the four flags of green silk hanging from the flagstaff on the dome of the grand temple of Debal fort which protected the rulers and residents of Debal from the enemy. So long as the flags atop the temple remained in position, the army of Dahir and the people of Debal will continue to fight. But if the Arabs could bring down the charmed flags and the flagstaff of the temple, the army will accept defeat. Eventually it was this betrayal which led to the defeat of Dahir. Next day bin Qasim ordered the catapult engineer, one Jaubat, to bring down the charmed temple flagstaff, while the Arab warriors mounted a fierce attack from four directions. As soon as the flagstaff was broken by the fussilades of stones shot through the catapult, Dahir's army lost heart and opened the gate of the town. The people of Debal prayed for mercy. But as instructed by Hajjaj, the Arab army continued to slaughter the citizens for three days during which no quarter was given nor requests for mercy entertained. While the campaign in Sind was continuing, Hajjaj received the head of the vanquished king, 60,000 slaves and the mandatory royal one fifth of the plundered wealth. He offered special prayers of thanksgiving to Allah. A proclamation asked the people of Sind to embrace Islam to save themselves from slaughter. The foregoing narrative of the Arab conquest of Sindh is largely based on a Persian translation of the *Chachnama* or *Tarikh-i-Hind wa Sind* by Muhammad 'Ali bin Hamid (Kufi) written in early thirteenth century. As pointed out by V.S. Naipaul, the *Chachnama* is Arab or Muslim genre writing, 'a pleasant story of conquest' and it was written five hundred years after the conquest of Sindh.[7] Unfortunately the officially doled out versions of the history of Sindh by the present day Pakistani rulers routinely describe the Arab invasion and the conquest of Sindh by bin Qasim in 711-713 A.D. as an event which liberated the Sindhi masses from Hindu tyranny and oppressive Brahminical caste-rule thereby ushering in an era of unprecedented social equality, which is incorrect. Even the translated version of *Chachnama* reveals a pirate-like conquest that wreaked havoc on the local populations, transferring a considerable volume of plundered wealth such as gold, silver, and jewellry and also slaves, as a tribute to Hajjaj. Mohammad bin Qasim and his military commanders also greatly profited from the conquest, enriching themselves at the expense of the local population. Another history of the period, *the Futuh-i Bulda'n* by Ahmad bin Yahya bin Jabir, (892-893 A.D.), which is relatively far less older than *Chachnama* describes how some of the victories in Sindh were achieved by the destruction (or salinization) of vital aquaducts that starved the populations of drinking water, leading to their surrender.[8] Both these historical documents describe the slaying of able-bodied soldiers and other townsmen and the taking of women and children as slaves in large numbers. According to Dr. B.R. Ambedkar, where Mohammed Bin Qasim found that Hindus objected to forcible conversion, he put all men above the age of 17 to slaughter and ordered all others, including women and children, to be enslaved. The temple of Hindus was looted and the rich booty was divided equally among the soldiers, after one-fifth, the legal portion meant for the Hajjaj, the ruler, had been set aside.[9] That is the true story of the defeat and ignominy suffered at the hands of Arab invaders by the forbears of the people of Sindh. No wonder, G.M. Syed and some other proud Sindhi Muslims, refused to eulogise the conquest of Sindh by the Arabs.

With the looting of its savings of gold and silver and other assets and the annual demands for tribute (estimated at a million dirhams annually) it is not surprising that Sindh was culturally and economically eclipsed by Gujarat and Rajasthan—its eastern neighbours which escaped such devastation.[10] What is remarkable about the contemporary records of history is the irrefutable evidence of forcible mass conversions. Conversion to Islam was offered as an option to escape death to the defeated populations. It was also presumed that conversion to Islam would be taken as a token of surrender and willingness to pay tribute to the new authorities and a sign that the political suzerainty of the victors would not be challenged. The same methodology of forcible conversion had been successfully used earlier by the Arab conquerors in Iran and several other parts of the Middle East.

After partition of the sub-continent, the fundamentalist Muslim historians and rulers of Pakistan have been putting forth a viewpoint that the conquest of Sindh by Mohammed bin Qasim was a grand event and that the advent of Islam ushered in an era of great social equality and promoted education and learning on a grand scale. This claim has to be viewed against the backdrop of Pakistan's origin as a theocratic Islamic State based on the philosophy of rabid hatred of the Hindus. Interestingly, Raja Dahir belonged to the illustrious clan of Mohiyal Brahmins. According to a legend, a Mohiyal ruler of West Asia had rushed his army, under prince Rahab Datta, to help the beleagured Imam Hussain, grandson of Prophet Muhammad in the year 680 A.D. (61 Hijri) in the famous battle of Karbala, located in today's Iraq on the banks of river Euphrates. Imam Hussain who led a small force was son of Fatima and Ali bin Abu Talib and was a grandson of prophet Muhammad. At Karbala, a large army mobilised by Yazid, a descendant of the Umayyad tribe, had beseiged a relatively smaller army of Arab Muslims led by Imam Hussain. Yazid had directed the latter to submit to his authority which Hussain refused to do and joined the battle against Yazid. Imam Hussain put up a brave fight but in the ensuing battle he was killed and his small army routed at Karbala and the head of Imam Hussain was sent to the Ummayad Caliph Yazid. It is said that in the battle of Karbala, fighting shoulder to shoulder with Imam Hussain, the Mohiyal Brahmin prince Rahab Datta (perhaps his correct name was Raghav Datta) and his soldiers too, had perished. Imam Hussain is regarded as a great martyr in the cause of Islam and his sacrifice is commemorated every year by Muslims as a day of mourning, i.e., Moharram. That explains why Mohiyal Brahmins are sometime referred to as Hussaini Brahmins by Muslim historians. Apparently at that time there were some regions or principalities in the Middle East which were ruled by the Mohiyals. But subsequently in the great Islamic wave of rapid conquests the Mohiyal rulers were forced to flee to Afghanistan and India. In the history of medieval India there are references to a dynasty of Shahi or Shahiya Brahmins who ruled over several parts of Afghanistan and North Western India (now a part of Pakistan). The last Hindu Shahiya king of Kabul, Bhimapal, was killed in 1026 A.D., after the advent of Islam and the rise of Ghazanvi rulers. The Shahiya rulers had offered stiff resistance from the fastness of Khyber Pass to Muslim invaders for decades. Finally in the eleventh century the Shahiya kingdom was overrun by the Muslim rulers of Ghazni. It may be recalled that just a hundred years prior to the reign of Dahir, Sind was ruled by Rajput Rajas who had embraced Buddhism. Attention may be drawn to the views of a Sindhi historian and political activist of Pakistan, G.M. Syed, who was jailed in 1964 for eulogising the great ancient civilisation of Sindh and praising Raja Dahir and earlier Rajput rulers of Sindh for their just and liberal secular views and tolerance. According to G. M. Syed, during Dahir's reign people of various faiths co-existed peacefully throughout Sindh. While the Hindus had their Mandirs, the Parsis (Zoroastrians) had their fire-temples, the Buddhists their Viharas and Stupas and the Arab Muslims, who had been given permission to settle down along the coast, had their mosques. G.M. Syed came to the conclusion that the primary motivation for Arab invasion of Sind was the ire of the Umayyad Caliphs against local rulers for having given shelter to Zoroastrian nobles and generals after their defeat in Persia at the hands of Arabs. This possibility, howsoever remote, cannot be ruled out totally, because of the existence of several pockets of resistance led by stray groups of Sassanid warriors in Iran who continued to have support of the left-behind Zoroastrian population in rural areas. Perhaps Umayyad rulers, aware as they were of the military history of Persia and the prowess shown by Zoroastrian nobles in the battlefield while conquering Arab lands, wanted to forestall the possibility of a Persian-Sindhi alliance being forged for fighting the Arab armies. One conjecture is that the Umayyad caliphate decided to attack Sindh before any such alliance could take shape but that seems rather far fetched. According to a more reliable version, given by Dr B. R. Ambedkar in his book, *Pakistan or Partition of India*, the expedition by Muhammad bin Qasim was of punitive character and had been undertaken to punish Raja Dahir of Sindh who had refused to make amends for the seizure of an Arab ship at Debal, an important seaport of Sindh.[11] But there might be another aim, too. That was to strike a blow at the idolatry and polytheism of Hindus and establishing Islam in India. After subjugating the Zoroastrians and securing their eastern flank by the annexation of Sindh, the Arabs mounted campaigns against other neighbouring civilizations and carried out a whirlwind conquest of the Persian-ruled Mesapotamia (Iraq), the Roman-ruled Syria and enslaved the entire Northern Africa, right from Egypt, which was predominantly populated by the Christians, to Morocco. Thus within one hundred years of the death of Prophet Muhammad, the Arabs had seized the southern and eastern shores of Mediterranean, including most of the Iberian peninsula, the modern Spain, and destroyed almost all old civilizations of the region. After converting the Moors and the Berbers of Africa to Islam and rallying them to their ranks, the Arab armies started knocking at the doors of Italy and France. It must be admitted that the great Arab-conquests from seventh to tenth centuries owed a great deal to the gutsy and inspirational leadership of Prophet Muhammad who had guided them to the path of "holy wars" which they continued to wage relentlessly, even though the Prophet was no longer alive to personally lead them in campaigns. The Syrian capital of Damascus became the seat of the vast Umayyad Caliphate and the Arab empire stretched from Sindh in Hindustan (India) in the east, through Iran, Mesapotamia, Egypt, Maghreb and Morocco to the eastern shores of Atlantic of which the Iberian peninsula (modern Spain) was an important outpost. Soon the rapidly advancing armies of the Arabs and Berbers posed a grave threat to the Christian civilization of Europe. It is interesting to note that in the circumstances somewhat similar to those prevalent today, in the eighth century too, the Christian Europe had lived under the shadow of fear because of the repeated onslaughts of advancing Islamic armies the tales of whose exploits caused trepidation all over Europe. In the year 711 A.D. the Iberian peninsula, referred to by the Arabic name of Al Andalus by Muslim historians, witnessed a bloody battle in which the Visigothic army of Spanish Christians led by King Roderick, was routed by the Muslim troops, mostly Berbers and Arabs, which were commanded by the Umayyad Commander Tariq Ibn Ziyad, a manumitted slave. This was followed by another invasion of Europe by a larger force led by the Umayyad Amir, Musa Ibn Nusayr and all those towns and cities of Iberia which resisted Arab occupation were systematically plundered and destroyed. Spurred by the Jihadi zeal of spreading the prophet's message all over the world, the Arab armies had evolved the tradition of carrying fire and sword in their wake into the regions captured by them. Their Iberian campaigns were no exception. It may be recalled that during the dark middle ages the pre-Islamic tribal tradition of Bedouin brigandage, widely practised in the desert of Arabia, came to be woven into the concept of jihad. Consequently, it was a standard norm for Muslim warriors to plunder the cities and carry away the riches of the defeated nations as booty. After consolidating their control over Iberian peninsula, in 732 A.D. the Arabs crossed the Pyrenees and mounted an armed expedition under Abd ar Rahman to capture the land of Franks or Firangs, the modern France. According to both Latin and Arabic historical sources, Abd ar-Rahman's aim was not merely to plunder the Dar-ul-Harb, the land of conflict, ruled by the infidels but to conquer and subjugate the entire Christian world. As recorded in the *Futuh Misr* by Ibn Abd al-Hakam, an Arab historian (c. 803-71), the Muslims defeated the Christian army of Eudo at Bordeaux, then ransacked the city and took a great deal of booty including gems and pearls, encrusted golden jewellery, etc. But soon thereafter when the Muslim army led by Abd ar Rahman, Governor of Spain, moved further ahead into the land of Franks, i.e., France, they were intercepted and engaged by a large French army led by Austrasian Mayor, Charles, in a fierce battle on the road connecting Tours and Poitiers and were decisively defeated and put to flight. Abd ar Rahman was killed. After Charles won the war against invading Muslims at Tours-Poitiers he earned the title 'Martel', i.e., the Hammer. Thus the battle of Tours-Poitiers, fought and won by the French Christian army on Saturday the 10th October 732 A.D., was the first turning point in the history of Europe as well as resurgent Islam – the former succeeded in saving Europe's Christian civilization, while the mighty Muslim army tasted its first defeat at the hands of Christian Europe and was humbled by the Franks, called 'firangs' by Muslims. For Christians it was a very significant victory, especially when one considers it in the light of the record of successful armed campaigns of Muslims leading to their political and cultural dominance along the entire eastern and southern shores of the Mediterranean. The blitz of Islam's conquests of Iran, Sindh, Syria, Mesapotamia and the north African coastline right upto Morocco, in the seventh and eighth centuries had led to imposition of Arab culture on the previously Christian and non-Muslim populace of these lands. With the defeat of the Visigothic army of Spanish Christians by the Muslims in the battle of Rio Barbate in 711 A.D., the former were doomed to live in servitude for seven long centuries before Spain could regain freedom. Interestingly in the matter of long record of slavery the Christian Spain comes second, just behind the Hindu civilization, which remained in the captivity of alien rulers for almost nine hundred years, seven hundred years under the Muslims and almost two hundred years under the British.

The "Reconquista" of their motherland by the Spaniards could be completed only after seven hundred years long fierce struggle when they drove out the Moors from Granada in the year 1492. That was just a few months before Columbus received official blessings for his voyage across the Atlantic. The Spanish warriors spearheading the 'Reconquista' were as ruthless as were the Muslim invaders 700 years ago. Churches remodelled into mosques were reconverted and many freshly built mosques were destroyed. The sole architectural exception was the beautiful Alhambra mosque. There were organised reconversions of European Muslims to Christianity. After being ruled by the Moors for almost 400 years, in 1147 Lissabona (i.e., Lisbon, the capital of modern Portugal) was overrun. The Christian army promised to spare the lives of the defending Moors if they surrendered but after the town fell the promise was violated and the Moors were killed in large numbers. Ultimately the Moors were systematically driven out across the Mediterranian; emigration, conversion or death were the only options given to them. In other words the Spaniards treated the Moors and Arabs in much the same manner in which the invading Muslim hordes had treated the Spanish people some 700 years ago.

Thus Europe escaped subjugation by the warriors of Islam largely due to the resounding victory of the French army in the battle of Tours-Poitiers, also known as the battle of Tours in October 732. Had Charles Martel suffered defeat at Tours-Poitiers and met the fate which befell the Visigothic King Roderick in the battle of Rio Barbate at the hands of the Muslims, the history of Europe and Christianity could have been different. In fact the entire world history would have taken a different turn! The significance of the Battle of Tours has been topic of much debate. In 1776 Edward Gibbon wrote in his celebrated treatise, *The Decline and Fall of the Roman Empire*, a famous, but colourful, passage about the event saying that "A victorious line of march had been prolonged above a thousand miles from the rock of Gibraltor to the banks of the Loire; the repetition of an equal space would have carried the Saracens to the confines of Poland and the Highlands of Scotland; the Rhine is no more impassable than the Nile or Euphrates and the Arabian fleet might have sailed without a naval combat into the mouth of the Thames. Perhaps the interpretation of the Quran would now be taught in the schools of Oxford and her pulpits might demonstrate to a circumcised people the sanctity and truth of the revelation of Muhammed." The noted historian, William E. Watson, expressed the view that the importance of the battle of Tours has been exaggerated, implying that even if Charles Martel had lost, the Europe might still have mustered the strength to repel the Muslim invaders. But historians like Edward Creasy held a different view. They felt that it was unlikely that a lesser man could have succeeded where his superior had failed. Similar views were expressed by the well known French historians, M.Guizot and Mme. Guizot de Witt, who wrote in 1869 about the battle of Tours that "it was a struggle between East and West, South and North, Asia and Europe, the Gospel and the Koran, and we now say, on a general consideration of events, peoples, ages, that the civilization of the world depended on it."[12]

The crusades waged by the coalition of European kings from eleventh to thirteenth centuries were an attempt to retake from the Muslims the holy city of Jerusalem, most sacred to Christians, it being the site of the crucification of Jesus Christ. They did not succeed but were able to considerably thwart Islam's design to conquer Europe. A few centuries later, Europe was able to carve out a number of Christian-ruled states in West Asia which led to the conquests of many Arab nations. Even after the massive defeat of the Serbs by Ottoman Turks in 1389 at Kosovo where thousands of Serb warriors laid down their lives, Europe refused to submit to the invading Muslim armies. In 1396 a large expedition mounted by king Sigismund of Hungary to save the Balkans from Turkish onslaught had received support of many Christian kings and knights of Europe. But they were defeated in the battle of Nicopolis (i.e., Nikopol) on the banks of Danube. Islam continued to be entrenched in eastern Europe as a politico-religious force and Turks were able to consolidate their hold on the Balkans. But their ambition to capture the heartland of Europe was finally put paid in the seventeenth century. To defeat and plunder the rich and famous kingdom of Hapsburg rulers of Austria, a leading dynasty of Christian Europe, the Ottoman Turks started making preparations from March 1683 onwards to attack Vienna which they had covetously eyed all along but had failed to conquer in 1529. In June 1683 the Turkish army invaded Austria and King Leopald and his court were forced to flee to Passau. On July 14, 1683, the Turks reached the outskirts of Vienna and laid seige to that great capital of Hapsburgs. The final battle was joined on September 12, 1683. This was one of the most important battles in the history of Europe and its outcome had a profound long term effect on the history of the continent— perhaps on the history of the entire mankind. On one side was arraigned the formidable Turkish army along with fifteen thousand Tartars lined up on their side, led by Grand Vizier Kara Mustafa, an Ottoman commander. On the other side were a far less numerous combination of German, Austrian and Polish troops, gallantly led by King Jan Sobieski of Poland. The latter were greatly helped by a determined group of residents of Vienna who had erected fortified barricades to block several breaches made by the Turks in a bid to enter the city. Sobieski had marched with his troops from Krakow to Vienna with a vow to proceed "to wage a Holy War, and with God's help to give back the old freedom to beseiged Vienna and thereby help wavering Christendom". And he succeeded splendidly. Jan Sobieski came to be looked upon not only as the saviour of Vienna but the saviour of the entire Europe from the depredations of Turks. The defeat of Ottoman army at Vienna in 1683 became the second turning point in the history of Europe; it ranked next only to the victory of Charles Martel in the battle of Tours in 732 A.D. After the defeat of Turks at Vienna in 1683 the history of militant Islam has been that of tremendous downswing in their fortunes. Thence onwards they met several successive reverses at the hands of the European civilization during the next two centuries, as is evident from the formidable count of the subjugation of several Muslim countries and territories in the eighteenth and nineteenth centuries. These had been earlier overrun and annexed by the armies of Islam. This fact has always rankled in the minds of Islamic societies and on this score the Islamists continue to bear a massive grudge against the Christian civilization. On a rational examination, however, the grievance of the Islamists against the Christian civilization is found to be rather shallow and specious. The Islamists conveniently forget that originally they and their forebears, too, had captured all these countries from the hapless peoples and indigenous rulers of those lands through the medium of wars – most of which were quite brutal and bloody. True, the re-conquering European armies also indulged in large scale violence and repression. But in sharp contrast to the oppressive rule of most Muslim kings, the acts of repression committed by the Christian Europe were far less severe.

The conflict between Islam and Christianity has a fairly long and chequered history of almost 1400 years. It is not a new phenomenon nor a discovery. But credit must be given to Samuel Huntington for bringing up the topical subject of the growing Islamist threat in an objective and analytical manner, supported by empirical studies and devoted research. He has drawn attention to a geo-political phenomenon of gigantic dimensions, the jihadi terror, which is already upon us. The battle-lines are already drawn. The present civilizational clash is bound to have wide repercussions on *the future imperfect* of the mankind, whichever way the wind might blow—irrespective of the fact whether the universal civilization wins or Islam emerges victorious in this historic clash. From the very beginning, Islam has been a militarily expansionist and war-oriented religion. For centuries, say for almost one thousand years, it remained involved in a number of wars with every other civilization in Asia, Africa and Europe. Apart from the destruction and unsung exit of the Jewish civilization from Arabian lands, the other important civilizations attacked by Islam were those of Mesapotamia, Byzantine and Egypt which were totally annihilated and wiped out, while the three non-Semitic but culturally sublimated and "tolerant" religions, namely the Zoroastrian, the Buddhist and the Hinduism, all highly advanced in terms of education, science, culture and arts, were roundly defeated by Islam in successive wars and driven to the margin of history. In the aftermath of one thousand years of relentless civilizational clashes in Asia the Zoroastrians stood virtually decimated, Hindus barely managed to survive, *albeit* badly battered, bruised and mauled, while Buddhism totally disappeared from the Middle East, Afghanistan, Central Asia and a number of south Asian countries. The Christian Europe was the only civilization which withstood the successive mighty onslaughts of Islam. It speaks volumes for the qualities of unity, grit and perseverance displayed by the Christian Europe - found woefully lacking among the contemporary Zoroastrian rulers of Persia or the Hindu rulers of the Indian sub-continent. It was a formidable combination of these qualities which enabled the Christians to successfully push back the advancing Islamic armies. Finally through crusades they carried forward the battle right into the Arab camp by coalescing the formerly divided legions of Europe's Christian kings into a tough coalition. They not only repulsed the repetitive attacks of Islamic campaigners, both of Arabs as well as Turks, but defeated them steadily and surely, in a convincing manner in a series of battles from twelfth century onwards.

The Crusades, as many as eight, waged between 1095 and 1270 A.D. by the coalition of European kings finally managed to turn the tables on the expansionist designs of Muslim armies to overrun Europe. Although the third crusade led by King Richard, the Lion-hearted, ended in a fiasco in July 1192 with his defeat at the hands of Saladin outside Jafa, very close to Jerusalem, the Christian Europe did not throw in the towel. They continued to strive for reaching Jerusalem by mounting more crusades. The real importance of crusades lay in bringing about a unity of purpose between the

Christian kings of Europe which enabled the Spaniards to throw out the Moors in the thirteenth century and subsequently led to the total rout of the Ottoman army at Vienna in 1683. Unlike the Zoroastrians and the Hindus, the European civilization emerged a winner largely because of their far-sighted strategy of forming a 'coalition' of the Christian rulers of Europe to fight the onslaught of militant Islam. The Zoroastrians, the Hindus and the Buddhists failed to realize that Islam was a powerful union of scores of countries, all bound by one single faith, which was committed single-mindedly to destroying all neighbouring civilisations. But Christian Europe had a better perception; they knew that Islam was a powerful union of all Muslim countries which could destroy Christianity just as they had decimated many other civilizations, in case the former chose to fight the menace separately, as independent nations. So they banded together and fought back - despite their multifarious internal feuds and endless squabbles! The contrast in attitudes has been aptly described by Naipaul in his book, *Among The Believers : An Islamic Journey*. He compares the conquest of the Hindu kingdom of Sind by Arabs with the conquest of Mexico and other Latin American countries by the Spanish conquistadores and points out that the theme of both campaigns was the same: the destruction by an imperialist power, with a strong sense of mission and a wide knowledge about the world, of a remote unintelligent and uninformed culture that knows only itself and doesn't understand with whom it is fighting.[13] The world-conquerors have a wider view and objective. Their men are bound together by a larger idea. The people to be conquered live in isolation; they see less, know less and have fragmented societies which are ready to be taken over. Interestingly, both in Mexico in 1519 and Sindh in 710 A.D. the will of the losing people had been weakened by the prophecies of the impending conquest.[14] The Hindu and the Buddhist rulers had neither any sound knowledge of the great unity of Islam, the fact that 'Ummah' was a global union nor could they make any strategic assessment of the aggressor's resolve to ruthlessly over-run all civilizations of neighbouring countries. That spelt their doom. The Christian kings of Europe knew better. It looks as though even today, in the twenty-first century, the Christian West represented by the Geroge Bush and Tony Blair duo, is more wide awake and better attuned than most oriental countries to meet the threat of international Islamist terrorism. No great wisdom is needed to know that the Islamic concept of 'ummah' is a sort of permanently bonded union, a transnational corporation much more vigorous and powerful than a mere 'coalition' in as much as the Islamists have a ready all-time union of their co-religionists all over the world for achieving their common objective, namely waging a holy war. In almost every respect and on every count, a militant transnational corporation based on religious affinity and flush with funds could be a formidable expansionist mechanism, much more powerful than a coalition. The strategy of George Bush to form a 'world coalition' to fight Islamist 'union' is not something new. It is a copy of the coalition of the Christian Europe formed in the tenth and eleventh centuries. But one must eschew the temptation of labelling it 'old hat'. The coalition of George Bush is a refined, sophisticated and enlarged version of the coalition of the European rulers constituted in the medieval times to stave off the Islamic threat. It is a coalition of the entire democratic civil society believing in equality and modernity.

Finally, much to the chagrin of Islamic world, between eighteenth and twentieth centuries the European powers managed to establish their supremacy by capturing a number of Muslim countries in the Middle East, Central Asia and Africa and put paid to the jihadi fervour of Islam - at least temporarily for a few hundred years. Beginning from 1798 when the Dutch seized direct control of the East Indies, most of which now constitute Indonesia, and right upto 1941-1946 when the U.K. and the Soviet Russia gobbled up between themselves Iran, the West had waged a number of successful wars against Muslim countries and annexed nearly thirty territories enumerated below, all ruled by the Muslims, causing a massive setback and heart-burn to the Muslims.[15]

Sl No.	Year	Islamic Countries Or Territories Annexed by European Powers.
1.	1798	Dutch occupation of East Indies
2.	1820	Qatar and Trucial Oman became British protectorates
3.	1830-57	Algeria was conquered by the French
4.	1834-59	Caucasus was annexed by Russia
5.	1839	Aden was annexed by Britain
6.	1846-64	Valley of Syr Darya was annexed by Russia
7.	1853-65	Russia captured Tashkent
8.	1856	Oudh (ruled by a Muslim Nawab) was annexed to British India
9.	1857	Demise of Mughal empire of India - India taken over by the British
10.	1866-72	Conquest of Bukhara and Samarkand by Russia
11.	1873-87	Uzbekistan was seized by Russia
12.	1875-76	Kohkand annexed by Russia
13.	1881-83	Tunisia was conquered by the French
14.	1873-87	Occupation of Egypt by the British
15.	1885-90	Conquest of Eritrea by Italy
16.	1890	Conquest of Senegal by France
17.	1891-99	Conquest of Upper Niger and Ivory Coast by France
18.	1891	Muscat became a British Protectorate
19.	1895	Annexation of Pamir Plateau area by Russia
20.	1898	Conquest of Sudan by the British
21.	1900	Conquest of Chad by France
22.	1906	Sultanates of northern Nigeria became British Protectorates
23.	1912-30	Italy conquered Tripolitana and Cyrenaica
24.	1912	Morocco conquered by France and Spain

25.	1914	Kuwait became British Protectorate
26.	1919-21	Greece seized Smyrna province of Turkey
27.	1919-21	Turkish territory of Anatolaya was seized by Italy
28.	1919-21	Cilician Province of Turkey occupied by France
29.	1920	Syria and Lebanon came under French mandate
30.	1941-46	Britain and Russia occupied Iran

The Russo-Turkish war of 1877 and the Greco-Turkish war of 1897 were major setbacks for Islam. The turbulence in the Muslim world further increased with the Italian invasion of Tripoli in October 1911 and the Balkans wars of 1912 and 1913. After the defeat of the Ottoman Caliphate of Turkey in 1918, it was sunset time for Islam when the Turkish government asked for an armistice which was signed at Mudros on October 30, 1918, and Constantinople was occupied by the British in December the same year. As a follow-up of the treaties made during the war, the Italian troops landed at Adalia on April 29, 1919, and the Greeks also joined on May 15, 1919. After vanquishing the Ottomans and seizing their capital Constantinople, the British and the French partitioned a large part of the Turkish empire between themselves. Three new states were formed under three new names. Two of these, Iraq and Palestine, came under British rule, while the third state, called Syria, went under the French rule. Later on many of the 30 conquered countries either became protectorates of their European rulers or acquired semi-independent or independent status. But the humiliation of losing out to Christianity continues to torment Muslim scholars and clerics even today. Evidently the antagonism between the Islamic and Western civilizations has festered for several centuries. Iranian scholar and diplomat Fereydoun Hoveyda argues that Islamic civilization has been impeded since the twelfth century as a result of major crisis and confrontations with Christendom.[16] The Crusaders occupied the Levant and the Holy Land and established Christian states in the areas claimed by Islam, while in the Iberian Peninsula a Christian coalition slowly but decisively began the campaign to evict the Muslims from Spain and Portugal.[17] According to Bodansky, mysticism, militancy and the quest for perpetual jihad have become the rallying cry of the latest generation of Islamist militants. *Jihad* which literally means "striving", refers to a holy war undertaken to further the rule of Islam over contested lands, particularly Muslim lands occupied by non-Muslims who consider any land ever conquered by Islam as theirs forever and so also the territories having a significant Muslim population even if those are controlled by the non-Muslims.[18] Therefore the disintegration of the Turkish empire in the twenthieth century was a serious setback to the might of Islam. Before the outbreak of World War I in 1914, Turkey had lost her provinces in the Europe during the two Balkan wars. Consequent upon the dismemberment of the Turkish empire, the Ottoman Caliphate came to be abolished. That was another major blow to the pride of Muslims. The fact that Islam has lost many countries and regions to the Christian west during the last 200 years and was repetitively humbled and deprived of its grandeur of middle ages by western civilization has always rankled in the minds of Muslim scholars, intellectuals and fundamentalists, as reflected in Iqbal's highly readable poem "Shikwa". To an average Indian, Iqbal is better known as the author of "*Saare Jahan Se Accha, Hindustan Hamara*", a magnificent poem which he had written when he was just 18 or 19 years old. Excepting the educated classes not many Indians know that it was Iqbal who had sown the seeds of India's partition on the ground that Muslims were a separate nation who could not live with the Hindus in the same country. The first clear expression of the idea is to be found in an address to the Muslim League in 1930 by Sir Mohammed Iqbal. He had mainly in mind what is now West Pakistan.[19] Iqbal was the idealogue who conceptualised the Islamic state of Pakistan and for that important reason he is held in great esteem in Pakistan and universally revered by many terrorist groups of Pakistan Occupied Kashmir (PoK). He was an intellectual and a poet.His poetry is full of wonderful imagery and superb diction. In his magnum opus, 'Shikwa', which means "the Lament", Iqbal makes a passionate and soulful supplication to Allah for restoration of the old glory and grandeur of Islam and complains about the plight and humiliation of "the faithful" all over the world. Those were the years when Islam was in the sunset mode. While analysing the causes of the growth of radical Islam, it would be interesting to understand the import and the impact of the forceful message contained in Iqbal's 'Shikwa'. His lament about the declining fortunes of Islam, and resonant references to the intrepid spirit and courage of Muslim warriors in waging wars against the infidels and idolaters created a new awakening among the Muslims of the sub-continent and in the Arab lands of West Asia and even in the far away Indonesia. The 'Shikwa' was considered as a clarion call to the faithful and widely acclaimed after it was translated into Arabic by Effendi. Iqbal recalled the old glory of Muslim warriors when they overran many continents and made "the rich and the powerful" bite dust, while singing "*shaan aankhon mein na jachti thi jahandaron ki, kalma padhate thei ham chhaon mein talwaron ki*". Translated into English it meant that the Muslims did not like the hegemony of the rich and the powerful and waged wars while saying their prayers, i.e. Kalma, in the battlefield. Looks like as though Iqbal had the dream vision of Islam's ongoing war against today's prosperous and powerful America, when he wrote those lines. Iqbal sang paens to the valour of Muslim warriors, bold horsemen, in galloping across the continents from one victory to another through deserts and oceans to spread the message of the Prophet and narrated how they had extinguished the fire of Zoroastrian temples, humbled and subjugated Khyber Pass and destroyed idols and vanquished the idol worshippers worldwide. But now they were down and out because they had foresaken the path shown by the Prophet. The soul stirring inspiration provided by Iqbal's Shikwa to radical Islamists across the globe was experienced by V.S. Naipaul in 1979-80, even prior to Afghan jihad and Laden's rise to fame, in the far away Bandung in Indonesia when he met Imaduddin, an Engineer turned Islamist instructor at the mosque-cum-madarasa of the Institute of Technology, during a three days course in "Islamic mental training". After recitation of some verses of Quran, Imaduddin was called upon to read a poem. Imaduddin told Naipaul that the poem he was going to read was by Iqbal and that during the last session of mental training he always closed the course by reading that poem by Iqbal. He had chosen it because it is very soul-stirring. It was written in Urdu, as Naipaul knew, had been translated into Arabic by Effendi and from Arabic version translated into Indonesian by Mohammed Natsir. Iqbal was the idealogue of Pakistan, while Natsir was once the leader of the banned radical Muslim party of Indonesia. Imaduddin explained the poem to Naipaul and then began to read and he was totally transformed. Giving a graphic account of the impact of the poem on Imaduddin's personality, Naipaul points out that all his social graces and humour were submerged in this new personality, not of an actor or puppet-master but of a Mullah in the mosque, reciting the Quran on some religious day. Imaduddin had said the poem was emotional; and as he read, his voice broke. At times he seemed about to sob as if in anguish, perhaps thinking of hell, heaven and redemption. The theme of Iqbal's poem, as Naipaul understood, was, how without the Prophet and knowledge of his mission, the world could be endured.[20] Thus Iqbal was not only the idealogue of Pakistan, he fathered Pakistan – Jinnah was merely Qaid-e-Azam. Iqbal also played a major inspirational role in promoting the pan-Islamic movement across the globe. His exhortations to the faithful were making waves among orthodox Muslims, long before the beginning of Afghan jihad when Osama bin Laden appeared on the scene. Successive Pakistani governments have faithfully carried forward Iqbal's mission, even when the going for them was tough. Of special interest to Islamic militants of Pakistan have been Iqbal's famous lines from another poem captioned '*Tarana*', which could be titled Tarana-e-Islam, in which he sang of the bonds of universal Islamic brotherhood and raised new visions of the victory of pan-Islamism by proclaiming "Muslim hain ham watan hai saara jahan hamara, Chin-o-Arab hamara, Hindustan hamara". Again," Teghon ke saye main ham pal kar jawan huey hain, Khanjar halal ka hai qaumi nishan hamara". Translated into English it means that "the entire world belongs to us, the Muslims; we have a claim on China and Arabia, and India too belongs to us. We, Muslims, have been brought up under the 'shade of swords' and for that reason the Halali dagger, or butcher's knife, represents the Nation of Islam". These famous lines of *Tarana* are music to the ears of jihadis being trained in Pakistan and Pak Occupied Kashmir (POK). Iqbal refers to the glorious history of Islam, its golden age when the valleys of Europe were overrun by the Muslim warriors and Christian churches had reverb rated with the echoes of 'Azan'—the Muezzin's call to the faithful for prayer. And those were the glorious days when Muslim soldiers used to bivouac in the gardens of Al Andalus, that is Spain. While concluding, Iqbal asserts that Muslims were not the kind who would ever submit to the infidels and that their reckless courage had been tested hundreds of times, when he boasts: "Batil se dabne wale aiye aasman nahin ham, sau bar kar chuka hai tu imtihan hamara." These were not mere words, nor mere poetry; this was an invocation to the revival of the long lost grandeur of Islam and the raw courage sought to be breathed into young Islamists. As mentioned in an article by Ardeshir Cowasjee, a renowned columnist of Pakistan, the singing of Tarana with verve by students is compulsory in all government schools of that country by a government fiat. In his another narrative, Naipaul has referred to the famous chant of Muslims encountered by him in Pakistan: "*darta nahin duniya mein Muslaman kisi se, ja poocch Ali se*", which means that "we, Muslims, fear no one, none at all. If you have a doubt, go and ask Ali (Prophet Muhammad's son-in-law)." The world must understand that it was this medieval gutsy spirit of martyrdom and resolve to fight in holy war which was responsible for the audicious terror attacks on WTC and Pentagon. It is this spirit of sacrifice and the glorification of suicidal martyrdom which has kept the Palestinian cauldron on the boil for the last fifty five years. It is this attitude of reckless courage which is responsible for multiple jihads in a number of countries. The macro picture revealed by the geographic composition of the detainees at Guantanamo Bay Naval Base shows that the contagion of militant Islam has already infected the bloodstream of at least forty two countries. That is the ground reality of Islam's long march. The ISI of Paksitan has lighted a prairie fire, with the help of Osama bin Laden, which will continue to burn and glow across the continents of Asia, Africa and Europe, from the Philippines and Indonesia to the Balkans, France and U.K., for decades to come. It is of little consequence whether bin Laden lives or dies. And to this fact file of civilization conflicts one may add a footnote that the U.S.A. too has a lurking Islamist problem in their backyard in the shape of the not-too-dormant Black Muslim movement led by that firebrand Black Muslim leader, Louis Farrakhan, who calls it "the Nation of Islam", that nomenclature being fully in tune with the concept of ummah and the Islamic thesis of the world being divided into two nations, one of the faithful and another of the infidels. The very concept of the 'nation of Islam' has a divisive connotation. It implies that the Muslims of America are a separate nation, "the nation of Islam', while the remaining Americans constitute another nation, i.e.,"the nation of Kufr" which means the land of infidels. In the decades to come the American scenario might well be overshadowed-by the two nation theory inherent in the theology of Islam which was skilfully honed by Iqbal in 1930 for creation of Pakistan. Incidentally, the entry of Louis Farrakhan into the U.K. has been banned because of his rabid racist pronouncements against the Jews.

The creation of Pakistan in 1947 revived the dreams of a resurgent Islam straddling the globe as a geopolitical force, just like the days of the yore—a wish strongly nurtured by the protagonists of radical Islam ever since the abolition of Ottoman (caliphate). Steadily a subterranean current of Islamic militancy was built up which gathered momentum in early 1970s and rekindled the pan-Islamic dream of restoring the long lost glory of Islam. In due course of time, Pakistan (to which, post 9/11, General Musharraf had alluded as the *'fortress of Islam'* in his speech on September 19, 2001) started assuming the leadership of the Islamic world as was evident from the major role it played in establishing the Organization of Islamic Countries (OIC) in 1971. By virtue of the size of Pakistan's population and its huge land-mass, it slowly but surely became the storm centre of the revival of radical Islam. Through sound diplomacy and by swearing total commitment to the revival of the puritanic Wahabi version of Islam, the Pakistani leadership was able to move very close to the Saudis. Ever since early 1960s, long before the Russian invasion of Afghanistan, the Pakistani establishment was busy building up an army of "holy warriors" to fight in the ongoing surreptitious war being waged in Kashmir. Later on they used the same strategy to consolidate their hold on Afghanistan when trouble started brewing in that country. In subsequent years for training hundreds of thousand jihadis the Pakistani Army and the ISI were able to enlist support of Saudi Arabia and the mighty CIA. Like most Muslims, bin Laden's world too, was shattered during the last days of 1979, when the Soviet Union invaded Afghanistan. Since World War II for the first time a non-Muslim country, Russia, had occupied a Muslim country. Pakistan again took the lead when an extraordinary meeting of foreign ministers of thirty-five Islamic states was called in Islamabad on January 27, 1980.[21] Those assembled strongly condemned the Soviet military aggression against the Afghan people and called for the immediate and unconditional withdrawal of all Soviet troops from Afghanistan. They also urged that no Muslim country should recognize the Soviet-installed Democratic Republic of Afghanistan (DRA).

Osama bin Laden was one of the first Arabs to proceed post haste to Afghanistan after the Soviet invasion. At the instance of the ISI he made plans for launching a jihad against the Russian occupation of Afghanistan. To that end he took help of the ISI, to carry out considerable organizational spadework. The infrastructure for training of jihadis was already available in Pakistan. Within a short time he succeeded in recruiting hordes of Pakistani youth from the ISI-sponsored local madarasas, and brought a few thousand Arab fighters into Pakistan. Some time he covered the travel costs of these volunteers to Pakistan and Afghanistan from his personal funds. With the blessings of the ISI in early 1980 bin Laden established Ma'sadat Al-Ansar, as the main base for Arab mujahideen in Afghanistan. Soon bin Laden came into contact with Sheikh AbdAllah Yussef Azzam, "who was a key figure in establishing what is today the International Legion of Islam", a highly proficient and dedicated hard core outfit of Islamist terrorists. Osama bin Laden, a qualified engineer and son of one of the wealthiest Saudi Arabs, soon established himself as a patron of jihad and along with Sheikh AbdAllah Azzam, his mentor, founded the Maktab-al Khidmat (or MAK, i.e. "Office of Services") at Peshawar in 1984 with active support of the Pakistani government. The MAK functioned as a recruiting centre for volunteers of the International Muslim Brigade to fight in Afghanistan. During the decade long conflict, the

MAK reportedly recruited, trained, equipped and financed approximately 40,000 to 50,000 jihadi warriors hailing from more than 50 countries across the globe. The ISI recruited another two lakh jihadis by extensive use of the services of Tablighi Jamaat, a radical Islamist missionary group based in Raiwind, near Lahore. Most recruits were from Pakistan, while quite a few thousand came from a number of north African countries like Algeria and Tunisia for joining the jihad. After success in their campaign in Afghanistan, thousands of these Mujahideen indoctrinated by the ISI, are now waging holy wars in several parts of the world, of which India (Kashmir), Chechenya, Dagestan, Bosnia, Tunisia, Algeria, Egypt, Palestine, Bangladesh, Malaysia, Indonesia and Philippines, are the prominent ones.

Due to tireless efforts of the ISI, and initiative of bin Laden, in early 1980s some 3,000 to 3,500 Arabs were brought to Pakistan for waging jihad against the Russians. Another 16,000 and 20,000 Islamist militants from more than twenty countries arrived in Pakistan during the late 1980s. Most of them were Arab Islamists but many were from diverse countries and places like Indonesia, Malaysia and the Philippines; there was a trickle of Bosnian Muslims and Kosovo Albanians from the then Yugoslavia.[22] Virtually all of these were Islamists committed to the liberation of their own countries and the establishment of Islamic regimes there. Unlike volunteers of the early 1980s to mid-1980s, the newcomers had no real interest in the liberation of Afghanistan. Most of them came to be trained and the ISI was happy to oblige.[23] The successive rulers of Pakistan took full advantage of the impact of Afghan crisis, resulting from Russian occupation, on American policy makers. By playing upon the fears of Americans about consolidation of communist hold in the region they were successful in enlisting the financial and ideological support of the CIA and Saudi Arabia to contain the Russian advance in Central Asia and the Middle East. But in the heart of the Pakistan's devout Islamist leadership the grand vision of Iqbal to restore the lost grandeur of Islam, nurtured since 1947, was always uppermost. That idea they never gave up, not even while dancing to the tune of the CIA. And the strategy worked fabulously well. It enabled the ISI to raise a huge army of Mujahideen, totally indoctrinated in the fundamentalist concept of jihad and committed to the cause of radical Islam. This jihadi movement launched in Pakistan for liberating Afghanistan was substantially funded by the flow of petro dollars from Saudi Arabia and other oil-rich Muslim countries but the biggest bucks for Afghan campaigns were provided by the ubiquitous CIA. The recruits for Afghan jihad came from a number of foreign lands and came to be known as' Afghan Arabs'. Interestingly, as pointed out by Peter L Bergen none of them was an Afghan and while most were Arabs, they also came from all over the Muslim world. Some were high school students who came on trips to the Afghan-Pakistan border, something which was not more than the equivalent of jihadi summer camp. Some were involved in support operations along the border, working for charities and hospitals. There were some who spent years in fierce battles against Russia.[24] The total number of guerrilas that would be operating on any given day would therefore not be below 35,000 and not above 1,75,000.[25] While analysing the dimensions of the huge manpower recruited and trained for campaign in Afghanistan and the role of the CIA and the Saudis in funding the war, Peter L. Bergen estimated that the maximum combined strengths of the various Afghan mujahideen factions averaged somewhere between 175,000 and 250,000 in any given year. These numbers clearly showed that the contribution of the Afghan Arabs' to the war against the Soviets was insignificant from the military point of view. "The war was won primarily with the blood of Afghans and secondarily with the treasure of the United States and Saudi Arabia, who between them provided approximately $6 billion in support".[26]

The radical Islam gained further ascendancy in politics under the dictatorship of General Zia, who utilized the American money and organizational skills of Musharraf, a Lt. General then, and Lt. General Mohammed Aziz, the then Director General of Inter Services Intelligence, for creating the Taliban to overrun Afghanistan. Under Zia ul Haq, Musharraf and Aziz created the Army of radical Islam to fight the Soviet troops in Afghanistan and diverted it to Jammu & Kashmir in 1992, after the collapse of the Najibullah Government in Kabul.[27] Today the jihadi forces in Pakistan and the Pak-Occupied Kashmir are spread far and wide. Although there are dozens of active militant Islamic groups based in Pakistan, the main operational outfits, indulging in violence in Kashmir and many parts of India, consist of the Harkat-ul-Mujahideen (HUM), the Lashkar-e-Tayeba (LeT), the Jaish-e-Mohammed (JEM) and the Al Badr. The first two are members of Osama bin Laden's International Islamic Front for Jihad against the U.S. and Israel.[28] Lately these outfits have been changing their names but the objectives remain unchanged. All these organisations are supported by the ISI and their ultimate aim is not only to overrun Jammu & Kashmir, but to destablize the Indian state with the long term objective of converting the entire sub-continent into Dar-ul-Islam. That is the goal which Pakistan has set before itself for which it is waging a "war of a thousand cuts" against India. Pakistani army has a pathological hostility against India and compulsive hatred for the Hindus. Their plan to wrest Kashmir is only the purported first milestone on Indian territory as part of their agenda for establishing global supremacy of Islam, the ultimate objective of the pan-Islamic movement. We tend to forget that General Musharraf, who authored the Kargil misadventure, told a Karachi audience just a few weeks after Mr. Vajpayee's Lahore bus ride that the Lahore Declaration was nothing but "hot air" and that "low intensity conflict with India would continue even if the Kashmir issue is resolved".[29] One has only to recall the recent speech, by General Musharraf's closest crony during the Kargil conflict, General Aziz Khan. He asserted that because of the religious and social values prevailing in India, relations could not be normalised even if the Kashmir dispute was resolved.[30] Similar views had been expressed by General Musharraf in the past, more than once. Despite its moral posturing, Pakistan continues to harbour the dream of carving out at least three states for Muslims in India – an indication to this effect is available from information revealed by terrorists apprehended in the Jammu and Kashmir region, according to a top officer of the Border Security Force.[31] There are reports that Pakistani military commanders and the ISI have been indulging in a covert operation to separate Jammu and Kashmir in the North, create a Muslim majority state in the North East and carve out another state on the same lines in the South. In order to fulfil its nefarious objective, the ISI has geared its commanders of various terrorist outfits to carry out frequent bombings all over the country. Activists of the Students of Islamic Movement of India (SIMI) members of Ahl-e Hadees and the vast network of the underworld don, Dawood Ibrahim, are being used for the purpose. Cadres of some of these organisations, especially SIMI, are being regularly trained for the purpose. They have been indoctrinated to such an extent that they often talk about balkanisation of India by carrying out large scale terrorist strikes. Similarly, Ahl-e Hadees, an organisation which once worked under the command of Abdul Karim Tunda, a Lashkar-e Tayeba operator, has surfaced again.This terrorist group was involved in the bomb blasts in Delhi in 1997 and has cadres of highly indoctrinated youths capable of carrying out bombings. According to the latest intelligence inputs, "the International Islamic Army", a newly formed terrorist group in neighbouring Sri Lanka has urged Muslims to take up arms. An offshoot of the Taliban and supporter of the fugitive Osama bin Laden, this group has been trying to gang up with militant outfits active in the Kashmir valley.[32]

Thus, the Islamists, led by the jihadi warriors of Pakistan and Saudi Arabia, have set their hearts on the goal of restoring the lost grandeur of Islam. For the loss of Islam's erstwhile supremacy, they squarely blame the Christian west. They are trying to restore the past glory of their faith by waging multiple holy wars in several countries, not realising that the ancient and medieval glory of all religions, including Hinduism, Buddhism, Christianity and Islam, lies buried deep in the sands of time! It is well nigh impossible to resurrect and restore the old glory of any religion in today's pluralistic world. But the problem really is with their warped mindset. Perhaps it is a Bedouin hangover of the medieval times which refuses to go. If the past resolves of Islamists could be taken as a guide, their foot soldiers will continue to wage no-holds-barred multiple jihads for decades to come. For the civil society it is going to be a long haul.

5

Long March of Islam

"A journey of a thousand miles begins with a single step."
– Lao Tsu, a Chinese Philosopher

Throughout history, jihad or the holy war against infidels, has been the *leit motif* of Islam. In the history of mankind no other religion or creed, ever expanded so much and so fast, as Islam did in the medieval times. Essentially though, it was a coercive spread of the faith of Prophet Muhammad through violent and bloody wars. The might of the sword of Islamic warriors backed by the raw courage of the faithful was the chief medium of its rapid growth in medieval times which saw Islam's emergence as a super power. That was a radical and ruthless Islam in the middle ages which countenanced no resistance to its forward march and those opposing its advancement were visited upon by swift retribution. But in the twelfth century and thence onward the Christian Europe, acting as a sort of coalition, turned the tables on the Islamic warriors. Although ultimately the crusades achieved very little in terms of territory, the alliance of Christian kings of Europe demonstrated their resolve and ability to carry the war right into the heartland of West Asia through successive campaigns against Islam's holy warriors. From twelfth century onwards Islam started losing its prime position to Christianity and in the eighteenth and nineteenth centuries the European nations, invigorated by the renaissance and industrial revolution, assumed the leadership role all over the world. The last century saw the vigorous revival of a resurgent and militant Islam worldwide. The spectacular long march of Islam across the globe during the last five decades and the manner of its striking roots in more than forty countries is one of the important success stories of the twentieth century. But the rapid advance of radical Islam during the last century did not receive adequate attention of modern historians, political analysts and think tanks for quite a few decades, despite the first alert being sounded by Sir Vidia Naipaul in early 1980s through his famous narrative, *Among the Believers: An Islamic Journey*. The western world woke up to the threat only in 1990s when Samuel Huntington gave a wake up call through a well researched paper on the subject. The very fact that in the early 1980s hundreds of thousand Muslim volunteers joined the jihad against the Soviets in Afghanistan and thereafter embarked on multiple jihads simultaneously in more than two dozen countries in different parts of the world demonstrated the resolve of the radical Islam to confront and overwhelm the universal civilization. In may be recalled that more than 760 Islamist terrorists from 42 countries had been arrested from Afghanistan during the war launched by the U.S. and that even now at least six hundred Muslim terrorists are being interrogated by the CIA and FBI at the Guantonamo Bay Naval Base Camp in the U.S.A.

The story of the revival of militant Islam has a long and colourful history which goes back to the first half of the twentieth century when certain events taking place on the sub-continent signalled the charting of a futuristic course of pan-Islamic movement across the globe. Public memory is proverbially short but shorter still is the memory of the western powers about a macro development in the geo-strategic confines of South Asia in late 1940s which foretold the contours of the big picture which we see today on the global screen. Not many political analysts might remember and perhaps those knowing too well, mostly based in the Indian sub-continent, might loathe to admit the unpleasant truth that the ongoing long march of radical Islam had begun as early as 1947, with a single step forward, namely the creation of Pakistan, on the plea that Muslims cannot co-exist with Hindus, Sikhs and Christians in the undivided India due to which it was imperative to give them a separate homeland. And since then the warriors of radical Islam across the globe have not looked back. When Allama Iqbal envisioned the creation of a separate homeland for the Muslims of the sub-continent and sang paens to the past glory of Islam in his poem Tarana, he laid the foundations of an aggressive pan-Islamic movement. Unfortunately at that time neither the British nor the Congress leadership, including the stalwarts like Pandit Jawaharlal Nehru, could read the writing on the wall nor assess the long-term consequences of the creation of Pakistan, not only for India but for the entire world. But at that very time India had an astute visionary and political pundit, Dr. B.R. Ambedkar, who had foreseen the shape of things to come. While analysing the causes for the sudden shift in the attitude of Jinnah and other Muslim League leaders in giving up the nationalist cause and instead opting for Pakistan, he found that the real explanation for the sudden transformation of the Muslim leaders was not any dishonest drift in their opinion. They saw in the creation of Pakistan the dawn of a new destiny the magnetism of which was so great that even men like Jinnah were unable to resist its pull. The new vision could be seen in a concrete form over the map. It provided to the Indian Muslims an opportunity for realizing their dream of linking with other Islamic States in the Middle East. With the separation of Pakistan from Hindustan and by joining Iran, Iraq, Arabia, Turkey and Egypt, the Muslims could form something like a confederation of Muslim countries extending from Constantinople down to Lahore.[1]

The creation of Pakistan in 1947 was thus the first step forward in the long march of the radical Islam. It laid strong foundations of the cult of secessionist movements in all those countries where Muslims constituted a sizeable proportion of the population and imparted a strong momentum and positive direction to the dormant pan-Islamic movement. Immediately after partition of the sub-continent, Pakistan started eyeing the State of Jammu & Kashmir, ruled by the Dogra ruler Hari Singh. The fact that the majority of the valley's population was Muslim but the ruler was a Hindu, had caused a great deal of consternation to the radical Muslim leaders of Pakistan. They decided to grab Kashmir by force and launched an operation code-named 'Operation Gulmarg' the plan for which was fully known to the British officers of the Pakistani army. At that time the senior officers and commanders of the three services in Pakistan as well as in India were British, and most of them had been interacting with each other. On October 20, 1947, a trained militia type force of 15,000 to 20,000 armed tribal raiders, all Pakistanis, supported by two divisions of Pakistani army, invaded Jammu & Kashmir and after overrunning many towns and villages, including Baramulla, rapidly moved towards Srinagar. These were ferocious and unruly armed tribesmen from North Western Province of Pakistan who, acting in concert with the Pakistani army, indulged in large scale killings, looting of property and molestation of hapless women. They laid waste and plundered a number of villages and towns, including Baramulla. Unable to counter the attack of the two divisions of regular Pakistani army with his limited troops and meagre military resources, Maharaja Hari Singh decided to accede to India and signed the Instrument of Accession on October 26, 1947. The next day, on October 27, Lord Mountbatten, Governor General of India, announced that India had accepted the accession of the State "to the Dominion of India". This announcement, followed by swift military operations mounted by the Indian Army in Jammu & Kashmir for repulsing the invading troops and tribesmen, caused a serious setback to the Pakistani plan for forcible annexation of the State. The accession of the State of Jammu and Kashmir to India was fully supported by Sheikh Mohammed Abdullah, leader of the National Conference, and also by an overwhelming majority of the people of the Jammu & Kashmir State. Soon a popular government was set up in Jammu under the stewardship of Sheikh Mohammed Abdullah who was easily the tallest political leader of Kashmir. Unfortunately the then Indian Prime Minister, Pt. Jawaharlal Nehru, had immense faith in Lord Mountbatten and that was what led to the Kashmir issue being taken to the United Nations. As recorded by V.P. Menon in his book, *The Integration of the Indian States*, Pandit Nehru had entrusted the responsibility for handling the matters concerning the accession of Jammu & Kashmir to Lord Mountbatten. There are reasons to believe the latter's commitment to the Indian cause was somewhat lukewarm - at least that is what it turned out to be. Some military strategists believe that the Government of U.K. was keen to prevent India's victory in Jammu & Kashmir. Fulfilment of this objective was facilitated by virtue of the Governor General of India, Lord Mountbatten, being the chairman of the Defence Committee of the Cabinet. There could be no other plausible reason for not allowing the Indian forces more time to proceed beyond Poonch-Uri-Domel axis ahead of which lay two strategic bridges of Domel and Kohala. Surprisingly excepting a few offensive sorties flown by the Indian Air Force, no worthwhile attempt was made to launch aggressive air attacks in support of the ground troops to force early eviction of Pakistani army and the accompanying hordes of tribal raiders.

According to V.P. Menon, within six days of the invaders entering the Kashmir, Lord Mountbatten had told him that a plebiscite would have to be held in Kashmir to ascertain the wishes of the people. In mid-December he pressed the Indian Government to complain to the United Nations about the Kashmir imbroglio. By referring the Kashmir issue to the United Nations and subsequently agreeing to ceasefire and the role of the United Nations Commission for India and Pakistan (UNCIP), India gave up the advantage which the army had leveraged by their superior tactical operations. Once the matter was referred to the United Nations it became more complex. By now it seems to have become almost intractable and has taken the shape of a festering sore. Unfortunately a ceasefire was called when the Indian Army had moved ahead very well, and were only a couple of weeks short of completing the operations for clearing the State of invaders. Meanwhile, the Pakistani army overran Muzaffarabad and Gilgit, including the adjoining areas. And on November 3, 1947, a British officer, Major Brown, Commandant of Gilgit Scouts, who had earlier in October 1947 staged a coup against the Dogra Governor of Gilgit, Brigadier Ghansar Singh, hoisted the Pakistan flag over Gilgit. Moving ahead, the Pakistani troops seized the difficult terrain of Baltistan and Skardu located on the northern tip of Kashmir, very close to the Chinese border. As a result of the reference made to the United Nations by the Indian Government, both India and Pakistan were called upon to state their respective versions of the events before the Truce Sub-Committee of the United Nations. In December 1949 talks were held at Karachi between the military representatives of the two countries and it was decided that neither country should supplement and consolidate its troops on either side of the ceasefire line. On January 5, 1949, a resolution was passed by the United Nations (Resolution No. 5) saying that to resolve the Kashmir dispute, a plebiscite may be held to ascertain the wishes of the people. Later on General McNaughton of Canada was named by the Security Council as the Informal Mediator on December 17, 1949, to prepare the ground for a plebiscite. The McNaughton formula proposed that:

(1) There should be an agreed programme of progressive reduction of armed forces on either side of the ceasefire line by withdrawal, disbandment and disarmament in such stages as not to cause fear to the people on either side of the ceasefire line;

(2) The programme of demilitarization should include the withdrawal from the State of Jammu and Kashmir of regular forces of Pakistan and withdrawal of the regular forces of India not required for the purpose of security and maintenance of local law and order on the Indian side of the ceasefire line;

(3) Also the reduction by disbanding local forces and militia of the State of Kashmir, and on the other side the Azad forces; administration of the northern area should, subject to United Nations supervision, be continued by the existing local authorities;

(4) When the agreed programme of demilitarization preparatory to the plebscite has been accomplished to the satisfaction of the United Nations representative, the Plebiscite Administrator should proceed ahead to exercise the functions assigned to him under the terms of the UNCIP Resolution of January 5 1949;

(5) A United Nations representative should be appointed by the Secretary General of the U.N. to supervise the completion of demilitarization and to

   (a) interpret the agreement reached by the parties,

   (b) determine the implementation of the demilitarization plan; and

(6) the U.N. representative should be authorised to make suggestions to the governments of India and Pakistan which, in his opinion, are likely to contribute to the expeditious and enduring solution of the Kashmir question, and place his good offices at their disposal.[2]

The McNaughton formula was palpably partisan but it had the support of the Anglo-American bloc which dominated the United Nations. It found favour with Pakistan, but was rejected by India because it totally ignored the fact that under the doctrine of Paramountcy, laid down by the British, once the ruler of the State of Jammu and Kashmir had signed the Instrument of Accession, legally and constitutionally, it became an integral part of India. Moreover, Pakistan was clearly the aggressor which fact was being overlooked by General McNaughton. The people of Jammu and Kashmir were very angry and hurt at the brutal manner in which the invading Pakistani troops and accompanying tribesmen had treated the Kashmiri population. Meanwhile, Bakshi Ghulam Mohammed, a close associate of Sheikh Abdullah, declared that so long as a single Kashmiri was alive the McNaughton formula will not be accepted. Mirza Afzal Beg, another prominent Kashmiri leader belonging to the National Conference, said that India will lose the friendship of Kashmir if she were to bow down before the pressure of Anglo-American bloc and accept, in any shape or form, the McNaughton formula which equated the aggressor with the aggressed.[3] Pakistani press launched a fierce campaign against Sheikh Abdullah following his statement in early November 1947 that the Pakistani invasion had made it clear to the people of Kashmir that the rapidly developing situation would not allow them any time and therefore they had either to suffer the fate of their kinsmen in Muzaffarabad, Baramulla and other towns and villages or seek help from somewhere. Under these difficult circumstances, both the Maharaja and the people of Kashmir requested the Government of India to accept the accession of Kashmir.[4]

The 1947 invasion of Jammu & Kashmir by the Pakistani army signalled their ulterior designs to continue their pre-independence attitude of hostility towards India and to capture Jammu & Kashmir. But since the brunt of that first onslaught was borne by Indians, to be more precise by the peaceful Kashmiris, the West took no notice of it. In fact, all along, sympathies of the western nations were misplaced and Pakistan's misdemeanour was never condemned. For decades the western powers refused to take cognizance of the ongoing ethnic cleansing in Kashmir by Pakistan sponsored terrorist groups, although they were quick to react to similar ethnic cleansing in the Balkans and other parts of the world. There is a general impression among the Western political analysts that the Pakistan sponsored militancy and cross-border infiltration into Jammu & Kashmir is a post-Laden phenomenon. But that is farthest from truth. According to B.L. Kak, a plan to raise groups of infiltrators in Pakistan for creating chaos in Indian Kashmir was taken up for detailed discussion for the first time on August 16, 1953 – two days after Pakistan's Independence Day and six years after India's partition —when a high level meeting of leaders from Pakistan and Pak-occupied Kashmir was held in Karachi under the chairmanship of Mohammed Ali, the then Prime Minister of Pakistan.[5] It was attended by Aziz Ahmed, Cabinet Secretary of Pakistan, three former Presidents of the so-called Azad Kashmir, Maulvi Yusuf Shah, Chaudhri Ghulam Abbas and K.H. Khurshid and Maulvi Noor-ud-Din, brother of Maulvi Yusuf Shah and uncle of Maulvi Mohammed Farooq, President of the Awami Action Committee of Kashmir.[6] Although Pakistan's Prime Minister tried to debate Pandit Nehru's plea for normalisation of relations between India and Pakistan, Chaudhri Ghulam Abbas interrupted the discussion and got up to recommend to the Prime Minster, Mohammed Ali, that Pakistan should organise at least twenty thousand armed infiltrators to be sent to Indian Kashmir in civillian clothes for creating widespread insurgency and chaos. That will create serious security problems for the Indian Government. This meeting had been organised to chalk out Pakistan's plan of action in the light of disturbances in the Indian Kashmir following Sheikh Abdullah's arrest. Subsequently, when war broke out between India and Pakistan in 1965, i.e., after a long spell of twelve years, the suggestion made by Ghulam Abbas in 1953, was implemented by sending thousands of armed guerrillas into Kashmir valley through unguarded stealth routes. On Pakistani side of the border burly Pathan soldiers were posted to ensure that no Pakistani infiltrator ran back. Some of the captured intruders told Indian military officers towards the end of August 1965 that infiltrators had been told by their masters that they would be shot dead if they returned to their camps in Pakistan.[7] On September 15, 1965, the Chief Minister of Jammu & Kashmir, G.M. Sadiq, informed the State Assembly that some infiltrators had tried to converge on the State capital, Srinagar. Soon it became clear that the Pak-sponsored intrusion had more serious dimensions. It transpired that many trained personnel of Pakistani army, equipped with modern weapons, had been infiltrated into the valley. Interrogation of the captured infiltrators confirmed that Pakistani army had trained nearly 10,000 people in sabotage, terrorism and subversive activities, even before the agreement regarding territorial dispute over Rann of Kutch had been signed.[8] At that time too, the Pakistan Government had tried to create a myth which had been reiterated in President Ayub Khan's broadcast on September 1, 1965 that the infiltrators were freedom fighters and that there was an internal revolt in Kashmir. No wonder, after a long gap of almost thirtyeight years, General Musharraf continues to parrot the same excuse. On August 14, 1965, the *Washington Post* said that reports from a variety of sources in Srinagar and the information gained from Kashmiri and Pakistani sources during visits to Rawalpindi, Peshawar and Karachi left little doubt that at least fifteen hundred Pakistani-officered commandos have crossed the ceasefire line since August 5, 1965.[9] Similarly on August 14, 1965, the *New York Times* reported that on the basis of most reports received, the infiltrators appeared to have been recruited from among the people of Azad Kashmir. This was clear from the fact that most of the prisoners captured did not speak the Kashmiri dialect. They spoke various Punjabi dialects normally used by the inhabitants of the extreme western sectors under Pakistani control. The *Daily Telegraph* reported on August 22, 1945, that this was a military operation launched from Pakistan with official connivance.[10] In fact, as early as May 17, 1965, the *Pakistan Times,* Lahore, had quoted Sardar Rahmatullah, a State Councillor, as having said that thousands of Razakars were ready to cross the ceasefire line and march into the Indian Kashmir to rescue their brethern.[11] Thus the Pakistani Army and the ISI have been deeply involved in the strategy of training jihadi warriors from early 1960s onwards—and not since 1979, as is generally believed by most Western commentators and several Indian political analysts. And guess since when had the Pakistani establishment been trying to enlist militant jihadis from radical Muslim countries of West Asia and Northern Africa for fighting against the Hindu India in Kashmir? According to the *Pakistan Times*, Lahore, of January 1, 1965, an Islamic activist Maulvi Farid Khan Ahmed had claimed that "There is a great fund of goodwill for Kashmir in North Africa and Middle-Eastern countries. Almost everywhere, the question being asked is when Pakistanis or Kashmiris will take up arms for the Valley's liberation". He claimed that the Defence Minister of a Muslim country had offered to personally participate in jihad if Kashmiris and Pakistanis launched it.[12] Apparently Maulvi Farid Khan, who used to travel often to the West Asian and Northern African countries, was closely associated with the Tablighi Jamaat, the services of which were subsequently harnessed in a big way to recruit committed volunteers from West Asian and North African countries for jihad against Russia. And after the Afghan jihad was over, these jihadis were ultimately pushed into Kashmir. Thus when the ISI and the Pakistani Government, headed by General Zia, joined hands with the CIA to train bin Laden's soldiers in 1979 to wage war against Russia, they already had under their belt twenty-five years long expertise in the dreadful business of terrorism. They were no novices and had been into the terror business since partition – or at least since early 1960s, having trained more than ten thousand jihadis even before 1965 for operating in Kashmir. The CIA, too, had enough experience of promoting subversion and sabotage from the days of Vietnam war. The novice, if any, in this strategic game, was bin Laden. But once initiated into the terror game, he learnt the ropes fast from the ISI which led him to the leadership role astutely but quietly. That arrangement suited the ISI. No efficient intelligence out fit, and the ISI is certainly one, would like to assume a high profile role in such activities having international ramifications. After all, anonymity is the hallmark of all successful intelligence operations.

At present Pakistan is the only country in the world possessing almost fifty years of long expertise in terror industry. During the last five decades it has been enlarged from a small home-grown business into an expansive export-oriented industry with branches all over the globe, cleverly nurtured through the Pakistani diaspora. The unwavering commitment of the Pakistani establishment, especially its army and the ISI, to the cause of radical Islam has been the single most important factor responsible for speeding up the long march of Islam during the last fifty years. What is most interesting is that both the KGB and the CIA, the two biggest intelligence outfits of Russia and America, the erstwhile two respective super powers of the cold war era, miserably failed to assess the deadly game being played for decades by Pakistan - a small time theocratic nation steeped in orthodoxy and obscurantism. And what was the result of the professional incompetence of the KGB and the CIA. Both Russia and the U.S.A. had to pay a heavy price in terms of human lives as well as economic prosperity. Following its defeat in Afghanistan at the hands of jihadi forces, the Russian state disintegrated and that country went into tailspin both politically and economically. America too suffered enormously. More than three thousand lives were lost on the Black Tueday, apart from massive financial and economic losses, and for a while the U.S. government was widely perceived as licking its wounds. Later on, after successful completion of the Afghan campaign, America appears to have gone into a belligerent overdrive and appears to be badly stuck in Iraq at least for now.

Undoubtedly bin Laden is an intrepid, resourceful and charismatic leader, with excellent organizational skills and totally committed to pan-Islamism. But the truth remains that bin Laden alone, unaided by the ISI and the Pakistani army, could not have achieved any substantial success. He had no infrastructure, much less the requisite trained manpower running into hundreds of thousand soldiers to take on the mighty Russian army. Without the total support of Pakistan's governmental machinery, on his own he could not have grabbed even a small strip of Afghan territory from the Russians. He was able to achieve all that he did, and then emerge as global hero of Islamists solely due to the massive support of the Pakistani government, especially the ISI and its army. It is as simple as that. Napolean was not far wrong when he solemnly pronounced that "the occasion produces the leader". Perhaps bin Laden was one more such occasion-created leader coming out from nowhere—just to meet the demands of the hour! Every militant movement needs a charismatic hero, a high profile role model and at the opportune time bin Laden appeared on the scene to lead the jihadi warriors. Apart from providing the ready-made infrastructure, the ground work for jihadi blitzkrieg first in Afghanistan and subsequently across the globe, was done entirely by the ISI and the Pakistani army. The latter had lent on the sly, thousands of its soldiers plus key officers to wage jihad—many of them were found fighting shoulder to shoulder along with the Taliban as late as 2001, when America attacked Afghanistan. In all fairness, the credit or discredit for the present jihadi long march ought to be given primarily to Pakistan.

Bin Laden and his cronies, once unhinged from Pakistan, as they are now, have been reduced to more or less 'terror-tape' tigers, due to lack of the much needed infrastructure, inadequacy of manpower and above all the absence of governmental support—at least for the time being. True, Al Qaeda has the capability to stage many spectacular terrorist attacks in a number of countries, as indeed they have done in Bali, Riyadh, Morocco, Jakarta and even in Istanbul, because of the vast network which they managed to build when they had total support of Pakistani government. Their ability to overrun any country or overthrow any government as they earlier did in Afghanistan, however, has been seriously impaired. The only two countries which they can hope to overrun or where coups can be staged possibly are Pakistan and Saudi Arabia because of the massive public support to Islamist ideology at the grassroots level and substantial Islamization of the state apparatus in these two countries, including their armies. There is near unanimity among the middle rank officers and lower rungs of Pakistani army for commitment to radical Islam and the concept of jihad. The proof is there for everyone to see. In recent months quite a few middle level officers of Pakistani army were arrested for being in league with terrorists groups, including Al Qaeda. No doubt, the regular rantings of Al Qaeda against America, India and Israel and sometimes even against Musharraf, cannot be totally ignored. These are alarming, because the terrorist groups led by Al Qaeda still have the capacity to launch terror attacks at will but they no longer wield the kind of clout which they enjoyed before the collapse of Taliban-ruled Afghanistan. Just now they seem to be holed up in the wilderness of Federally Administered Tribal Areas of Pakistan or they could be hiding even in the Pak occupied Kashmir. Cornered as they are, it is difficult to believe that Pakistan cannot capture them. They are certainly well within the reach of Pakistani army, if it wishes to go whole hog after them!

In regard to the grooming of the Al Qaeda and the Taliban, the basic truth is that the ISI and the Pakistani army had built up a huge infrastructure for training jihadis long before the Russian occupation of Afghanistan: the madarasas were there, many training camps were there and several Arms Bazars already existed to meet the requirements of Islamist warriors. Apart from being the storm centre of Islamist terror, what distinguishes Pakistan from other southasian countries is that it is a country awash with all kinds of weapons and armaments. Regular gun running and smuggling of weapons is big business in the rugged areas of Pakistan bordering Afghanstan.The gross abundance and easy availability of weapons in that country is to be seen to be believed. Today in the entire south Asia, Pakistan has easily the most heavily armed civillian population. The import of Sharia-based Wahabi Islam from Saudi Arabia and the joint endeavours of the ISI and the CIA for ousting the Russians from Afghanistan were financed by promoting cultivation of poppy and trafficking in drugs, notably the infamous heroin trade. Money flowed copiously into the coffers of terror groups as a result of the rapid growth of trafficking in narcotics. But drug addiction also grew very fast in certain areas of Pakistan and on a conservative estimate now Pakistan has around three million drug addicts. The deep roots of militancy in Pakistan were further strengthened by the blatant use of religion by General Zia ul Haq to create a fundamentalist polity for enlarging the support base of his army dictatorship with the help of mullahs. Fairly extensive facilities for training Islamic terrorists had been in existence in Pakistan since early 1960s. For decades Pakistan was using and expanding all these facilities silently and studiously for terror attacks in Kashmir and promoting insurgency in that State. When bin Laden plunged into the campaign against Russian presence in Afghanistan, all these facilities were placed at his disposal by the ISI. The entire spade work for launching jihad first in Afghanistan against the Soviets and subsequently in several other countries, with special emphasis on the Indian Kashmir, was thus master minded by the Inter-Services Intelligence of Pakistan (ISI) which had been rightly described by the Peshawar-based newspaper *Frontier Post* in May 1994 as the "invisible Government of Pakistan". Till 1970s the progress of the pan-Islamic movement remained somewhat tardy but nevertheless it was quite steady. Historically Islam has never been short of volunteers willing to die in Allah's cause because of the deep commitment of Muslims to the doctrine of jihad. In any case, Pakistan did have a large population, it being easily one of the largest Muslim countries. Therefore, dedicated manpower for jihad was never a problem. The main constraint was the inadequacy of financial resources. The financial muscle was provided by the sudden upsurge of unprecedented prosperity in Saudi Arabia and the adjoining Arab Sheikhdoms in early 1970s, after the 1967 Gulf War, due to sky-rocketing increase in petroleum prices and the emergence of OPEC as a powerful cartel. The Pakistan government immediately capitalized on the opportunity by enlisting the financial support of the Saudis and then roping in the CIA by playing upon the U.S. fear about the growing Russian influence in the region. Soon plans were afoot to oust the pro-Soviet regime in Kabul, a cause very close to the heart of the Americans. In doing so the ISI saw an opportunity to surreptitiously raise the pan-Islamic movement to a higher plateau by breathing a new fiery zeal among the youth of Muslim countries. The ultimate goal was to restore the lost grandeur of Islam on the world canvas. The American strategists were too naïve to comprehend the core of the Pakistani gameplan. Roughly some three hundred thousand to four hundred thousand jihadi volunteers were trained by the ISI and the Pakistani army during the late 1970s and early 1980s. After victory in their long campaign against Russia, many of these 'holy warriors' returned to their parent countries but a sizeable number was pushed into Kashmir and some contingents despatched to the new theatres of Islamic campaigns in Bosnia, Kosovo, Chechenya, Algeria, Indonesia and the Philippines where they have been waging multiple jihads. According to Mohammed Amir Rana, the well known Pakistani author of the book, *Jihad-e-Kashmir and Afghanistan*, even now Pakistan has 1.2 million trained militant youngmen possessing the experience of participation "in the activities of jihadi and religious organizations", while approximately thirty thousand had died in the holy war in Afghanistan and Kashmir.[13] This estimated strength of the jihadis spread across Pakistan tallies with the figure quoted in a New Delhi seminar by Prof. Satish Kumar, an expert political analyst. Most of them are reasonably well trained in the use of arms and armaments - some could be even battle-scarred. More importantly, they are willing cannon fodder, ready to die in jihad-like that Amrozi, the bomber of Kuta Beach in Bali who smilingly received his death sentence and the unrepentant Imam Samudra who shouted Allah-o-Akbar and pumped his clenched fist into the air, when death sentence was read out to him by an Indonesian court. The impressive numbers of trained jihadis spread all over Pakistan and their fanatic commitment to holy war underlines the dimensions of the ongoing long march of Islam. Simultaneously the flow of petro dollars was being used by the Saudis with the help of the ISI to finance the activities of the radical Islam by setting up thousands of religious seminaries, called madarasas, first in Pakistan, Indonesia and Afghanistan and thereafter throughout the length and breadth of Asia, Africa and Europe. These religious seminaries, especially the one in Peshawar called Haqqania Madarasa and another one located in the Binori mosque of Karachi, came very handy for waging jihad in Afghanistan in the 1980s. They supplied thousands of volunteers for Afghan jihad. But ultimately all seminaries became factories for producing terrorists and suicide bombers. For instance, the Haqqania produced a galaxy of ruthless Taliban group leaders and fighters. While exporting petroleum to the West, the Saudis steadfastly exported the fundamentalist version of Islam all over Asia and Africa with the help of the petro dollars earned from the West. Many Saudi fugitives even managed to set up terror shops in Europe and America, as a recent probe by the Federal Bureau of Investigation and the CIA has revealed. The edited 28 pages of the Congressional report on the events of 9/11, produced by a joint panel of the House and Senate intelligence committees, have created serious doubts about the complicity of some Saudi intelligence agents who were believed to have indirect contacts with at least two hijackers. People familiar with the report and who spoke on condition of not being named, said that the two Saudi citizens, Omar al-Bayoumi and Osama Bassnian, operated in a complex web of financial relationship with officials of the Saudi government. The sections that focus on them drew connections between the two men, two hijackers and Saudi officials.[14] In his latest best seller, *Sleeping with the Devil*, Robert Baer, a former CIA operator, has described Saudi Arabia as something of an irrational state—a place that has been spawning global terrorism even as it succumbs to an ancient and deep-seated isolationism, led by a royal family that cannot get out of its own greed. Baer has dwelt heavily on the funds being provided by the Saudi regime to innumerable mosque-schools, i.e., madarasas, that preach hatred of America and promote militancy and terrorism. But all this wisdom came to the Americans much later and at a heavy cost. And the Pakistani establishment promptly capitalized on the opportunity by enlisting the massive financial support of the Saudis—even that of the CIA on the plea of ousting the Soviets from Afghanistan. While the concept of ummah remained the sheet anchor of Islam's unique bonding because it ensures a never-drying stream of young volunteers, the Islamists soon spread their wings across to the Europe and the U.S.A. With the open support of Pakistani establishment they made the new frontiers of technology as the powerful driver of the core strategy to carry forward the message of jihad to the farthest corners of the world. For attaining their objective the storm- troopers of Islam made full use of the freedom of speech and expression available in the democratic countries of the Europe and the U.S.A. to promote their cause and win large support for fund raising and recruiting volunteers for their global project. How did the pan-Islamic movement spread so fast and so soon? The answer is the committed dedication of jihadi warriors plus the adoption of new technology by them. Radical Islam has taken full advantage of the latest technological developments for spreading its message to ummah in distant lands. The rapid advancements in digital communication, easy availability of the facility of internet and mushrooming of trans-continental television channels have placed a vast array of formidable tools in the hands of Jihadis. So the communication revolution spurred by technology, by annihilating the distance, has re-engineered the relationship between far away groups and communities in a thematic rather than spatial manner, thus bringing them closer. Owing to the rapid advancement of technology, in matters concerning dissemination of information and sharing of technology, the governments no longer count for much. Easy access through internet and availability of satellite phones have led to virtual demise of distance and blurring of national borders. The role of governments in the field of communication has been marginalized. Technology has made the traditional methods of communication irrelevant—the old concepts of distance and transnational borders are *passe*. Internet has facilitated quick exchange of information and made the tasks of horizontal and vertical integration of terrorist organizations easier thereby opening new opportunities for conspiracy and collaboration, through convergence, across the continents and oceans. In the process, the unique bonding of Muslim masses, called 'ummah', has been further strengthened by facilitating regular and quicker interaction thereby consolidating the command and control structure. Rapid organizational changes, speedy exchange of vital information and prompt decision-making have become easier and affordable; these have been the hallmark of several terror strikes. A number of jihadi oufits have registered presence on the Internet and hoisted their websites on which they regularly post their communiques and programmes, sometime even coded messages to ensure secrecy. The number of websites hoisted by the Islamists is legion. Most of these websites have been sending encrypted messages through Internet and are using satellite phones for directing reinforcements of weapons and manpower wherever required by the terrorist operators for accomplishing the tasks assigned to them. This was done on a fairly extensive scale during the Bosnian war when supplies of weapons and battle hardened groups of jihadis were rushed for tactical operations to Bosnia and other parts of Balkans from several Muslim countries, with the active support of the governments of Pakistan and Iran. In 1993 more than 150 battle hardened jihadis of Afghan vintage were seen to be operating in Bosnia and Kosovo. Apart from waging holy war against the Serbs, these jihadi groups indoctrinated Bosnian and Albanian Muslims in the fundamentals of radical Islam by preaching return to the purist Wahabi Islam through missionary activities called *da'wah*. The same strategy is being used extensively by the terror groups waging jihad in Chechenya and Jammu and Kashmir. Some Chechen rebels have been seen wearing caps and berets with the word 'Ghazwah' emblazoned across, just to revive and promote the jihadi fervour of the times of Prophet Muhammad.

New technology is also being used successfully for conveying secret strategic commands and directions to the terrorist outfits and Al Qaeda cells and action stations in far removed countries like Morocco, Saudi Arabia, Indonesia and the Philippines. To ensure that there is no easy snooping by the intelligence agencies, clever use of passwords is a standard practice. The Islamic websites have also been using Internet for beaming propaganda and spreading messages both to their co-religionists as well as to other communities. At one time it was believed that perhaps Hizb-ut Tehrir, an Islamist outfit, having its objective as the establishment of a Muslim caliphate, which should include the U.K., had been using an Islamic site based in the Imperial College, London, which was closed down only when complaints were made to the authorities. They subsequently set up their own site as "Hizb-ut Tehrir" on which they had been posting their literature and programmes including their scheduled meetings. Interestingly the Syrian Islamist idealogue Omar Bakri Mohammed, who had studied at Cairo's prestigious Al Azhar University, after his expulsion from Saudi Arabia in 1986, took asylum in the U.K. But Omar Bakri had a history. During his sojourn in the Middle East he had been associated with Islamist groups like Muslim Brotherhood of Syria and Egypt and Hizb-ut Tehrir, also known as Islamic Liberation Party. In due course of time Bakri enlisted the support of more like-minded radicals and founded the U.K. Branch of Hizb-ut Tehrir which took recourse to indoctrination of Muslims studying in the universities and started interacting with prominent members of the Muslim community for promoting the Islamist ideas. Hizb-ut Tehrir is an international fundamentalist organization which aims at establishing a Khilafat, i.e., a Muslim state based on sharia, all over the world, including the U.K., by obliterating transnational borders. According to the doctrine of Hizb-ut Tehrir, if necessary the Islam's Khilafat has to be established by waging jihad against 'the Kufr', i.e., the non-believers. In February 1996 Bakri broke away from Hizb-ut Tehrir and set up another radical outfit, Al Muhajiroun, which means 'the Immigrants' with the help of some like-minded Islamists, including one Farid Qasim, another Syrian-based in the U.K. Bakri soon proclaimed himself as a judge of the British Court of Sharia, meant for Britain-based Muslims, which believes in the dominance of sharia laws, as far as Muslims are concerned. Omar Bakri also happens to be the founder of Al Khalifa Publications, a publishing press dedicated to propagation of the philosophy of radical Islam. Hizb-ut Tehrir is highly critical of many Arab and Muslim regimes of the Middle East and Central Asia for which reason it has long been banned in a number of Muslim countries, especially in the Middle East. But it was not banned in the U.K. where it continued to flourish. Full use of technology, including Internet and print media, was made for propagating the goals of Al Muhajiruon and Hizb-ut Tehrir, thereby, making them as two high profile, proactive and most articulate organizations of Muslims in the U.K. Al Muhajiroun recently hit the headlines on the occasion of the second anniversary of 9/11 for praising the "Magnificient 19" hijackers of September 11 for terror attacks in New York and Washington as a commendable deed. They have an office in a business centre in Tottenham, London. Posters inside the room glorified the hijackers for making the U.S. "taste its own medicine". In the first week of September 2003 Al Muhajiroun held a press conference and public meeting at which the hijackers were described as 'Brave Warriors' who had made the ultimate sacrifice.

Similarly the Algeria-based GIA or the Algerian Armed Islamic Group, which was involved in several bombings and terrorist acts, had reportedly been operating their Internet directed command and control system from the U.K. for a long time. Israeli intelligence agencies were struggling for quite sometime to identify and destroy the highly sophisticated but decentralized multiple systems of command and control, devised by the notorious Hamas. At one time, the secret investigations by the FBI of America raised the suspicion that a part of the decentralised command system of Hamas could be located in Tampa in Florida. Subsequently it had allegedly moved to London where it started publishing "Filistine-al-Muslima", sort of a newsletter and carried out even some fund-raising activities. Similar extensive use of high tech gizmos, including Internet and satphones was done by the Pakistan-controlled terrorists for planning and executing the dastardly attack on the Indian Parliament on December 13, 2001, in which many security personnel laid down their lives to save the Members of Parliament and several Ministers trapped inside. The loyalty and commitment of the terrorists to Pakistan rang loud and clear when one of them, while spraying bullets and racing towards the main entrance, shouted "Pakistan Paindabad", i.e., 'long live Pakistan'. There could be no better proof of the complicity of Pakistan in that terror crime against the biggest democracy of the world. Interestingly while on their way to the Parliament House they even asked on the cell phone, one of their colleagues, who was left behind to watch the proceedings of the Parliament to inform which VIPs and how many Ministers were present in the House—too bad for them that their accomplice could never get back to them to convey that the Prime Minster was not there in the Parliament then. After the news of attack on Indian Parliament became known, there were celebrations in Lahore, Karachi and many other cities of Pakistan. Recently in April and May 2003 a sophisticated command system, though not a high tech one, set up by the Pakistan sponsored terror groups was destroyed by the Indian army during "Operation Sarap Vinash" in the Hill Kaka region of Surankote, Kashmir, after high profile operations. The command structure was being operated by the guerrilas of Lashkar-e-Tayebba for launching attacks on innocent civillians on the orders received from their "masters" located across the border in Pakistan and Pakistan-occupied Kashmir. They had put in place a regular wireless network to remain in constant touch with their masters on the other side of the border and had the facility of satphone, too. Similarly investigations into the assassination of Haren Pandya, a former Minister in the BJP Government of the Gujarat State, have revealed that the conspiracy was hatched entirely on the Internet.[15] According to the CBI, Internet cafes in Rajasthan and Gujarat were used by Asghar Ali, the accused who allegedly pulled the trigger on Pandya, to communicate with Rasool Khan Pathan, one of the chief masterminds, now in the hiding perhaps in Karachi, Pakistan, along with Mufti Sufiyan, a co-accused. Both Rasool Khan Pathan and Mufti Sufiyan had reportedly sent a number of youngmen to Pakistan for training in the use of firearms and explosives. Most Islamist terror outfits, especially Al Qaeda, have made full use of the modern tools like resource planning, strategic resource mobilization and acquisition and utilization of situation specific manpower, weapons and funds from the nearest countries or action stations, located hundred of miles away. Prima facie, the initial training for such in-depth use of technology had been provided by the Pakistani army to hand-picked group leaders of Al Qaeda who, in turn, trained several hundred lower cadres of jihadis. The new frontiers of technology have played a vital role in the jihadi long march. It is evident from the examples of Afghanistan, Bosnia, Chechenya, Palestine and Kashmir that terrorists have made extensive use of technology for strategic movement of men, moneys and materials for strengthening the Islamist campaigns. In short, the adoption of new technology has made tech-savvy terrorists a cut above the rest, even placed them a notch above the average soldier of security forces.

In addition, there were quite a few other geo-political developments all favouring the votaries of radical Islam. One important factor which contributed substantially to the spread of radical Islam was the Iranian revolution of 1979 which united the Muslims across the globe to wage jihad against the western powers, especially the U.S.A., to break their hegemony over the Islamic countries of the Middle East and central and southeast Asia. The Islamic revolution in Iran, like the French and Russian Revolutions with which it resembled in many ways, had a huge impact not only at home and among its own people but also among all the countries and peoples with whom it shared the fundamentalist ideology.[16] And like the earlier revolutions, and particularly the Russian one, it has its own network of agents and emissaries striving in various ways to further the cause of the revolution or at least the regime that seemed to embody it.[17] The success of the Iranian revolution was a great inspiration to the Islamists of Pakistan, Afghanistan, Palestine, Saudi Arabia and several North African countries.

The victory of jihadi groups in Afghanistan over the powerful Russian army in 1980s, achieved largely by the endeavours of the ISI and Pakistani army, albeit with substantial support of the CIA, both in terms of financial resources and tactical inputs, proved to be a shot in the arm of the Islamists. It gave them dream visions of grand success ahead. The militant factions of Taliban, warlords like Gulbudin Hekmatyar, the fundamentalist faction of Abu Sayyaf and several other groups, all trained by the ISI, were able to baptise their warriors, sharpen their terror tactics and combat skills in the Afghan war against Russia. The sudden collapse of the Russian power structure after the Afghan jihad and the resultant disintegration of the Soviet Union created a political vacuum in Central Asia thereby facilitating the emergence of radical Islam in several former Russian territories like Uzbekistan, Turkeminstan and Dagestan. In the Russian province of Chechenya it virtually led to a revolt against the Russian authority. The break-up of the Soviet Union opened up a new arena of religion-based faultline conflicts and ethnic strifes in quite a few Islam-dominated states which were formerly part of the Soviet Union. It has exposed the soft underbelly of Russia to the growing Islamist threat. The terrorist groups are likely to make full use of this opportunity to extend the field of their operations against Russia.

The success of terror tactics and prolonged guerrilla wars waged by multiple Islamic groups in Kosovo and Bosnia with the active support of Iran, Pakistan and a host of Muslim countries was an important milestone in the jihadi compaign. The subsequent defeat of Serb nationalists largely due to the intervention of NATO and the U.S.A. in the years 1998-99 resulting from incessant bombing of Serbia for nearly 2½ months gave a thumbs up signal to the jihadi forces across the globe. After the defeat of Ottoman Turks at Vienna in 1683, for the first time in the history of Europe, the warriors of Islam were able to score a credible victory in their religious and idealogical war against the Christian nations of Serbia and Croatia. It was the fulfilment of a long cherished ambition of the Islamists, worldwide. This success has invigorated the Muslim identity of Albania, Kosovo and Bosnia and the growing numbers of Muslims in Balkans are already consolidating themselves further.

The disastrous debacle and humiliation faced by the American troops in Somalia in October 1993 was another important event. It gave tremendous impetus to the growth of radical Islam across the globe. The ignominy heaped upon the U.S. troops by the militant Somali Islamists, aided by Iran and Islamists of Sudan, duly backed by the Al Qaeda, raised hopes among Muslims of an imminent victory of jihadi warriors over the West. As pointed out by Bernard Lewis, bin Laden and his associates repeatedly cited the American retreats from Vietnam, from Lebanon and the most important of all in their eyes the retreat from Somalia.[18] Bin Laden's views about the U.S. soldiers turning tails while facing jihadi warriors, expounded in an interview with John Miller of television channel, ABC News, on May 28, 1998, were interesting. He claimed that in the last decade there was a visible decline in the strength of America and the combat capacity of American soldiers, who could only wage cold wars but were unfit to fight long wars. This, he claimed, was proved in Beirut when the U.S. Marines fled after two explosions and ran away in less than twenty-four hours. The same story was repeated in Somalia where Islamic warriors were surprised at the low morale of American soldiers. After receiving a few blows, they ran away in defeat and forgot all about the U.S. being the world leader. Finally, he claimed, that Americans ran away from Somalia, dragging their corpses after suffering a shameful defeat.[19]

Operation 'Caustic Brimstone", as the Somalia campaign was dubbed, turned out to be a major setback to the prestige of America. Although prima facie it appeared to be a successful operation, the general perception was otherwise, because of the horrid finale shown on television in which the corpses of U.S. soldiers were dragged across the town by Somali guerillas. In Washington, Defence Secretary Les Aspin was most unhappy. The toll of casualties read: 18 Americans and 1 Malaysian dead, 84 Americans and 7 Malaysians wounded, 312 Somalis dead and 814 wounded.[20] While on the face of it the Americans had successfully carried out their mission of capturing some senior leaders of Somali militia, the world did not view it as such. The American public were shocked when they saw on television the pictures of the captured pilot Michael Durant, badly wounded and beaten, in agony. More revolting still was what the Somalis did to the five dead, including Seargents Gordon and Shugart. The bodies were defiled, one of them being dragged naked through the streets of Mogadishu in front of the CNN camera by jubilant Somalis.[21] Thus the turning of a victory into defeat through the medium of television visuals, became a great morale booster for the Islamists.

The Islamists have also been making full use of the freedom of speech and expression and of belief, faith and worship available in democratic countries. By taking advantage of the freedom of speech and expression, greatly valued in the U.K. and most other western countries, a statement was put out in a London-based Arabic newspaper, *Al-Quds al-Arabi*, on February 23, 1998, directing all Muslims worldwide to kill Americans and Jews. The historic statement was simply a typical call for jihad issued by bin Laden and his associates and among its signatories were Ayman al-Zawahiri of Jihad of Egypt, Abu-Yasir Rifa'i Ahmed Taha of Egyptian Islamic Group, Shaykh Mir Hamzah, Secretary of Jamiat-ul-Ulema-e-Pakistan and Fazlur Rahman of the Jihad Movement in Bangladesh. This pronouncement was more or less a religious ruling or "fatwa" issued against 'the crusaders and Jews', whether civillians or military men. Issuing such threats publicly, through print media, would have been a taboo, almost impossible, in the totalitarian Muslim regimes of the Middle East and Central Asia. But it could be easily done and was conveniently done, in a free democratic society like the United Kingdom. This "fatwa" or declaration of war against the crusading Christians and Jews was extensively broadcast across the world by several television channels thereby raising the stature of bin Laden in the eyes of militant Muslims in scores of countries. Subsequently after 9/11, bin Laden's Al-Qaeda group, in October 2001, added the name of 'Hindu India' to the list of the communities and nations marked for being targeted by the Jihadi groups. In a video-taped message, released through Al-Jazeera television network, an unnamed Al-Qaeda spokesman added that the "U.S. support to the Hindus against the Muslims of Kashmir" to the familiar list of grievances that include the U.S. presence in Saudi Arabia, the Palestinian issue and the situation in Iraq.[22] This happened immediately after the U.S. froze the assets of Jaish-e-Mohammed which reacted by alleging that the freezing of its funds had been done at the behest of Indian Government which was in cahoots with America. The announcement that the so-called 'Hindu India' had been added to the target-countries of jihad announced by the Al Qaeda made banner headlines in the Indian and Pakistani newspapers and was beamed all over by television channels. The news proved to be a shot in the arm of Lashkar-e-Tayyeba terrorists operating from Pakistan. It is anybody's guess whether or not the subsequent December 13, 2001 attack on the Indian Parliament was a sequel to the threats issued to the 'Hindu India' by the Al-Qaeda and Jaish-Mohammed, two well-known terrorist outfits.

Although India has a surfeit of columnists and analysts who try to underplay the threat of Islamist terror, Al Qaeda and its allied terror groups have no qualms about targetting 'the Hindu India'. They have done it time and again from Kashmir to Kanya Kumari. Recently on the second anniversary of 9/11 an Al Qaeda tape showing bin Laden and his close associate, Ayman Al Zawhiri, was released by Al Jazeera which spat venom against the Hindus. It is a chilling reminder to the Indian people of the future dangers from Islamist terrorists. After September 11, 2001, it is for the second time that the Hindu India has featured prominently in an Al Qaeda tape. Although a major portion of the tape was directed against General Musharraf, who was dubbed as "traitor Musharraf" for betraying Islam and choking the jihad in Kashmir, there were many provocative references against India, warning the Pakistanis of the day when they will "wake up from their slumber to find Hindu soldiers" raiding their homes "in complicity with the Americans". It has an ominous ring of the likelihood of a new terror storm blowing across India in the shape of more serial bombings and killings. Close on the heels of Laden's taped terror came the pronouncement made by the notorious Jaish-e-Mohammed of Pakistan to kill the top leaders of India. It is well known that India has hundreds of active ISI modules and moles in the local population. Without the latter's active support the kinds of bomb blasts which Mumbai has been witnessing could not have occurred with such daring and impunity. Laden's tape and Jaish's open threat should give enough food for thought to all those critics who proclaim that the Islamic threat to the country is being exaggerated. The message of terrorists is loud and clear: The Christian America, the Hindu India and the Jewish Israel are the enemies of Islam and will therefore remain on the hit list of Al Qaeda and related militant Islamist groups. It may be recalled that the radical Islam has been aggressively hostile to these three civilizations now for almost one thousand years.

In making jihad a global phenomenon the audio-visual media too have played a key role. The daily menu of the heroics of Islamic warriors attacking and killing the so-called 'kafirs', the numerous battles waged by Klashnikov crazy mujahideens and the flashbacks of young Muslim lads coming forward as suicide bombers, served on the television and in print media, have been providing grist to the mill of Muslim militancy. The visuals of the frequent bloody strifes in hotspots of faultline clashes across Palestine, Indonesia, Chechenya, Afghanistan and Kashmir, regularly shown by the television channels, CNN, BBC and Al Jazeera, have imparted a new vigour to the resolve of jihadi Muslims, worldwide. For instance, the broadcasting of the so-called bin Laden tapes at intervals by Al Jazeera has helped in rallying massive support of the faithful to the cause of the ongoing jihad in several countries. It has to be acknowledged that the audio visual media has become a powerful tool, a great unifying force for like-minded Islamists; it has contributed substantially to spreading the cult of suicide bombings. For Islamist martyrs the ideal of carrying the Quran in one hand and a Kalashnikov in the other has become the standard badge of honour. The arrest and subsequent conviction by the trial court in America of a 34 years old Kashmir-born truck driver, Iyman Faris alias Mohammed Rauf, now a naturalised U.S. citizen, a few months ago for plotting to blow up New York's Brooklyn Bridge and launch another unspecified attack in Washington, gives an insight into the modus operandi of Muslim terrorists. Faris had reportedly travelled in late 2000 and subsequently to Pakistan and Afghanistan, where on one occasion he claims to have met Osama bin Laden and his senior lieutenants, one of whom was Khalid Sheikh Mohammed, who was captured on March 1, 2003 in Pakistan. Investigation revealed that Faris was living a "double life" of a truck driver as well as of an Al Qaeda operator. The latter assignment included carrying cash for Al Qaeda, providing vital information about 'ultralight' aircraft and scouting equipment for blowing up railroad tracks and cutting suspension bridge cables. Faris who had been earlier in touch with Al Qaeda leaders, had one more confederate based in America who sent coded messages for him to a senior Al Qaeda operative in Pakistan between April 2002 and March 2003. During his trip to Pakistan in late 2000, Faris had also met an unnamed friend he had known since the Soviet-Afghanistan war in the mid-1980s. Together the two had travelled to an Al Qaeda training camp in Afghanistan, where that friend of Faris, described as bin Laden's "right foot" was involved for providing supplies of materials to Al Qaeda. In 2002 Faris met Khalid Sheikh Mohammed to whom he delivered a bag containing cash and cellphones. On being told by Faris that he worked as a truck driver, involving deliveries of consignments to cargo planes, Khalid Sheikh Mohammed told him that he was interested in cargo planes because they would hold 'more weight and more fuel'. Khalid Mohammed had informed Iyman Faris that Al Qaeda was planning two simultaneous operations in New York city and Washington D.C. and asked him to obtain "gas cutters" to sever the bridge cables and the tools to damage the rail road tracks. He was further advised to refer to the torches as gas stations and the tools as mechanics shops in the communications sent by him. Faris tried to look for gas cutters on the Internet and asked a friend about them but did not succeed and sent a coded message to Khalid Mohammed. He also carried out a recce of the Brooklyn Bridge in early 2003 and concluded that the plot would fail because of the sound security and structure of the bridge and then sent another coded message to his unnamed friend saying that "the weather was too hot". The following three tasks had been assigned to Iyman Faris:

1. Researching ultra-light planes as means of escape for terror operatives, which task he managed to accomplish at an Internet café in Karachi.
2. Ordering 2000 lightweight sleeping bags from a factory which were duly shipped to Al Qaeda in Afghanistan.
3. In December 2001, Faris helped Al Qaeda and managed to obtain extensions for half a dozen air tickets for Al Qaeda operators planning to visit Yemen.

The arrest of Faris also exposed the close links between Al Qaeda and the Tablighi Jamaat, a radical Muslim missionary outfit, indulging in proselytizing activities all over the world. Not many U.S. intelligence agencies knew that the two organisations had been brought close to each other by the ISI during the Afghan campaign against the Soviet Russia. It was a simple task because the Tablighi Jamaat is a Pakistan-based radical missionary group enjoying enormous popularity and high visibility in that country. One of the Al Qaeda's first assignment for the truck driver, Iyman Faris, named in a terrorist plot to target and destroy the Brooklyn Bridge, was to visit a travel agency while he was in Pakistan in late 2001 to have some old airline tickets re-issued. Because the tickets were not in his name, Iyman Faris needed an explanation to validate his request. Investigators say he used the one that other Qaeda recruits have relied on to disguise their intentions: he pretended to be a member of Tablighi Jamaat, a fraternity of travelling Muslim preachers that is well known in Pakistan and other Muslim countries.[23] The services of Tablighi Jamaat were specially sought by the ISI of Pakistan for recruiting 'committed Islamic volunteers' both from Pakistan and North African countries in 1970s and 1980s to wage holy war against the Soviets in Afghanistan. It is a 75-year old pan-Islamic Wahabi organisation, which originated in India, but is now headquartered in Raiwind (near Lahore) in Pakistan where it wields huge influence due to official patronage and regular liaison with the ISI and the Pakistani Army. It was only after the Black Tuesday that the Tablighi Jamaat attracted attention of American security agencies. It has been used either as part of a cover story like that of Faris or as a springboard for leaping into militancy, as in the case of John Walker Lindh, an American, serving term for aiding the Taliban. Interrogation of John Walker Lindh revealed that his path to militancy began in California, where he met Tabligh missionaries in 1999 after converting to Islam. He joined them on a proselytizing tour but soon left them behind. One year after his association with Tablighi Jamaat mission, looking for a place to study Islam, Mr Lindh contacted one of his visiting Tabligh preachers, who enrolled him in a madarasa or religious school, in Pakistan. It was there that Lindh became convinced that he should help the Taliban. He then signed up for a military training camp that ultimately sent him to fight American and Northern Alliance forces in Afghanistan. He was captured there.[24] The Tabligh is fairly well entrenched in America. According to Michael J. Heimbach, the Deputy Chief of the FBI's International Terrorism Section, Tablighi Jamaat have a significant presence in the United States and it was known that Al Qaeda had used them for recruiting, now and in the past. Another senior law enforcement official described the group as a natural entrée, a method of gathering people together having common interest in Islam. The official added that the extremists use that as an assessment tool to evaluate individuals with particular zealousness and interest in going beyond what is offered.[25] Similarly in another case six Yemeni-American men from Lackawanna, a Buffalo suburb, had told some friends a similar story—that they were going to Pakistan in the spring of 2001 for religious training with the Tablighi Jamaat. But once in Pakistan, the men went on to take military training at an Al Qaeda camp in Afghanistan. This only shows how a number of Islamist moles and Al Qaeda Sleeper cells have been established in almost all democratic countries and open societies, including the U.S.A. and the U.K. Of course, India has been pock-marked by hundreds of ISI modules and terrorist action stations of radical Islam now for several decades. It is well known that Al Qaeda and allied terror groups have organised a very efficient system of operations through networking, by using Pakistan as their focal point. As a modest estimate, the Sleeper Cells established by Al Qaeda and its associate outfits are said to exist in at least fifty countries - some analysts place the number as high as eighty nations, both Islamic and non-Islamic included. These Cells, manned by trusted battle-hardened operators, can be readily converted into action stations at short notice through the medium of Internet, and satellite telephones.

It is obvious that the long march of Islam will continue to be a multi-pronged and low-intensity no-holds-barred war, more specifically as series of violent incidents staged at irregular intervals, in which several groups of fundamentalist Islamic terrorists, guerrillas, drug smuggling Muslim gangsters, indoctrinated insurgents and highly motivated ethnic tribal factions like the Moro Islamists of Southern Phillipines, Arab militants and Pakistani veterans are likely to play a key role. Having started their long march almost five decades ago, the radical Islam is in no frantic hurry. They know that the dynamics of demography and the resolute commitment of millions of Muslims in more than forty countries to die in the cause of jihad have been working in their favour. The universal civilization ought to realize that Islamists are not going to wage a large scale war by involving regular armies of Muslim nations like Pakistan or Iran or by regrouping the soldiers of Islam, spread in many countries, most of whom are Pakistanis, Arabs, and Afghans—at least not until they are able to develop and deploy nuclear weapons in support of their jihadi long march. With the successful completion of the U.S.—led military campaigns in Afghanistan and Iraq, the possibility of Islamic countries taking recourse to conventional warfare is practically over—perhaps for all times to come. At present no country in the world, leave alone Pakistan and Iran or any other combination of Muslim countries, is in a position to match the military strength of the USA. But even though the RMA,i.e. Revolution in Military Affairs, has catapulted America into the exclusive one-member club of hyper-power, there will always be the threat of Islam's suicide bombers trying to use a 'dirty nuke bomb' or other rudimentary radioactive weapons against the universal civilization for inflicting mass casualties—perhaps more specifically against America, India and Israel. The Islamists have abundantly demonstrated their determination and long reach by staging the 9/11 attack on the WTC by using hijacked planes as deadly weapons, by using suicide squads for targeting the Indian Parliament in New

Delhi on December 13, 2001, in broad daylight and subsequent spectacular bombings in Bali, Morocco and Saudi Arabia and Turkey. As disclosed by the Russian first Deputy Foreign Minister, Vyacheslav Trubnikov, both Russia and the U.S. now see the threat of Pakistani nuclear weapons falling into the hands of terrorists as no more purely a theoretical possibility, implying that it was quite a possibility. The two countries have been repeatedly discussing the issue. The threat of Pakistani nuclear weapons falling into the hands of terrorists is growing because of the presence of large number of extremist groups in Pakistan. The matter deserves attention of the world community. It will be always necessary to keep in mind the grim possibility of some fundamentalist Army commanders of Pakistan suddenly seizing control of Pak nukes and then taking the extreme step of attacking India and Israel, the two most hated countries in their immediate neighbourhood. They could perhaps mount a suicidal nuclear attack even against the American troops and the CIA functionaries based in and around Pakistan and Afghanistan. At the same time the test-firing by Iran of their medium range missile 'Shahab 3' in July 2003, in the presence of their supremo, Ayatollah Khomeini, should alert the world to the possibility of Pakistan and Iran joining hands in the near future in a renewed bid to advance the cause of radical Islam by pooling their nuclear assets and technical know-how. Shahab-3 is a medium range ballistic missile having a range of 1300 kilometers and can reportedly carry a warhead weighing 700 to 1300 kgs. It has brought Israel within the target range of the fundamentalist Iranian regime. The long-term implications of Shahab-3 for India are being studied but may not be made public. In the Persian language, 'Shahab' means a "meteor". For sometime past, Iran has been under pressure from the International Atomic Energy Agency (IAEA) Director, Mohammed El Baradei, to allow surprise inspection of its nuclear facilities. The IAEA has been advising Iran to sign and ratify an additional protocol to the Nuclear Non-Proliferation Treaty. But Iran is quite reluctant. The reasons are obvious.

By virtue of its commitment to radical Islam, Pakistan has always played a key role in the propagation of jihadi culture. Looking to the praise which the U.S. President and Collin Powell have been showering on Musharraf for helping them fight the Al Qaeda, often describing Pakistan as a 'stalwart ally', many Indians presume that perhaps Washington is not fully aware of Pakistan's role in international Islamist terrorism. But that presumption is wrong. A mere glance at the comments of senior analysts in the U.S. media and occasional proceedings of the congressional committees will convince anyone that Pentagon has complete knowledge of the active role of the Pakistani and Saudi regimes in fuelling the Islamic jihad. A question often asked during animated discussions in the drawing rooms of New Delhi is that why and how did the fundamentalist Pakistan government, headed by a jingoist army General, manage to jump on to the bandwagon of America's fierce campaign to destroy the global advancement of Islamist cause? The answer is the TINA factor. Neither Pakistan, nor the U.S.A. had any alternative. It is a marriage of convenience. The immediate need of the U.S.A. was to secure a firm and multi-pronged toehold in Pakistan for the twin purposes of mounting a no-holds-barred aerial-cum-ground assault on Afghanistan, where bin Laden and his legions were well entrenched and to set up within Pakistan an extensive network of electronic intelligence, supported by multiple teams of seasoned ground operators, to maintain a hawkish vigil. The CIA is fully aware that Pakistan is teeming with scores of militant outfits and thousands of armed jihadis committed to radical Islam. Although India had offered to help the U.S.A., the latter's foremost priority was to secure a number of high perching places in Pakistan for maintaining a long term watch on that country and its neighbourhood. Otherwise their operations could end up in a fiasco. Moreover, the Americans knew that, by virtue of being a vibrant democracy, it was impossible for them to secure any bases in India nor was the Indian political class purchasable or pliable. In sharp contrast, Pakistan under Musharraf was available—at least temporarily, may be for a few years. And therefore when Collin Powell came calling on phone, Pakistan's military dictator had no option but to submit to America's demands. The U.S. request was virtually a stern command. And another reason for the American decision to virtually 'buy out' Musharraf could be the realization that the direct launching of a war against a country of Pakistan's size would require enormous resource mobilization, apart from committing more than half a million defence personnel and sink several billion dollar worth equipment in a war which could turn out to be a long drawn affair. Even for attacking the teeny weeny Afghan army, known as the Taliban, the U.S.A. had to make a month-long preparation, canvass and rally the support of world opinion to form a global coalition of the willing nations to fight the threat of Islamist terror. Even so during the operations in Afghanistan there were anxious moments, sometimes days and weeks of grave doubt, when it looked that the progress on ground in the war against Taliban was painfully slow. But for the mobilization of troops of the Northern Alliance, the U.S.A. could not have easily captured Kabul. Even carpet bombing does not guarantee physical control on the ground. And if the U.S. had to attack Pakistan, a country much bigger in size and nuclear-armed, flaunting nearly a million strong army, including the Rangers and para military outfits, they might have had to take at least six months or more for preparation. Obviously they chose the path of least resistance, by securing Pakistan as the launching pad for operations in Afghanistan by promising economic aid and other doles. That was the major predicament facing the U.S.A. which restrained them from attacking Pakistan. Since Vietnam war the American public has been mortally afraid of body bags and so is the U.S. government.

It may be recalled that in his famous speech of September 19, 2001 pledging total support to the U.S.A. in the war against terror, Musharraf had boldly referred to Pakistan as the "fortress of Islam" which expression fits that nation very well in view of the pivotal role it has played in promoting the radical Islamist ideology since its birth in 1947. After all, the Pakistani army had fathered the Taliban and ultimately managed to secure Afghanistan through a regime change, making it more or less an adjunct of Pakistan. The aim was to secure "strategic depth" for Pakistan in order to wage war against the so-called 'Hindu India', an eventuality which the military leadership of Pakistan considers inevitable. As a prominent India-baiter of Pakistani army, Musharraf was the chief architect of the plot to capture Afghanistan, to secure strategic depth. What made him join the U.S.-led coalition can be assessed from the alternatives open to him and the sombre ground reality after Black Tuesday. Musharraf was fully aware of Pakistan's deep involvement in the international Islamist terror enterprise and knew that the details thereof had been known to the U.S. Not long ago when the former U.S. President Bill Clinton, visited India in March, 2000, and during return journey stopped over for a day in Pakistan, the American intelligence officials were quite apprehensive about his security. As a measure of abundant security precaution they decided to stage a 'dummy run' before landing Airforce One, carrying Bill Clinton, at Islamabad. The Pentagon knew about the close liaison between Pakistani Army, Al Qaeda and the Taliban and the deep inroads which Islamic militancy had made into the state apparatus and the fundamentalist societal structure of that country. Anyway post 9/11 Musharraf knew too well that if he declined to help the U.S.A., all those cruise missiles and daisy-cutter bombs which devastated Afghanistan, would rain on Pakistan and reduce all military installations and all major cities to rubble ! He loved Taliban from the innermost depths of his heart and wanted to save them, but dare not help beyond a point. And then he had an urgent twofold agenda: first to protect Pakistan's nuclear assets; and second to stay on course to keep alive the insurgency in Jammu and Kashmir for ensuring that the army and the mullahs were happy. Indian political analysts seem to have forgotten that in his speech of September 19, 2001, Musharraf had recounted certain important concerns which made him join the world coalition against terror.[26]

The first concern listed by Musharraf in his speech was to ensure the security of Pakistan and avert any external threat. The second was to work towards the revival of economy. Third concern was to protect Pakistan's strategic nuclear and missile assets. And the fourth concern was to remain steadfastly committed to "the Kashmir cause". He specifically referred to the fact that "some scholars and religious leaders are inclined towards taking emotional decisions." While countering their viewpoint, he reminded them of "the events of the first six years of the history of Islam." Musharraf is no greenhorn; he is a shrewd strategist, as was demonstrated by him when he ousted Nawaz Sharif in a bloodless coup.

Musharraf also reminded the people of Pakistan that the Islamic calendar started with the Prophet's migration. The significance of migration was clear from the fact that the Prophet went from Meccah to Medina. He migrated to save Islam. Migration was not, God forbid, an act of cowardice. First, the Prophet had signed the Charter of Medinah (Meesaq-e-Medinah) to keep peace with the Jews at a time when he was facing the hostile non-believers of Mecca. It was an act of sagacity. This treaty remained effective for six years during which three battles were fought with non-believers of Mecca – the battles of Badr, Uhud and Khandaq. The Muslims emerged victorious in these battles with the Makkahns because the Prophet had signed a treaty with the Jews to ensure peace on that front.[27] By implication he reasoned that if Prophet Muhammad, when hard pressed, could sign an opportunistic treaty with the Jews (i.e. the Charter of Medinah), it was perfectly kosher for Pakistan at this juncture to join hands with America. Musharraf asserted that there was a lesson in this historic episode of Islamic history. "The lesson was that when there is a crisis situation, the path of wisdom is better than the path of emotions. Therefore we have to take a strategic decision". The question of weakness of faith or cowardice did not arise.[28] He further emphasized the need for pragmatism by referring to Islam's history for compromising with principles by alluding to the treaty of Hudabiyah, signed by the Prophet in 628 A.D. with his enemies, the Makkahns (rulers of Mecca) for keeping peace with them when he was engaged in a war with the Jews. Later on the treaty of Hudabiyah was aborgated before its expiry when the Muslims sensed that the right time to attack Mecca had come. In the subsequent battles the Jews were vanquished and finally banished from Medinah. In dwelling upon the example of the Prophet's treaty of Hudabiyah, Musharraf had taken cue from a speech made by Yasser Arafat in May 1995 before his Palestinian-Arab constituency to justify his negotiations with Israel by referring to the strategem used by the Prophet who later on repudiated the treaty of Hudabiyah, perhaps eighteen months before its expiry. By referring to the repudiation by the Prophet of that opportunistic treaty, Musharraf sent out a clear and loud signal to the people and the Pakistani army that he was joining the world coalition led by America solely because of the adverse circumstances in which Pakistan was placed. Implicit in his statement of September 19, 2001, was an assurance that he would try to repudiate the commitment to the world coalition as soon as the circumstances changed in favour of Pakistan. There is a significant commonality between the pronouncement made by Yasser Arafat in 1995 and that made by Musharraf in September 2001. Both proclaimed that they would honour their commitments but in practice neither did. Yasser Arafat continued to hobnob with the Palestinian terror groups like the Hamas and Islamic Jihad and gave them both shelter and support, mostly on the sly till he was exposed by the Israelis and then George Bush sidelined him. Musharraf has been using the same scheming technique of sheltering the Al Qaeda and Taliban leadership and allied terror outfits in Pakistan, right under the nose of the U.S.A. But George Bush is yet to catch him in the act of cheating and double dealing! The important aspect of Musharraf's speech in which he publicly said that he was making a compromise with his principles by joining the U.S.-led coalition, with an implicit rider that he could repudiate it when the circumstances turned favourable, did not receive much attention of the western political analysts and media or for that matter, even a critical scrutiny by the American think-tanks. Similarly neither the Indian political analysts nor our hyper-active media mandarins bothered to examine what Musharraf was saying and what could be his game plan. But one must be fair to Musharraf; he minced no words in spelling out his compulsions as well his ultimate intentions. It was time that the Pentagon realized that the wily fox that he is, Musharraf has every intention of reneging on the promise he made to Collin Powell. But he will do that only at an opportune time. The reference by him to the compromise made by the Prophet with his enemy when the former was in dire straits but subsequently reneging on the treaty as soon as he had an upper hand, is pregnant with several possibilities. Surely in his speech he gave a subtle public assurance to this effect to the people of Pakistan as well. It is learnt that his confidants in the Pakistani army feel fully reassured about Musharraf's ultimate intent to make an about-turn at the appropriate juncture. But for his public commitment and his tacit, but sure, assurance to the army, Musharraf's continuance in power would have been impossible. At heart, Musharraf remains a faithful jihadi soldier of Islam down to his toes. In his speech, he had also referred to his friends' worry about the fate of Afghanistan. His immense love for Taliban oozed overwhelmingly in his speech when he said that he and his government were much more worried about Afghanistan and Taliban. He went on record saying that he had done a lot for Afghanistan and Taliban when the entire world was against them. He met about twenty to twenty-five world leaders and spoke to each one of them in favour of Taliban and requested that sanctions should not be imposed on Afghanistan.[29] He went on to assure his Pakistani audience that "we are trying our best to come out of this critical situation without any damage to Afghanistan and the Taliban." "This is my earnest endeavour and with the blessings of Allah I will continue to seek a way out."[30] But Americans just won't spare Al Qaeda and the Taliban despite whatever Musharraf tried to do. They carpet-bombed Afghanistan and tried to destroy the Taliban lock, stock and barrel. It is a different matter that many leading lights of Al Qaeda and Taliban continue to be sheltered in Pakistan by the ISI - and perhaps with the knowledge of Musharraf himself. Now they are growing both in size and strength.

Many Pakistani political analysts and columnists have been lamenting that Musharraf did not try to secure a better economic and financial deal from America in lieu of the services most humbly rendered and the consequential enormous loss suffered by Pakistan's economy. It has been pointed out that between 1951 and 1981 the U.S.A. had provided $5 billion as direct economic aid to Pakistan, while General Zia had negotiated $3.2 billion as assistance for 1981-1985, and another $4 billion for subsequent six years, in return for Pakistan's help in the anti-Russian war in Afghanistan. Apart from the bilateral economic aid, at that time the U.S. had helped Pakistan get additional funds from the IMF and the World Bank. But critics forget that the two situations are not comparable. They forget that in the current global scenario the Pakistani establishment has been virtually in the dock because of their neck-deep complicity in promoting and exporting Islamist terror. On earlier occasions there was no such ignominous charge against Pakistan. After Black

Tuesday, Pakistan dare not refuse to meet the demands made by America nor was there any time for negotiations to seek a better financial deal. For Musharraf it was a question of saving his own skin and protecting Pakistan from being bombed out by the mighty U.S. war machine. All his options were closed. Beggars could not be choosers. Pakistani columnists ought to thank Musharraf for managing to divert the fury of U.S.A.'s aerial arsenal to Afghanistan, a country which was made the sacrificial lamb. But for Musharraf's abject surrender, the Washington would have come down on him as well as Pakistan with the proverbial ton of bricks, albeit in the shape of cruise missiles and daisy-cutters.

Perhaps it was a great civilizational tragedy or call it a quirk of destiny, that the innocent people of Afghanistan got bombed out and were ravaged for no fault of theirs by the relentless fury of America's B-52 bombers and cruise missiles. Every one knew that the vast majority of Afghans were no better than mere captives of the Pakistani army and the ISI and that the Afghan territory had been seized through the Taliban by Pakistan as an extension of their own country. Logically all those missiles and bombs which killed thousands of Afghans and destroyed their hearths and homes should have rained on Pakistan which was the birth place of both the Taliban and the Al Qaeda and where mujahideen were trained in hundreds of ISI-run terror-training camps for decades. After the exit of Russians from Afghan soil as soon as the Americans turned their back, the Pakistani establishment in pursuit of their goal of strategic depth managed to enslave the Afghan people through a cleverly manipulated regime-change in which the Taliban took charge of Afghanistan. That was how a fundamentalist Islamic dictatorship was foisted on the innocent and gullible populace of that country by Pakistan.

The Pakistan-sponsored Islamist terror is now like a genie out of the bottle; it cannot be pushed back. Before attempting a conflict resolution at national and international levels, the concerned nation-states forming part of the universal civilization have to fight the menace jointly on multiple fronts and destroy the roots of terrorism. Otherwise it will devour a number of nation-states, especially of the soft variety and also those which have become *effete* because of their ageing populations. Unless engaged frontally and combatted globally, the ongoing terrorism has the potential of causing immense damage to the civil society and universal civilizational values. It needs to be understood that the two nation theory is implicit in the orthopraxy of Islam when it makes the division of the world into two distinctly opposite and perpetually conflicting camps: the "us" and the "them", namely the 'faithful' and the "infidels". Islamic theology is divisive by virtue of being antithetical to the modern concept of 'nation-state'. It unequivocally proclaims that the world consists of two entities, namely the Nation of Islam and the Nation of 'Kufr'- the latter entity being inclusive of all non-Muslim religions and countries. In that sense, the concept of two-nation theory, about which there have been endless debates in Indian media, has been inbuilt into the rigid, but expansive, philosophy of Islam. That explains why Muslims everywhere start demanding the right to secede and form a separate country, long before their numbers approach the majority status. Alija Izetbegovich of Bosnia has been openly saying so, at least for the last three decades. Recent events have shown that not only the concept of jihad against 'kafirs' is an integral part of the theology of Islam, it is deeply ingrained in the psyche of a large majority of Muslims, including scholars and intellectuals of the community. The theocratic state of Pakistan, created in 1947 by the British by partitioning the Indian sub-continent on the ground that the Hindu and the Muslims were two separate nations and therefore Muslims could not live with the Hindu majority, stands out as the role model for radical Islamists to seek secession from the parent countries. For protagonists of radical Islam, decades ago Pakistan had emerged as the first major milestone on the jihadi highway. Since then many new encampments have been established in Palestine, Bosnia, Kosovo, Chechenya, Indonesia and the Philippines on the long route charted for attaining the goal envisaged by the Islamists. Currently numerous jihads are being waged in several countries across the globe and the faithful hope to establish more milestones of success on the pattern of Pakistan—with every successive victory which they secure. Pakistan has been the breeding ground of Islamist doctrine ever since 1947 when the British decided to divide and quit the sub-continent, leaving behind a bloody trail of murders, mayhem and plunder, the like of which were never witnessed in the human history. While India, despite its overwhelming population of Hindus and Sikhs (which stood at approximately 85% post partition, as against approximately 82% today) opted for a modern, secular and multi-cultural State guaranteeing equal rights to all citizens, Pakistan emerged as an Islamic theocracy—despite Jinnah's pretentious claim of believing in secularism. Every ruler of Pakistan, from Liaqat Ali Khan to General Yahya Khan, Zulfiqar Ali Bhutto, General Zia-ul-Haq, Benazir Bhutto and Nawaz Sharif to General Mushraff have unabashedly stoked the fires of Muslim fundamentalism and invoked the time-honoured Islamic doctrine of jihad against India for one reason or the other, mostly using Kashmir as an excuse.

In retrospect, one gets the impression that the creation of Pakistan and the latter's attack on Jammu & Kashmir in the year 1947, following the partition, signaled the revival of the radical Islamic philosophy of aggression and marked the beginnings of their long march to conquer the world. During the last five decades, Pakistan has been in the vanguard of every pan-Islamic movement to wage holy wars in support of all sorts of Muslim claims in different parts of the world. It is not for nothing that Musharraf calls Pakistan the *'Fortress of Islam'*. One must give the devil his due. It is entirely due to the tireless efforts of the Pakistani leadership and tremendous organizational inputs provided by its Army and the ISI, that the radical Islam has advanced so soon and thus far and continues to burst upon the world horizon in successive multiple waves of violence and terror. Courtesy Pakistan's strategic planning, now the jihadi movement has acquired hundreds of thousand armed foot soldiers worldwide and their long march has become a formidable force to reckon with.

The first wave of Islamist terror started around 1969-70 with the spectacular hijacking of three aeroplanes by the Palestinian terrorists, just a few years before the massacre of Israeli athletes at Munich Olympics in 1972. These terrorist strikes were occasioned by the expulsion of Palestine's radical Islamists by Jordan. The forced-out hordes of radical Palestinians, scattered across the West Asia, started a series of retaliatory terrorist campaigns, including frequent attacks on the Israelis. Abu Jihad, a trusted lieutenant of Yasser Araft, emerged as the kingpin of the first wave of Islamist terrorism spawned by the Palestinian conflict. On August 30, 1993, Israel agreed to give a limited autonomy to Palestinians following which on September 13, 1993, the historic accord between Israel and the P.L.O. was signed at Washington granting limited Palestinian self-rule in Gaza and West Bank, which had been occupied by Israel in the "Six Days War" in 1967. But while the Palestinian Liberation Organization which had masterminded this terrorist movement, announced their abandoning of terror in 1993, a more radical Islamist outfit 'the Hamas' emerged on the scene and took over as the principal opponent of Israel to continue open recourse to terror as a means. Till recent times Hamas has been opposing any proposal for peace with Israel, short of the creation of an independent Palestinian state, on the terms set by its leadership. For a while Hamas agreed to hold back their notorious suicide bomb attacks but soon restarted its 'mission mayhem'. The second wave of Islamist terror came in early 1980s in the shape of Afghan jihad to oust the Soviets from Kabul when more than two hundred thousand militant Muslims from several countries, an overwhelming majority of whom were from Pakistan, indoctrinated by Mullahs, trained and armed with the funds provided by the CIA and the strategic political support of U.S.A. and Saudi Arabia were let loose on the Russian troops. Osama bin Laden and his infamous Al Qaeda, in tandem with the ISI of Pakistan, played a pivotal role in the Afghan jihad. The success in Afghan jihad whetted the appetite of the leaders of radical Islam, especially Osama bin Laden and his associates and collaborators in the Pakistani establishment. We have seen that how, after overthrowing the pro-Russian Najibullah regime in Afghanistan the rabid jihadis, led by hordes of Arab Afghans swearing allegiance to bin Laden, fanned out worldwide to a number of countries to push forward their long march. The result is there in the open, for everyone to see.

The big picture of geo-political faultline conflicts shows that since 1990s there have seen outbreaks of parallel jihadi movements in more than twenty countries enumerated in Appendix-II[31], including Bosnia, Albania, Macedonia, Croatia, Turkey, Algeria, Tunisia,

Somalia, Sudan, Egypt, Yemen, Palestine, Chechenya (Russia), Dagestan, Uzbekistan, Kyrgystan, India (including Jammu & Kashmir), Bangladesh, Malaysia, Indonesia and Philippines. In these countries the rumblings caused by the footfalls of terrorists can be heard all over. The governments and the people of each one of these countries have been drawn into relentless bloody conflicts with radical Islam which has been trying to destablize these nations by bleeding them white through organised politico-religious upheavals and the resultant financial strain. By now all these countries, dotted with cells of Al Qaeda and allied terrorist organisations have become important camping sites on the route charted by Jihadis for their long march. The terror cells in these countries are also being used as operational "action stations" of mujahideen. This is done by promoting internal subversion by establishing one or more militant outfits for radicalizing the local Muslim populations and then motivitating the younger generation to get involved in terrorist activities and terror tactics. In India, the emergence of SIMI (Students Islamic Movement of India), the Muslim Defence Force, Deendar Anjuman and innumerable fundamentalist and terrorist outfits operating in Jammu & Kashmir, North East and southern India, are typical examples of the clandestine work being done by the suspected Al Qaeda affiliated terrorist cells and action stations. The strategy of engineering internal faultline conflicts by fomenting inter-communal and intra-cultural strifes has considerably helped the Islam in its long march. At micro level the well-planned establishment of terror cells by Al Qaeda or similar other militant outfits, mostly based in Pakistan, has been in progress at a fast pace for the last twenty years or more in several countries, including the U.S.A., the U.K., the Netherlands, Germany, India, Bangladesh, Malayasia and Indonesia. These Cells, mostly manned by four to five committed jihadis, have become pivots of organised militancy and are regularly used both for collection and dissemination of vital information and provide safe havens for sheltering the designated terrorists, before or after the launching of attacks. One of the duties enjoined on the Terror Cells is to remain on the look out for Islamic causes which are then used for spreading disaffection among Muslims and thereby build a provocative atmosphere of hate and rage. The Al Qaeda cells-cum-action stations are like important buckle-links on the zig-zag route charted by jihadis for their ongoing long march. Pakistan has been the storm-centre of this new radical phenomenon, albeit massively aided by the Saudi regime, and even by the fundamentalist Iranian regime. Buoyed by the heady appetiser of successful jihad in Afghanistan, the rulers of Pakistan have been cleverly using hundreds of thousands armed jihadis, drawn from more than two dozen countries, for fighting a series of renewed high profile war of terror in the above mentioned countries. The third wave of terror, revealing its global dimensions and the long reach, was launched by bin Laden on 9/11 with vicious attacks on the twin towers and the Pentagon. This was the first major attack by the Islamist terrorists on America, that is on American soil. Undoubtedly it took a very heavy toll of more than three thousand lives. It naturally angered the Pentagon and the American people no end. Yet America decided to sign up the Pakistani establishment, headed by Musharraf, as its key ally in the war against terrorism. And after the U.S. victory against radical Islamists in Afghanistan and Iraq, came the FBI disclosure that the source of money used in the 9/11 attack was funnelled from Pakistan asserting that it underscored the necessity to take conclusive steps at ensuring an end to terror links in the region.[32] The FBI investigators had traced the funding for the World Trade Centre twin tower attacks to Al Qaeda accounts in Pakistan.[33] According to an FBI report the investigators traced the origin of the funding of 9/11 back to financial accounts in Pakistan, where high ranking and well known Al Qaeda operatives played a major role in moving the money forward, eventually into the hands of the hijackers located in the U.S. According to FBI estimates the September 11, 2001 attacks cost between $175,000 and $250,000. That money which paid for flight training, travel and other expenses, flowed to the hijackers through associates in Germany and the United Arab Emirates. Those associates reported to Khalid Sheikh Mohammed who managed much of the planning for the attacks from Pakistan.[34]

But the Indian intelligence agencies had known all along that Pakistan was playing a pivotal role in planning, promoting and financing of all terrorist activities through the ISI (Inter Services

Intelligence) because India had been been subjected to innumerable such attacks during the last two decades. After two unsuccessful attempts to seize Kashmir by force, in the years 1947 and 1965, Pakistan has devised the strategy of waging a proxy war against India through cross-border terrorism and to bleed India by what is known as the war of 'a thousand cuts'. According to the *South Asian Intelligence Review*, a well known Delhi-based group of analysts, this proxy war claimed 26,226 lives between 1988 and 2000 in an estimated 43,956 incidents of violence. Of these casualties 10,310 (40 per cent) were civillians, 3,520 (13 per cent) security personnel, and 12,396 (47 per cent) terrorists.[35] And this campaign of Islamic jihad continues to take its heavy toll in India, notwithstanding the claims of grand success made by the U.S.A. in containing the terror across the globe. Just take a look at some of the examples of the so-called grand success of the world coalition. During the year 2002 there were 2 successive attacks, in a single year, on the historically famous Raghunath temple in Jammu on March 30, 2002, and November 24, 2002, a brutal attack on the families of Army personnel living in Kaluchak residential complex (Jammu) in May 2002, plus a bloody attack on the Akshardham temple in Gandhinagar, Gujarat, on September 24, 2002. There were a series of bomb blasts in Mumbai, the commercial capital of India, later on. And before that during 2002 itself quite a few daring attempts were made to stage similar terrorist strikes in New Delhi, the Indian capital. These were clear manifestations of the Pakistan sponsored jihadi's nefarious designs to destroy the Indian civilization (Hindu civilization) which has long been its target, almost for more than nine hundred years now. Earlier on August 6, 2002, Muslim terrorists had launched an unprovoked vicious attack on innocent and unarmed Hindu yatris going for pilgrimage to the Amarnath cave in which nearly a dozen Hindus were killed and over 37 injured. In fact, by now attacks on the Amarnath Yatris are almost a regular annual feature. The year 2003 saw even an attack on the Hindu pilgrims going to Vaishnodevi temple in Jammu. Hundreds of Hindu temples all over the country, starting with the Ram temple at Ayodhaya to Goddess Vaishnodevi in Jammu, Somnath and Ambaji temples in Gujarat, Tirupathi temple in Andhra, Jagannath temple at

Puri (Orissa) and the Lakshminarayan Mandir (Birla Mandir) and Hanuman Mandir in Delhi are under continuous threat of the radical Islamists who have murder in their minds. This creates confusion and anger in the minds of law abiding civil population and leads to a law and order problem in many cities.

According to the U.S. State Department's latest report, titled "Patterns of Global Terrorism", India has been the world's worst victim country in terms of terror. India was subjected to over 67 terrorists attacks in 2002, compared with nine in Israel and seven on the West Bank.[36] The report also notes that extremist violence in Kashmir fuelled by infiltration from Pakistan across the Line of Control threatened to become flashpoint for a wider India-Pakistan conflict during most of the year.[37] After recording these facts the report glosses over Pakistan's role by referring to it as a "key ally" in Washington' anti-terror campaign. It was also lauded for handing over 500 suspected Al Qaida and Taliban suspects. Perhaps in order to maintain its military and intelligence bases in Pakistan, America has adopted a softer approach on Pak leadership. It is a known fact that many radical outfits have continued to function in Pakistan and Pak-Occupied Kashmir, after changing their names. These facts are well known to Washington but the U.S. seems to be having its own compulsions for not going against Pakistan.

For decades the Pakistani rulers and their army, which always had the final say in the running of that country, kept on promoting fundamentalism and the militant Jihadi culture with the help of American funds and active connivance of the CIA. Finally in mid-1990s Pakistan was able to bring about a "*regime change*" in Afghanistan and set up a radical Islamic government headed by the Talibans, a protégé of Al Qaeda. That is how the tyrannical rule of militant Talibans was foisted on Afghan people. The Taliban government was all along nurtured and groomed by the ISI and Pakistani army with a view to holding Afghanistan as a hostage, for use as natural extension of Pakistan so as to provide it with "strategic depth" in the event of a war with India. Pakistani army has always believed in the inevitability of war with India for fulfilment of their wild dreams of ruling over Hindu India once again, as Muslims had done in the past—something about which successive Pakistan rulers have been gloating for decades. The establishment of a network of thousands of madarasas, the Islamic seminaries, initially designed to indoctrinate and motivate the students, i.e., the Taliban, in the fundamentalist ideology of Islam, for waging 'holy war' against heathen Russians, was an important step by Pakistan towards launching a mission jihad worldwide. Bin Laden soon laid the foundations of Al Qaeda with the full support of ISI and backing of the military establishment of Pakistan and managed to set up hundreds of 'Terror Cells' in more than 50 countries by funneling petro dollars received from Saudi Arabia and other Sheikhdoms through numerous Islamic charities. And the ISI worked overtime to set up scores of well-equipped training camps to arm and train militant Jihadi volunteers recruited from more than 20 countries, including Pakistan, Afghanistan, Saudi Arabia, Algeria, Bangladesh and a few even from the U.K. and the U.S.A. Most of these training camps were positioned in Afghanistan, the adjoining border areas of Pakistan and Pak-occupied Kashmir. For strategically advancing this long-cherished goal of Pakistan's founding fathers fulsome credit must be given to the genius of the leading lights of Pakistan's ISI and that country's Army leadership for training and galvanising hundreds of thousand Muslim volunteers, coming from diverse socio-political background, and recruited from far away countries, into a cohesive Islamic army of Jihadis. These warriors have already joined the long march on the Jihadi highway across Asia, Africa and Europe, as charted out by the ISI, with the blessings of Al Qaeda. Since 1998 jihad has been openly declared against the infidels, namely the Christian west, the Hindu India, the Jewish state of Israel, and heathen Russians in Chechenya. In other words, the die has been cast and it might turn out to be a no-holds-barred civilizational conflict, all over the world.

Surely bin Laden has played an important role by assuming leadership of this long march. But frankly, the entire spadework was done by the Pakistani leadership, their committed Islamist cadres of the ISI, who despite decades of trials and tribulations of adversity through which Pakistan had to plod along quite often, stayed tenaciously focussed on their goal of restoring the medieval glory of Islam. While plans of the proposed global 'long march' by the Islamists were being rehearsed and finalised by the Pakistani establishment and bin Laden in the rugged mountainous regions of Afghanistan and Pakistan, the American establishment slumbered and remained totally bereft of any futuristic vision of the likely events. Could they be so lackadaisical that they had no idea about what the ISI was planning on the ground? And all this time the Afghan jihad was gaining support in Washington and more money was being appropriated for covert and not-so-covert support for the Afghan mujahideen.[38] The United States was convinced that it was supporting a genuine national struggle albeit with a strong Islamic foundation and Islamabad went to great lengths to ensure that the United States did not discover first hand the kind of mujahideen the American tax payers were sponsoring. Toward this end the CIA was isolated by the ISI from the training infrastructure it financed.[39] Although Bodansky is quite convinced of this fact on the basis of the testimony of Brigadier Mohammad Yousaf, then head of the ISI's Afghan Bureau, it is very difficult to believe that the ISI, which ate out of the hands of CIA, could have bluffed the latter so easily and effectively. There is a widespread belief in Pakistan that everything in that country is managed by the grace of Allah, America and Army—in that order. It is therefore inconceivable, that the CIA could not know the ISI's game plan of training thousands of Muslim jihadis for launching a series of jihads all over the world in a number of countries. If that is true then at least in this clever cover up of their ultimate design, the ISI top brass proved to be superior to their American counterparts. Brigadier Yousaf emphasized that the ISI was the sole provider of training in Pakistan and Afghanistan and that no "American or Chinese instructor was ever involved in giving training of any kind of weapon or equipment to the mujahideen.[40] In any case, the CIA ought to have known better because they were funding the radical Islamist outfits and their operatives had actively helped the successive Pakistan governments in training and equipping young mujahideen for fighting the Russians and their communist stooges in Afghanistan, to throw them out. After accomplishing that task, the hordes of Jihadi outfits were let loose on hapless Kashmiris for carrying out ethnic cleansing. In due course of time Pakistan was transformed from being the epicentre to the status of the storm-centre of Islamist terrorism. The journey of Islamist terror from Pakistan to Afghanistan was quick, almost meteoric, and finally led to the ignominous exit of the Russians from Kabul in 1988-89. And finally Afghanistan, the chosen land of 'strategic depth' for Pakistani Army, started producing thousands of armed Jihadis in Islamic seminaries and training camps set up by the ISI and nurtured by Al Qaeda. Soon the growing numbers of trained Jihadis started clogging the assembly line and the output became far in excess of what could be gainfully employed in Kashmir Valley, or deployed for Jihad against the so-called Hindu India. Consequently the Islamist outfits, groomed by the ISI, accumulated a big exportable surplus of thousands of mujahideen, moulded and manufactured in hundreds of terror factories of Pakistan and Afghanistan. A sizeable spill over of these jihadi warriors was despatched to Chechenya, Bosnia, Kosovo, Indonesia, Malaysia and even to the far away Mindnao and Sulu Islands of Philippines. Let us not forget that the dreaded Abu Sayyaf band of Moro jihadis, giving sleepless nights to the Christian President of Phillipines, Gloria Macapagal Arroya, are a product of Pakistani training camps patronised by the ISI and financed by the CIA. The ruthless leader of this militant group, originally known as Professor Abdul Rasul Sayyaf, was an Afghan intellectual belonging to the Ittihad party who had established himself in Peshawar, Pakistan, which became his home. He was inspired almost entirely by the ultra conservative Wahabi ideology of Saudi Arabia. This was a core group of jihadi warriors comprising several hundred guerrillas who fought the Russians in Afghanistan. After the end of Afghan war, they moved from their Peshawar base to the southern Philippines where they operated under the name of Abu Sayyaf group to fuel the Moro Muslim terrorism in collaboration with moro Islamic Liberation Front. In the 1990s it was the most violent and radical Islamist group in the Far East, using its CIA and ISI training to harass, attack and murder Christian priests, wealthy non-Muslim plantation owners, merchants and local government officials in the southern Philippines island of Mindnao.[41] Meanwhile by early 1998, driven by their hatred of America and Israel, the P.L.O. (Palestine Liberation Organisation), the Iranian regime, and Iraq led by Saddam Hussein, had all cosied up to each other and joined hands for promoting Islamist terror worldwide, including India. Apparently the Indian government did not come to know of this fact, or perhaps they conveniently ignored it because of our tradition of having infinite faith in the friendship of the Islamic regimes of the Middle East. For instance, India had always lionised the PLO which organisation had acted as pioneers in promoting Islamist terror, especially against Israel. We even ignored that several PLO leaders had been associated with the radical Muslim Brotherhood in their younger years. They were most receptive to the call for international jihad and had started sending some of their most promising radical youth to the terrorist camps in Pakistan for special training. It may be recalled that Yasser Arafat had made a fiery speech on October 15, 1985, proclaiming commitment to jihad or holy war. His military chief, Khalil al-Wazir, popularly known as Abu Jihad, was the first one to claim that Islam's terrorism was the "wave of the future", and subsequent events proved that prophetic indeed were his words. Within 15 years Abu Jihad's wave of the future had metamorphosed into an *Intercontinental Islamist Terror Missile*, which crossed both the Mediterranean and the Atlantic and hit the U.S.A. In early 1995 a number of secret meetings were held in Khartoum, Sudan, and some other locations to coordinate terrorist activities between high ranking intelligence officers of the terror sponsoring Muslim nations and some of these were attended by bin Laden, Palestinian leaders of HAMAS, representatives of Egypt's Islamic Jihad, Algeria's AIS and GIA and Qazi Hussein Ahmad of Islamic Jihad in Pakistan, and certain plans were finalized. In one of these meetings it was decided to establish a number of new offices all over the world to aggressively promote international Islamic movement. The new offices were meant for carrying forward the Islamist agenda and among other things the operations in Kashmir and other parts of India, Afghanistan and Albania and Kosovo were entrusted to the headquarters at Karachi. Simultaneously the office at Teheran was also assigned the task of supporting the operations in Central Asia, India and Bosnia.[42] Apparently there was some sort of an overlap in the allocation of responsibilities. That could be due to the priority accorded to the task of advancing the goal of radical Islam both in Bosnia and

India—two Islamist missions in which Iran and Pakistan had come together because of Al Qaeda. In early 1998, hectic efforts were made in the Middle East to forge unity among all major Muslim countries to meet the growing challenge of the U.S.A. and Israel in the region The turning point occurred in Feb. 1998 with the formalization of the strategic cooperation between Iraq, Iran, Syria and Egypt.[43]

There is a widely held wrong belief in India that Iraq being a secular nation, never joined hands with Iran and other fundamentalist countries of Middle East to promote terror. Nothing could be farther from truth. Sensing imminent U.S. intervention in the region, in middle of January 1998 Iran had sent out clandestine messages to all its neighbours, including Iraq, urging closer cooperation and coordination. Baghdad reacted quickly, by suggesting the formation of a common front against the American build-up. Baghdad also offered various concessions to entice Tehran and promised to cut support for the Iraq-based Iranian opposition group, the Mujahideen-ul-Khalq, and showed willingness to re-examine Iran's demand for some $100 billion in compensation for the Iran-Iraq War.[44] As pointed out by Bodansky, in January 1998 Muhammad Said al-Sahaf, Iraq's Foreign Minister and Saddam's secret Emissary, who earned quite a bit of notoriety during the 'Operation Iraqi Freedom' by colourfully trying to out-lie Goebbles and became a source of merriment to television viewers, had visited Tehran and signed a memorandum of understanding with Kamal Kharrazi, his Iranian counterpart. Later on it was followed up by a visit by Saddam's son Qusey and Rafia Daham al-Takriti, chief of Iraqi general intelligence, to meet Iranian Intelligence Minister in the border town of al Shalamja and the two delegations reached agreement on certain key points, including sponsoring joint terrorist operations.[45] They even carried out some joint surveys. Among other things, in all probability they also agreed to escalate any American attack on Iraq into a regional war against Israel – that promise of reprisals against the Jews remained a total non-starter during the recent Iraq war.

Subsequently Azzam's famous 'Dua' to Allah and Laden's declaration of jihad in early 1998 were loud pronouncements of their intent to attack American people and their interests everywhere.

But even that did not bother the U.S. establishment which kept on slumbering till 1998 when Osama bin Laden issued an edict announcing the "classic" Islamic call for Jihad against the Americans and the Jews. For a while it did attract the attention of the U.S. President, Bill Clinton, in August 1998. But ultimately like all jolly good Yankees, after ordering the launching of a score plus cruise missiles which hit a few training camps of Al Qaeda in Afghanistan nearabout Khost on August 20, 1998, Clinton soon reverted to his favourite pastime!

Come September 2001, and lo and behold, much to the bewilderment of the CIA and America's large retinue of defence strategists and security analysts, the deadly reach of Pakistan's exportable surplus of jihadis hit the U.S.A. like a raging tornado. And finally on 9/11 the dastardly terrorist attacks woke up the Pentagon from its deep slumber, but only when it escaped being bombed out. Perhaps that was for good reasons too, because most terrorists always prefer to bite first the hand that feeds them. Surely, the CIA with its vast expertise in espionage and counter-espionage plus archives full of case studies should have known better when it chose to pump in billions of dollars for training hundreds of thousand holy warriors through the ISI and the Pakistani Army. The denouement was graphically described by the *Washington Post on* December 30, 2001, when it highlighted the end result of Pakistan's Zia ul Haq joining as America's foremost ally and the CIA openly recruiting Islamic warriors from Egypt, Saudi Arabia, Sudan and Algeria for holy war in Afghanistan to oust Russians. The result was that radical Islam went into overdrive because its superpower ally and mentor funnelled support to Mujahideen. Ronald Reagan feted them on the White House lawns and the Saudis and Pakistan's Inter Service Intelligence became partners in the project. The U.S. saw in this game a double advantage of thwarting the Russians in Afghanistan and diverting militant Islam away from the Middle East to fight in Afghanistan. Withdrawal of Russian troops from Afghanistan in February 1989 was a dramatic turning point and good news. Unfortunately what should have been an unalloyed victory for the U.S.-Saudi strategy of diverting and controlling the new energies of militant Islam, however, gave birth to a new "transnational terrorist force."

It was astounding that the Americans did not know that only a fundamentalist state like Pakistan, born out of the unremitting hatred of the infidels, alone could act as a legitimate midwife to the birth of Islamist terror. For sure, the Americans had missed out on their radar screen the blips showing the zeal with which the founding fathers of Pakistan had mounted a violent campaign for ethnic cleansing of the Hindus and the Sikhs first from that country in 1947 and later on from Jammu & Kashmir - two important events that set the tone for the growth of radical Islam across the globe. Historically the process of ethnic cleansing by driving out, converting and killing the Hindus has been going on in northern parts of the Indian sub-continent, now for centuries, ever since Muhammad bin Qasim and Mahmud of Ghazni invaded the Indian sub-continent. At the time of creation of Pakistan there was a sizeable population of Hindus and Sikhs in that country. But just within 2 years, most of them were either driven out to India or killed or converted to Islam. Just 150 years back, there was a considerable Hindu and Sikh population in Afghanistan but no more today.[46] The last chapter of the systematic ethnic cleansing was concluded when Pakistan came into being and subsequently in recent years the ethnic cleansing programme was conducted in the valley and areas of J&K Doda, Rajouri and a few other districts of Jammu region.[47] This sustained campaign of ethnic cleansing in Jammu & Kashmir, fully supported by the Pakistani establishment, continues till date. The real challenge to the Indian state has come from the failure of successive governments to analyse and assess the menace of radical Islam which has already made massive inroads into various parts of the country. The overarching display of sympathy by almost every party across the political spectrum, often in defence of the known subversive outfits like the SIMI and Deendar Anjuman has made it even more difficult to identify and uproot the deeply planted cells of terrorists because even a long overdue and legitimate action against them is often protested and played up by some leftist groups as discriminatory and vindictive. The failure of the country's political leadership to squarely confront and destroy the terrorists operating both within India and in the neighbouring Pakistan bodes ill for the future of the country. The ouster of Saddam Hussein and the U.S.

occupation of Iraq have further fuelled the anger of Islamists of the sub-continent, thus making the task more difficult.

Post 9/11 there has been no perceptible change in the ground situation in Pakistan, even after General Musharraf pledged his total support to the U.S. in war against terrorism on September 19, 2001 and became a frontline ally of America. In March 2003, while speaking in New Delhi on "Reassessing Pakistan as a long term strategic threat", Prof. Satish Kumar, a well known expert on international relations presented a research document containing a candid appraisal of the situation. Prof. Kumar's conclusion, empirically supported by facts and figures, was that the long term challenge which our hostile neighbour, dominated and ruled by a rogue military establishment, poses not only to us but to the entire neighbourhood was enormous. Prof. Kumar drew attention to the fact that the armed forces dominate every sector of national life in Pakistan ranging from toppling the elected governments to controlling the real estate, investments in stock market, producing electricity and taking over the jobs normally meant for civil services. His analysis of the malaise of Islamic extremism emanating from Pakistan is very illuminating. He draws "a parallel between the ideologies of the Al Qaeda and Osama bin Laden on the one hand and the ISI-supported Maulana Masood Azhar on the other".[48] According to Prof. Kumar the 'jihadi infrastructure' in Pakistan is largely intact and now includes 40,000 to 50,000 madarasas, with an estimated two million students. There are today 200,000 armed jihadis in Pakistan, backed by over one million young people, jihad- oriented but not yet armed.[49] Astonishingly these estimates of the presence of Jihadi warriors within Pakistan are fairly close to the figures given by Mohammed Amir Rana in his book, *Jihad-e-Kashmir and Afghanistan*. Prof. Kumar draws attention to a poll in Pakistan some time ago which showed 88 percent of the people believe that the Quran and the Sunnah should be the source of all laws in Pakistan; 84 per cent of those polled agree that Pakistan's security interests were served by supporting jihadi outfits in "Occupied Jammu & Kashmir" (i.e. Indian Kashmir). In such a socio-political scenario how can democracy strike roots? According to Prof. Kumar, there are two reasons which make Pakistani military believe that despite India's vastly superior conventional military and economic strength, they can continue to bleed India in Kashmir and elsewhere.

First, from 1987 onwards India has been deterred from responding militarily to its provocations because of the fear of nuclear escalation. Second, the Pakistani army is somehow convinced that it has the support of the United States not only in ruling the country but also in receiving American economic and military assistance, despite their provocations to India. Unfortunately this old belief may no longer be valid looking to the fact that lately the U.S.A. has not only allowed Israel to sell Phalcon early warning system along with several other tech-savvy weapons systems to India but also blessed the growing defence and political ties between the two democratic countries. Prof. Kumar also referred to the growing trend of Islamisation within the army and quoted in support of his thesis the assessment of the well known American scholar Stephen Cohen according to whom the present arrangement of a military led or influenced government will prevail indefinitely but not transform Pakistan. Rebuilding weakened institutions is pointless if the central operating principles of the Pakistani establishment remain hatred and distrust of India and intolerance of diversity at home.[50]

Now at long last there are some positive signs that lately America's neo-conservatives are becoming wary of Pakistan's attempts to hoodwink the West and carry on with its old agenda of promoting terror. They are worried about the resurgence of the Taliban ideology in Afghanistan because of Pakistan's support.

6

Global Demographic Portents

> Well, you'd better start swimming or you will
> sink like a stone oh the times, they are changing ....
>
> – Bob Dylan

The unprecedented resurgence of radical Islam during the last five decades has been facilitated by certain major geo-political developments, of which demography is the foremost. Changes in the population profiles of a number of countries, reflecting a sharp growth in the population of Muslims across the globe during the twentieth century, has given a big boost to the ideology of radical Islam. Three important factors have contributed to the increase in Muslim population. First, the Muslim societies have higher fertility rates due to non-acceptance of contraceptives because of the religious diktats of clerics who often use the scriptures to thwart the propagation of the small family norm. As a rule, most Islamic societies have remained steeped in orthodoxy. Therefore traditionally the Mullahs and Maulvis have always exercised strong influence on the Muslim masses. Their 'fatwas' against the small family norm and endorsements thereof by the community leaders have always carried considerable weight with the faithful. Secondly, the absence of female emancipation in Muslim societies and their non-empowerment leads to a higher fertility rate resulting in rapid growth in numbers. Lastly, extensive proselytizing activities of a number of Islamic missionary groups, especially the Tablighi Jamaat, a well-known rabid radical outfit, which has its main focus on the Indian sub-continent, south-east Asia and North Africa, brings substantial accretions to the numbers of Muslims by conversions every year, particularly in Africa and south Asia. Tablighi Jamaat has been winning new converts even in many countries of Europe, e.g., France, Germany and Spain. The sharp increase in Muslim population has led to a sharp growth in the number of mosques and religious seminaries not only in Asia and Africa but even in the Europe which was till recently the heartland of secular Christian ethos. For instance, in Spain more than 100 new mosques have come up within the last few years, while there are 2000 mosques and prayer centres in Germany and a new one opening almost every day.[1]

The galloping growth of radical Islam owes a great deal to the extensive propagation of pan-Islamic movement for restoring the long lost glory of Islam, undertaken by the theocratic state of Pakistan during the last fifty years. As highlighted by Sir Pendrel Moon in his narrative, *Divide and Quit*, the two-nation theory was first put forth by Syed Ahmed Khan in 1888 when he visualised a situation in which two separate countries for the Hindus and the Muslims will have to be formed after the departure of the British from the sub-continent.[2] But nothing much happened on the Indian sub continent during the next thirty years. After World War I, the freedom movement launched by the Indian National Congress gathered momentum in the 1920s and early 1930s and the possibility of independence from the British rule or getting dominion status under the British suzerainty rose somewhat sharply. At that stage Allama Iqbal envisioned the creation of an Islamic state for Indian Muslims by partitioning India. Like Syed Ahmed he, too, argued that Islam was a separate nation, different from all other faiths, due to which reason Muslims could not live in peace and amity with the Hindus in India. He reasoned that it was time for the Muslims to demand a separate homeland. Basically the views expressed by Sir Syed Ahmed in 1888, by Iqbal in 1930, by Chaudhary Rehmat Ali in 1940 and Alija Izetbegovich of Bosnia in 1970 have the same refrain—that the Muslims are a separate nation and due to cultural differences they cannot live with other religious groups in the same country. So they must secede and carve out their own homeland by forcing partition of the parent country. It is remarkable that for almost eight decades, from 1888 to 1970, from Syed Ahmed to

Iqbal to Alija Izetbegovich, there has been no change in the thinking of Islamic leadership. If anything, during the last eighty years their attitude has hardened across the globe leading to major socio-religious upheavals.

In the course of the twentieth century, Christianity swept through the continent of Africa where the proportion of Christians in the population rose to nearly 45 per cent from less than 10 per cent in 1900. Christians have also made significant gains in several countries of Asia, especially South Korea and Indonesia.[3] During the same period, Muslims have considerably increased their share in the world, going up from 12 per cent in 1900 to about 19 per cent in 1990. Their proportion in the population has improved in almost every part of the world; the gains have been especially significant in parts of Africa and in Indonesia in Asia.[4] Both in terms of absolute numbers and percentage increase the gains of Muslim community have been much more sizeable. No other religious group has registered such rapid growth in numbers. The phenomenal rise in the population of Muslims took place both in the Muslim majority countries as well as in other nation states where Muslims happened to be in minority. Today Islam is the fastest growing religion in the world—even way ahead of Christianity. This major demographic change is likely to have far-reaching consequences on the future of mankind, especially for those nations which are part of the universal civilization. An important aspect of this explosive growth of Muslim population is that radical Islamic groups are now fully alive to the fact that their numbers are growing very fast and that Muslims will soon constitute almost one-third of the world population by the year 2025 A.D., or even earlier. This has given a big boost to the morale and ego of Islamists whose leadership and ranks now hope to rule over the entire world, say after a few decades. We are aware how inter-civilizational conflicts in the former Yugoslav republics have played havoc with the political stability of Serbia, Croatia, Kosovo and Bosnia Herzegovina. The single most important factor leading to these conflicts, however, was the demographic change that took place in Kosovo and Bosnia.[5] Kosovo was an autonomous province within the Serbian republic having the de facto powers of six Yugoslav republics excepting the right to secede. In 1961 its population was 67 per cent Albanian Muslims and 24 per cent Orthodox Serbs. As the Albanian birth rate was the highest in Europe, Kosovo became easily the most densely populated area of Yugoslavia. By 1980s almost 50 per cent of the Albanians were less than 20 years old. In view of the growing Muslim numbers Serbs emigrated from Kosovo in search of better economic opportunities to Belgrade and elsewhere. As a result, in 1991 Kosovo was 90 per cent Muslim and 10 per cent Serb.[6] Serbs tend to view Kosovo sort of their holy land, it being the site among other things, of the great historic battle on June 28, 1389, when they went down bravely fighting the Turks and as a result, suffered Ottoman rule for almost five centuries.[7] Ultimately due to sheer decline in numbers Kosovo was lost to the Serbs. Something similar happened in Bosnia. In 1961 the Serbs constituted 43 per cent and the Muslims 26 per cent of the population of Bosnia-Herzegovina. By 1991 the population ratios were exactly reversed. Serbs had dropped to 31 per cent and the Muslims had risen to 44 per cent. During those thirty years the numbers of Croats went down from 22 per cent to 17 per cent. Unfortunately, ethnic growth of one group resulted in ethnic cleansing by the other.[8] The population changes in the Balkans have destabilized the geo-political equation between various countries of the region. Actually few other regions in the world, over the centuries, have been equally affected by population displacements. In modern times very few other regions bled out such a large proportion of its inhabitants. Jonas Widgren, a population migration expert, stated at the Europe's Council of Parliamentary Assembly Conference in September 2000, that the issue of population displacements and migration flows in the Balkans has to be considered in a wider European security perspective. Movements from the states in the region affect the security situation in the Balkans as well as in the entire Western Europe. Its security paradigm needs immediate attention of both the European Union and the NATO.[9] According to the estimates of the International Centre for Migration Policy Development, near about 15 per cent of the population of the Balkan peninsula with its 75 million inhabitants have involuntarily been on the move since the political changes by the end of the 1980's, a very high percentage by international standards. Population displacements are an effect of political instability and they create in themselves further instability."[10] It is believed that bin Laden and his top deputy, Ayman al-Zawahiri, with help from Iran, had recruited and trained quite a few brigades of blond, blue-eyed Bosnians and indoctrinated them for martyrdom in Islamist cause. Iran and Al Qaida terrorist network began recruiting and training Bosnian Muslims more than 10 years ago for war against Orthodox Christian Serbs and Catholic Croats in an effort to expand the Muslim base in Eastern Europe.[11] According to the former Congressional terrorism expert, Yossef Bodansky, there are many blond, blue-eyed Slavs among these Bosnian Islamists. Thousands of them were trained by the mujahideen and ultimately a number of them joined the international brigades.[12] Apparently dismantling the jihadists' training camps in the Balkans, after imposing peace plans that included power-sharing by the Muslims, was not considered a priority by the U.S. government. Therefore the sponsors of Islamic campaigns there have not decommissioned the jihadist forces in Bosnia, Albania and elsewhere in the region. According to a 1992 report, Islam experienced an exceptional renaissance in Communist Yugoslavia in the mid-1970s. The revival increased the number of mosques throughout Bosnia-Herzegovina and led to a growing number of local youths being sent for higher Islamic studies in the Middle East, especially Iran, where in the Islamist classes of seminaries radical mullahs used to include some 250 Bosnians every year. A former government terrorism expert, who spoke on the condition of anonymity, said Iran was at the core of recruiting and mobilizing training of terrorists with Iraq, Pakistan and Syria playing key support roles. A report drawn up by the Task Force on Terrorism and Unconventional Warfare of the U.S. House of Representatives (TFTUW), found that the then Yugoslav government in Belgrade was quite concerned when it saw that within its 40 percent Muslim population there were groups of Islamic terrorists operating against the West and that Yugoslav Muslim youths were being drawn to emulating and cooperating with Arab terrorists.[13] The Ayatollahs and Mullahs of Iran always looked at the Balkans as a prize to be won for the glory of Allah. The report revealed that Iran had declared the battleground of Bosnia-Herzegovina as a "microcosm" for resisting the West's war on Islam and had called for reinforcements from Islamic nations which included highly trained and combat-proven volunteers from Iran, Afghanistan, Lebanon and other countries. Bodansky, who was the director of the TFTUW, disclosed that bin Laden and al-Zawahiri also played a pivotal role in deploying and concealing the elite Islamist terror groups brought from around the Middle East and inducting them into the Bosnian army by setting up humanitarian front organizations to explain their presence.[14] Although the U.S.-led Dayton Accords of 1995 called for foreign Muslim fighters to leave Bosnia, the majority of mujahideen scheduled to have left Bosnia still continue to serve in the army ranks of the Bosnia-Herzegovina. The mujahideen are divided into three clusters of operational units, while a fourth cluster is directly engaged in terror acts and other covert special operations. The TFTUW report revealed that special military units were built around a hard core of foreign mujahideen, while the rest of the troops were Bosnian Islamists. Presently training is being provided by the mujahideen who should have left Bosnia under the Dayton Accords and who, according to Bodansky, were activating Bosnian Islamists by reminding them that without jihadist support, "there would not have been a Muslim Bosnia ……. We helped you, you come and fight for us."[15] A *Washington Post* report said that the Bosnian village of Bocinja Donja, which has 60 to 100 former mujahideen Islamic guerrilas from the Middle East, came under scrutiny when U.S. law-enforcement authorities discovered that a handful of these men who have visited or lived in the area were associated with a suspected terrorist plot to bomb targets in the United States on New Year's Day of 2000. Bodansky, whose topical book, *The High Cost of Peace*, is a strong criticism of what he describes as the failed U.S. policy in the Middle East, feels that the U.S. policy lacks the forcefulness in dealing with the mujahideen problem in Bosnia by not forcing them out of that country, as envisaged by Dayton Accords. The failure to act allowed the Islamist military brigades to maintain bases in Bosnia and they continue to recruit and train Muslim forces for terrorist acts.[16] The continued presence of a large number of hard core foreign holy warriors adds a new dimension to the demographic turmoil spread all over the

Balkans which can explode again. The countries located in the region have lived through a series of faultline conflicts caused by civilizational frictions between Muslims and Orthodox Christians. There is hardly any possibility of the religious conflicts in this region dying down in the near future. Another notable example of the far-reaching consequences of the religion-based civilizational faultline conflicts, caused by demographic shifts, is that of Lebanon, where the Maronite Christians have become a helpless minority in their own homeland, the land of their ancestors, within a short spell of sixty years - something similar to what has been progressively taking place in India's north-eastern state of Assam. The collapse in the early 1970s of the thirty year old constitutional order in Lebanon, under the National Pact of 1943, was in large part a result of the dramatic increase in the Muslim population compared to that of Maronite Christians. In the not-too-distant past Lebanon was a Christian majority nation. But within seven decades the Muslim numbers rapidly outgrew the Christian population thereby converting it into a Muslim majority state. In the year 1900 Christians constituted approximately 77 per cent of Lebanon's population while Muslims were barely 21 per cent.[17] By the year 1932 the Christians were reduced to near about 55 per cent. According to a 1943 agreement between Maronite Christians and the Muslims it was decided that the political authority will be shared by the two religious groups in proportion to their respective national populations. Posts of top ministers were to be shared in the ratio of six to five between Christians and Muslims corresponding to their population recorded in Lebanon's 1932 census. During the next twenty-five years Lebanon's demographic profile underwent a sea change in favour of Muslims. The result was that by 1975 Lebanon became a Muslim majority country. At present, the Christian population is approximately 30-35 per cent - their percentage could be even less. That is how an erstwhile Christian majority country, surrounded on all sides by Islamic nations, was completely swamped by the fast growing numbers of Muslims. Buoyed by the growth in their numbers, the Lebanese Muslims managed to successfully curb the political rights and ambitions of the Maronite Christians for a share in power by waging a devastating civil war from 1975 to 1990 in which the

Muslims emerged victorious. Due to the huge squeeze caused by the growing numbers of Muslims and their increased aggression, since 1975 thousands of Lebanese Christians have been moving out every year to the U.S.A. and other countries, mostly in Europe. The squeeze on the Christian community in the Middle East is for real. Even in the Christ-nativity town of Bethlehem, the Islamization of which is actively backed by Yasser Arafat, Christians have lost their majority as never before in the history. In Jerusalem, now Christians constitute barely two per cent and face near extinction.[18]

As a rule, all demographic changes resulting in major alterations in the percentage of populations of different religious or cultural groups have the potential to increase social tensions and consequential friction between the interacting religious communities within that country or region and sometime even far beyond the region. Historically this broad principle tends to apply with greater validity where the demographically gaining community happens to be the Muslims. Whenever there was a noticeable increase in the percentage of Muslims in a region or state, socio-religious conflicts have invariably led to bloody confrontations, as is evident from the events which took place in Kosovo, Bosnia, Serbia, Chechenya, Cyprus and Indonesia, etc. It has been experienced that even a sizeable increase in the proportion of Muslims in any country or region, leads to a loud clamour, often culminating in a violent struggle,for a separate homeland by dividing that nation, even before Muslims attain the near majority status. Examples of Pakistan and similar secessionist movements launched in Cyprus, Bosnia, Kosovo, Chechenya, Jammu & Kashmir and the Philippines support the above conclusion. As stated by Huntington, Islam is a more absolutist faith—even more than the Christianity.[19] It combines religion with politics and draws a sharp line between those living in the Dar-ul-Islam and those in the Dar-ul-Harb. The result is that Confucians, Buddhists, Hindus and Christians have less difficulty in adapting to and living with each other than any one of these has in adapting to and living with Muslims. For instance, ethnic Chinese have been an economically dominant minority in most Southeast Asian countries. Yet they have been successfully assimilated into the societies of Buddhist Thailand and the Catholic Philippines. There are practically no instances of anti-Chinese violence by the majority groups in those countries. In sharp contrast, anti-Chinese riots and violence have been frequently occurring in Muslim Indonesia and Muslim Malaysia, and the role of Chinese in those societies remains a potentially explosive issue in the manner in which it is not in Thailand and the Philippines.[20]

The global advance of radical Islam backed by international Islamist terror groups and the rapid growth of Muslim population during the last century are likely to hasten the pace of faultline conflicts in certain regions of the world which have been plagued by religious strifes for centuries. One such important region is the Middle East, or the West Asia, which has witnessed a series of multiple wars during the latter half of twentieth century. The tiny Jewish nation of Israel, occupying a 470 kms long and 135 kms wide stretch, which constitutes a meagre 0.20 per cent of the total area of Arab lands, is surrounded on three sides by hostile Muslim countries which have been trying to destroy it. According to Israel's Central Bureau of Statistics, at the end of the year 1996 the country's population was 5,764,000 showing an increase of 2.6 per cent over the end of the year 1995. Israel's demographic profile in 1995 was 80.8 per cent Jews, 14.6 percent Muslims, 2.9 per cent Christians and 1.7 per cent Druze. The growth rate had dropped to.01 percent, i.e., 1/10th of 1 per cent in 1996 due to reduced immigration, with only 69,000 new residents coming during the year.[21] During the last eight years there has been a nominal change in the demographic profile. The present population of Israel is estimated at 6.4 millions of which 79.2 per cent are Jews and 20.08 per cent being Muslims, Christians and Druze. For decades the state of Israel has been facing gross acts of terrorism unleashed by the Palestinian groups like Hamas, Islamic Jihad and Martyrs of Al Aqsa.

The conflict between the Jews and the Palestinian Muslims is a modern phenomenon but it has a hoary historical past stretching right up to the times of Prophet Muhammad who had thrown out a number of Jewish tribes, including Banu Nazir, Banu Kunaika, Banu Khaibar and some others from Medina and the adjoining Arab lands. The Jewish claim to this land is based on the Biblical promise to Abraham and his descendants on the ground that it was the historical site of the Jewish kingdom of Israel to which they will ultimately return. The ancient kingdom of Israel was destroyed by the Romans. They received another blow subsequently in the seventh century when most Jewish tribes were pushed out from their ancestral lands by the warriors of Islam. With the growth of national consciousness in the nineteenth century the Jews started coming together in search of a nation state of their own. The area comprising the cities of Jerusalem, Hebron, Safad and Tiberias and nearabout where most Jews were concentrated was the most logical and optimal choice. At that time it was part of Palestine, which was ruled by the Ottomans. The Zionist movement began in 1882 with the first wave of European Jews migrating to Palestine. Before their arrival, most Jews living in Jerusalem and the cities around it observed traditional, orthodox religious practices and spent their time studying religious texts and depended on the charity of the prosperous world Jewry for their survival. Their attachment to the holy land and to the seat of their faith, Jerusalem, was very deep and religious. But they were not involved in the Zionist movement which began in Europe and soon gathered momentum, after Theodor Herzl brought up the idea in his seminal pamphlet of 1896 title *'Der Judenstaat'*. During his stay in Paris as a correspondent of Vienna's *Neue Freie Prese,* Herzl had heard a French Crowd shout "Death to Jews" at the trial of a Jewish army officer on trumped up charges of selling some military secrets to an enemy agent. Herzl thought over the reasons for such intense hostility against Jews in Europe, and came to the conclusion that the establishment of a sovereign Jewish state was the only solution to the problem of wide spread anti-Semitism in Europe. His writings on the need for a Jewish homeland led to the organization of the first Zionist Congress in Basle in 1897 where it was resolved to seek the creation of a homestead for the Jews "in Palestine secured by public law." Herzl could visit Palestine only once, just one year after the Basle Declaration, when after a private audience at Constantinople with German king, Kaiser Wilhelm II, he proceeded to Jaffa (a city of Israel, located close to Jerusalem) and led an official Zionist delegation to king Kaiser Wilhelm II in Jerusalem.

By the time World War I broke out in 1914, the population of Jews in Palestine, mostly around Jerusalem, had risen to sixty thousand. Although in terms of the Balfour Declaration of 1919, the British agreed to the creation of the Jewish state of Israel, the promise materialized only in 1948 and that too when the Zionists took up arms to carve out their homeland. The modern state of Israel was born on May 14, 1948, with war raging all round, almost fifty-one years after the first Zionist Congress. The declaration of the creation of the Jewish homeland was read out by David ben Gurion, while standing beneath an impressive portrait of Theodor Herzl.

Since its birth in 1948, Israel has been caught in the throes of violent clashes and there is hardly any sign of resolution or abatement of the Israel-Arab faultline conflict. In addition, this region with practically little tradition of democracy, except Israel, has been the breeding ground of Islamist terrorism. It continues to play home to a number of notorious terror groups like Al-Gama'a Islamiyya, Jihad Group, Muslim Brotherhood, Hamas, Palestinian Islamic Jihad, Martyrs of Al Aqsa, PLO, Islamic Change Movement (Jihadi wing of Arabian Peninsula), International Muslim Brotherhood and many more similar outfits hostile to Israel. Many of these terrorist organizations have openly vowed to destroy Israel and stamp out Jewry from the land of its birth. Surrounded as the state of Israel is on all side by hostile Muslim neighbours, it is set to face a major demographic problem in the decades ahead. Since 1990 more than 600,000 immigrants have arrived in Israel, the majority from the former Soviet Union.[22] Since the Palestinian population in the former occupied territories in 1996 was estimated at between 2.2 million and 2.4 million, it meant that in the former mandate of Palestine (both Israel and the future Palestine state) there were close to 3.5 million Muslims and Christians. Since the Palestinians in the occupied territories have one of the highest birth rates in the world, while the Israelis have one of the lowest, it is only a matter of time before the Palestinians inside Israel's borders and in territories under its control outnumber the Jews. Once the state of Palestine is born, tens of thousands Palestinians living in Syria, Lebanon and Jordan as refugees will return. Whenever a final settlement takes place between Israel and Palestinians at least half of the Palestinian diaspora will seek to return, making Jews an instant minority within the borders of the former mandate of Palestine. It could even happen earlier because of the nearly invisible Jewish emigration to the U.S.A. and other countries. The extent of Jewish emigration could only be estimated by comparing the difference between those who arrived and those who departed from Israel's Ben Gurion airport, because the government does not disclose the emigration rate of Jews. That showed that the departures over the years were 600,000 higher than the arrivals. The Israeli government's practice is to continue to count Jewish emigrants as residents of Israel so long as they visit Israel at least once every four years which strategy keeps the figure of Jewish population at a higher level.[23] At the same time the steady trickle of native-born Israelis leaving for the U.S., Canada and Australia for years now is being replaced by a stream of immigrants to Israel from the former Soviet Union who are moving in because they could not get decent jobs there. There could be 700,000 Israelis living in the United States alone in 1996. If most of them are counted as residents of Israel by the Bureau of Statistics, it would mean approximately 4 million Jews permanently living in Israel in 1996. It is, however, a sensitive subject and the Israeli government is simply wishing it away. Yet all admit that there will be more Muslims and Christians than Jews within the former mandate of Palestine by the year 2010. That is a reality which cannot be ignored. The Labor Party believes in living with the growing Muslim population within Israel's borders, but fencing off the much larger Muslim and Christian communities in the West Bank and Gaza into a Palestinian state. But the ruling right wing party headed by Ariel Sharon, has set its heart on building a massive 350 km long fence barrier despite a U.S. threat to reduce $9 billion in loan guarantees. Washington feels that the project prejudges the likely borders that should be decided in negotiations. Yet the construction work to complete the fence, something like an impregnable barrier cutting into Palestinian territory, is progressing at a fast pace to separate the West Bank from the main state of Israel. Despite the United States misgivings about the proposed barrier, Israeli government claims that the fence is absolutely essential to keep out the suicide bombers and terrorists. Palestinians call it a new "Berlin Wall" that cuts deep into the territory they want for their state. In the third week of October 2003, the United Nations General Assembly passed a resolution with an overwhelming majority, calling the sprawling network of fences and walls a contradiction to international law and directing Israel to stop and reverse its construction on Palestinian lands. But Israel vowed its resolve to continue the project saying that "the fence will continue being built and we will go on taking care of the security of Israel's citizens".[24] Obviously the less realistic Likud Party wants to keep all of the mandate, from the Mediterranean to the Dead Sea, which would give the Jewish population full national rights as an occupation authority over an even larger Muslim and Christian population with no rights at all.[25] Wiser after the experience of stepped up terror attacks by Hamas, the Martyrs of Al Aqsa and other militant groups, the Israelis appear to be preparing for a long drawn out confrontation in the coming years. It is difficult to find fault with Israel for constructing the security fence because of the growing cult of suicide bombers and galloping Palestinian population. The threat of Palestinian numbers outpacing the Jews is a real one. In the circumstances, it looks almost certain that for decades to come West Asia will continue to be a prime faultline conflict and war-prone region. The latest demographic changes in and around Israel will keep the Middle East on boil, and the region might continue to be a hotspot of perennial faultline conflicts for many more decades to come.

Surprisingly except Muslims, no other religious civilizational or political group has shown awareness of the significance of the latest demographic changes and their likely impact on the future of the democratic world. It is only now, post 9/11, that Pentagon has woken up to the threat which looms large on the world horizon. The manner in which Pakistan sponsored extremist groups have pushed forward their global agenda of jihad against the West and other democratic regimes like Israel and India, has raised serious apprehensions about the compatibility of certain aspects of the Islamic civilization with the democratic world which values freedom of religion, pluralism and tolerance, above everything else. Although the world has moved ahead at a galloping pace since the times of

Prophet Muhammad, somehow the Islamic societies continue to live in their fourteen hundred years old time-warp. The political ideals of Muslims across the globe remain inexorably focussed on their scriptures and look to the Quran and the Sharia for guidance even in matters concerning the day-to-day political governance and the rights and duties of the common people, both Muslims and non-Muslims, living and working in Muslim majority regimes. This often leads to friction between those believing in freedom and democratic values and views of the clergy.

As a latest example, one has just to look at what is happening in Iraq, after Saddam Hussein's defeat. There have been demonstrations in many towns, including Najaf and Baghdad, demanding that the new constitution of Iraq should be written in accordance with the wishes of the Shia clerics and cast in the mould of Islamic scriptures – on the pattern of Iran. This attitude, totally negating the choice of democracy and modernity in the scheme of governance, sums up the present day crisis of Muslim societies in many parts of the world. Most Muslim countries are ruled by despotic kings or military dictators. Experience shows that even if there are free and fair elections in Islamic countries, the torch-bearers of radical Islam are sure to emerge as winners. It happened recently in Pakistan where in the provincial elections of North Western Frontier Province and Baluchistan, suspected to be rigged in favour of a pro-Musharraf faction, the pro-Taliban fundamentalist party, opposed to Musharraf, known as the Muttahida Majlis-e Amal, won hands down. It also happened in the Muslim majority states of Northern Nigeria. In the hitherto moderate Malaysia, the PAS (Malaysia's Islamic Party) headed by Nik Aziz, has been gaining ground. Till a few years ago PAS was a small player in the Malaysian politics rooted largely in Kelantan province where it was in power. But in the year 1999 it captured another state, Terengganu, adjoining Kelantan and increased its tally threefold in the country's Parliament by winning 27 out of 193 seat. That demonstrates the growing hold of fundamentalist groups over Muslim masses even in the democratic or partially democratic countries. One has to see the deep imprint of rapidly growing orthodoxy in Kota Baharu, the capital of Kelantan in Malayasia where a beginning has been made by the government by banning drinking of alcoholic beverages by Muslims and shuttering the night clubs and bars. When during the day the Muezzin calls the faithful to prayers, the stores in the city switch off their music blaring stereos. All big stores and supermarkets have separate checkout counters for men and women so as to avoid any contact between the sexes.

Last five decades of the twentieth century have witnessed large scale religious revival across the globe among the adherents of various faiths. But religious revival has been the strongest in Muslim societies. A trend which has been a matter of concern to the world civilization is the pronounced tendency towards violence accompanied by the rising crescendo of the battle cry of jihad. This has re-stirred and reinforced the centuries old differences between various religious and cultural groups. The populations of two major proselytizing religions, the Christians and the Muslims, have increased substantially during the last hundred years. In the year 1900, the Christians were estimated at 26.9 per cent of the world population which grew in 1980 to 30 per cent. It meant an annual increase of 3.1 per cent. Muslims grew more sharply, from 12.4 per cent in 1900 to 16.5 per cent, as per another estimate by 18 per cent in 1980.[26] "In the long run, however, Muhammad wins out", avers Huntington, because the Christianity grows primarily by conversion, Islam both by conversion as well as reproduction.[27] An example of the high reproduction rate of Muslims could be bin Laden, the role model of the resurgent Islamic youth, who is one of some 65 children of a Saudi construction magnate, Mohammed bin Laden.[28] Accoding to another version, given by John Gray in his book, *Al Qaeda and What It means to be Modern*, Osama bin Laden is one of the 52 children of his father. Whatever the truth, the figures prove high reproduction rate of the Muslims. Bin Laden's father had a number of wives but never more than four at a time, as ordained by Islamic scriptures. Islam allows marrying new wives, while divorcing the old ones, subject to the rider that a Muslim should not have more than four wives at any time.

Reverting to the subject of population growth, it may be pointed out that the percentage of Christians in the world peaked at about 30 per cent in the 1980s, then levelled off, and is now declining.

It will probably approximate to 25 per cent of the world population by 2025.[29] Due to their extremely high growth rate the numbers of Muslims are likely to touch 30 per cent of the world's population by 2025 and might grow further till the end of the present century. In addition to the higher reproductive rate, Muslims have fine-tuned the art of proselytization far more effectively than the Christian missionaries. The conversions to Islam in Africa, Asia and Europe alone are winning hundreds of thousand new entrants to Islam every year. A great deal of spadework in this connection has been done by the Tablighi Jamaat, an international Islamic missionary entity, which has its headquarters at Raiwind, near Lahore, in Pakistan, where it enjoys massive state patronage plus the support of the ISI. The Tablighi Jamaat, which receives huge funds from the Saudi regime and other Muslim countries, including Pakistan, has been working feverishly at grassroots level to win converts in India, Bangladesh, South-east Asia and Africa for the last fifty years. It has a number of offices in Europe, especially in France, Germany, Balkans, and perhaps in the U.K. as well. Tabligh has a sizeable presence in the U.S.A. where they had held a large conference in Chicago, Illinois, in 1988 when it managed to attract over six thousands Muslims from around the world.[30] A Pakistani scholar, Mumtaz Ahmed, felt that this was perhaps the largest gathering of Muslims ever in North America.[31] Fundamentalist clerics have been preaching militant Islam from thousands of mosques which now dot the Asian, African, European and American landscape. And the result is that frequent killings of innocent civilians in Israel, Chechenya, Indonesia, Kashmir and the Philippines by xenophobic jihadi suicide bombers are increasing by the day.

Far more grim is the global demographic scene. A massive wave of rising Muslim populations across the globe, almost unprecedented in history, is building up. A large percentage of them will be young and therefore more aggressive and violence-prone. Apparently till now neither many nations nor demographers nor world statesmen have taken note of this very significant phenomenon which could alter the geopolitical equations across the globe. There are, however, reasons to believe that the Pentagon, especially the Neo-conservative strategists, are seized of this development. An assessment of the impact of the fast-paced demographic changes in the profile of Muslim population during the next three to five decades which could cause multiple faultline conflicts gives an inkling of the mankind's future imperfect, if one considers the latest population trends.

The population growth rates (per annum) and total fertility rates (per woman) of Muslim countries are far above of those of non-Muslim countries. For instance, Saudi Arabia, the role model of the Islamic universe, has a growth rate of 3.38 and fertility rate of 6.15 per woman. Comparable figures for some other countries are Yemen: growth rate 3.42 and fertility rate 6.82; Afghanistan: growth rate 3.38 and fertility rate 5.6; Syria: growth rate 2.45 and fertility rate 3.72; Nigeria: growth rate 2.53 and fertility rate 5.4; Pakistan: growth rate 2.01 and fertility rate 4.1, Bangladesh: growth rate 2.06 and fertility rate 3.17. Similarly Iraq has a growth rate of 2.8, Libya 2.4, Indonesia 1.5, Malaysia 1.9, Morocco 1.64 and Tanzania 1.72 per cent. Most of these growth rates and fertility rates are well above the population replacement level; some like those of Saudi Arabia, Yemen, Afghanistan, Nigeria, Sudan and Somalia are abnormally high compared with non-Muslim countries—almost higher by mile-long margins.[32]

In sharp contrast the growth rates (per annum) and fertility rates (per woman) of non-Muslim countries are way below those of the Muslim nations, enumerated above. The United Kingdom has a growth rate of 0.3 and fertility rate of 1.66, France a growth rate of 0.42 and fertility rate of 1.85, Italy a growth rate of 1.37 and fertility rate of 1.26, Germany a growth rate of 0.04 and fertility rate of 1.37, Spain a growth rate of 0.16 and fertility rate of 1.26 and Russia, trapped in a population freefall, has a negative growth rate of –0.3 per cent and fertility rate of 1.33 per woman. Australia has a growth rate of 0.22 and fertility rate of 1.41 per woman. India has a growth rate of 1.47 per cent and fertility rate of 2.91 per woman (as compared to Pakistan's growth rate of 2.01 and fertility rate of 4.1 and that of Bangladesh's growth rate of 2.06 and fertility rate of 3.17). China has a growth rate of 0.6 per cent and fertility rate of 1.66 per woman. The growth rate of the United States of America is 0.5 per cent.[33] These figures reflect the dimensions of the demographic conflicts likely to overshadow the future of democratic societies.

Within non-Muslim countries, too, there are substantial differences in the population growth rates and fertility rates of Muslims and non-Muslims—perhaps because of the scriptural sanction accorded to Muslims to have multiple wives, though not more that four at one time. The second reason is the huge gender discrimination resulting in non-emancipation and non-empowerment of woman in Islamic societies. For instance, in India the population growth rates of Muslims for the decadal census years 1981-1991 was almost fifty per cent higher than that of the Hindus and the Buddhists. Similarly the population growth rates of Muslims in the U.S.A., the U.K. and many other countries are much higher than those of other religious groups. There are reasons to believe that the relatively higher population growth rate and fertility rate of France, when compared to the neighbouring countries like Germany and Italy, could be due to the influx of a large number of Muslims from North African countries, who are believed to have a higher growth rate than French Christians. Among European countries, France has the largest concentration of Muslim population. It is already heading for a faultline conflict over the question of Muslim girls insisting on wearing head scarves (called "hijab") in schools and the practice of Muslim women wearing the veil in public.

This massive build up of the growing Muslim population in North Africa, the Middle East and the South East Asia has already started unfolding its wings and is spreading through the phenomenon of large scale movement of Muslims from one country to another, from one region to another and even from one continent to another. Growing numbers of human beings in any corner of the world invariably tend to seek extra space to settle down, requires more food, grab new and bigger economic opportunities to earn livelihood and, above all, show a greater urge to seek recognition in the country's affairs and the comity of nations through the sheer size and strength of their numbers. For these reasons the growing numbers become restive and aggressive. That is a universal truth.

No one can deny that Muslim population is growing across the globe exponentially, almost at the rate of 2.9 % per year which is much higher than the overall growth rate of the world population at approximately 2.3 % per annum, including Muslim population. In the Maghrib (i.e., Algeria, Tunisia, Libya and Morocco) between 1965 and 1990, a short spell of 25 years, the population almost doubled, from 29.8 million to 59 millions. In the same period, Egypt's population increased from 29.4 million to 52.4 million. Both Maghrib and Egypt are totally Muslim territories. The population of Muslims in North African countries and the Middle East is truly bursting at the seams and many are steadily migrating in large numbers to Europe. Anyone visiting Europe can notice it, experience it and feel it.

In Central Asia between 1970 and 1993, population grew at an annual rate of 2.9 per cent in Tajikistan, 2.6 per cent in Uzbekistan, 2.5 per cent in Turkmenistan, and 1.9 per cent in Kyrgyzia. In the 1970s the demographic balance in the Soviet Union shifted drastically, with Muslims increasing by 24 per cent in a decade, while Russian christians increased by only 6.5 per ent. Thus the decadal increase in Muslim population was almost four times the increase in the population of Christians in terms of percentage.

In early 1990s, the fertility rate of women in the Russian Federation was 1.5, while in the Muslim Central Asian nations, former members of the U.S.S.R., the rate was about 4.4 and the rate of the net population increase (crude birth rate minus crude death rate) in the late 1980s in the latter countries was almost five to six times that in Russia.[34] In 1980s Chechens increased by 26 per cent and Chechenya was one of the most densely populated places in Russia, its high birth rate producing both migrants and fighters.[35] In Russia the population—most Russians are Christians—is declining so precipitously that in January 2001 the Russian cabinet called for emergency measures to arrest what has been described as "the self-genocidal pattern of the last two generations".[36] Despite growing pressure the Russian President Vladimir Putin declined to legalize polygamy, a measure that had been proposed by ultra-nationalist, Vladimir Zhirinovsky.[37] Others supported Zhirinovsky in promoting such a startling remedy for Russia's "birth dearth" perhaps alarmed by the growing Muslims in Chechenya and other areas. Zhirinovsky's faction called for a new family policy that would permit up to five wives per man - apparently a kind of one-upmanship over the

Muslims who are allowed four wives by the Quran. More wives, he reasoned, would lead to quick population growth. But the ludicrous suggestion to opt for polygamy was rejected. It was a laughable ante-diluvian proposition, made ostensibly in the belief that polygamy will step up the Russian (read the Christian) population growth to match the galloping Muslim numbers in Chechenya and the adjoining countries, mostly former constituents of the Soviet Union. Interestingly, the demographers looking at the population charts have dubbed the crisis "The Russian Cross".[38] In the year 2000 Russia's population fell by 900,000. Vladimir Kulakov, a population researcher notes that Russia's population is declining at an alarming rate for an industrialized country; it is down from 148 million three years ago to 145 million at present – a decline of three millions in three years. A study released by the state statistics agency, Goskomstat, painted a grim demographic scenario for Russia. Russia's population is imploding and could be slashed to half by 2050, making the country unable to man its economy or defend its borders. According to Anatoly Vishnevasky, head of the Centre for Demography and Human Resources, Moscow, Russia's ambitions are those of a great state, but they are no longer supported by demographic data. "There are too few Russians being born each year, and too many working adults are dying. It is a long term disaster".[39] Russia's workforce has declined by 12 million over the past decade, and is likely to fall by another 10 million by 2015. Deaths among men are about seven times higher than among women. Russian men don't live up to retirement, and Russian women are having fewer babies. The birthrate is currently 1.1 children per woman, far short of the 2.4 kids per woman that would be needed to sustain the population at zero growth.[40] According to Goskomstat's optimistic projections, Russia's population will plummet from the present 145 million to just 102 million by 2050. The agency's pessimistic scenario would see it cut by half, to 77 million. Most of Russia's Asian territories are heavily under-populated. It is already a problem to find labour for agriculture and industry in many parts of Russia. And how would Russia defend its vast borders without young soldiers? To stem the numbers haemorrhage, Russians must produce 2 million babies per year. But only 1.2 million babies are born each year. The Russian President, Vladmir Putin and his cabinet have stressed that the population crisis represents an economic threat. Fewer people means fewer workers and fewer soldiers. Russia's population has fallen from 149 million a decade ago to just over 144 million today. Male life expectancy now stands at 59 years, with the average Russian woman living upto 72 years.[41] Demographic experts say that the country is losing one million of its population annually and the nose-diving is accelerating. The whole regions of Siberia and the Russian far east are already depopulated and new deserts are appearing even in former black earth regions of central Russia, according to Lev Gudkov, a demographer with the Russian Centre for Public Opinion Research. It is felt that Russia will not be able to maintain its industry, agriculture or the size of armed forces at this rate. Ever since the collapse of U.S.S.R., mortality rates among young males have risen to levels never before seen in peacetime. Mr Gudkov predicts that there could be one pensioner for every worker in Russia within 20 years. Not even a rich economy could survive that kind of strain.[42] Russian women, who are as well-educated and career-oriented very much like their Western counterparts, have been having fewer children since 1970s. Unike some other Western countries which compensate for lower birth rates by permitting immigration which keeps the economies growing and tax revenues flush, Russia did not have an immigration policy till now. Faced with a free fall in population at this juncture 'replacement migration' seems to be the only alternative. But the issue is politically so sensitive that Russian leadership dare not even discuss it. The proposed solution has been resisted even after the fall of the Iron Curtain because it can lead to immigration from the neighbouring Muslim countries and China which would be unacceptable to the Russian society. According to Yevgeny Krasinyev, head of the migration studies at the official Institute of Social and Economic Population Studies in Moscow, the only acceptable sources of immigrants were the Russian speaking populations of former Soviet countries in the Commonwealth of Independent States.[43] A tentative proposal to allow immigration restricted to five million Russian-speaking people from the adjoining CIS states over the next few years is being considered as a temporary replacement strategy to tackle the problem of manpower shortage. Such indeed is the plight of Russia trapped in a serious depopulation crisis that it does not have enough youth to run its factories and farms.

The fast approaching global waves of the Muslim population, especially in the southeast Asia, Middle East and North Africa, along with the manifestly disastrous consequences of the Russia's "do it yourself genocide" should serve as eye openers to the family planning enthusiasts of India. The current economic stagnation of the ageing Europe and its inability to look after its pensioners must be read as a timely warning. The overall demographic changes resulting from a declining population could lead to some very complex and far reaching geo-political and economic consequences. The demographic change starts slowly, almost imperceptibly, and initially remains unnoticed. Most governments tend to ignore it. Once the declining trend builds up for a few decades it transforms into a strong current which becomes difficult to reverse. For example, in India this 110 years old trend has come to be highlighted only now due to the determined efforts of some demographers. Even now not many political leaders and intellectuals are aware of its long term implications for the future of the country.

First, once a regular trend of falling fertility rate has been established, it becomes very difficult, almost impossible, to reverse it. That is the experience worldwide. Any quick increase in population becomes almost impossible, even through the incentive of cash bonuses now being offered in many European countries. The obstacles to bringing about a rapid population increase in an ageing country are formidable. Once the proportion of old people, both men and women, has grown beyond a certain threshold, with a corresponding decline in the proportion and numbers of the young, there is no easy possibility of any rapid growth in population. Old men and women cannot procreate, while the proportion and numbers of young men and women gets shrunk too much, rendering it too ineffective for bringing about any noticeable surge in the number of births. In initial stages, the population growth compounds at a very slow rate – until it gathers momentum through a surge in the youthful population which takes, on an average, at least twenty years to materialize. Another constraint, a major one, is that the decisions about having more children or fewer children, depend largely upon the wishes of the individuals or the concerned couples. Governments can offer only incentives.

Second, fewer young people resulting from a population squeeze, will mean that there would be a shortage of young soldiers and officers who constitute the backbone of a country's armed forces. Countries like Russia, China, the U.S.A., India and Australia, having vast borders and far too big coastlines will find it extremely difficult to find enough young men and women for strengthening their defence preparedness, in case they blindly follow the ongoing trend of birth control through family planning. Both Russia and Germany are at present facing this problem because of the unimaginative population policies followed in the not so distant past – say thirty or forty years ago.

Third, declining numbers of young population means lower productivity and a lower GDP growth. It also means a smaller production of goods and services and lesser farm produce as well as a lower saving rate. Not many people realize that the capacity to save is a function of a person's productivity level and his earnings accruing therefrom. Again the level of investment, based on internal savings, is directly related to the total quantum of savings made by the individuals, the government and the corporates. A person's as well a nation's savings rate tends to increase or decrease depending on the pace of economic development and growth of Gross Domestic Product.

Thus a fertility rate, lower than the replacement level, has very serious implications both for a country's economic development and its defence preparedness. It may be recalled that Russia was the first country to legalize abortion in 1920. On reconsideration the Government reversed its policy in 1936 and prohibited abortions. But due to public clamour it was again legalized in 1955. Russia has perhaps the highest abortion rate in the world. Two abortions are performed for every three pregnancies, according to official figures. Russia's demographic death throes are a warning to all nations – particularly those with similar declining rates of fertility, Italy and Spain among them, caused by a virulent abortion and condom culture. Nations that ignore the agony of a depopulating Russia, might follow her to the brink of extinction. Mass migrations of other ethnic groups invariably try to move into sparsely populated lands in search of new territories and natural resources.[44]

Vladmir Putin has been quick to recognize this threat. He is trying to tackle the grave crisis. The tragedy is that a long-term secular trend of declining fertility now conclusively established in Russia will be difficult to reverse. It will be a herculean task. Perhaps another solution to the threat of depopulation is to return to some sort of sexual morality. The governments of developing nations like India should try to learn from the Russian depopulation crisis. Wisdom lies in evolving strategic population policies specific to the development and defence needs which will strengthen the trend towards raising small families but not too small families either. The long-term objective should be twofold: first to meet the requirements of a developing economy; and second, to ensure effective defence preparedness. Strategic policies should be evolved which will ensure the fertility rate is maintained well above the replacement level of 2.1. Again if the future religion based conflicts are to be avoided, the population policy should ensure that the burden of family planning is equitably shared by all communities and religious groups. A sensible population policy would be the one which will ensure that there is enough working manpower available to provide a regular supply of young healthy men and women for the country's defence services and also that there is no shortage of enough working hands available within the country to run the nation's factories, farms and transport systems for sustaining a steady pace of growth in the GDP and the overall national productivity, both in the industry and the agriculture. A conscious effort should be made to ensure that the country does not fall into the trap of a declining population crisis like the one facing the ageing Europe and the shrinking Russia—graphically described as the "Do-it-yourself-genocide".

During the coming decades the increasing population in the Muslim heartlands will also significantly impact the countries and regions where Muslims are in minority. In some countries like Macedonia, the Muslims are likely to become a majority within next twenty to forty years because of their higher fertility rate—just as it happened in Lebanon. According to the latest figures given in the CIA's

Worldfact Book, the percentage of Muslims in Macedonia has now sharply risen to 30, while that of Christians is steeply down to 67. The comparative percentages in the year 1900 were 8.39% Muslims and 90.67% Christians.[45] The result of a sharp upswing in Muslim population was that the year 2001 saw a violent Muslim uprising led by the Albanians who have been silently trooping into Macedonia, just as Bangladeshis have been entering India. All major demographic changes like these, first faced by Lebanon and now taking toll in Macedonia are likely to upset the geo-political balance even in the adjoining countries and accentuate faultline conflicts resulting in tectonic socio-political upheavals.

According to Oriana Fallaci, a well known political analyst and author, today Europe has more than 16 million Muslims and their numbers are growing fast. She bemoans that the Europe was no longer Europe. It looks like a province of Islam, as Spain and Portugal were at the time of the Moors. It hosts almost 16 million Muslim immigrants and teems with mullahs, mosques, burqas and chadors and perhaps hosts thousands of terrorists.[46] It seems that after fifty years from now the Italian population will stand greatly reduced. The United Nations has virtually called a red alert with shocking statistics: the average number of children an Italian woman could expect to bear in her life time is now down to 1.2. By 2050, Italy's 56 million people are likely to thin down to 40 million.[47] Islam is already the second religion of almost every European state - the only exceptions being European countries like Azerbaijan and Albania where it is already the majority religion. Fertility rates across Europe are now so low that the continent's population is likely to drop markedly over the next 50 years. In fact, these bald statistics are being looked at with horror by much of the white western Europe—their women just aren't having enough babies any more. From the United Kingdom to almost every country of the mainland Europe, a message has gone out that it is time to produce more babies to move out of the trap of "birth dearth". Several European governments are suddenly announcing baby bonuses which is a cash in hand scheme somewhat successfully tried in France and Sweden. Now the baby bonus scheme has been adopted by Italy too.[48] The U.N. whose past population projections have been fairly accurate, predicts that the world's population will increase from over 6 billion in 2000 to just 8.9 billion by 2050 and might stabilize around that level. During the same period, however, the population of the 27 countries that should be members of the EU (European Union) by 2007 is likely to fall by 6% from 486 million to 454 million. For countries with particularly lower fertility rates, the decline is dramatic. By 2050 Spain's population may drop from 40 million to 37 million. Germany, which currently has a population of around 80 million, could find itself with just 25 million inhabitants by the end of the century, according to recent projections by the Deutsche Bank, which adds that even assuming a statistically high annual immigration intake of 250,000, Germany's overall population could decline to about 50 million by 2100. If these trends continue, by 2020, or even earlier, more than ten per cent of the Europeans could be Muslims. The percentage could even rise higher because of the likelihood of increased migration from North African countries and West Asia because of the growing pressure on their economies due to rapid increase in population of those two regions. The southern tip of Europe is separated from North Africa only by the Mediteranean. The changing demographic picture has produced enormous political uncertainty in Europe due to fears of being outnumbered by immigrant Muslims. At the same time, the problem has other fall outs in the economic sphere. Due to the phenomenon of ageing population, Europe has been economically stagnant almost for the last three years. The governments have no option but to enforce unprecedented cutbacks in pensions and social benefits. This led to crowds of angry demonstrators marching in European countries whose governments, reacting to the shift from youth to the aged, are moving to reduce social services, including the pensions that millions have been counting on for their golden years.[49] One study by William Frey, a demographer at the Brookings Institution in Washington, predicts that the median age in the United States in 2050 will be 35.4, only a very slight increase from what it is now. In Europe, by contrast, it is expected to rise to 52.3 from 37.7 years.[50] The likely meaning of this "stunning difference," as the British weekly, *The Economist*, called the growing demographic disparity between Europe and the United States, is that American power - economic and military—will continue to grow relative to Europe's, which will also decline in comparison with other parts of the world like China, India and Latin America.[51] With its population not only ageing but shrinking as well, Europe seems to face two broad possibilities: either it will have to make up the population shortfall by substantial increases in immigration, which would almost surely create new political tensions in countries where anti-immigrant parties have gained strength in recent years or it will have to accept the fact of becoming older and smaller and therefore, as some have been warning, far less influential in world affairs.[52] Underlining the seriousness of the problem created by large ageing population, Bernd Raffelhuschen, a member of the German governmental commission studying pension reform said that just now Germany had two working people supporting one retired person. By the year 2035 or so, every working hand will support one retired person.[53]

But the biggest problem facing the Europe is the growing fear, perhaps a genuine fear, of being outnumbered by the immigrant Muslims in the long run. It has caused much disquiet in many countries of western and southern Europe where it has become a highly emotive topic. The fear could manifest itself in the form of violence as was witnessed during rioting in some parts of England in the summer of 2001. In June 2003 a booklet was circulated by a U.K.-based think tank 'Civitas' which warned against the growing threat from Islamists. It urged British Muslims "to accept values of liberal democracy as Hindus, Sikhs and others" have done.[54] The think- tank advised that fanatical religious leaders who preach hatred of Western values should be prevented from coming to work in British mosques and felt that radical Islam was incompatible with democratic values and should be disavowed by the British Muslims. It also called for an immediate reform of the immigration procedures to prevent any more influx of Islamist idealogues. Two central concepts from traditional Islam, Sharia and Jihad, have been revived and extended by modern Islamists in ways which were incompatible with the U.N. Universal Declaration of Human Rights, said the report titled *The West, Islam and Islamism.*[55] The traditionally liberal and secular societies of Europe have seen an increase in support for far-rightist political parties in recent years, like France's National

Front led by Le Pen, the Northern League in Italy, the Freedom Party in Austria, the Pim Fortuyn List in the Netherlands and the People's Party in Denmark. The only European countries which are growing in population are Muslim Albania and Catholic Malta. Countries like Spain are trying to restrict entry of migrants through their borders and are contemplating stricter scrutiny of migrants and even some action against third world countries from where they come or the countries through which they pass. What has caused greater concern to the strategic thinkers and political analysts is the steep decline in the fertility rates all across the Europe: it is 1.21 in Italy, 1.19 in Spain, 1.34 in Germany, almost everywhere below the replacement level of 2.1. The precipitous decline in fertility rate bodes ill for the future of Europe. The fact that the population of democratic countries is declining has generated a fear that many of the European countries will be overwhelmed by the growing Muslim numbers in the decades ahead. It had been highlighted as early as November 1997 that 79 countries worldwide were declining both economically and militarily because of low birthrates. By the year 2015, an estimated 67% of all people will live in countries with fertility rates at or below replacement level.[56] The fearsome rumblings of the declining fertility rate are being felt as far away as Australia where fertility rate has fallen to 1.8 per woman. Australian National University demographer, Peter McDonald, said Australia's low fertility rate could cause a 40% decline in population over the next century, dropping to less than 11 millions.[57] Peter McDonald further stated that the falling fertility rates in the Europe and Japan were resulting in massive growth of ageing populations which governments could not afford.[58] Federal Opposition spokesman on population, Martin Ferguson, asserted that Australia's Labor Party would establish an Office of Population. Couples will have to produce more babies. Otherwise Australia would face serious demographic problems—by 2021 there will be one retired person for every 3½ working.[59] In Australia, too, the declining fertility rate threatens to become a roadblock for rapid development. Additionally the fast growing population of Muslims in the neighbouring Indonesia and militancy in the Philippines has been causing a certain degree of anxiety to the political leadership. The gravity of the situation could be assessed from the fact that on April 19, 1999, Victorian Premier Mr. Kennet told an audience of school girls that Australian women were not producing enough babies. He told students of Melbourne's prestigious MacRobertson Girls' High School that while surrounded by near neighbours having huge populations, Australian women produced only 1.8 children each on average. Australia has an ageing population and "women were not producing enough children to simply maintain the desired population levels," Mr Kennett told the giggling girls.[60] We have seen the far-reaching consequences of the rapid demographic changes on the socio-political fortunes of several countries and continents. The faultline conflicts which rocked Lebanon and the Balkans, solely due to certain changes in the religious complexion of populations, are recent history. Lately, the indigenous inhabitants of Europe and Russia are finding it difficult to cope with the problem of rapidly declining populations. Their economies as well as defence preparedness are under serious pressure.

How does India fare in the overall demographic scenario? Just now, India might appear to be placed in a fairly comfortable position. But that is both a temporary and illusory respite. In another three to five decades India, too, is likely to be caught in a demographic bind, because a secular trend of decline in the population of Indian religionists (i.e. the Hindus, the Sikhs and the Buddhists) has already been established during the last 110 years which is now gathering momentum. Recently three demographers and sociologists, Dr. A.P. Joshi, M.D. Srinivas and J.K. Bajaj have carried out an in-depth research into the changing demographic profile of India. They have analysed the increases and declines in the religious population of the undivided sub-continent (i.e., India, as it existed before 1947), the population trends in the present Indian state and in the states of Pakistan and Bangladesh, and attempted to make demographic projections for the future. Some conclusions arrived by the three researchers by means of empirical studies might raise the hackles of the self-styled secularist academia because of the emerging prominent trait of rapid growth of Muslim population in percentage terms. The study titled *Religious Demography of India*, published by the Centre for Policy Studies, Chennai (India), highlights the likely far-reaching changes in the religious complexion of India's population during the next four to five decades. The most important conclusion arrived at by the study is that the fertility rate of Muslims in India as well as Pakistan is substantially higher than that of the Hindus—the term used by the researchers is 'Indian Religionists' which includes the Hindus, the Sikhs, the Jains and the Buddhists. An analysis of the census data of pre-independence era, from 1891 to 1941 shows that in every census the number of children per woman of childbearing age for Muslims was at least 12 per cent higher than that of the Hindus. For the year 1901, the difference was 20 per cent.[61] Another striking feature is the prominent long-term trend of continuous rise in the percentages of Muslim and Christian population for six decades, i.e., from 1881 to 1941 in undivided India, i.e. the pre- independence era. During those sixty years, the population of Indian Religionists, i.e., the Hindus, the Sikhs and the Buddhists, declined from approximately 79 per cent to 73.67 per cent in the sub-continent, while that of the Muslims increased from approximately from 20 per cent to 24.3 per cent in undivided India and of the Christians from 0.71 per cent to 1.9 per cent. Among Indian Religionists, the only group which gained were the Sikhs whose proportion rose from 0.74 to 1.46 per cent during those six decades.[62] The post-independence census data of the Indian Union for the past four decades, from 1951 to 1991, reveals that in percentage terms the population of the Indian Religionists (the Hindus, the Sikhs and the Buddhists) declined from 87.2 per cent in 1951 to 85 per cent in 1991, while that of the Muslims rose sharply from 10.4 per cent to 12.5 per cent during the same period. The percentage of the Christian population remained almost static, it being 2.33 per cent in 1951 and 2.32 per cent in 1991.[63]

The most noticeable aspect is the persistent decline in the proportion of Indian Religionists in the population of the Indian sub-continent (i.e., India, Pakistan and Bangladesh bracketted together) throughout the long span of 110 years from 1881 to 1991. What should cause concern is the finding that the decline not only continues but also became sharper after partition. In the 60 years span between 1881-1941, the proportion of the followers of Indian religions declined by 5.5 per cent, from 79.32 to 73.81 per cent.

In the forty years after partition, between 1951-1991, the proportion of Indian Religionists declined by another 5.06 per cent from 73.09 to 68.03 per cent.[64] The defining feature of the religious demography of the Indian sub-continent during the last 110 years for which census data is available is the distinctly lower growth of followers of Indian religions as compared to Muslims and Christians. Between 1881 and 1991, the population of Indian Religionists in the sub-continent grew by a factor of 3.7, while that of Muslims grew at 6.5 times and Christians by as much as 12.3 times.[65] Such substantial differences in the rates of growth persisting over such a long period have led to the percentage of Indian Religionists in the population of the sub-continent (i.e India, Pakistan and Bangladesh) declining from about 79.3 per cent in 1881 to 68.0 per cent in 1991. The percentage of Muslims during the same period rose from about 20 to 30 per cent and that of Christians from 0.7 to 2.0 per cent.[66] The share of Indian Religionists in the population of the sub-continent thus dropped by more than 11 percentage points and of Other Religionists increased correspondingly. Such large changes in the religious composition of a compact geographical region could lead to grave consequences for the Indian people. Similar changes had led to partition of the country in 1947. Persistence of these differentials will cause significant changes in the religious profile of the sub-continent.[67] These could cause serious religion-based conflicts. According to the census report of 1991, the population of Muslims in the Indian union has shown an overall growth of 32.76 per cent during the decade between 1981 and 1991 which is far higher than the average national growth rate of 23.79 per cent. The census figures of 1981-91 showed that Muslims comprised 12.12 per cent of the country's total population of over 81.61 million.[68] The Hindus on the other hand recorded a slower rate growth at 22.78 per cent during that decade and now constitute only 82 per cent of India's total population. It meant that in percentage terms during the decade the overall growth rate of Muslims was almost one and a half times that of Hindus. At this rate it is only a matter of time, say four to five decades for demographic changes to cause a chain reaction of multiple faultline conflicts of the kind which overtook Lebanon and Bosnia, leading to civil wars there. To a serious student of Indian polity, it should be obvious that lately in India there has been a sharp increase in the hostility between the two communities. Perhaps the increasing incidence of religion-based faultline conflicts in several parts of India could be ascribed to the sharp demographic changes, more than any other development. The higher fertility rate of Muslims apart, the last three decades have seen a massive illegal immigration of Bangladeshi Muslims which has led to a big increase in communal tension and socio-political fissures in many parts of the country, especially in Assam and other parts of north-eastern India. It can be safely presumed that the trend will gather momentum in the years ahead, as it did in Lebanon, Bosnia and Macedonia. Unfortunately in most developing countries, including India, there is little awareness among people that during the last ten years the thinking about the goal of family planning has radically changed. The focus has distinctly shifted from mere reduction in the numbers of new borns to the welfare of the child and the mother. Countries like India must work at a fast pace for eradication of illiteracy, ensure provision of quality education to its sons and daughters, matching the very best in the world, and mount an all out campaign to rid the society of obscurantism and sloth. Only then can India move ahead. According to Catholic Family and Human Rights Institute, between 1900 and 2000 A.D., world population grew from 1.6 billion to 6.1 billion persons. While, the world population increased nearly four times, the world's real gross domestic product increased 20 to 40 times, allowing the world to not only sustain a four-fold population increase, but also to do so at a vastly higher standard of living.[69]

Along with the phenomenal demographic changes resulting from a higher fertility rate of Muslims, the last four decades have witnessed large scale mass movement of people across many countries and continents. But the scale of movement of Muslims from their traditional geographical regions, where they are in majority, to other regions and countries where they constitute a minority group has been very high and almost dramatic. It is basically due to their exploding population numbers caused by high birth rates. There has been an influx of a large number of Muslims from several countries of Asia and Africa into Europe, U.S.A., Canada, Australia and other areas. Also there has been a huge movement of Muslims from Bangladesh into India. The numbers of illegal Bangladeshi immigrants and their progeny in India, mostly Muslims, is now estimated to be approximately 30 million. Large scale migration of Muslims has already disturbed the demographic equilibrium in certain sensitive regions of the world of which the Balkans, western Europe and India appear to be the worst affected. In India this development has already raised communal tensions—and perhaps, in Europe, too if that frank and outspoken author of Italian origin, Oriana Fallaci, is to be believed.

America has been a multi-religious and multi-ethnic country all along. During the last three decades it has witnessed a sharp increase in the population of Muslims, largely through immigration. It is believed that the numbers of Muslims in the United States grew sixfold between 1972 and 1990. According to one estimate, in North America the Muslim birthrate is nearly three times the average U.S. family. Muslims now form the largest minority religion in the United States with an estimated 6 million followers.[70] An estimated 400,000 Muslims live in the Chicago area. The number of mosques in America has grown from a relatively small number in 1960 to more than 2,000 today, according to Ibrahim Hooper, a spokesman for the Council of American-Islamic Relations. Chicago has nearly 90 mosques and the number of Muslim families in Naperville has nearly doubled to 500 in the past five years, according to Kareem Irfan of the Council of Greater Chicago. Though the claim that there are six million Muslims in the U.S.A. is being contested, the fact that there has been a massive increase in their numbers lately, remains uncontested. Writing in *National Review*, Steven A. Camarota, points out that the number of Middle Eastern immigrants in the U.S. has grown eightfold from 1970 to 2000, and is expected to double again by 2010.[71] This growth could have significant repercussions for America's homeland security and might even impact the U.S. support for Israel.[72] Then there are serious long-term implications. The Centre for Immigration Studies has issued a report of this group of immigrants, based on Census Bureau data in which Middle East is broadly defined as running roughly from Morocco to Pakistan. While the overall size of the foreign-born population has tripled since 1970 and now stands at 31 million, the number of immigrants from the Middle East increased more than twice as fast – from fewer than 200,000 in 1970 to nearly 1.5 million in 2000.[73] The INS (Immigration and Naturalization Service) estimates that about 10 per cent or nearly 150,000 of them are illegal aliens. The new Middle Eastern immigrants are not just more numerous than the old but also very different in religion. Till 1960s the Middle Eastern immigrants were mostly Christian Arabs from Lebanon or Armenians, Assyrians, Greeks and other Christian minorities fleeing from predominently Muslim countries. In 1970 only 15 percent of Middle Eastern immigrants were Muslims, but by 2000, the percentage grew to almost 73 percent. Between 1970 and 1990, the population of Christians in the U.S.A. declined from approximately 91 per cent to 85.69 per cent, while that of Muslims increased from 0.38 per cent to 1.40 per cent.[74] But this trend of rapid increase in Muslim population of U.S.A. is now likely to be reversed because of the operation of a stringent legislation, effective January 2003, requiring all migrants from 12 Muslim countries and North Korea, deemed to be potential source of terrorism, to register themselves with the Immigration and Naturalisation Service. Natives of Afghanistan, Algeria, Bahrain, Eritrea, Lebanon, Morocco, Oman, Qatar, Somalia, Tunisia, U.A.E., Yemen and North Korea, in the age group 16 to 45 years will be fingerprinted and photographed and their visa documents inspected. Unofficially a big squeeze is also being applied on intending migrants even from friendly countries like Pakistan and Saudi Arabia as a measure of national security. The new registration procedure is in line with the revised rules now being applied to scrutinise applications for visa from several Muslim countries. The measure has been welcomed by the American public who are convinced that in the context of the growing menace of international Islamist terrorism, it is perfectly legitimate to keep out the citizens of countries which may harbour terrorists. There were some complaints that in trying to enforce the new law vigorously, the INS officers in South California sometimes arrested, handcuffed and detained several hundred men and boys, for suspected immigration law violations because they happened to be suspected from terror-sponsoring countries. It is believed that more than 13,000 of the Arab and Muslim men who came forward earlier this year to register with immigration authorities - roughly 16 per cent of the total - may now face deportation.[75] Only a handful have been linked to terrorism. But of the 82,000 who registered, more than 13,000 have been found to be living in the country illegally. Many had hoped to win leniency by registering and demonstrating their willingness to cooperate with the government's campaign against terror. The men were not promised special treatment, however, and officials believe most of them will be expelled in what is likely to the largest wave of deportations after the September 11, 2001 attacks. The government has initiated deportation proceedings, and in immigrant communities across the country, an exodus has already begun.[76] The acting Director for Interior Enforcement at the Department of Homeland Security, Jim Chaparro, clarified that there has been a major shift in priorities. He said that some people may not like the change, but that is what the U.S.A. needs to do. If a loophole can be exploited by an immigrant, it can also be exploited by a terrorist.[77] Miffed by the harsh measures, some Attorneys for immigrants have also accused officials of practising selective enforcement by targeting immigrants from Arab and Muslim countries. But the Bush administration is not bothered. It is going ahead with rigorous implementation of all Homeland Security measures. Over a period of time these measures will slow down the growth of Muslim population in the U.S.A. by impacting the immigration from Islamic nations.

At the same time, the Pentagon is very alive to the problem of depopulation facing the Europe and Russia. In late 1980s, the U.S. Department of Defence had commissioned quite a few studies into the effects of worldwide population trends for assessing America's ability to influence events abroad. One of these was published in a summary form in the Spring 1989 issue of the *Washington Quarterly*, a journal of the influential Centre for Strategic and International Studies. The overview, which had been compiled by Gregory D. Foster, an Instructor at the National Defence University in Washington, was described in the publication as having been drawn, sometime verbatim, "from the commissioned papers" which were presented to the Commission on Integrated Long-Term Strategy, under directions of the Office of the Director of Net Assessment at Department Of Defence.[78] The study was prefaced with the critical observations that the circumstances do not permit Americans the luxury of ignoring events until they occur simply because the tools of prognosis at their disposal are rather ill-developed. In fact, the looming resource constraints required higher levels of prescience by the United States in handling its global affairs. It was therefore necessary, even if a little daunting, to look once again into the future, may be to the end of the first decade of the next century, to assess the importance of the matters concerning the world population to the security interests of the United States.

The report alerted the Pentagon to the stark reality that "demographic developments promise to have a material effect on the general complexion of the world" during the next two decades.[79] By the year 2010 the world will have roughly 7 billion inhabitants of which 81 per cent will reside in the Third World. On the important issue of demography affecting the size and composition of military establishments around the world it underlined two important aspects. First, declining fertility rates will make it increasingly difficult for the United States and its NATO allies to maintain their defence forces at current levels. Second, high fertility rates in developing countries, if not matched by a commensurate growth of jobs, could lead to expanded military establishments in the affected countries as an alternative to arrest unemployment. In other words, where labour forces are significantly under-employed, military establishments may have a built-in momentum to capitalize on the unused manpower for purposes of both internal and external security. While population changes may or may not alter the international balance of power over the next two decades, it looked almost certain that the types of conflicts likely to predominate in the years ahead will be manpower-intensive regional conflicts. That might give more power and influence to the developing countries over a period of time.[80] Some other important conclusions reached by the study were as follows:

1. Today's wealthy nations will be burdened increasingly by the growing needs of the elderly. The numbers of 65 years of age or older will increase from the present 286 million to 418 million by 2000 AD, and the trend will be more pronounced in the developed world, where the median age by the year 2025 will be almost 39, as against 30 or less

in the developing nations. Ageing results in reduction in productivity and increases the chances of economic stagnation. It leads to a high ratio of retirees to workers thereby demanding increased taxation to meet the social security expenditures.

2. Armed forces will have to compete with other sectors more intensively both for manpower and money. But in overall terms less money will be available because of shrinkage of the productive population base. Such a scenario will have quite an adverse effect on Japan and the countries which are members of NATO.[81]

3. The population of the United States, which is presently the fourth most populous nation in the world, will begin declining in early twenty-first century, and by 2010 A.D., its population share which was six per cent in 1950, will plummet to four percent. The numbers of U.S. citizens in the 18-24 years age bracket peaked in 1981 at 30.5 million, and will decline. Nearly 39 million elderly persons are expected to live in the U.S. by 2010, up from approximately 14.5 million in 1955. That will mean more competition between the military, the colleges and civilian employers for filling vacancies and require significantly higher pay packets to those joining defence services. That will put a serious squeeze on the federal budget.

4. In Europe the declining population will pose severe problems. The military research document said that the growth of population of ethnic Europeans will fall below 0.2 per cent around 2000 and decline close to zero by 2025. By that year four important European states now among the sixteen most populous nations of the world—Germany, Italy, the U.K. and France—will go down in rankings. France is expected to rank twenty-fifth in total population by that time; others will rank yet lower. In West Germany the birthrate has fallen to unprecedented low levels. It was at a level 35 to 40 per cent below replacement. Thus West Germany's actual population could

decline by over 2 million between 1989 and 2010. Despite unification of the East and West Germany, the demographic situation for Germans continues to be grim. Perhaps by 2030, non-workers will outnumber workers in Germany. In term of the numbers of potential troops available, Germany is cited as an example of the future hardships that await the superpowers of today.

5. Similarly Russia will also face serious problems of low fertility and ageing. As already discussed Russia is just now trapped in a self-made depopulation crisis. Its political role in the comity of nations will go down substantially and so will its military prowess, unless it manages to shore up its population numbers which the Russian President Vladimir Putin is trying to do now.

6. The increasing disparities between the rich and the poor nations and regions might produce new geo-political problems which could take the form of either accelerated international migration or higher levels of hostility towards the western nations. The most critical migration activity will occur where areas of low economic growth happen to be located in close proximity to the areas of high economic growth, just as Europe is located close to North Africa and the Middle East and the United States is close to the Caribbean Bay basin. Where immigrants cannot be easily assimilated due to cultural differences, or any other reason, and where they are perceived to be usurping the employment opportunities of the citizens of the host countries, political instability might increase.

7. Population growth in the Middle East is likely to pose increased risks for the U.S. interests in that area. The region's population, estimated at 233 million in 1987, was expected to reach 418 million by 2010. Two large Muslim countries, Egypt and Iran, will add 35 million and 49 million numbers respectively by 2010. In this region any attempt to decrease the fertility rate faces strong opposition. More specifically Iran, Iraq, Kuwait, Libya, Qatar, Saudi

Arabia, the U.A.E., Bahrain and Palestinians prefer high population growth rates. Population in this region is growing at a fast pace.

8. Between 1988 and 2010 the population of the African continent will double to more than 1.2 billion and between 1985- 2030 the total increase in Africa will be 1.1 billion. Also due to high fertility rate Nigeria's population, 103 million in 1988, is likely to double by 2009 and quadruple by 2035 thus adding 312 million people to the world population in 50 years. By 2035 A.D. Nigeria is likely to surpass both the U.S.A. and Russia to become the third or fourth largest country in the world, in terms of population.

High birth rates lead to large increases in the size of the economically active population (EAP) and if the distribution of global resources remains unchanged in the face of such far-reaching demographic changes, it could result in waves of rising discontent and conflicts across the globe.

A second military report on demographic trends was prepared in 1991 for the U.S. Army Conference on Long Range Planning, by Nicholas Eberstadt of the Harvard University Centre for Population Studies. According to Eberstadt, who is also a Visiting Scholar at the American Enterprise Institute, the changing demography of the world constitutes a major threat to western domination. The study, which was reprinted in the Summer 1991 edition of the Council on Foreign Relations journal, *Foreign Affairs*, pointed out that virtually all current population projections anticipate comparatively slow population growth in developed regions, that is Europe, Russia, Japan, North America, etc., and correspondingly higher growth for the less developed regions, which means the rest of the world. If these trends continue for another generation or two, the consequences for the balance of world power could be enormous.

A very important conclusion, based on the statistics culled from the Development Research Centre at the Organization of Economic Cooperation and Development (OECD), was that per capita income in most developing countries has risen with population increases thus giving those nations a vastly greater share of global prosperity.

Citing the examples of Asian and Latin American countries, the study acknowledged that the per capita output in those regions rose by a factor of more than four between 1900 and 1987. Though the population of nine Asian countries in the sample more than tripled during this period and the population of six Latin American countries rose nearly seven times, the per capita output rose more dramatically —by a factor of more than three for the Asian group and by nearly five for the Latin American group. Briefly, taking the Latin American example, the population increased nearly seven-fold in the first eight decades of the twentieth century, while per capita income rose by a factor of five, meaning thirty-five times. It showed that the period saw Latin American nations on the average enjoying a thirty-five fold increase in wealth – as a result of having seven times more people and an average gross national product five times greater, on a per person basis. Like the earlier study of the Department of Defence, the U.S. Army Conference cautioned that the presently powerful nations will, as populations age and shrink, gradually lose the ability to direct and mould the politics and culture of the world. The 1991 military report had cited some examples of far-reaching geopolitical impact resulting from demographic changes. In Lebanon the political changes were the inevitable result of the fertility differences between the Christian and Muslim population groups. A 1943 agreement, known as the National Pact, stipulated that political power will be shared between the two religious groups, the Christians and the Muslims, in accordance with their respective strength in the national population. Top ministers were to be divided in a six-to-five ratio between the Christians and the Muslims (including the Druze sect), corresponding to the population ratios reported in Lebanon's 1932 census. Subsequent population counts however showed a pronounced difference between the Christian and Muslim fertility. In early 1970s the Christian community had a declining fertility rate of less than four children per woman, while the Muslims had an estimated fertility rate of six children per woman. The result : by 1975 Lebanon came to be widely believed to have become a Muslim majority country. Similar geopolitical results are visible in South Africa where the Whites at one time constituted slightly more than one- fifth of that country's enumerated population. That proportion fell to one-seventh by early 1980s and by 2020 the white population will dwindle to one-ninth of the total population. The current sea-change in South Africa's political scenario might not have been wholly motivated by the demographic developments but it might as well be based on informed calculations about the likely population changes.

According to the above cited two defence studies, population growth, if handled intelligently, can work in a country's favour in a variety of ways. First by increasing the numbers of economically active persons for increasing the GDP. Second, by enlarging the mass base from which the army and defence services can select the most suitable soldiers and airmen. Third, by generally increasing the influence and the political status of the country in the comity of nations. Another comparative advantage will be added if a country's potential political adversaries are caught in a relatively slow population growth or a free fall mode as Russia is—and Germany likely to follow suit. In fact, the 1988 study prepared for the Defence Department called for a huge commitment of resources for intelligent planning of population to safeguard the interests of America.

The 1988 CSIS (Centre for Strategic and International Studies) summary acknowledged that population trends are difficult to project because of unknown factors which can affect both fertility and mortality. The report forcefully projected that good population management is an important component of defence strategy. Indeed, the report accords population planning a level of importance that is essentially "equal to the development and procurement of advanced weapons."[82]

Since the beginning of the twentieth century there has been a rapid decline in the fertility rate of most developed countries. When the fertility falls so low that a nation starts producing smaller numbers of young people, the elderly tend to become a disproportionately larger percentage of the population. That leads to a situation in which the GDP has to be produced by a smaller percentage than in the past thus causing a shrinkage of the economy. A slowing down of the economy also entails a decrease in the rate of saving, a function directly correlated to a person's ability to earn, which in turn has a bearing on his capacity to save. That is why pensioners and other old persons are seldom able to save anything much. In the long run an ageing population leads to a declining gross domestic product and will result in economic stagnation. This demographic trend has another downside, though at present only for the western civilization. The population of western countries, especially in Europe, is top heavy in the sense that the proportion of elderly persons is high while that of the young is low.

But the position in the predominantly Muslim countries is just the reverse. For instance, today more than half the population of Algeria is under the age of twenty and the situation is almost similar in most other Muslim dominated countries. This trend has at least five-far reaching implications.

First, a younger population will reproduce more and thereby perpetuate the increase in the numbers of Muslims thereby carrying forward the growing numbers and also the percentage increases in their population at least for the next five decades - and perhaps even into the next millenium. At this rate, by 2100 A.D. or perhaps earlier, Muslim population numbers will overwhelm a major portion of the globe.

Second, an ageing population tends to be introspective, slow and sluggish, incapable of fruitful economic activity and therefore solely dependent on the youthful component. In sharp contrast, the young population is more energetic, economically productive, inventive and innovative.

Third, a youthful population is bound to be more aggressive and violence-prone as well. The aggressive and more violence-prone tendency of young population might not bode well for many countries or even regions, because the end-result of increasing numbers of youthful Islamists will depend on how strong or fragile is the political structure and defence capability of the affected country or the region. The growing young members will demand more space, food and greater say in governance and aggressively assert themselves.

Fourth, the overall impact of a youthful population will not always remain confined to the concerned country or region. By its energetic, aggressive and volatile nature a youthful population is likely to cause major societal upheavals and affect the economy and the socio-political structure not only of the concerned country but all around in a particular region or even across continents like Europe or a country like India, due to the accelerating force of "push" factor inherent in the process of migration, which if allowed to go unchecked for a long time, tends to establish itself as a secular trend through the sheer force of momentum. The history of mankind is a witness to this demographic phenomenon. Balkans and Lebanon are two classic examples of the socio-political destabilization caused by the push factor. Macedonian Christians are likely to become "push-overs" in their homeland in the near future entirely due to the operation of this "push" factor! Nearer home we have the ready example of Assam where the local population has been pushed to the wall by Bangladeshis.

Fifth, all economic development is a function of the human resource—a more dignified name for manpower or working population. Anyone having a rudimentary knowledge of economics knows that every farm, factory and industry depends on manpower —preferably knowledge-soaked youthful manpower possessing the latest technological skills. In the realm of economic development one area of long-term significance is the science of demography on which much work has been done by the United Nations.[83] As per these studies done by the U.N. the world is likely to face significant demographic challenges during the next 25 years. If one ignores migration, for maintaining a stable population a country requires every female to give birth to 2.1 children—the extra 0.1 to take care of infant mortality and imbalances in the male-female ratio. Interestingly in nearly every developed country, excepting the U.S. (which has a fertility rate of 2.05), the fertility rate is significantly below 2.1.[84] As we have seen, the Muslim countries, by and large, have the highest fertility rates.

The de-population crises facing the ageing Europe and declining Russia, trapped in a free-fall of numbers, should be taken as a grim warning by the nations across the globe—particularly those with similar declining rates of population: Italy, Spain and Germany among other European countries. For a change, at long last some of these nations are now waking up by offering cash bonuses to those couples who opt to make more babies. This unexpected crisis has several futuristic lessons for many developing countries excessively obsessed with family planning. Demography is a very complex science pregnant with serious long-term consequences which has the potential to alter the destinies of many a nation in future, as indeed it has done in the past of which Lebanon and Bosnia are the latest ones—with Macedonia and some other countries of the Balkans heading further in that direction.

The long march of radical Islam is a reality. In view of the growing commitment of Muslim youth to jihad and the oncoming avalanche of the burgeoning population of Muslims across the globe, there is a strong possibility of outbreak of serious faultline conflicts and societal upheavals in many demographically vulnerable regions of the world. At least four strategic regions can be straightaway identified which are likely to face multiple faultline conflicts, mostly religion-based, and in each one of these Islam is sure to be one of the warring groups. We have seen that West Asia or Middle East is one such important area where a deep and long standing civilizational conflict between the state of Israel and the adjoining Arab Muslim countries has been in progress now for the last fifty five years. The current faultline conflict between Israel and the Palestinians, the latter uncopromisingly backed by the militant Muslim neighbours, is not only likely to continue, but might as well escalate in the years ahead because of the likely massive surge in the population of Muslims in the West Asian countries surrounding Israel. That will make life more difficult for Israelis who are already driven to the wall—literally forced to raising an impregnable wall for their security—now exasperatingly battling to secure the survival of the Jewish homeland.

The second major area of faultline conflicts is likely to be the Balkans and the southern and western European countries which have experienced a sharp upswing in Muslim population and rapid mushrooming of mosques and seminaries all over. The Balkans is already a highly destabilized region ever since 1912 when the first Balkans War broke out which was followed by a second Balkans war in the year 1913. Since then the Balkans has been in a state of perennial turmoil. The massive growth in the population of

Muslims in Albania and their overflow into the erstwhile Yugoslavia has been the source of major population changes in the entire Balkans. The sharp increase in the numbers of Muslims in the region which has been rocked by a series of violent conflicts has serious implications for other neighbouring countries. During the last decade several European countries, especially Spain, France, Italy, Germany and Netherlands have experienced large accretions to the population of Muslims. Even the United Kingdom has been substantially affected. What has been causing greater concern, however, is the huge growth of radical Islamist outfits in almost all these countries. This has naturally raised hackles of the indigenous Christian populace and resultantly some right wing political activists, hostile to Islamists, have come to occupy a part of the central political space in many countries. Needless to mention, the entire Balkan region and many of the countries of southern and western Europe are likely to face growing faultline conflicts in the near future. In France a raucous controversy over the wearing of veil by Muslim women and head scarves by school girls is gathering momentum. The situation is likely to get more exacerbated because of the growing possibility of large scale migration of young Muslims from North African countries which have been witnessing mammoth population growth. The eastern and southern coastlines of Mediterranean have seen numerous flows of population-migration and religion-based conflicts from the times predating the crusades when Islamic warriors overran the entire North Africa and conquered the Iberian Peninsula, the modern Spain. The defeat of the Christian Byzantine empire by the Turks and the fall of Constantinople to Turks some 550 years ago was a major victory for Islam. It was renamed Istanbul in 1453 by the Turks. Since then the movement of Muslims from the West Asian and North African countries to Europe has been sort of a regular trend. Now that the population of West Asia and North Africa is threatening to burst at the seams, the migration to Europe has been steadily increasing. As it gathers momentum within the next two decades, it is likely to cause major faultline conflicts in the tinderbox called the Balkans and all around in southern and western Europe. Unless a workable solution is evolved, the hordes of young and violence-prone migrants from

North Africa and West Asia have the potential to destabilize a major portion of the European continent.

The third likely region of dangerous climactic faultline conflicts, some of which could be exceptionally turbulent is likely to be the Indian sub-continent. Ultimately, say in three to four decades, the Indian sub-continent could become a hotspot of religion-based faultline conflicts due to a sharp growth in the population of Muslims, with a correspondingly steep decline in the percentage of Hindus and other Indian Religionists. The massive silent invasion of Bangla-Muslims through India's porous borders has been further fuelling religious tensions in the country. If one adds to this, the mayhem being created by growing terrorist attacks in certain parts of the country, largely due to Pakistan-sponsored radical outfits, the scenario looks quite grim. The situation is already becoming difficult because of the rapid strides made by the long march of radical Islam, entrenched in two theocratic nations of the sub-continent, located to our west and the east. Both these countries Pakistan, in the west, and Bangladesh in the east, have higher fertility rates as well as population growth rates. The threat posed by the radical Islamic ideology is already manifest in the multifold increase in the terrorist attacks across the country, mostly engineered by the ISI, often with the help of local moles. The Pakistani establishment makes no pretence of innocence in the matter and gleefully describes it as "the war of a thousand cuts". Their avowed aim is to bleed and balkanize India. They will not mind to wait, say for another forty or fifty years, in the hope that meanwhile due to growing dissensions and divisive politics, the Indian nation will become more soft and an easy take-over target. In many recent terror crimes there has been some degree of participation by Indian citizens—one might call them the loony fringe. These developments have increased the communal divide between the two communities, the Hindus and the Muslims. The increased hostility has already caused an upswing in the religion-based faultline conflicts visible all over the country.

The fourth region of such conflicts is likely to be Central Asia, the soft under belly of Russia, because of the latest demographic developments in that region. The population of Russia is now more or less in a free fall, while its Muslim province of Chechenya has the highest fertility rate—literally overflowing with Muslim numbers. Similarly the numbers of Muslims in the former constituent-States of the Soviet Union, e.g., Dagestan, Turkmenistan, Uzbekistan and Azerbaijan, are growing rapidly—much faster than the Christian Russia. The free fall in the population of Russia coupled with the growing Muslim population in its province of Chechenya and neighbouring Muslim countries, located in Russia's south, have the potential to destabilize the entire region, once faultline conflicts gather momentum. Deeply conscious as they are of their superiority in the numbers game, the Islamist are already raring to go. A jihad against Russia is already in progress in Chechenya which is the most heavily populated province of Russia, and the rumblings of an Islamist upsurge brewing in Dagestan can be easily heard. The contagion has already spread to Turkmenistan and Uzbekistan where fundamentalist Islam is growing well and fast. It is merely a matter of time before the Islamists up their ante and launch multiple jihads all along the soft under belly of Russia in search of new horizons and pastures greener. The lure of vast uncultivated lands and abandoned farms in Russian hinterland will surely invite predators from some of the neighbouring Muslim countries, and even from China.

Though not in the immediate future, ultimately two more regions might also become the battleground of religion-based conflicts. These are the African continent and Australia. According to the CIA Worldfact Book, Nigeria has at present a population of approximately 134 millions of which Muslims constitute about 50 per cent (up from 43.89 percent in 1990 and from 25.93 per cent in 1900). The Christians are now down to 40 per cent (from 45.44 per cent in 1990 and 43 percent in 1970).[85] Nigeria has a history of several violent faultline conflicts between the Muslims and the Christians quite a few of which occurred in the recent times. With Muslims already having attained the majority status, the incidence of religion-based conflicts is bound to grow rapidly. Nigeria has a very high fertility rate, mostly among its component of Muslim population and according to some demographic estimates its population will cross 520 million mark by 2035 A.D. when it could become the third largest country in population, ranking just behind

India and China. That could plunge the entire African continent, especially the nations having majority of Christian populations, into a major turmoil.

Similarly Indonesia could be another area of concern, especially for the nearby Australia which is facing the problem of declining population. According to the CIA Worldfact Book, Indonesia at present has a population count of approximately 235 million with Muslims forming nearly 87-88 per cent of the total population, up from 54.71 per cent in 1990 and from 40 per cent in 1900, after separation of the Christian state of East Timor.[86] The rising Islamic militancy sweeping Indonesia and the tide of the rising Muslim population have been causing a kind of trepidation among the Australian politicians about the future of their country. They still remember the caustic-tongued jibe of Mahathir Mohammed that Australia was "some sort of transplant from another region". The bombing of the Kuta beach resort in October 2002 by Islamists which took a heavy toll of Australian tourists came to them as a rude shock. Australia is virtually a continent with a total population of approximately 22 millions, a very low population density of three persons per square kilometre and vast coastline. Its huge natural resources, open spaces, plenty of cultivable land and sparse population could invite large scale migration from the nearby Indonesia which is already teeming with growing numbers. Unless the Indonesian government manages to turn off the overflowing tap of Islamist fundamentalism, the threat of faultline conflicts with Australia will continue to darken the south-eastern horizon.

Forecasting future events on the basis of empirical studies is a tough call, especially for researchers who are mere mortals, and not always endowed with the necessary political vision and wisdom. It is indeed one of the most difficult tasks, more suited to the eclectic genius of the futurologists, if we leave out of reckoning the tribe of crystal ball-gazers, astrologers and south sayers. Yet even at the risk of being branded as a prophet of doom, it would be prudent to warn the civil society that according to the emerging demographical pattern, the people living in the aforementioned four regions of the world are likely to face a high degree of socio-religious turbulence, even civil wars, in the coming decades.

Therefore, some strategy, some effective mechanism, for conflict resolution has to be evolved and put in place to meet the challenge of Islamist aggression, or call it reckless terror, supported by that powerful transnational union called ummah. If one goes by the present trend of demographic changes, the next three or four decades could emerge as the defining phase of international Islamist terror - say, a kind of make or break situation for the Islamists as well as the civilized world. The problem could assume gigantic dimensions in at least four regions because of the likely onslaught of massive migration from North Africa and the Middle East into the Balkans and southern Europe and the likely spurt in the movement of Muslims from Chechenya, Dagestan, Azerbaijan, Turkmenistan and Uzbekistan into a depopulating Russia. Just add to this bleak world outlook the high fertility rate of Indian Muslims and the havoc being played with India's socio-economic fabric by the relentless silent invasion of Bangladeshis. That should reflect the big picture of the shape of things to come. Most nations remain glued to the micro picture of their own country, believing that the raging storm all around will bypass them. But that does not happen in this interdependent world order. It is therefore imperative for the concerned nations to constantly monitor the developments in their neighbourhood nations, watch and analyse the macro picture and develop meaningful survival strategies. Since Islamic ummah is the biggest politico-religious union of more than three score countries across the world, comprising almost 1.2 billion numbers plus massive petro funds, no single nation, howsoever big and powerful, including the United States, can meet the growing Islamic threat of terror single-handedly. According to an exhaustive study made by Loretta Napoleoni in a seminal research work, *Modern Jehad*, the financial world of terror has access to a whopping $ 1.5 trillion, which constitutes five per cent of the world GDP—and several times that of India's GDP.[87] Frankly, the enormously higher reproductive rate of Muslims worldwide alone has the potential of plunging several soft states into chaos in the not-too-distant future. Many of these like Russia, India and the Philippines are already being regularly bled and debilitated by successive waves of terrorist attacks promoting serious faultline conflicts. One such example was the Godhra train holocaust and the resulting communal carnage in the state of Gujarat. During the last few years a number of religion-based faultline clashes have taken place with increasing frequency in the state of Maharashtra, Hyderabad city and many other locations across the country.

Compared to monarchies and dictatorships, democracies can be very fragile while facing aggressive opponents. Apart from recourse to a violent coup, a debilitated democratic regime can be undermined, or overthrown simply by the numbers game expressed in terms of votes. In the arithmetic of universal franchise based on one-man-one-vote formula, sharp changes in the religious composition of a country's population can play a decisive role in radically altering the political dispensation. And once the forces of radical Islam attain an upper hand due to the facility of demographic changes, they will not hesitate to enforce a fundamentalist regime based on Sharia. Apparently the civil society has not learned any lessons from the tragedies of Lebanon and the Balkans, especially the latter region which has been rocked by successive bloody civil wars. It needs to be analysed that how and why a die-hard communist and secularist like Slobodan Milosevic turned into a rabid Muslim hating Serb. All communists are committed secularists and Milosevic was no exception. Then what made him go after the Muslim Kosovars and Bosnians in a big way. The answer is simple. When Milosevic and other comrades in his government saw that the future of the Serbian civilization was in grave danger and that the entire Serb nation was likely to be overwhelmed by the rising tide of the Muslim numbers, they lost mental balance and openly acquiesced in acts of ethnic cleansing committed by the Serb militia and army. In 1980s due to frequent violent protests and riots by Albanian and Kosovar Muslims the persecution of the Serb minority had risen sharply. There were large scale religion-based riots involving the killings, property damage, rapes and wanton harassment of the Serbs who claimed that the threat to them was of genocidal proportions. In 1986 the plight of the Kosovo Serbs led to a declaration by two hundred leading Serbian intellectual, political leaders including several prominent communists, defence service officers and the editor of the liberal opposition journal *Praxis* demanding that the government should take effective steps to prevent genocide of Serbs in Kosovo. These developments led to total transformation of Milosevic and other communist leaders from secularists into staunch nationalists. Milosevic also saw in it an opportunity to became a popular Serb leader. On June 28, 1989 he visited Kosovo together with one million Serbs including a host of national leaders and intellectuals, including many communists, on the occasion of the 600th anniversary of the great battle fought with Turks in which thousands of Serb youths had laid down their lives. Milosevic gave a call to save the Serb nation which was hailed throughout Serbia. Kosovo could more appropriately be described as the Haldighati of Serbs. For centuries the Serb countryside used to resonate with the ballads and ditties of the heroic exploits of the Serb youth who had laid down their lives while defending their motherland and religious faith in the battle of Kosovo in 1389.

The tragedy of the Balkans has an important lesson for mankind, especially the future generations. Frequent religion-based faultline conflicts will break out with increasing frequency in all those countries which are likely to be overwhelmed by the fast paced growth of Muslim population. The numbers of Muslims are on a massive roll almost globally, at least in four continents. It is somewhat premature to say that ultimately radical Islam will achieve through the medium of producing more babies, courtesy the scriptural sanction for multiple wives, a dominant position in the world. That has the potential of securing for them a facile win over democracies which they might not be able to attain otherwise through holy wars. If we go by the dynamics of the latest global demographic trends and the resolve of jihadi militants to continue their long march, there is a strong possibility of such a denouement, perhaps any time during the latter half of the present century.

It is time that the world leaders understood that by virtue of their growing population, in the near future the Muslims are going to be a major force to reckon with which could make the Islamists emerge as a global super power, even to the exclusion of the secular Christian nations led by the U.S.A. For India the threat is more specific. We must not forget that every democratic country is governed by the great numbers game, called elections, based on universal franchise. And the future demographic developments hold the key to that great numbers game as far as India is concerned.

7

Dynamics of India's Demography

"Those who do not learn from history are condemned to repeat it".

– George Santayana

The Indian sub-continent has witnessed certain major demographic changes during the twentieth century which will have far-reaching consequences for the future of the Indian people. Unfortunately the gravity of these population changes has not received any worthwhile attention of our political class. Recently a very detailed and illuminating demographic study has been carried out by Dr. A.P. Joshi, M.D. Srinivas and J.K. Bajaj giving an insight into the latest trends in India's population. The voluminous study, based on empirical research, shows that according to the pattern of demographic changes which have occurred during the twentieth century, the Indian civilization is already under tremendous squeeze, if not under a virtual siege. It could meet a fate similar to that of Lebanon and parts of the Balkans where the majority community was reduced to minority status by demographic changes within a few decades. In India a secular trend of continuous decline in the population of Indian religionists (a term devised by the researchers to include Hindus, Sikhs, Jains and Buddhists) in percentage terms has been conclusively established over a period of 110 years, i.e., from 1881 to 1991. What is more alarming is that this trend has gathered speed after partition of the country in 1947.

The census data of six decades, from 1881 to 1941, reveals that in British India, i.e., before partition, the percentage of Indian

Religionists declined from 78.958 percent to 73.671, while that of Muslims increased from 19.969 percent to 24.280.[1] The total population of India in these sixty years grew at a compounding rate of 0.74 percent per annum. Population of the adherents of religions of Indian origin rose at a somewhat lower rate of 0.62 percent per annum, while that of other Religionists rose almost twice as fast, at a rate of 1.14 percent per annum. Amongst adherents of Other Religions, Christians grew the fastest with an average annual growth rate of 2.41 percent; Muslims, the largest community in this group, recorded a rate of growth of 1.07 percent per annum, three fourths higher than that of Hindus.[2]

Between 1901 to 1941, the population figures for the Indian Union (i.e., Bharat) show that the population of Indian Religionists declined from 86.640 to 84.438 percent, while that of Muslims rose from 12.209 percent to 13.380 in four decades.[3] Indian Union conducted its first census after independence and partition in 1951. Since then regular census has been taken every ten years. An analysis of the census data for the four decades, from 1951 to 1991, shows that the total population of the Indian Religionists rose from 315,001,000 to 720,100,000, while that of the Muslims rose from 37,661,000 to 106,552,000. Thus in terms of percentage, the population of Indian Religionists declined from 87.237 in 1951 to 85.088 in 1991, while that of Muslims increased from 10.430 to 12.590 per cent during those forty years. In post-independence era, in percentage terms the population of Christians remained almost static, it being 2.334 per cent in 1951 and 2.322 in 1991.[4] As a consequence of partition, the proportion of the Indian Religionists in Indian Union increased by about 3 percentage points between 1941 and 1951 and that of the Muslims declined by about the same percentage. But the most significant point is that in the forty years between 1951 and 1991, the proportion of Indian Religionists has continuously declined; by 1991 the relative proportion of Indian Religionists and Muslims has come nearer to the proportion that prevailed in 1941, before partition.[5] After independence the population of the Indian Union continued to grow at a slower rate than that of Pakistan and Bangladesh. And, within the Indian Union, Indian Religionists continued to have a lower rate of growth than that of the Muslims, though they almost caught up with the Christians. Between 1941 and 1951, the proportion of Indian Religionists in Indian Union temporarily increased from 84.44 to 87.24 per cent - primarily due to massive influx of non-Muslims from Pakistan. In the forty years between 1951 and 1991, it has come down to 85.09 per cent. The proportion of Muslims during the same period has increased from 10.43 to 12.59 percent, thus reaching near the pre-partition level of 13.38 percent recorded in 1941. The proportion of Christians has not changed significantly in these forty years.[6] The growth of Muslims and Christians has not been uniform over the whole of the Indian Union. The increases are concentrated in various pockets; this has led to the formation of several clusters within Indian Union, where the proportion of Indian Religionists in the population is getting sharply eroded.[7]

The rapidly changing population profile of Assam, West Bengal, Bihar and Uttar Pradesh should be a matter of concern to everyone, especially those political leaders who have national stature and share a futuristic perspective of the country's unity and integriy. For instance, in Assam within eight decades from 1901 and 1991, the percentage of Indian Religionists registered a steep decline of 26.30 points, falling from 84.55 to 68.25 percent, while that of the Muslims almost doubled, rising spectacularly from 15.03 to 28.43 percent.[8] At least in four districts of Dhubri, Barpeta, Hailakundi and Karimganj Muslims are reported to have become the majority community. Quite a few more districts are likely to follow suit in another decade. Similarly in West Bengal, Muslims have reportedly become majority community in at least two districts of Murshidabad and Malda, while West Dinajpur and Birbhum may soon follow suit. Again certain districts of Uttar Pradesh like Rampur, Bijnor, Moradabad, Saharanpur, Muzaffarnagar and Bareily are likely to become Muslim majority districts within the next one or two decades. In Bihar, Muslims are already an overwhelming majority in Kishanganj district with a 65.91 percent share in population, while some other districts like Araria, Katihar, Sahibganj, Darbhanga and Pashchimi Champaran have witnessed rapid growth in their numbers and percentage.

In the sensitive border state of Assam, which has witnessed numerous faultline conflicts, the decline in the share of Indian Religionists has been almost phenomenal. Their proportion has been dwindling continuously from decade to decade since 1901; it was 84.55 percent in 1901, declined to 75.80 percent by 1931 and further to 73.32 percent in 1951, when the proportion of Indian Religionists increased almost everywhere else as result of partition causing millions of Hindus and Sikhs to migrate from the neighbouring country, which later on split into Pakistan and Bangladesh.[9] During 1951-1991, the Indian Religionists in Assam lost another five percentage points, with their population declining to 68.25 percent in 1991. Thus between 1901 and 1991, the share of Indian Religionists has declined by more than 16 percentage points; about two-thirds of the decline took place in the period before independence and the remaining one-third in the four decades since then. Muslims and Christians have both gained at the cost of the Indian Religionists, the share of the Muslims in Assam has risen from 15.03 per cent in 1901 to 28.43 per cent in 1991, and that of the Christians from 0.41 to 3.32 per cent in the same period.[10] The fast pace of the growth of Muslim population in Assam has the potential of converting it into a Muslim majority state within the next twenty to thirty years time because of the operation of twin causative factors of their higher fertility rate and the unabated influx of Bangladeshis. The fate of the Hindus in West Bengal is only a shade better. In that State, the proportion of Indian Religionists declined from 70.18 per cent in 1901 to 69.29 per cent in 1931; it rose to 79.85 per cent in 1951 mainly as a result of partition, and in the four decades following independence and partition, it has declined by 3.6 percentage points to 75.82 per cent in 1991. The corresponding share of Muslims in State's population has increased from 19.46 per cent in 1951 to 23.61 per cent.[11] Similar trends of rapid decline in the percentage of the Hindu population and the substantial increase in the percentage of the Muslims have also been established in the States of Bihar and Uttar Pradesh, both of which constitute the heartland of India. The latest census data for the decade ending 2001, showing the religious break up of the population patterns in various States, is yet to be published. But on the basis of the past secular trend, it can be categorically stated that the population figures of Assam, West Bengal and the communally sensitive States of Uttar Pradesh and Bihar will reflect a further rise in the proportion of Muslims and a corresponding decline in the numbers of Hindus. Most demographers admit this. The conclusions reached in the research study titled *Religious Demography of India* are not new. The trend was quite visible in the census figures of 1991. It has been re-confirmed now. When presented with a map and statistical chart, only a cynic can remain unaffected by the alarming growth of Muslim presence in the border belt comprising Bahraich, Gonda, Basti, Gorakhpur and Deoria of eastern U.P., Champaran, Muzzafarpur, Darbhanga, Saharsa, Purnia and Santhal Parganas districts of Bihar; West Dinajpur, Malda, Birbhum and Murshidabad of West Bengal, and Goalpara, Kamrup, Darrang and Nagaon of Assam.[12] Muslim population in this belt is said to touch 28 per cent, a decadal increase of seven per cent, in four decades. Other pockets of high Muslim growth include western U.P., Cachar (Assam) and Kolkata (West Bengal).[13]

By limiting their analysis to bare statistical parameters, the researchers have refrained from commenting on some controversial socio-economic and cultural issues which India might face as a result of these population changes. Even while avoiding the issue of India's failure to assert its civilisational ethos after independence, they have candidly pointed out that religion, particularly the large presence of a religious community in compact border regions, was the cause of partition less than six decades ago.[14] The research has conclusively established the rapid growth of Muslim numbers along the country's sensitive borders which could spell trouble in the decades ahead from the law and order point of view. Clearly there is a message in the statistics which India can ill-afford to ignore. The lesson of history is that many a monotheistic creed, especially the Islam, has always found it difficult to peacefully co-exist with other religious groups. We need to recognise the gravity of the situation, defend our civilisational identity and take pride in our national genius.[15]

Ordinarily a moderate population growth of any religious group, in terms of percentage or absolute numbers, need not cause alarm.

But when such rapid growth in numbers, having the potential to radically alter the demographic religious balance in a country, is accompanied by multiple acts of terror and killings in the name of holy war or 'jihad', the concerned nation must sit up, take notice and counter the menace. The jihad being waged against India by the ISI of Pakistan and allied outfits like Al Qaeda and Lashkar-e-Tayyeba is a fact of contemporary history. And there is more to it. Not many Indians know that a Pakistan-sponsored terrorist organization of Bangladesh is now laying claim to West Bengal. The fundamentalist Islamist outfit, Shahadat-e al- Hikima, the formation of which was announced by its chief Syed Kawsar Hussain Siddique, on February 6, 2003, has been propagating that it considers West Bengal as a part of Bangladesh and advocates its occupation by the latter.[16] It is reported to have been funded by the underworld don, Dawood Ibrahim, now at long last declared by the U.S.A. as an international terrorist, by sending an instalment of Rs.140 crore Takas, for anti-India terrorist activities. Although on paper this terrorist outfit has been banned by the Bangladesh government, it continues to be quite active and is believed to be running many terrorist training camps at the behest of the ISI, in the area around Rajshahi. They are propagating the ideology of claiming West Bengal, as part of the Muslim Bangladesh, with the support of the ISI and Al Qaeda. It is well known that Dawood Ibrahim was responsible for the 1993 serial bomb blasts in Mumbai in which hundreds of innocent people were killed. The launch of Shahadat-e al-Hikima at the instance of the ISI has to be viewed in the light of the growing talibanization of Bangladesh and rapid growth in the activities of the ISI and Al Qaeda in that country. Dawood Ibrahim, wanted since long time by India in many cases of terrorism, including Mumbai bomb blasts, is a known protégé of the ISI. He has been sheltered and protected by the ISI and Pakistan government now for more than one decade.

As the proportion of Muslim population increases and that of Hindus declines further, say during the next 30 or 40 years, the incidence of faultline conflicts between the two major communities, the Hindus and the Muslims, is likely to increase dramatically. Not learning this simple lesson from the history of civil wars in Lebanon and the Balkans could be a major political failure and blunder, especially with the backdrop of the events leading to India's partition on religious grounds. The history of Lebanon is a classic example of a devastating politico-religious civil war caused by the massive population changes resulting from fertility differences between the Christian and Muslim population groups. The epoch-making geopolitical transformation took barely fifty years to complete. Not many Indians know that in the year 1900 the Maronite Christians constituted 77.32 per cent of Lebanon's population, while Muslims were barely 20.49 percent.[17] During the next four decades the proportion of Muslims rose rapidly, coming close to parity with Christians. In terms of a 1943 agreement, known as the National Pact of Lebanon, it was decided to share the political authority between the two religious groups, the Christians and the Muslims, in proportion to their respective strength in the national population. Posts of top ministers were apportioned between the Christians and the Muslims in a six-to-five ratio, as per the figures revealed in the country's 1932 census. At that time the Christians had a thin majority of approximately nine per cent over the Muslims. The two important top posts of the President and the Prime Minister were to be shared by the two communities, the President being a Christian and the Prime Minister a Muslim. Subsequent population counts showed a pronounced difference between the Christian and Muslim fertility. Despite widespread awakening among Maronite Christians, who were more alert and better educated, and efforts of their clergy and community leaders to motivate them to have more babies, the declining trend in the fertility of Christians could not be reversed. In early 1970s the Christian community had a declining fertility rate of less than four children per woman, while Muslims had an estimated fertility rate of six children per woman. By then the percentage of Christians had fallen to 53.71, from 77.32 in 1900. After that it was a steep downhill slide for the Christian numbers. By 1975 Lebanon became a Muslim majority country. As a warning of the coming events casting their shadow before, the faultline conflicts between the two groups had already started rising sharply prior to the climactic demographic change. Even before Muslims acquired the majority status, ferocious civil war had started raging throughout the country wreaking havoc on the civillian population —just as it happened in Kosovo and Bosnia regions of the Balkans. Ultimately the heavily armed Lebanese Muslim militias, raising the battle cry of jihad and supported by various Muslim countries surrounding Lebanon, emerged victorious in the 1990s. Since then the Christians are being squeezed out of that country. Luckily they happen to be the well-educated, adventurous types and have a number of Christian countries to turn to. Ever since 1970s, Christians have been migrating out, under the growing threat of an aggressive Muslim majority. The demographic profile of Indonesia has been similarly tilting in favour of the Muslims, their proportion in population having gone up from 40 per cent in 1900 to almost 55 percent in 1990.[18] They are now estimated at 75 to 80 per cent of the total population. No wonder at present Indonesia is in the grip of radical Islam; this happened largely due to the vast demographic changes. Nigeria, too, is at present witnessing growing hostility and faultline conflicts between the Christians and the Muslims, because in percentage terms the population of Muslims has increased from 25.93 in 1900 to 43.89 in 1990.[19] Rapid growth in the numbers of Muslims is now a worldwide phenomenon in most countries and their population often tends to outpace other religious groups almost universally. At this rate, Macedonia in Europe and India in Asia, could be the next two target countries for take-over or partial take-over by the Islamist jihadis, unless some other factors intervene in the meantime. Demography, as we know, is a complex science. Apart from the high fertility rate of the Muslims, Macedonia is facing the problem of large scale Muslim influx from Albania and Bosnia both of which have the highest fertility rates in Europe. The same factors have been operating in the rapidly changing demographic profile of India. Both Pakistan and Bangladesh have a higher fertility rate than India.

Basically it is due to the dynamics of demography that Muslims feel confident that the "21st century will be the century of Islam" —as emphasized by Akbar S. Ahmed, a Pakistani scholar, who lectures at the Ibn Khaldun Chair of Islamic Studies, American University, Washington D.C.[20] He draws attention to the fact that there are nearly 1.3 billion Muslims living in 55 countries, one of them being nuclear. Another one-third live in non-Muslim countries, while about 25 million Muslims live in the West, including 7 million in the U.S.A. and two million in the U.K. Their world population is the fastest growing across the globe and that Islam in one religion which is on collision course with all other world religions. He seems to take pride in the fact that due to a unique combination of geo-political factors, Islam is in confrontation with all "the major world religions: Judaism in the Middle East, Christianity in the Balkans, Chechenya, Nigeria, Sudan and sporadically in the Philippines and Indonesia; Hinduism in South Asia and after the Taliban blew up the statues in Bamiyan, Buddhism."[21]

Despite Islam being pitted against every major world religion, a vast majority of the Muslims believe that ultimately Islam will emerge as victorious because they consider it to be a superior faith which ensures its ready acceptability and popularity. But that kind of claim is also made by the votaries of many other religions, including Christianity and Buddhism. Actually the core of the strong belief of Islamists in the invincibility of their faith comes from the widespread consciousness about their fast growing numbers across the globe and willingness of the faithful to court martyrdom while waging jihad. Most Islamic scholars seldom fail to sing paens to the long record of the conquests made by the warriors of Islam in medieval times through holy wars and repose enormous confidence in the growing tribe of suicide bombers among Muslims which they feel will surely make them victorious in this holy war.

India has a nine hundred years long history of repetitive conflicts with Islam which dates back to the eighth century when Arabs set their foot on the Indian soil. Even when the Mughal empire was at its zenith, the resistance to the alien rule and culture at the grass root level continued to surface every now and then, in one form or another, like it did under the leadership of Rana Pratap in Rajasthan, Shivaji in Maharashtra and Guru Gobind Singh in the Punjab. Additionally there is an unfortunate legacy of communal riots which continued to erupt from time to time in various parts of the sub-continent during the British rule, right from 1889 onwards till the partition in 1947. Huntington calls these religious clashes as faultline conflicts. The long tortuous history of communal riots in India during the decades preceding the partition and the two examples of the dire fate which overtook Lebanon and the former composite state of Yugoslavia in the Balkans underline the strong likelihood of the religion-based faultline conflicts plaguing the Indian sub-continent in the decades to come. Historically, changes in the population profiles of different religious groups have often been the main source of communal divide, faultline conflicts and dismemberment of countries. The phenomenon of partition or dismemberment of a country becomes a greater possibility wherever the population gain is in favour of the Muslims. Huntington has exemplified how demographic changes tend to create tensions between the concerned religious groups because of the identity crisis. For dealing with identity crisis, what counts for most people are the relationships based on blood and belief, faith and family. Most people rally to those with similar ancestry, religion, language, values and institutions and tend to distance themselves from those with different ones.[22] The events of Balkans illustrate this point succinctly. During the Cold War, Greece and Turkey were in the NATO, Bulgaria and Romania were part of the Warsaw Pact. But once Cold War was over, all these alignments broke and gave way to civilizational ties rooted in Islam and Orthodoxy. The Balkans leaders now talk of forging a Greek-Serb-Bulgarian Orthodox Christian alliance. The Prime Minister of Greece feels that the Balkans wars have revived the resonance of their old Orthodox bond. It was dormant, but now due to the latest developments in the Balkans, it is again taking shape. In difficult times people seek identity and roots in search of security to defend themselves. Similar thoughts were echoed by Serbia's main opposition party which felt that the situation in south-eastern Europe will soon require the formation of a new Balkans alliance of Orthodox Christian countries, including Serbia, Bulgaria and Greece, in order to resist the encroachment of Islam.[23] In an overview of the emerging scenario of faultline conflicts, Huntington points out that in Russia Orthodox Belarus, Moldova and Ukraine will gravitate towards Russia, while Armenians and Azeris will fight each other. The Russian army will fight Muslim fundamentalists in Chechenya and Tajikistan. The neighbouring Muslim countries (part of the former Soviet Union) will try to develop economic and political relationships between themselves and with their Muslim neighbours. Turkey, Iran and Saudi Arabia will continue to work for cultivating relations with these new Muslim states. In the Indian subcontinent, India and Pakistan will remain at loggerheads over Kashmir where fighting will intensify, and within India, new conflicts will arise between the Muslim and the Hindu fundamentalists.[24]

Like the Balkans and Lebanon, India too has a long history of religion-based faultline conflicts, often referred to as communal disturbances. It has become fashionable to blame the British rule for the almost perennial hostility between the Hindus and the Muslims, as reflected in the frequent outbreaks of communal riots. But that is incorrect. Surely the British rulers did practise the policy of divide and rule, epitomised in the Roman motto, *Divide et impera*, and in the process tried to favour the Muslims. But that alone cannot explain the ferocity of the Hindu-Muslim riots witnessed throughout the British rule. It must be admitted that the Hindu-Muslim discord is firmly rooted in the Indian history of one millenium. It cannot be wished away peremptorily. The Europeans had come to India as merchants, while Islam entered India's northern border as an aggressor. The conquest it undertook was not merely territorial but religious.[25] Ever since 327 B C when Alexander invaded India there have been many invasions notably by Bactrian Greeks, Sakas, Kushans and Huns which could do no more than injuring India physically. But they did not traumatise the collective psyche of the Indian people.[26] Unlike Muslim invaders, the Greeks and the Kushans did not take recourse to mass killings and plunder of innocent masses nor did they try to decimate the religious and cultural ethos of the Indian society. But the Islamic invaders were of a different genre. They subjected the Indian masses to large scale oppression for centuries, including recourse to forcible conversions, the scars of which are deeply entrenched in the Indian psyche. Hindus find it difficult to forget that traumatic past. And unfortunately, many Muslims of the sub-continent who are mostly descendants of the Hindus forcibly converted during the oppressive alien rule, often brag about having ruled over Hindus for centuries, not realising the truth about their own roots. That creates further complications, and promotes greater hostility between the two communities. The classical example of one such vitriolic outburst was that of Zulfiqar Ali Bhutto, a former Prime Minister of Pakistan, who once boasted that Muslims had ruled over cowardly Hindus for one thousand years and that they would do so again. A befitting reply to that morbid statement was given by the late Justice M.C. Chhagla, himself a Muslim, by reminding Bhutto that by hurling abuses at the Hindus, he was only denigrating his own forefathers. Truth also dawned upon Bhutto but only when death stared him in the face during imprisonment by General Zia. It was only then that Bhutto poignantly remembered the great tradition of truth and tolerance cultivated by the great Indian civilization, dating back to the times of Ashoka the Great and even earlier. In that twilight hour of his life, Bhutto realized the telling difference between the sublimated civilizational values of the Indian culture, in sharp contrast with the brutal sub-cultural practices imported from the alien lands of Arabia and the Middle East.

Many historians, mostly left oriented, often overlook the truth and even try to distort history by emphasizing that before the arrival of the British there were no communal riots. It is difficult to guess whether such assertions are made due to sheer naivette or by deliberate design. They ignore the basic fact that during the long spell of Muslim rule there could be no question of any communal disturbances or riots in India because the Hindus had been totally subjugated by the Muslim rulers. Occasionally there was some resistance to Muslim oppression in some far away corner but that was sporadic, and mostly symbolic. The backbone of the Hindu resistance had been broken and their will to fight the tyranny severely restricted. Even the gutsy Maratha warriors had lost to the marauding troops of Ahmed Shah Abdali in 1761 in the third battle of Panipat. So where was the question of the Hindus ever daring to start a communal riot, leave alone opposing the ruling Muslim community on any issue? The very thought is preposterous. There were occasional communal confrontations during the Muslim rule, too. But there could be no rioting by the Hindus. Any attempt on the part of the Hindus to assert their legitimate rights or act against the wishes of the neighbourhood Muslims, was treated as an uprising and put down with a heavy hand and often followed by strong reprisals. This had happened off and on even in the vicinity of Delhi, in the area now called Mewat. Ultimately the headstrong and turbulent Mewatis, both Rajput and Jat Hindus, were tamed by the medium of repression and then forced to convert to Islam. The same thing happened to Malkana Rajputs in the rural belt of Agra. The Hindus of Katihar in Bihar and several other parts of India faced similar persecution. The average Hindu was just not allowed to assert his rights nor permitted any self-respect. Owing to the overload of abject slavery and persecution carried by generations of Hindus, their guts were in tatters and excepting pockets of resistance here and there, say in Maharashtra which had undergone a Hindu resurgence under Shivaji or parts of Rajasthan where the folklore of valiant Rana Pratap who had the daring to cross swords with the army of mighty Akbar, sometimes made Hindus hold their head high. A number of historians, ranging from Lanepool, Titus and R.C. Majumdar to Will Durant have graphically described how Indian civilization was ravaged and plundered under the Muslim rule. A large numbers of Hindus were forcibly converted to Islam. Those wanting to escape conversion had to pay the impost called jiziya. As a result of the oppressive policies practised by the alien rulers, millions of Indians were reduced to the status of hewers of wood and drawers of water. The sole exception to the overall atmosphere of shame and sullenness of the Hindu society were the Sikhs of Punjab whom the great Guru Gobind Singh had infused with a new vigour to oppose tyranny and defend not only their motherland but also protect the meek and submissive Hindu masses from among whom they had been moulded into Khalsa. It was only after the rise of the Sikh power in Punjab that the annual blight of invaders and looters descending into India from across the Khyber and Bolan passes stopped playing havoc with the hapless populace. Not only did the Sikh warriors led by generals like Hari Singh Nalwa and Sham Singh Atariwala put the fear of God into the hearts of invaders, for a change they also trounced the belligerent Afghans and made king Shujah of Afghanistan pay an annual tribute, ban cow slaughter and return the plundered gates of the historic Somnath temple. The Sikhs demonstrated how a motivated people, fired with the zeal to re-win their lost pride and honour, could turn the tide against bands of ruthless marauders.

Who can forget that when the Pandits of Kashmir valley, came under severe pressure, on orders of Aurangzeb either to convert to Islam or face death, they rushed to Guru Tegh Bahadur, father of Guru Gobind Singh, for the shelter and succour of his temporal and spiritual strength to escape Aurangzeb's wrath. Sometime a question is asked that why did the Sikh soldiers of Punjab support the British rulers during the mutiny of 1857, also described as the first war of India's independence. The answer is simple. Having borne the brunt of the despotic Muslim rule for centuries, Sikhs had the farsight to discern that it was better to suffer the privations of serving under the British than to allow the horrors of Muslim rule to revisit India. It was only after 1857 that a mass awakening seized the sullen Hindu masses which ultimately gave birth to the concept of Indian nationalism which, for all practical purposes, came up as the resurgent Hindu nationalism. The truth is that the phenomenon of communal riots started in the late nineteenth century only after Hindus regained their lost confidence and self-respect under the British rule as a result of the enlightenment acquired from western education which enabled them to stand up to communal fanaticism. To that extent perhaps our leftist friends might like to blame the Hindu community, more than the British rulers, for mustering the courage to stand up for their self-respect when Muslims were no longer the rulers. In doing so perhaps they will be nearer to truth.

Throughout British rule religious disturbances broke out with unabated fury almost every year. For example, between 1889-93, seven disturbances broke out in Bombay (now Maharashtra), 46 in Bengal, 9 in N.W.P. (North West Province) and Oudh (present Uttar Pradesh), 17 in Madras (which comprised Tamil Nadu, parts of Andhra, Kerala and Ganjam district of Orissa), 1 in Punjab and 3 in Hyderabad. Again between 1923-26, riots broke out at 71 places and were responsible for over 3000 injured and 260 deaths.[27] According to the opinion of the masses these disturbances broke out on such issues as cow-killing; playing of music before mosques; the construction and demolition of mosques; coincidence of Hindu and Muslim festivals; obstruction in each other's place of worship and in festivals. But the educated classes attributed these to such causes as the increasing heat of religious, political and race discussion, which could be seen from the struggle for government posts, the question of separate representation; the proximity of census; the growing irritation of Muslims with the Swadeshi agitation coupled with agrarian and social disturbances; Muslim extra-territorial sympathies and lastly to the missionary or proselytizing movements.[28] In November 1912, serious Hindu-Muslim disturbances took place in Ajodhya (Ayodhaya) and Faizabad in the United Provinces (i.e., present U.P.) over the sacrifice of cows on the occasion of the Id-uz-Zuha. In October 1916 two serious Hindu Muslim disturbances occurred in the Patna District on the occasion of Bakr-Id.[29]

The communal situation deteriorated substantially after the Moplah rebellion of 1920 caused by the Khilafat Committee's call for jihad in which the Hindus suffered enormously. Thereafter frequency of communal riots began to rise sharply. Though there was lull in 1922-23, the relations between the two communities were strained throughout 1923-24. One of the worst communal riots took place in Kohat (N.W.F.P.) on September 9 and 10, 1924 in which total casualties were 155 killed and many wounded. As a result of the reign of terror the whole Hindu population was evacuated from Kohat. They could return only after several weeks, when it was agreed to drop prosecutions against the rioters.[30] In the summer months of 1924 there was a distressing number of riots. In July, severe fighting broke out between the Hindus and the Muslims in Delhi resulting in serious casualties. In the same month there was again an outbreak of riot at Nagpur. August was even worse. There were riots at Lahore, Lucknow, Moradabad, Bhagalpur and Nagpur in British India; while a severe affray took place at Gulbarga in the Nizam's dominion. The months of September-October saw severe fighting at Lucknow, Shahjahanpur, Kakinada and Allahabad. In 1925-26 the antagonism between the Hindus and the Muslims became more widespread. A very significant feature of the Hindu-Muslim rioting which took place during this period was its wide distribution and its occurrence, in some cases, in small villages.[31] In his lucid treatise, Pakistan or Partition of India, Dr. Ambedkar has given graphic details of many communal riots which took place year after year in various parts of the country, in the decades following the Moplah rebellion and during subsequent years, before the actual partition of the country. Once in a while the British might have favoured a particular community but there is no empirical evidence to support the oft-repeated allegation that they were responsible for promoting communal strife between the two communities, excepting the solitary instance of the Direct Action Day rioting in August, 1946, in Calcutta. It is a fact that communal riots were a regular feature of the Indian political scene from the eighties of the nineteenth century right up to the year of the partition of the country, i.e., 1947. The years 1946 and 1947 witnessed the biggest communal carnage ever witnessed in the istory of modern world. What was more shameful was that neither the British nor the Congress leadership did anything worthwhile to prevent it, although the country had already been awash with communal frenzy for the previous two years. The threat of massive communal clashes was looming large over the horizon of the sub-continent since the Calcutta killings of August 16, 1946, when the Muslim League gave a call for jihad against the Hindus. The threat of communal carnage was so obvious that even the blind could see it, smell it and feel it in the air! But no preventive strategy was devised. Looking to the past history of communal conflicts and the latest demographic changes taking place in the sub-continent, the phenomenon of growing communal tensions and recrudescence of faultline religious conflicts is likely to pose a formidable challenge to the Indian state in the near future—say at the most within the next two to three decades. The growing tension and mutual suspicion between the two communities is already in the air because of repetitive attacks by the Islamist terrorists on innocent civilians, Hindu yatris and on the temples of Raghunathji in Jammu and Akshardham in Gujarat. In the recent years the continued influx of Bangladeshi Muslims into India has further muddied the communal scene. According to a rough estimate there could be approximately thirty million Bangladeshi migrants and their progeny in India and their silent invasion through the porous border continues unabated. The serious dimensions of the problem were highlighted by Bibhuti Bhusan Nandy, a retired senior officer of the Cabinet Secretariat in a well-researched study published sometime ago.[32] He drew attention to an incisive analysis of the 1991 Bangladesh census statistics by

Sarifa Begum, a Bangla demographer, which showed that the estimated 104.7 million population of Bangladesh in 1991 had excluded 9-10 millions from the computation. Additionally the census figures were at odds with the Bangladesh government's own projection of a population of 112-114 million in 1991 and the UNDP (United Nations Development Programme) estimate of 116-117 million. Sarifa Begum rightly attributed the 'missing millions' to unregistered 'out-migration'.[33] From the estimates projected by Sarifa Begum, it is clear that between the census decade of 1981-1991 approximately 14 to 15 million Bangladeshis had entered India. There was a sizeable presence of Bangla immigrants in India even before 1981—many stayed on after 1971 war which had led to the liberation of Bangladesh. Many more continued to pour in. But they were mainly concentrated in Assam, West Bengal and parts of Bihar and U.P. till 1980-82 when a massive influx of Bangladeshis started. Between 1980-1991 millions of them managed to spread almost all over India. By now their presence in metropolitan cities like Delhi, Mumbai and Kolkata and numerous small townships runs into millions. Official estimates place the number of Bangladeshis in Delhi at more than 13 lakhs. Mumbai has even a larger number, while Kolkata may have nearabout two million or more. Their deportation has become almost impossible, as admitted by Delhi Police while responding to a High Court directive. They cited various reasons including political pressure and the non-cooperation from corrupt officials. This was stated in a sealed affidavit which the Delhi police filed before the High Court.[34] The 13 lakh illegal Bangladeshi migrants have managed to acquire documents like ration cards, passports and voter identity cards to avail civic facilities which rightful citizens are being deprived of.[35] Illegal Bangla immigrants have also settled in large numbers in cities like Patna, Lucknow, Jaipur, Ajmer, Ahmedabad, and many other towns. India's Defence Minster, George Fernandes, during his visit to Chandigarh on September 27, 2003, confirmed that a large number of Bangladeshis were entering India and altering the demographic character of the North-eastern States. According to the information given to him by the Eastern Command over one lakh Bangladeshis were entering India every year.[36] The influx of Bangladeshi Muslims has been depriving millions of economically backward and poor Indian wage earners, and small farmers, of their work-a-day employment and meagre land holdings thereby putting an economic squeeze on the poorest of the poor groups in India.

Unfortunately there has been no realization of the important fact that the illegal migrants from Bangladesh are not qualified professionals nor educated individuals. They are essentially poor wretches who are unable to earn a subsistence wage in their own country. Almost the entire lot of Bangla-Muslim immigrants are illiterate and unskilled petty wage earners owing to which the first victims of their influx are the poorest local Indian labourers and land-tillers who are elbowed out of their professions and lands. In most cases the immigrants start by offering to work on a lower wage and then gradually worm their way up and spread their wings. This process has been creating tensions both on economic and religious grounds in several parts of the country. Unfortunately our self-centred politicians do not realize that by out-migrating between 20 to 30 million poor and illiterate miserable wage-earners and their progeny (which too must be in millions by now), the Bangladesh government has transferred approximately fifteen to twenty percent of their poverty and an equal percentage of illiteracy to India. This has added to the economic burden of the Indian people and increased unemployment, while to Bangladesh it has provided corresponding relief both in economic growth and promotion of literacy in that country. Interestingly, the political parties sustaining their growth through the culture of minority vote bank comprising Bangladeshis are guilty of depriving the poorest of the poor Indian citizens of their bread and butter. The Bangla immigration has been pushing down the poverty stricken marginalized Indians, mostly in Bengal and other poor states like Orissa, Assam and Bihar, into deeper depths of penury. By denying the problem of Bangladeshi influx the Communists, Marxists and other leftist outfits have been functioning in a manner totally inimical to the interests of the weaker sections of society in whose name they have always captured political power. Another important implication of this ever-growing problem is that the continuing silent invasion of Bangladeshis has become a major obstacle in raising the threshhold level of poverty in the country, especially in West Bengal, Assam and Orissa. Their growing numbers have acted as a drag on India's economic development. But this out-migration of approximately 30 million people has given a big push to the prosperity of Bangladesh and upgraded that country's GDP and literacy level, almost dramatically. If this massive immigration was curbed, the per capita income of the states like Assam, West Bengal, Tripura, Meghalaya, etc., would have risen much faster. The slow pace of illiteracy eradication, too, is a direct result of this illegal invasion. No Indian economist has tried to assess the economic cost of Bangla influx. Unfortunately most Indian intellectuals do not want to understand this simple 'cause-and-effect' economic phenomenon resulting from illegal entry of 20 to 30 million aliens and the resultant crushing economic burden on India. One of the main reasons of the higher incidence of poverty and hunger in Assam, West Bengal, Bihar, Orissa and U.P. is the growth of Bangladeshi numbers. It can be safely presumed that in addition to the 15 million immigrants who entered India during the census decade of 1981-1991, as estimated by Sarifa Begum, an additional 15 lakhs must have entered during the last 12 years. And if we take into account the numbers which were present in India before 1981 and their progeny, the real figure could cross 30 million. The faultline conflicts likely to arise from unlawful entry of 20-25 million Bangladeshis during the last thirty years, can be ignored only at grave peril to the Indian nation. After lying for decades to their voters, mostly the poor, in a style remniscent of Goebbels, finally even the Communist Party (Marxist) and leftists who had always glossed over this problem because of their commitment to vote-bank politics, conceded in July 2003 that the illegal migration of Bangladeshis has acquired alarming proportions. This marked quite an about-turn by a party which shrugged off fears about Bangladeshis pouring into different parts of the state as an "anti-Muslim campaign."[37] The changed tune, sung by the CPM's state secretary, Anil Biswas, was apparently caused by the dawn of wisdom on the new Chief Minister of West Bengal, Buddhadeb Bhattacharya. Unlike his ultra-secular predecessor, Jyoti Basu, the present Chief Minster candidly admitted that the Central Government's fears of demographic crisis in the border districts of West Bengal and the resultant consequences for the state's security and economic development were true and that this problem deserves attention. The crass administrative ineptitude and inexcusable lack of political will, on the part of successive state governments and even governments at the Centre, is responsible for this gigantic problem which is already causing faultline tremors from north-eastern India to Delhi and Maharashtra. It has become a serious threat to India's national security because now Bangladesh is the commonest route being used by Islamist terrorists for entering India. The persistent denials by Bangladesh Government of the fact of illegal immigration stands fully rebutted by the research carried out by Sarifa Begum, one of their own demographers. The much higher growth rates in Indian districts bordering Bangladesh and significantly lower growth rates in the adjoining areas, extremely low growth in Hindu-concentrated districts and population explosion in urban pockets of West Bengal confirmed the finding. Some statistics tellingly illustrate the point : Greater Jessore and Greater Khulna districts in Bangladesh registered 1.97 and 1.58 per cent growth respectively as against 3.16 per cent in the adjoining North 24 Parganas. Greater Mymensingh had a growth rate of 1.82 per cent against 3.84 per cent in the adjacent Garo Hills district in Meghalaya. Greater Comilla district (Bangladesh) showed 1.89 per cent growth rate against 3.36 per cent in Tripura. Many semi-urban areas of West Bengal have witnessed a virtual population explosion—Gobardanga (8.64 per cent), Khardah (9.5), Raiganj (13.93), Ashoknagar (7.45) Mekhliganj (7.98) and Tufanganj (22.45) —against the 2.45 per cent state average.[38] Like all Muslims, Bangladeshis have a higher fertility rate because of non-acceptance of the small family norm on religious grounds. The massive influx of Bangla Muslims during the last three decades has caused a sharp increase in communal tension and socio-political fissures in Assam and other parts of north-eastern India. This changed demography and the communal balance of the border districts has been generating inter-ethnic and inter-religious tensions. In West Bengal, many Hindus of remote villages in the border belt have been relocating themselves in towns for better security and protection.[39] The resentment against Bangla-immigration now appears to be rising dangerously in India's north-east. Recently an organisation by the name 'the North-East People's Forum' was set up to find ways and means for countering the menace. During his inaugural address on September 19, 2003, at Guwahati in Assam, P.A. Sangma, former Speaker of the Lok Sabha, disclosed that Osama bin Laden was directly financing over 400 madarasas in Bangladesh, which were "training more than 25,000 people to become part of suicide squads". He asserted that he was saying this with full authority, as it was conveyed to him "by the Chairman of the Parliamentarians Committee of South-East Asian Countries, Professor Kabir Choudhry, who is from Bangladesh". An alarming aspect of the problem is that a large number of youth from Assam and other north-eastern states have also joined them. During the last two years, more than 500 non-government organisations have come up in Bangladesh which are preaching fundamentalism.[40] Sangma, who is Vice-Chairman of the Parliamentarians' Committee of Southeast Asian Countries, emphasized that "we cannot remain a silent spectator to the political developments in the neighbouring countries". He clarified that it was not Bangladesh but Pakistan which was using Bangla territory to create unrest in India and reminded the audience that at the time of Bangladesh's liberation, the then Prime Minister of Pakistan, Z.A. Bhutto, had remarked that the war had just begun; it will continue for the next one hundred years. Incidentally, Sangma is not a Hindu. He is a practising Christian and a patriot of the highest order.

As pointed out by Bibhuti Bhusan Nandy, the presence of nearly 15 per cent of another country's population in India underscores the significant erosion of our national sovereignty. It is a pity that India has no say in "who comes in and who stays on in this country". In Assam and West Bengal, votes by foreigners decisively influence election results in an increasingly large number of parliamentary and state assembly constituencies. The rise of Islamic fundamentalism and spread of the jehadi spirit in Bangladesh have turned the illegal immigrants into a potent source of subversion.[41]

Some analysts believe that the number of illegal Bangla immigrants who entered India during the last three decades plus the sum total of their subsequent fast growing progeny, due to high fertility rate, could be larger than the total births prevented in a span of five years through the family planning campaign in the country. That kind of large influx of migrants could lead to huge socio-economic upheavals resulting in a repetition of the kind of communal strife witnessed in the pre-partition years. It is a foreboding scenario. If the communal confrontation gathers momentum, there could be eruption of large scale faultline conflicts in various parts of the country, just as had happened in the twenties, thirties and forties of the last century when Hindu Muslim riots became order of the day. The last three decades have already witnessed increased polarisation between the two communities. The causes for this growing divide are many and varied, including the Ayodhaya imbroglio and the long standing objection of Muslims to the singing of Vande Matram which they have continued to oppose right from the pre-partition days. The persistent opposition of Muslim groups to a uniform civil code and the resurgence of radical Islam manifesting itself in relentless bomb blasts across the country, including the frequent killings of innocent and unarmed pilgrims proceeding to Amarnath and Vaishnodevi are just straws in the wind. These ghastly events are already causing both grief and anger among Hindus. Unfortunately many media analysts and columnists have a tendency to turn Nelson's eye to the ground realities. It has become fashionable among them to blame the concept of Hindutava and the so-called Hindu militancy for the growth of communal politics in the country. Their understanding of this serious problem and the issues involved is both superficial and simplistic; it only shows their enormous bias. With their eyes wide shut they can't see the long list of Hindu temples throughout the country which are being security protected from attacks by terrorists—including the famous Tirumala temple situated in the far away south. They pretend not to know that in recent years a number of temples have been attacked, including Akshardham and the famous Raghunath temple of Jammu. The latter was attacked twice. If a Press Trust of India report is to be believed, even the make-shift Ram temple at Ayodhya is under threat of attack by Lashkar-e Tayyeba jihadis.[42] The leftists remain heartlessly unmoved by the senseless killings of innocent, unarmed Hindu pilgrims to Amarnath, year after year, almost on a regular basis, and the recent killings of those going to Vaishnodevi. Even after writing and reading so much about the death and destruction caused by more than half a dozen bomb blasts which rocked Mumbai between December 2002 and August 2003, they continue to blame Hindus and the Hindutava wave for the communal unrest sweeping the country. It is surprising how any rational and even minimally educated person can miss the vital point that a major part of the turmoil taking place in the Hindu society is not the creation of the forces of Hindutava. It is a direct consequence of the depredations of the protagonists of radical Islam operating from Pakistan and Bangladesh, and some supporters of their cause embedded in the Indian society—howsoever small their numbers might be. One such example is Dr. Jalees Ansari, originally a medico from Mumbai's V.N. Desai Hospital, now involved in more than thirty bombings across the country and presently lodged in the Ajmer jail. He is a typical supporter of the jihadi campaign. He is an Indian, but a member of the Ahl-e Hadees, a puritannical Islamic outfit. Ansari believes in waging jihad against kafirs and has become a role model for many motivated Muslim youth for terrorist acts. Dr. Ansari has many comrades. One of them is C.A.M. Basheer, an engineer from Kerala. Another is Janab, full name Tahir Ali Nisar Ahmed, a close confidante of Ansari, who is a specialist in making bombs. Both are on the run. There are many more like Dr. Ansari and Janab in Mumbai, Malegaon, Solapur, Hyderabad, Delhi and even in Bangalore. A handful have been caught, others are still at large.

Among those charged with the bombing of a local train of Mumbai in December 2002, are educated Muslims, a chemical engineer, a doctor and a computer expert—all three of them are educated professionals with good family backgrounds. None of them was unemployed, none lived in poverty and none belonged to Gujarat or Kashmir. The clue to their proclivity for terror lies in the fact that they are all committed to the Islamic doctrine of jihad. Investigations into the twin bomb blasts in Mumbai on August 25, 2003, in which 53 persons were killed and 153 injured, have revealed that Hyderabad has become the hub of terrorist activities. It has acquired the contours of a city infested with hundreds of terrorists. In Pandya murder case also the trail of the dastardly crime had led the police to Hyderabad. Mumbai and Delhi have been the prime targets of terrorist attacks in recent years—perhaps Mumbai has been a notch higher in the target list. Frankly speaking, so many terror attacks across the country could not have taken place without some kind of local support. And dozens of such attacks, including those on pilgrims and temples, were taking place even before the Gujarat riots. It is no use shutting one's eyes to the inconvenient truth. Apart from the promptings by the ISI, the roots of the growing trend among Muslim youth of India towards jihadi ideology lie in the continuing propagation of the fundamentalist version of Islam by several leaders of the community and their staunch opposition to modernity. They insist on maintaining total supremacy of Sharia and orthodoxy. On September 21, 2003, the Uttar Pradesh Chapter of Jamiat Ulema-e-Hind (JUH) had organized a 20,000 strong Jalsa-e-Alam rally at Jyotiba Phule Stadium, Lucknow, to voice the concerns of the Indian Muslims.[43] Some of the views aired by the speakers were quite bizarre as well as somewhat frightening, as would be seen from a sample reproduced below:

1. Set up Sharia Panchayats for settling disputes between Muslims.
2. Killing of infidels is jihad.
3. Religious madarasas be established in every village throughout the country.
4. Globally there are attacks against mosques, madarasas, Quran and such Islamic symbols as beard, veil and Islamic dress code. They want to discourage Islamic norms and want everyone to be brought in the mainstream.
5. Fight the evil of co-education.
6. TV channels glamorising vulgarity have badly affected the Islamic culture. It has discouraged the purdah system. Muslim women should stick to purdah strictly.
7. The country, in fact, belongs to the minorities who together constitute the majority.

This action plan of the Jamiat, or their charter, did not differ much from the manifesto of the Taliban. That indeed was the essence of the goals set forth by the Jamiat Ulema-e-Hind.[44] The assertion that India belongs to the minorities who together constitute the majority reveals a dangerous anti-Hindu mindset. If this is the line of thinking of the so-called moderate Muslims today when Hindus are still in a comfortable majority, one shudders to think of what would happen to India when the Muslims grow to the near parity status in terms of population. At this rally were present some of the leading lights of India's several political parties - the Congress, the Bahujan Samaj Party and the Samajwadi Party.[45] None of them objected to the half-truths, none showed the daring to contradict the communal rhetoric and the retrograde agenda being propagated among the Muslim masses to poison their minds. A similar action plan was advocated in the presidential address of Amir Al-Hind Hazrat Molana Syed Asad Madani, President, Jamiat Ulema-e-Hind (JUH) at Delhi on March 9, 2003. Incidentally in the year 1999 in Assam, the Goalpara district Vice-President of Jamiat-e-Ulema-e-Hind, Maulana Mohammed Muslim Ali alias Muslimuddin, had been arrested for sending Muslim youth to Pakistan to undergo arms training. He had visited Pakistan on five occasions and five passports, including bogus ones, were seized from him. He was also the chief organiser of the Harkat-ul Mujahideen in Assam.[46]

When such are the beliefs and thoughts of the leading lights of the Muslim community, how can one hope to promote communal harmony in India? It is shocking that even today the so-called moderate organizations like the Jamiat-al Ulema-e Hind are doggedly following a fundamentalist agenda similar to the one propagated and followed by the Muslim League 57 years ago, before the partition. Is it any wonder than that radical Muslim outfits like the SIMI (Students Islamic Movement of India) and Deendar Anjuman have been working overtime to achieve the ultimate Islamist goal of transforming India into Dar-ul Islam? It may be recalled that during the first four decades of the twentieth century numerous attempts were made, mostly at the intiative of Gandhiji, to forge unity between Hindus and Muslims—sometime even by appeasing the latter. But all such attempts failed miserably and finally the communal situation took a turn for the worse. Even after independence, the communal problem and the resultant societal tensions have been with us now for almost fifty years, excepting a brief spell of five to ten years immediately following the partition. Subsequent to the rapid growth of fundamentalist Islam across the globe and multiple Pakistan sponsored terror attacks in Jammu & Kashmir, Mumbai, Delhi, Ahmedabad, Coimbatore and other parts of India, the hostility between the two communities has reached a new high. Unless the Muslim society opts for modernity and tolerance there is little likelihood of any rapprochement. Surprisingly the stand of the Muslim leadership and their flock on many crucial issues has not changed a wee bit even after independence. They continue to refuse to sing Vande Matram in schools and at public functions, insist on slaughtering cows on religious grounds, as a matter of right, and have been staunchly opposing the introduction of a uniform civil code. On these sensitive issues even today the position of Muslims remains the same as it was one hundred years ago. More importantly, Muslims are not prepared to modernise their madarasas or modify the teaching of the hatred-promoting subjects like jihad to young children. So long as the concepts like jihad and ghanima, i.e. plunder, continue to be taught in madarasas there is little hope of achieving a unity of mind between the two communities. If you talk to a Muslim cleric, a Maulvi, and seek his views for excluding the subject of jihad from the instructions he imparts to his pupils, he becomes furious and asserts that jihad is a part of the Quranic teaching and giving it up will be an act of blasphemy. When you address the same question to an educated and enlightened Muslim, he informs you that just as the philosophy of 'karma' is central to the teachings of the Gita, the theological concept of jihad is an integral part of Muslim scriptures. Both insist in their own way that the teaching of jihad to children cannot be modified. Both affirm that jihad is a very important aspect of Islamic faith. That is also the position taken by scholars like M.J. Akbar. So long as the glory of jihad against the Kafirs or infidels continues to be taught to young Muslims as part of their religious instruction, their hatred against the Hindus will continue to grow and smoulder. In such circumstances, there can be no real understanding between the two communities. A great deal of effort has been made during the last one hundred years to bring about Hindu-Muslim unity or at least evolve a formula for peaceful co-existence between the two groups but all those efforts failed. And that was how Pakistan was born. In this matter the Indian polity appears to have reached almost a dead end. A simple example will illustrate the crux of the Hindu-Muslim problem. Anyone can sing from any temple or a Gurdwara, Gandhi's favourite hymn, his favourite bhajan, "*Ishwar Allah tero naam, sab ko sanmati de bhagwan*" emphasizing the inherent unity of all religions, that there was only one God and that Ishwar and Allah were His two names. Indeed this bhajan (i.e., hymn) is regularly sung during prayers in many temples and Hindu homes, too. You can sing it with utmost abandon in any Gurdwara - and perhaps in a non-orthodox Church too. But no Muslim dare say from the pulpit of a mosque that Ishwar and Allah were two names of the same God who is one entity, though the wise worship Him in many ways. Any Muslim saying so in a mosque runs the risk of being lynched to death. In a nutshell, that rigidity of Muslims, that refusal to acknowledge that Ishwar and Allah were the names of the same God, that kind of extreme intolerance of another person's viewpoint is the crux of the centuries-old Hindu Muslim problem-the main cause of faultline conflicts. Mahatma Gandhi, too, had a first hand taste of this kind of extreme intolerance of Muslims when after the notorious Noakhali riots of October 1946, in which thousands of Hindus lost their lives and property, he went there to preach peace and amity between the two communities. In his book titled *To The Protagonist of Pakistan* Gandhiji has narrated how during his daily meeting at Masimpur (Noakhali), on January 8, 1947, he found to his dismay that a number of Muslims had left when "*Ramanama* was taken at the prayer." Addressing the gathering after the prayer was over, he expressed unhappiness that his Muslim brothers had gone away. He was told that Muslims left because they did not like taking *Ramanama*. Gandhiji felt sad that Muslims thought that God could only be called by the name 'Khuda'. He realized then that the cause of all that happened during the Noakhali riots was that kind of intolerance of the religious beliefs of other people. He remarked that Hindus might be small in numbers, but the Muslims should know that *Ramanama* and the name of Khuda were the same. He said that he was told that in Pakistan everyone will be allowed to follow his own religion, but what he had just seen in Masimpur was something else.

He felt sorry that Hindus of Masimpur were expected to forget their Hindu faith and required to address God as Khuda.[47]

History is an eloquent witness to the fact that the Hindu civilization has always been exceptionally tolerant and peaceful, both by tradition and temperament. Frankly, the Hindu response to frequent senseless killings by jihadis often borders on pusillanimity, especially if you consider the fact that despite massive ethnic cleansing in Kashmir Valley, resulting in the killings of unarmed Kashmiri Hindus by Islamic terrorists and the ouster of more than three hundred thousand Hindus, no radical outfit like Gujarat Revenge Force was ever launched, nor any retaliatory attacks ever planned. Let the leftists name any other country in the world where the majority community has stoically suffered the kind of ethnic cleansing of their kinsmen, as Hindus have tolerated in the violent Valley.

How is it that the RSS and Hindu Mahasabha could not influence the Hindu mind at the time of independence to opt for the creation of a theocratic Hindu Rashtra, when in the aftermath of partition, the country was abuzz with gory tales of bloodbath and the wounds of partition were raw? How is it that now, fiftysix years after independence, the Hindu society has come to be seized with the Hindutava wave? Surprisingly most political commentators and columnists are not prepared to analyse and comprehend this vital sea-change in the thought processes of the Hindu society. They do not understand the simple fact that when partition took place, the majority of Hindus had believed that they were putting behind them the old sordid era of religion-based strifes and genuinely looked forward to living peacefully in the years ahead. The Hindu majority had deliberately opted for a secular democratic system—and decisively rejected the theocratic concept of Hindu Rashtra in the earnest belief that the Muslims opting to stay behind in India will whole heartedly subscribe to the secular ideal, give up their divisive postures and respect the principles enshrined in the Indian Constitution, including the Directive Principles of the State Policy. But unfortunately that did not happen and the fundamentalist clergy and an equally fundamentalist political leadership continued to rule the hearts and minds of the Muslims. That is the real tragedy. Our over-reactive columnist should understand that the religion-based unrest in the Hindu society being witnessed today is nothing more than mere "Hindu response" to the threat of Islamist militancy reflected in the long standing call for jihad against 'Hindu India' given by the ISI of Pakistan decades ago, repeated by bin Laden and the Taliban in 1998, and brashly sought to be implemented by Pakistan President Musharraf in Kargil in 1999. This response is the spontaneous reaction of a beseiged and beleaguered civilization, ravaged and plundered for centuries by ruthless invaders.

The Islamist threat is deeply embedded in the Hindu psyche and comes from the hearts of millions of ordinary rustic Hindus, certainly not part of the intellectual elite to which most of the political analysts and columnists belong. A mere glance at the blood drenched history of medieval India will convince anyone of the grossness of the terror and trauma which Indian masses had gone through during those dark centuries. Such indeed has been the impact of that harrowing experience, that in the present times, the Hindu masses hear the eerie echoes of their troubled past in every bomb blast, every attack on Hindu temples and unarmed pilgrims, and on hearing every battle cry of jihad. When they see that countrywide hundreds of temples have to be security protected to save them from Islamist attacks and that even festivals like Dashehra and Deepawali are threatened with jihadi bombings, in their subconscious they are reminded of the fate of thousands of temples destroyed by Jihadi invaders in the not too-distant past. Not many people are aware that in the light of attacks on Akshardham and Raghunathji temples, the security of the Tirumala temple is sought to be hugely upgraded. Plans are afoot to import light weight pistols from Israel, a bomb disposal squad and special scanners have been inducted and the feasibility of providing bulletproof glass enclosures in front of the queuing space leading to the temple 'mahadwaram' is underway.[48] In doing all that the Hindus are not acting as a schizoid group; they are being just practical in responding to the threat of jihadis of whose destructive mindset they have been aware for many centuries. Can anyone believe that the Islamist threat to the Hindu way of life will not register in the minds of lakhs of devotees praying at the Amarnath shrine or Vaishnodevi, or at the Tirupati temple? And the same threat perception and security apparatus is visible at hundreds of temples across the country, including Siddhi Vinayak in Mumbai, Somnath and Ambaji in Gujarat, Hanuman Mandir and Laxminarayan and Kalkaji temples in Delhi. Will it not strike a responsive chord for Hindutva in the hearts and minds of temple-going Hindu worshippers? When an entire civilization is threatened by bombers, there is bound to be some mass response. Seeing gunmen at the temple gates, even young children accompanying their parents are known to have asked uncomfortable searching questions. There are, however, some self-styled intellectuals who fail to understand this simple truth from which the natural Hindu response emanates. Perhaps they do not understand the phenomenon of stress-related human response to threatening situations.

The spiralling of terrorist attacks across the country, relflected in the successive bombings in Mumbai, have substantially contributed to the growing communal divide. Every act of terrorism acts as chilling reminder of the dark centuries when thousands of chained and manacled Indian slaves were carried over the Hindu Kush mountains for sale in the bazaars of Ghazni, Kabul and Baghdad. Many of these scarry episodes have been vividly described by several eminent historians, as highlighted by Dr. Ambedkar in his book, *Pakistan or the Partition of India*. As pointed out by Dr. Ambedkar, Mahmud Ghazanvi "not only destroyed temples but made it a policy to make slaves of the Hindus conquered". In the words of the well known historian Dr Titus: "Mahmud seems to have made the slaughter of infidels, the destruction of their temples, the capturing of slaves, and the plundering of wealth of the people the main objects of his raids. On the occasion of his first raid he is said to have taken much booty; and half million Hindus, 'beautiful men and women' were reduced to slavery and taken back to Ghazni."[49]

Later when Mahmud seized Kanauj, in A.D. 1017, he took so much booty and so many prisoners that the fingers of those who counted them would have tired. Describing how common Indian slaves had become in Gazni and Central Asia after the campaign of A.D. 1019, the historian of the time recorded that the number of prisoners may be conceived from the fact that each one was sold for two to ten dirhams. These were afterwards taken to Gazni, and the merchants came from distant cities to purchase them.[50] These are only two of the hundreds of similar instances cited by chapter and verse, in book after book, by innumerable prominent historians—many of them Muslims.

It was not for nothing that at the time of partition Dr. Ambedkar advised his followers, the Scheduled Castes, who happened to be trapped inside Pakistan, to come over to India by such means as may be available to them. He further told the scheduled caste people that it would be fatal for them, whether in Pakistan or in Hyderabad, to place faith in Muslims or the Muslim League. He regretted that it had become a habit with the Scheduled Castes to look up upon Muslims as their friends simply because they dislike the Hindus which was a mistaken view.[51] At the time of partition, Dr. Ambedkar was by far the most aware politician. He could anticipate the likely fate of the Hindus and the Sikhs left behind in Pakistan. After all it was he who had forcefully argued for a well organized exchange of population of minorities on the pattern of the Balkans, in his above quoted book in 1946. He had cited examples of similar exchange of populations worked out by Turkey and Greece and other countries of the Balkans after the second Balkans war in 1913 to minimize the sufferings of the left-behind minorities. He had forcefully advocated organized exchange of population by pointing out that despite insertion of constitutional safeguards the problems of minorities in the Balkans and Turkey could not be resolved until the three concerned nations, Greece, Turkey and Bulgaria devised a plan for organized exchange of population. The presumption that constitutional safeguards or protection by the concerned states would be able to protect the minorities was proved wrong. Only organized exchange of population could afford protection to the minorities trapped in the hostile environs. He forcefully argued that experience showed that safeguards did not save the minorities but only the exchange of population did save them. The task undertaken by the three concerned nations was a major one for such small countries, involving transfer of twenty million people from one location to another. Those countries felt that the consideration of communal peace and saving lives must outweigh every other consideration. If those three small countries could do it, there was no reason to believe that Indian and Pakistan could not do so. To quote Dr.

Ambedkar, "the transfer of minorities is the only lasting remedy for communal peace. If small countries with limited resources like Greece, Turkey and Bulgaria, were capable of such an undertaking there is no reason to suppose that what they did cannot be accomplished by Indians."[52]

If only someone had listened to the wise counsel of Ambedkar, millions of innocent people would have escaped being butchered and plundered in the maelstrom of communal frenzy let loose by the Muslim League in the name of jihad in 1946-47. In the words of the famous historian Will Durant, "the Mohammedan conquest of India is probably the bloodiest story of history". He calls it a discouraging tale, for its only lesson was that civilization is a precarious thing, whose delicate complex of order and liberty, culture and peace could be overthrown at any time by barbarians invading from without or multiplying within.[53] The threat to Indian civilization from outside, that is Pakistan and Bangladesh, is open and widely understood. But it is anybody's guess how great is the threat which thirty plus radical Islamists outfits pose from within. As pointed out by Francois Gautier, the massacre of six million Jews by Hitler and the persecution they suffered all over the world in the last 15 centuries has been meticulously recorded after 1945 and has been enshrined not only in history books, but also in the Holocaust museums, the most famous of these being the one in Washington D.C. The Hindus too have suffered a terrible holocaust, probably without parallel in human history. Drawing attention to the naming of a mountain system nearly 1000 miles long and 200 miles wide located between Amu Darya Valley and Indus valley as Hindu Kush, he points out that it is a reminder of the days when the Hindu slaves from the Indian sub-continent died in harsh Afghan mountains while being transported to Moslem courts of Central Asia.[54] Encyclopaedia Britannica mentions "that the name HinduKush first appears in 1333 A.D. in the writings of Ibn Battutah, the medieval Berber traveller who said the name meant "Hindu Killer", a meaning still given by Afghan mountain dwellers." Unlike the Jewish holocaust, the exact toll in the Hindu genocide suggested by the name Hindu Kush is not available. Encyclopaedia Britannica mentions that Mughal emperor Akbar ordered the massacre of nearly 30,000 captured

Rajput Hindus on February 24, 1568 A.D., after the battle for Chittor, a number confirmed by Abul Fazl, Akbar's court historian.[55]

Apparently the frightening echoes of that oppressive past and the memories of the killings which took place during the 1947 jihad launched for the creation of Pakistan and the mayhem caused by the ongoing jihad, have become unforgettable memories for the Hindus. Despite grave provocations by Islamist bombers, the Hindus continue to be tolerant. Surprisingly attempts continue to be made, every now and then to confound the gullible masses about the real intentions of the organizations like the SIMI (Students Islamic Movement of India), Al Umma of S.A. Basha, notorious for Coimbatore serial bomb blasts, the Muslim Defence Force, Ahl-e-Hadees, Deendar Anjuman, All India Jihad Committee, Islamic Liberation Army of Assam, Gujarat Revenge Force and dozens of similar radical outfits by covering up their ugly design of converting India into Dar-ul-Islam. Their activities continue to raise temperature across the country and naturally fuel and foment Hindu fundamentalism. Incidentally, more than thirty radical Islamist outfits are already operating in India, a number equal to more than two-thirds of similar radical groups in Pakistan, as is evident from Appendix-II. It is no secret that most of these Islamist outfits have been operating at the behest of the ISI of Pakistan. But they have substantial local roots as well—and Pakistani officialdom openly boasts about it.

At a meeting which a senior official of the Indian Foreign Service had with a group of prominent Pakistanis in a South Asian capital, a close associate of Musharraf bluntly remarked that if India believed that it could ignore its differences with Pakistan and move ahead economically, his country would have no difficulty in taking steps to retard India's economic progress. What a strange attitude? And a few years ago a former Director General of the ISI had told the same retired official that Pakistan would see to it that the jihad in Kashmir draws support from Muslims all across India. That was in response to an assertion that Muslims of India were proud of the secular ethos of their country.[56] One simply marvels at those who keep on saying that there is no Al Qaeda presence in India. Is it necessary for a bomber or AK 47 wielding terrorist to wear a badge of allegiance to Al Qaeda to identify himself or to proclaim his evil intentions? Al Qaeda is nothing but a jihadi philosophy which imbues a Muslim with an urge to kill the so-called infidels and wage jihad. All those who manufacture and explode bombs, all those who collaborate for attacking temples and carry AK 47s to murder innocent pilgrims are *ipso facto* members of Al Qaeda and are potential ISI agents. They are, all of them, subscribers to the Taliban philosophy. It is not incumbent upon an Al Qaeda mujahid or an activist of SIMI or Al Umma to make a pilgrimage to Guantonamo Bay Naval Base to earn his jihadi spurs! His killer action is the badge of Jihadi honour, good enough to make him an Al Qaeda operator. The Indian Government should have in the first instance itself, banned such organisations and the funds to such organisations should have been immediately frozen. It is quite difficult to cite any instance of any Hindu or any Hindu organisation attacking and killing Muslim pilgrims proceeding to Ajmer, leave alone those boarding planes for going to Haj in Arabia. The Indian Government permits them to undertake such visits and help them carry out their religious obligations. Another strange fact is that, after the commitment of a heinous terrorist crime, a Muslim organisation comes forward and claims credit for spreading anarchy. Such mentality deserves highest condemnation by the civil society.

Till eighth century India exhibited an astonishing panoply of excellence in arts, sciences, mathematics, culture and civilizational values of a high order. That period has been rightly described as the golden age of Hinduism. But from eighth century onwards the meteoric rise of Islam from the arid deserts of Arabia broke the placid calm of the sub-continent by making repeated knocks at the western gates of the country. The intrepid, but ruthless soldiers of Islam led by Mohammed bin Qasim, made their intentions to destroy the Indian civilization known first by overrunning the Hindu kingdom of Sind in 713 A.D. The conquest of Sind was followed by breaching the natural barriers of the Khyber and Bolan passes in the north-west of the country by Mahmud of Ghazni in the eleventh century. He killed thousands of innocent Indians by labelling them as infidels and laid waste the northern plains.

Long before the rise of Islam the suzerainty of Indian rulers extended right up to the region called Gandhara (Kandhar in modern Afghanistan) and far beyond upto Vaahic Pradesh, now called Balkh i.e., Bacteria. In Indian folklore the people of Gandhara called Gandharvas, were known for their fair complexion, statutesque looks and proficiency in arts and culture. Even today the Gandhara school of arts occupies a distinct pride of place in the realm of Indo-Aryan art. The kingdom of Gandhara was established by Prince Taksha, the grandson of Raja Bharat of Ayodhya and its borders stretched right from Takshashila (Taxila) to Tashkent, which name is a corrupt form of Taksha Khand, located in the present day Uzbekistan. In the classical Indian epic, Mahabharata, queen Gandhari, daughter of the king of Gandhara and wife of the blind king Dhritarashtra, occupies a prominent place.

From eighth century onwards for nearly nine hundred years the Indian civilization was pilloried and ravaged by a series of onslaughts by Muslim invaders as a result of which it descended into the abyss of slavery and abject poverty due to the incessant loot and plunder. Alluding to that era of darkness, the famous historian A.L. Basham has written that before the Muslim rule over India this country was "the wonder of the world" and that was how India attracted "the tourists and looters from everywhere." According to Rizwan Salim, the wrecking of Hindu temples went on from the early years of the eighth century to well past 1700 A.D., a period of almost 1000 years.[57] Every Muslim ruler of Delhi (or Governor of the Province) spent most of his time fighting the Hindu kings in the north and the south, the east and the west. And almost every Muslim Sultan and his army commanders indulged in large scale looting and destruction of Hindu temples and idols. The temples were also the citadels of beautiful and wonderful Hindu art and architecture which, with the destruction of the temples, got lost to the future generations. The invaders also slaughtered a lot of Hindus. The evidence of the ferocity with which the Muslim invaders struck at the sculptures of gods and goddesses, demons and apsaras, kings and queens, dancers and musicians is frightful.[58] Rizwan continues, savages at a very low level of civilisation and no culture worth the name began entering India from the early eighth century onwards. Islamic invaders demolished Hindu temples, shattered unaccountable sculpture and idols, plundered innumerable palaces and forts of the Hindu kings, killed vast number of Hindu men and carried off Hindu women. This story, the educated—and the lot of even the illiterate Indians—know very well. History books recount it in remarkable detail. But many in the world may not know that the alien Muslim marauders destroyed the historical evolution of the earth's most mentally advanced civilisation, the most richly imaginative culture and the most vigorously creative society. Tenth century Hindustan was far advanced than its contemporaries in the East and the West for its achievements in the realms of philosophy and scientific theorising, mathematics and knowledge of nature's workings. Hindus of the early medieval period were unquestionably superior in many things than the Chinese, the Persians (including the Sassanians), the Romans and the Byzantines of the immediate preceding centuries.[59]

Before the onslaught of Muslim invasions, India was a very prosperous and rich country. The wealth of the country reached its peak under Chandragupta Maurya and Harsha Vardhan. Yuan Chwang (also known as Hiuen Tsang) described an Indian city as beautified with gardens and pools and adorned with institutes of letters and arts; the inhabitants were well off and there were families with great wealth; fruits and flowers were abundant. The people had a refined appearance and dressed in glossy attire. They were clear and suggestive in discourse, though equally divided between orthodoxy and heterodoxy.[60] Earlier, when during the reign of Chandragupta Maurya, Megasthenes came to Pataliputra as Ambassador of Seleucus Nicator, Greek king of Syria, he was amazed to find a civilization which he found to his surprise, as entirely equal to their own. The absence of slavery in India struck him as a favourable contrast with his own nation. Although the people were divided into castes according to occupations, they accepted these divisions as natural. They lived happily enough, was his verdict.[61] The oldest of the two thousand cities of northern India in Chandragupta's time was Taxila (a corrupt form of Takshshila). It was situated approximately twenty miles northwest of the modern Rawalpindi. Arrian describes it as "a large and prosperous city". According to Strabo, "it is large and has most excellent laws." It was both a military and university town, strategically situated on the main road to West Asia and containing the most famous of the several universities possessed by India at that time. Students flocked to Taxila as in the Middle Ages they flocked to Paris; there all the arts and sciences could be studied under eminent professors, and the medical school especially was held in high repute throughout the Oriental world.[62] The excavations of Sir John Marshall on the site of Taxila have unearthed delicately carved stones, highly polished statuary, coins as old as 600 B.C., and glassware of a quality never bettered later in India. In the words of Vincent Smith, a high degree of material civilization had been attained and that all the arts and crafts incident to the life of a wealthy, cultured city were familiar.[63]

India's contribution in the field of mathematics was enormous. For making complex calculations the Hindus had developed a system of mathematics superior than Greeks, in every respect except geometry. The concept of 'zero', the so-called Arabic numerals and the decimal system were devised by the Indians and then learnt from them by Arabic scholars. The miscalled "Arabic" numerals are found on the Rock Edicts of Ashoka (256 B.C.), a thousand years before their occurrence in the Arabic literature.[64] It may be recalled that in Arabic a numeral is called "Hindsa", which clearly denotes its origin from Hind that is India. The decimal system was known to Aryabhata and Brahmagupta long before its appearance in the writings of Arabs and the Syrians. The Chinese learnt it from the Buddhist missionaries.

Similarly, Algebra was developed apparently quite independently, by both the Hindus and the Greeks. Its Arabic name, 'al-jabr' meaning adjustment, indicates that it came to Europe from the Arabs, but the latter took it from India. The great Hindu leaders in this field, as in astronomy, were Aryabhata, Brahmagupta and Bhaskara. It was Bhaskara who invented the radical sign and many algebraic symbols. These clever mathematicians conceptualized a negative quantity, without which the algebra would have been quite impossible. They were the first to find the square-root of '2', and solved in eighth century A.D., indeterminate equations of the second degree that were unknown to Europe until the days of Euler, a thousand years later.[65] The pinnacle of the glory of Hindu science and literature was their wonderful ability to weave the drab science of mathematics with the imagery of sensuous poetry. Will Durant praises the Hindus for expressing their science in poetic form and imparted to mathematical problems a grace characteristic of India's Golden Age, as reflected in the following two simple equations of Hindu algebra:

"Out of a swarm of bees one-fifth part settled on a Kadamba blossom; one third on a Silindra flower; three times the difference of those numbers flew to the bloom of Kutaja. One bee, which remained, hovered about in the air. Tell me, charming woman, the number of bees."

"Eight rubies, ten emeralds, and a hundred pearls, which are in thy ear-ring, my beloved, were purchased by me for an equal amount; and the sum of the prices of the three sorts of gems was less than half a hundred, tell me the price of each, auspicious woman".[66]

These examples further show that in ancient Indian society, women were held in high esteem, considered "auspicious" and even invited to solve novel algebraic equations, while being lavishly admired for their beauty, intellect and charm. They participated fully in arts, sciences and literary discourses as equal partners.

Rizwan Salim points out that the followers of Siva and Vishnu on the sub-continent had created for themselves a society more mentally evolved, more joyous and prosperous than what had been attained by the Jews, Christians and the Muslims. Medieval India, until the Islamic invaders destroyed it, was history's most richly imaginative culture and one of the five most advanced civilisations of all times. Ancient Hindu sculpture is vigorous and sensual in the highest degree - more fascinating than human figural art created anywhere on earth. Only statues created by classical Greek artists may be placed in the same class as Hindu temple sculpture. The Gothic art of cathedrals in France is perhaps the only other religious architecture wich could be considered to be comparable with the intricate architecture of the Hindu temples.[67]

In his outspoken critique of the damage caused by invaders to the ancient Indian civilization, Rizwan Salim continues: "Giving proof of the resentment that men belonging to an inferior civilisation feel upon encountering a superior civilisation of individuals with a more refined culture, Islamic invaders from Arabia and western Asia broke and burned everything beautiful they came across in Hindustan". Instead of attracting the so-called Hindu "infidels" to Islam by setting personal example, they just built a number of mosques at the sites of torn down temples and foolishly pretended that they had triumphed over the minds and culture of the Hindus.[68] The stones and columns of Hindu temples can be seen to have been incorporated into the architecture of several mosques.[69]

In this context, out of sheer curiosity, one question comes to mind. Could it be that the root cause of the widespread poverty which stalks the Indian countryside and the pain of hunger and deprivation stamped for centuries on the foreheads of the successive generations of emaciated millions, lies in the relentless plunder of wealth from the hearths and homes of Indian citizens and the treasuries of Indian kings by the waves of successive invaders? An insight into the strategy adopted to impoverish the Indians has been highlighted by the renowned historian, Will Durant, by highlighting that the policy of the Sultans was clearly sketched by Alauddin, who required his advisers to draw up rules and regulations for grinding down the Hindus and depriving them of that wealth and property which fostered disaffection and rebellion. Half of the gross produce of the soil was collected by the government; native rulers had taken up one sixth. According to a Muslim historian no Hindu, could hold his head high and in their houses no sign of gold or silver was to be seen and blows, confinement in the stocks, imprisonment and chains were all employed to enforce payments. When one of the advisers of Allauddin protested against this policy, the Sultan answered:"Oh, Doctor, thou art a learned man, but thou hast no experience; I am an unlettered man, but I have a great deal. Be assured then, that Hindus will never become submissive and obedient till they are reduced to poverty."[70]

Broadly, the same policy was followed by all successive alien rulers, except perhaps Akbar. If an in-depth research, based on empirical data of the likely quantum of wealth plundered during one thousand years of alien rule is made, perhaps the answer to the above question, tugging at every Indian's heart, might be in the affirmative.

We have seen that the dice of demography is heavily loaded against the Indian civilization because of the double jeopardy caused by the rapidly declining proportion of Indian Religionists, that is the Hindus, the Sikhs and the Buddhists, in the population of India during the last 110 years and the massive silent invasion of Bangladeshis during the last thirty years. Over a period of time, say during the next three or four decades, the deadly combination of these two factors has the potential of pushing India into chaotic and civil war-like conditions similar to those witnessed in Lebanon in 1970s and the erstwhile state of Yugoslavia in the not too distant past. To a serious student of the political scenario of the sub-continent, it should be obvious that lately India has witnessed a sharp increase in hostility between the Hindus and the Muslims. Even hitherto relatively calm and peaceful south Indian states like Tamil Nadu, Karnataka and Kerala have witnessed a sharp upswing in communal clashes. This sudden increase in the incidence of religion-based faultline conflicts, recently noticed in several parts of the country, can be ascribed to the rapid demographic changes, more than any other development.

During the last decade there has been a radical change in the thinking about the goals of population planning. In the modified approach, the focus has distinctly shifted from mere reduction in the numbers of new borns to protection of the child and the mother and their welfare. The old theory of opting for family planning as a quick fix for poverty alleviation, based on the Malthusian syndrome, is getting eroded. By now it has become an old cliche abandoned even by the UNDP (United Nations Development Programme).

It is being increasingly recognized that quality human resource or manpower is the most important component of all economic activity, including scientific research, inventions, new technologies and innovative thinking. Basically, manpower is what sustains the running of all farms, factories and transport systems. It holds the key to a country's economic development, much more than any other factor. Again, human resource is the motivator for innumerable multi-disciplinary research projects launched across the globe to explore the new frontiers of science and technology. It requires no great wisdom to know that the size of a country's Gross Domestic

Product (GDP) has a direct correlation with the size of its working population. A country having a high proportion of young, energetic and productive manpower will have a more robust economic growth than the one which has a disproportinately heavy burden of old people and pensioners. Similarly the quantum and percentage of savings in a country are a function of the size of its working population. Young working people are able to produce more, earn more and have higher disposable incomes compared to old people and pensioners. Therefore they are able to save more and invest more. It is a truism that countries having large youthful populations tend to have higher savings rate than those having a larger proportion of the elderly. The economic stagnation and slow down in the GDP growth, lately witnessed in most European countries and Japan, is a direct consequence of their declining numbers of working manpower and the growing burden of looking after ageing populations and pensioners. Apart from the inability of the old people to contribute much to the country's productive activity, the governments have to look after them by incurring expenditure on their social security and welfare.

It needs to be realized that young manpower is the single most important contributory factor for defence preparedness of every nation, the critical requirement being to provide a steady supply of youthful soldiers and officers to the defence forces for ensuring territorial integrity of the country and defending its borders. The importance of this aspect can be gauged from the fact that a military report commissioned by the U.S. Department of Defence on the subject *Population Control as a Military Issue* went to the extent of according "population control activities a level of importance that is essentially equal to the development and procurement of advanced weapons." The alarming free fall in the population of Russia and the plight of many European countries like Germany, burdened by the growing retinues of pensioners, have alerted the demographers and population experts, even of the United Nations, to the hazards of lop-sided emphasis on population control solely for reducing the birth rates. A new U.N. report studying the effects of population growth on the environment provides information that challenges some of the most fundamental assumptions of population control, assumptions used to justify sterlization, abortion and contraception.[71] A report on the subject, *World Population Monitoring* by the Population Division of the Economic and Social Affairs, emphasizes that many of the most dire predictions about the consequences of population growth have proved unfounded and remain unlikely to occur even if the world population rises to 8.9 billion by 2050.[72] In March 2002, the U.N. had convened a meeting of demographers to discuss whether the fertility of developing countries like India and Brazil will continue to fall, perhaps even reaching the extremely low fertility rates found in many developed nations. The Population Division of the Department of Economic and Social Affairs concluded that it is altogether likely that the fertility of much of the world will sink well below replacement level, which is 2.1 children per woman. Population Division reported at the meeting that before 2050, eighty percent of the world population will be projected to have below replacement fertility. In the light of this new assessment, the Population Division has reduced its 2100 A.D. projection for India by 600 million people.[73] Overall, the U.N. now believes that 74 countries, including India, will follow this pattern of drastic fertility reduction. And there is a note of warning, too. Some demographers fear that an anti-natal ethos, which is promoted by the contraceptive movement, may be impossible to reverse once it gets entrenched in a society and that fertility rates will continue to fall well below 2.1 children per woman in such countries. This phenomenon is already being experienced in many countries. The Population Division has been steadfast in its assertion that the fertility decline that has already occurred in countries such as Italy, Spain and Japan is beginning to have profoundly negative implications for those societies. The ever-increasing proportion of older people will overtax social security systems, pension funds and health care facilities. In a recent report, the Population Division concluded that even massive migration may not save these countries from the problems associated with below-replacement level fertility.[74]

Looking at the fate of Russia and many European countries, it is time India woke up to the future threat of declining youthful manpower, in case the present single-track population control policy is continued. Demography should not be used solely as a tool for arresting population growth. It is a complex and multi-faceted science which should be used for meeting the growing needs of a country for economic development, defence preparedness, requirements of internal security and maintaining peace within the country and in the immediate neighbourhood. It is fallacious to presume that an increase in population per se is a roadblock to the prosperity and economic development of any country, much less a resurgent nation like India, which has just now found its bearings in the realm of economic progress. A few examples will expose the gaping holes in that theory. India has a population density of 324 persons per sq. km. which is a shade lower than the population density of 335 persons per sq. km of Japan. But India is a poor nation, while Japan is rich and prosperous. Netherlands has approximately four time the population density of its former colony, Indonesia. But Indonesia continues to be poor, while Netherlands is highly prosperous. Is it not extraordinary that Bolivia with its 5 persons per sq. km is poor and therefore overpopulated, but Hong Kong with its huge population density is not poor nor overpopulated? Let us take the nearer home example of Singapore, a highly prosperous country, which has a massive population density of 5088 persons per sq. km., as against 324 persons per sq. km. in India. On top of it, Singapore has practically little natural resources like iron ore, coal or petroleum; nor does it have a bubbling green hinterland growing huge crops of corn and fruits. But in terms of economic development and prosperity, Singapore is several decades ahead of India—just recall how in the post-World War II years Singapore was an island of poverty and squalor. And the irony of the situation is that Singapore government is keen to increase the population of their small country further for which reasons they are offering incentives to their youth to marry early and raise families. Singaporean males are even being encouraged to bring brides from Vietnam because the latter prefer to raise children rather than rushing into the modern rat race for high profile jobs. The aim of the Singapore government is not to lose the momentum of fast track economic development which they have built by dint of sheer hard work and promoting technical education. At the same time, Singapore has been looking forward to welcoming high calibre professional immigrants from other countries for this very reason. It is therefore difficult to accept the thesis that an increasing population by itself is a liability. On the other hand, the history of economic development of several nations shows that a growth in the working population of a country has the potential to drive up the rate of its economic growth. Three most important determinants of economic development are the EAP (Economically Active Population), capital accumulation and adoption of the latest technology. Luckily India is blessed with all these important attributes. *The path to 2050* is the title of an excellent economic research paper released by Goldman Sachs in the first week of October 2003. The paper analyses the prospects for economic growth of four leading emerging market economies (BRIC i.e., Brazil, Russia, India and China) and demonstrates, by using demographic projections and other parameters, that the economies of these countries are growing faster than the economies of G-6 (U.S., U.K., France, Germany, Italy and Japan) and that how this growth differential will shift the balance of economic power. The BRIC's economies are likely to become much larger force in the global economy much faster than most investors currently anticipate.[75] According to this research paper, among the BRIC economies, it is actually India that has the potential to show the fastest growth over the next 30 to 50 years, not China. In fact, by 2010 India should be growing faster than China with the growth differential only increasing over time. This is driven largely by the demographic dividend which India is likely to reap over the coming decades, with a sharp surge in its EAP, or working-age population.[76] This is of course a two-edged sword, either we as a country create enough employment to absorb this huge surge in working age people and join the ranks of the global economic powers or we run the risk of falling into social chaos and anarchy. In that sense, India's destiny will be made or broken within the next 20 years. The gainful employment of this demographic dividend, or lack of it, will determine the economic and social fate of our country.[77] Most economists concede that population increase by itself is not an obstacle to economic development; on the contrary, it is more of an asset by virtue of being one of the important determinants of economic growth. But an illiterate and unskilled population is surely a major obstacle to development. For India the two biggest roadblocks to speedy economic growth are illiteracy and obscurantism. It is time to launch a frontal campaign to eradicate these two major evils which have been acting as a drag on the pace of our economic development. The truth boils down to this. Simply because of our own monumental failure during the last fifty six years to achieve total literacy and make every Indian an educated and skilled citizen, some woolly headed experts are trying to raise the bogey of over-population as a smokescreen, by ignoring the well known enlightened path of economic development, despite population growth.

We have seen in the previous chapter how the U.S. policy makers have been commissioning purposeful research studies about the demographical changes taking place across the world and studying their likely impact not only on the future of their country, but all over the world, especially in the realm of economic development, defence preparedness and the changing geo-political configuration across the globe. It is high time that in India, too, a mechanism was established to undertake comparable strategic demographic studies concerning various important aspects of national security, economic development and defence preparedness with special reference to the future strategic role of India in southeast Asia and the Middle East. Such population studies analysing long term impact of demographic changes in the sub-continent and immediate neighbourhood should be undertaken regularly, at least once in five years, and if necessary, even at shorter intervals.

It is imperative for the Indian nation to avoid the repeat of the demographic disaster which overtook Lebanon and the Balkans and now threatens Macedonia. We must not forget that even democracies are sustained by the number game expressed in terms of votes. Unless there is a mass awareness among the people about the likely demographic disaster, in this number game of one-man one-vote, the dynamics of demography could turn the tables on the Indian civilization, say by the day after—that is within a short span of thirty to forty years. A political analyst wrote sometime ago that it would take more than 360 years for Hindus to lose their majority status in India, thus suggesting that there was no cause for alarm. What an observation, what vision? The columnist conveniently overlooked three important facts. First, the calculations made by him were totally fuzzy; the apocalypse can visit India much earlier. Second, 360 years is a very short span in the history of a civilization. It certainly is not such a long time-frame that it could be easily ignored? As a rule, civilizations are reckoned in terms of dozens of millennia and far beyond. And lastly, our own experience of the birth of Pakistan shows that a determined violent and secession-oriented minority group of 25 per cent can engineer major faultline conflicts by taking recourse to organized violence and create civil war-like conditions. Apart from our own history, the events of Lebanon and the Balkans conclusively support this premise.

The dilemma facing the peace loving democratic nations, belonging to the universal civilization, has been vividly described by Bernard Lewis when he wrote that in this respect the democrats are at a disadvantage, because their ideology requires them, even when in power, to give freedom and rights to the Islamist opposition. The Islamists, when in power, are under no such obligation. On the contrary, their principles require them to suppress what they see as impious and subversive activities.[78]. "For Islamists, democracy, expressing the will of the people, is the road to power but it is a one-way road, on which there is no return, no rejection of the sovereignty of God, as exercised through His chosen representatives". Their electoral policy has been classically summarized as "One man (men only) one vote, once."[79]

For Indian civilization, reeling under the onslaught of jihad declared by the Pakistan-sponsored terrorists, these adverse population trends have acquired a definitive meaning—perhaps even sinister overtones. Any further adverse changes in the population ratios will speed up the communal divide, promote bigger faultline conflicts and then might lead to chaos and civil war-like conditions in the years ahead. There is yet more cause for serious concern. Such religion-based faultline conflicts in the sub-continent could assume almost diabolical dimensions because of the huge size of Hindu population. As the proportion of the Hindus declines, the incidence of such conflicts will tend to rise almost dramatically. That was how it happened in

Lebanon and the Balkans. Even when the population of the Hindus in certain states or all over the country, is reduced to the near minority status, the ferocity of faultline conflicts raging in the sub-continent could be very intense, much more intense than what was experienced in Lebanon and the Balkans, because of the sheer size of the Hindu population in absolute numbers. The Hindu numbers are already approaching one billion mark. The estimated population of Lebanon is around 40 lakhs, while that of the Balkans region is around 7.5 crores. Both population numbers could be described as peanuts, in comparison with the total population of the Indian sub-continent. God forbid, if unrest and violence seizes such a huge mass of 1.5 billion human beings (roughly, estimated population of India after 3-4 decades), one shudders to think of the likely damage to India's future generations and national progress—even colossal harm to the entire world civilization. It may be recalled that as a result of the growing religion-base faultline conflicts in the Balkans approximately 15 per cent of the total population of the Balkans peninsula region had to involuntarily move from one place to another since 1980s.[80] These figures of involuntary displacement of the population of the Balkans, compiled by the International Center for Migration Policy Development, speak for themselves. If 15 per cent, or even 10 per cent, of a total population of 1.5 billion human beings was forced to involuntarily move from one place to another due to faultline conflicts it will be a catastrophe and mayhem unparalleled in the history of mankind. Therefore any major changes in the demographic profile of India, say after 3 or 4 decades, could lead to a major global disaster. It is therefore imperative for the present political leadership of India to watch out and secure the interests of the future generations by evolving an effective preventive strategy. It is a critically sensitive subject on which there is a pressing need for total political consensus at the national level. Our composite national leadership dare not fail in this task; they must not. Let it not be said later on about the Indian leadership, as was sarcastically remarked about the tragedy of Lebanon, that the owl of Minerva began its flight only when total darkness had enveloped the skies.

8

Democracy, Modernity and Tolerance

"Those wanting to improve democracy in their countries should not wait for permission."

– Bulent Ecevit, a former Turkish Prime Minister

Every religion has its own societal ethos and civilizational moorings, its angularities, aberrations and strong and weak points. Neither Islam nor Hinduism nor Christianity could be an exception to this general rule. For instance, the Hindu society has many glaring modernity deficits, even serious societal infirmities, like the pernicious practice of untouchability and the evils of the caste-based discrimination, dowry system, etc., which have been eating into the vitals of Hindu civilization. Many scriptural texts of Manu Smriti and even Purusha Sukta of Rig Veda have been questioned and continue to be the subject-matter of serious controversies among the Hindu scholars, intellectuals and enlightened reformist. Surely, the same is true of other civilizations and religious groups like Christianity and Buddhism.

Similarly the Islamic theology has certain distinctive characteristics some of which appear to have contributed substantially to the growing friction between the Islamic and other civilizations because of Islam's mismatch with many universally accepted societal norms. The political ethos of Muslims across the globe derive their sustenance from the spiritual contents of the Quran and the Sharia with the result that Islamic nations continue to look to their scriptures and the clergy for the norms concerning the mode of governance, including the laws relating to public order, administration of justice and the rights of citizens. With the backdrop of Islamic scriptures forming the basis of every adminstrative and legal function, most Islamic rulers and their Muslim subjects consider the government as a monolithic fusion of religion and the state, as ordained by the Prophet. That implies that the rulers cannot make any departure from the norms and the procedures laid down by the Sharia. No amount of modernization or development of progressive ideals can supercede whatever is written in the Islamic scriptures. There is a wide divide between the democratic ideals of equality and freedom, rights of citizens, individual liberty and pluralism cherished by the universal civilization and the rigid format of governance envisaged by the clergy-centric and anti-pluralistic Islamic tradition. As a rule, most Islamic societies have remained isolated from the international mainstream of civilizational values and modern societal ethos because of the widespread absence of democracy, preponderance of orthodoxy and a disproportionately higher level of intolerance for all other faiths and religious beliefs. In order to ensure an objective examination of the issues involved and promote a healthy discourse we might refer to these as modernity deficits or institutional obstacles to harmonious co-existence of Islamic societies with modern civilizational groups across the globe.

Democracy is by far the most open and people-friendly system of government, based as it is on the principle of universal franchise, equality and freedom. It guarantees equal rights to every citizen irrespective of race, religion, sex, colour or cultural ethos and has therefore come to be identified with socio-economic progress. In modern democracies, supreme authority is exercised for the most part by the representatives elected to the legislatures by the citizens. Accordingly, democracy has been famously defined as the government of the people, by the people and for the people. It is a system which entitles the citizens to have the freedom of speech and expression, equality before the law and the right to worship according to his or her belief. In all democratic countries the ultimate power vests in the people who play a major role in the governance of the country. Members of the legislature or the lawmakers are elected by the people on the principle of one-man (or woman), one-vote. The executive head of the government is either elected from among the members of the legislature by majority vote, as in the United Kingdom and India, or he or she might be elected directly by the people, as is the system in America and some other countries. It is a simple pro-people system but unfortunately there is a singular absence of democracy in most Islamic countries, excepting Turkey and Malaysia which are like two islands of diluted democracy in the Islamic world. In Turkey the democratic polity is guided by the Turkish army. Although Mahathir Mohammed, former Prime Minister of Malaysia claimed to be a popular democratic leader, his commitment to democracy has been often questioned. Despite being a highly successful leader of a Muslim country, he often acted in an autocratic manner. For instance, he had no compunction in arbitrarily prosecuting and imprisoning, on charges believed to be trumped up, his Deputy Prime Minister, Anwar, whose arrest and trial not only stunned the Malaysian people but was also frowned upon by the world community. He was also accused of openly resorting to manifest discrimination against the native Chinese minority. In the process of implementing his populist Bhumiputra policy for giving preferential treatment to Malaysians he had deprived hundreds of ethnic Chinese of their businesses which were taken over by several leading Malaysian families. Recently, after his retirement, Mahathir Mohammed launched a diatribe against the Jews, alleging that they were ruling the world by proxy, mainly in a bid to play to the gallery. The statement was widely seen to be in poor taste.

The standard practice of governance in most Muslim countries is either by monarchs or by dictators, mostly army generals. In April 2003, after the ouster of the Baathist dictator, Saddam Hussein, the Editor of the *Yemen Times* had addressed an open letter to the rulers of Arabian nations captioned 'Dear Oppressive Arab Leaders' which was a telling commentary on lack of democracy in Arab countries. It indicated how disconnected the leaders of most Muslim nations are from their people. It also reflected the enormous yearning for democracy in the Middle East. The open letter warned them that the gap between the rulers and the ruled was huge and was getting wider. It made an impassioned plea for giving freedom and justice to the people by citing the example of Saddam Hussein who did not allow any freedom to his people and was ultimately toppled by a super power because he did not have popular support. It warned the Arab rulers that unless they treated their people in a better manner, eventually they might also meet the fate of Saddam Hussein sooner or later. They were advised to understand, before it became too late, that they could survive only if they managed to earn the love and appreciation of their people. They cannot hope to survive merely by winning the goodwill of the U.S.A. or any other country, howsoever powerful that country might be. The 'open letter' exhorted the Arab leaders saying: "It is your people, whom you should trust. ..... Allow freedoms. Establish justice. Allow peace and then rely on your people when the moment of truth comes."[1]

The absence of democratic tradition is the single most important reason for lack of modernity in Islamic nations. It is also responsible for their intolerance of other people's religious beliefs. The Middle East and the Central Asia have a number of Muslim countries, all woefully lacking in democratic tradition. For instance, Saudia Arabia, despite substantial economic prosperity heralded by the oil boom, has remained trapped in the centuries old feudal obscurantism. According to a recent announcement, for the first time in the kingdom's history muncipal elections might be held in the year 2004—and that too for only fifty percent of the seats in the municipal councils. Hopefully women may also be allowed to vote. If that happens it will be a big step forward towards women's emancipation because presently women are not allowed to drive cars or travel on their own without written permission of their male guardians.

Although Pakistan, Bangladesh and Indonesia have a veneer of democracy, the essence of democratic tradition has not been able to strike deep roots there. These Muslim nations, like several others, have been alternating between limping democracy and military dictatorship from time to time. The history of democracy shows that there are some societies, mostly illiberal nations, dominated by rigid dogmatic groups like the former Nazis or the Communist dictatorships or fundamentalist nations, which inhibit their capability to develop and nurture democratic institutions. Democracy presupposes the acceptance of certain civilizational values. Peaceful co-existence by different socio-religious groups on equal terms, allowing the citizens professing different faiths to worship freely in their own way, freedom of speech and expression and acceptance of pluralism and multi-ethnicity are the basic postulates of democracy. While discussing the conditions necessary for successful functioning of parliamentary democracy, Dr. Ambedkar, who was one of the members of the Constituent Assembly which wrote the Indian Constitution, had drawn attention to certain tenets of Islam which stand in the way of modernisation and democratisation of Muslim societies. One of these, according to him, is the tenet which says that in a country which is not ruled by Muslims, wherever there is a conflict between the Muslim law and the law of the land, the former must prevail over the latter in relation to the lives of Muslims and a Muslim will be justified in obeying the Muslim law and defying the law of the land.[2] Again the Islamic doctrine of jihad or holy war, against infidels also runs counter to the values for which democracy stands. Dr Ambedkar further pointed out that according to Muslim canon law the world is divided into two camps, Dar-ul-Islam (abode of peace) and Dar-ul-Harb (abode of war). A country is Dar-ul-Islam when it is ruled by Muslims. A country becomes Dar-ul-Harb when Muslims only reside in it, but are not rulers of it. That being the canon law of Islam, India cannot be the common motherland of both of the Hindus and the Muslims. It can be the land of the Muslims, but it cannot be the land of the "Hindus and the Musalmans living as equals". It can be the land of the Muslims only when it is Dar-ul Islam and is governed by them. The moment the land comes under the authority of a non-Muslim power, it ceases to be the land of the Muslims, because instead of being Dar-ul-Islam it becomes Dar-ul-Harb".[3] Then there is another tenet of Islam which runs contrary to the ideals of democracy and modernity : it is that Islam does not recognize territorial affinities.[4] The affinity enshrined in the concept of ummah is only religious and therefore extra-territorial. Threfore it is obvious that Islam is antithetical to the very idea of nation-state and for the same reason opposed to the evolution of a democratic polity.

Islamic societies differ from modern nation-states in several ways. Almost all Muslim societies place a great deal of emphasis on imparting rigorous religious education to children from the very young age of 4 or 5 years and the medium for this religious education is invariably the exclusivist theological school called "madarasa" or a religious seminary, where they are initiated into the tenets of Quran, the Sharia and the Hadith. For Muslim parents and clerics, the teaching of religious precepts to their children is the first and foremost priority and acquisition of knowledge of other subjects and sciences is a secondary consideration which can wait. The term madarasa is the Urdu or Persian equivalent of the English term 'school'. Thus a madarasa is basically an Islamic school, often attached to a mosque, where emphasis is solely on religious education, mostly concerning the Quran, the Hadith, the Sharia and their interpretation, referred to as 'tafseer'. The basic curriculum followed in madarasas is hugely steeped in Islamic theology, often described as 'Daras-e-Nizami'. Broadly, the instructions are imparted in Arabic—even in distant countries like Indonesia, Bangladesh and far away islands of Mindnao and Sulu located in southern Philippines. In Pakistan and India, in addition to Arabic, Urdu and Persian are also used as the medium of instruction. The major emphasis is on the philosophy of Islam, the basic precepts of the Quran and Hadith with special reference to the Prophet's personal life and examples, the Hikmat-e-Sharia (i.e., the Islamic personal law) and elementary mathematics. Special emphasis is placed on the history of Islam, the conquests by the warriors of Islam in the past and the related theological concepts of jihad, or holy war and the global fraternity called 'ummah'. In madarasa education there is a singular lack of pluralistic and secular ethos, scientific developments and democratic values, the sole emphasis being on the Quran and Sharia. Pakistan has thousands of madarasas, the figures given out vary from ten thousand to fifty thousand for the entire country. One of the famous madarasas in Pakistan, located in Peshawar is Haqqania, where more than 2800 male students ranging in age groups eight to thirty-five years study the Quran, the Hadith and Islamic history and Islamic jurisprudence. The madarasa is funded by wealthy Pakistanis, and devout, politically-oriented Muslims of the Gulf countries. There are no courses in the world history, English, mathematics and computers nor any emphasis on teaching science. According to Jeffrey Goldberg, the "Haqqania madarasa is in fact, a jihad factory".[5] The madarasas in Pakistan are not something unique. Madarasas are there in almost every Muslim country. A madarasa or an Islamic seminary is an old institution—a precursor of the Christian schools and colleges. There are one million students reportedly studying in Pakistan's more than 10,000 madarasas and militant Islam is at the core of most of these schools. But Haqqania is notable because it claims to have graduated more leaders of the Taliban than any other madarasas in the world. The Taliban hordes burst out of Kandhar in 1994 and during their quick march to Kabul, prohibited female education, fired lady doctors, assasinated homosexuals, staged public amputations and generally brought a bad name to the idealogy of the prophet in whose name they claimed to act.[6] The majority of Haqqania students come from Pakistan. That worries officials in Washington, Moscow,New Delhi and Jerusalem. Jeffrey Goldberg pointed out that Pakistan's Islamists were becoming more and more Talibanized, as some call it, largely due to the madarasas like Haqqania. As Pakistan also happens to possess nuclear weapons, many Islamic radicals claim that these weapons should become part of the arsenal being built for jihad. Haqqania students believe it too.[7] Maulana Sami-ul Haq, the Chancellor of Haqqania Madarasa, admitted that when the Taliban were faring badly in the battle against the Northern Alliance he had closed down the seminary and sent students to the front for waging holy war. Many Taliban and Al Qaeda leaders are graduates of Haqqania and other similar madarasas many of which are like mini-military academies where strategies for waging jihads against kafirs are evolved, preached and taught. For instance, the well-known terrorist Haroon Fazal was a scholar of the Koranic School in Comoros Islands and afterwards studied in Pakistan before he allegedly assisted in the terrorist strike on the U.S. Embassy at Nairobi in 1998. The main point is that the scriptural teachings of the kind preached in madarasas promote hatred against people belonging to other faiths. The Quran itself directs Muslims to wage holy war against idolators and promises just rewards, both in this world if one lives and in the other world, if one dies in jihad.

In Pakistani madarasas there is extra emphasis on comprehension of Allama Iqbal's "Shikwa" and even greater emphasis on regular singing of Iqbal's famous pan-Islamic poem titled "Tarana" which eulogises the glorious conquests of distant lands by the warriors of Islam in middle ages. "Tarana" also happens to be a great favourite of Jihadi terrorists undergoing training in militancy in the camps set up by the ISI and Pakistani army. This practice of opting for 'madarasa education' separates Muslim children from students of other communities at young age and tends to make them narrow minded, tunnel-visioned, and fundamentalists because of an overwhelming emphasis on the core tenets of Islam, including concepts like ummah and jihad and the ideal of paradise under the shade of swords. Studentship is the time when young minds can learn about the latest advances in science and technology, understand the beliefs, cultural mores and cardinal principles of other faiths, savour the multicultural social ethos and overcome prejudices, if any. But this does not happen in the exclusivist Islamic madarasas because of the absence of cross culture contacts and that leads to some kind of mental segregation of young Muslim minds. An example of the comparative school performance of Muslim and Hindu students in British India, almost four decades before partition of the sub-continent, gives an insight into the consequences of obsession with religious education in madarasas. A report on the Progress of Education in India (1907-1912) brought out that apart from social and historical aspects, there were other difficulties in promoting school education of Muslims. First, whereas the object of the young Hindu was to obtain an education which would fit him for an official or professional career, a young Muslim was not allowed to turn his thoughts to secular instruction until he had passed some years in going through a course of sacred learning because for him "the teaching of mosque must precede the lessons of the school." The Muslim boy, therefore, entered the school later than the Hindu. Secondly, he very often left school at an early age. The Muslim parents were usually poorer than their Hindu counterparts in the corresponding social position. A Muslim boy could not therefore receive thorough education. Thirdly, the Muslim parents often chose for their sons while at school an education which would secure for them an honoured place among the learned of his own community, rather than one which would command success in the modern professions or in official life.[8] These deficits of madarasa education, pointed out as early as 1907-1912, continue to plague the Muslim societies not only in India but across the globe even today. And post-partition, a change for the worse did occur in Pakistan, formerly a part of British India, where the mushrooming of madarasas promoted by the radical Islamists has taken a heavy toll on the quality of education and promoted fundamentalism. The creation of Pakistan and the subsequent long spells of army rule in that country proved to be a shot in the arm of radical Islam which thrives on the absence of democracy and amidst unending propagation of morbid hatred against Hindus not only in madarasas but even in the government-run schools. In an illuminating article by the well-known Pakistani columnist, Ardeshir Cowasjee, published in the '*Dawn*' (a reputed Karachi newspaper) and reprinted in the *Asian Age*, New Delhi, the author advised the President, General Musharraf, to first ensure that students in Pakistan were imparted enlightened and correct education and suggested a serious revamping of the present school curricula. He had drawn pointed attention to the fact that for the last eight years, since 1995, the objectives set out by the Ministry of Education in the national curriculum of school education emphasized that by the time the students complete Class V, they should understand the Hindu-Muslim differences, identify the forces working against Pakistan and India's evil designs and make speeches on jihad and shahadat (i.e.,importance of holy war and martyrdom). The students are also expected to promote an understanding of the Kashmir issue, to observe their fellow students and note their reaction to the wars with India and judge their spirit while they made speeches on jihad. Additionally, the students are also required to note the keeness and willingness of their classmates to recite *Tarana* at school functions.[9] Apparently the reference by Cowasjee is to Iqbal's *'Tarana'*, which is a somewhat rabid pan-Islamic poem, harking back to the past glory of Islam and claiming the ownership of India, China and Arabia for Muslims. It looks as though Iqbal's '*Tarana*' has lately been accorded the status of the second national anthem of Pakistan-thanks to the vigorous state-sponsored promotion of jihadi culture and build an anti-India tempo not only among the youth but even among the school children of Pakistan. Allama Iqbal's "*Shikwa*" and '*Tarana*' are hot favourites of Pakistani terrorists, too, and have been regularly sung with verve and gusto in the training camps run by the Jaish-e-Mohammed and Lashkar-e-Tayyeba. The phenomenol growth of madarasas is not limited to Pakistan and Afghanistan alone; it is the same story everywhere-in Bangladesh,

Malaysia, Indonesia, Philippines and even in the secular India. The increasing emphasis on converting every Muslim country into a rigid "Sharia-based Islamic state", if necessary through constitutional changes, otherwise by means of war, has led to the rapid growth of innumerable jihad-oriented Islamic seminaries. There are lakhs of madarasas multiplying all over the Islamic world and their numbers are growing exponentially; Pakistan alone is reported to have something like fify thousand madarasas (both big and small), while Bangladesh is believed to have another twenty to thirty thousand. Most of these madarasas, are factories of fundamentalism, basically devoted to indoctrinating the youngsters with radical Islam and mentally readying them for jihad. The number of madarasas in India too has multiplied exponentially, thanks to the funds donated by the Arab charities and resurgence of radical Islam. In India the number of madarasas was reported to be 88 in 1950.[10] According to the data given by Maqbool Ahmed in his book *Islamic Education*, their number was 30,000 in 1992. If the latter figure is correct, then there has been an unbelievable quantum jump. The number of madarasas in India multiplied more than 340 times in 42 years ! The exact number of madarasas in India at present is not known. According to some reports the overall number could be between forty and fifty thousand. At one time the government toyed with the idea of a legislation for compulsory registration of madarasas, as Pakistan has done. But it dare not do so because of the fear of criticism by the opposition which had carried out a sustained campaign even against passing of the Prevention of Terrorism Act. But the ground reality about the growth of madarasas in Indonesia is mind-boggling ; it reveals startling facts. According to the Indonesian Ministry of Religious Affairs' Office of Education Management Information System, there are 37,362 madarasas in the country in which about 5.6 million students study.[11] Of this, only 3,226 (8.6 per cent) with a million students are run by the state. These figures convincingly reveal Indonesia as a fertile ground for terrorist networks like the Al Qaeda to spawn in relative safety.[12] The bomb attack of October 2002 on tourists at Kuta beach in Bali, claiming more than 200 lives and the dreadful bombing of the J W Marriot Hotel in Jakarta on August 5, 2003 claiming 16 dead and 150 injured, are just straws in the wind. Looking at the massive jihadi fervour being built up among more than five million children studying in thousands of madarasas and the increasing influence of Jemmah Islamiah, there is a strong possibility of many more terrorist incidents being staged in Indonesia. Similarly there has been a big spurt in the establishment and promotion of madarasas in the neighbouring Bangladesh. The border areas, especially those contiguous to Bangladesh and Nepal have witnessed mushrooming of thousands of Islamic madarasas at a very rapid pace and these are mostly funded by the ISI, Saudi petro dollars and oil-rich Sheikhdoms of the Middle East. The Saudis have been playing the Wahabi card for quite some time now. It is estimated that during the last twenty years, the Saudis have spent a huge amount, approximately $100 billion, to promote Islamist philosophy at home and abroad. Only a part of that cash came from collections at mosques, schools, bazaars and other public places. The bulk of the funds came from the coffers of the Saudi treasury.[13] Bulk of this money is believed to have been spent on expanding madarasa education which in turn has promoted the jihadi cult in several countries. It is no less ironical that the very fundamentalist cult, funded and fuelled by Saudi petro dollars, now threatens to destroy the Saudi regime! A sporte of terror attacks in the recent months in the Saudi kingdom has given a rude jolt to the ruling clique.

Meanwhile, the madarasas of Pakistan and Afghanistan have already indoctrinated, trained and sent out thousands of militant mujahideen to various countries including the U.S.A., the U.K., Bosnia, Russia (especially in Chechenya), to India (Jammu & Kashmir), Bangladesh, Indonesia and the Philippines. Post May 12, 2003 night, when suicide bombers attacked housing complexes built for the westerners in Riyadh, some intellectuals tried to warn Saudis of the dangers of the home-grown terrorism. A few days prior to these bombings, Mansour Al-Nogidan, a former religious fanatic who has become fundamentalism's strongest Saudi intellectual critic wrote in a Saudi newspaper that Saudi Arabia suffers from a homemade brand of fanaticism propagated by members of the conservative Wahabi Islam.[14] There were more bombings in the second week of November 2003 targetting another housing complex on the outskirts of Riyadh which claimed many more innocent lives. The harmful effects of hard core fundamentalist teachings being imparted in religious seminaries called madarasas are now being recognized by the intellectuals and scholars of the Saudi society. Hamza Al-Muzini, a prominent Saudi linguistic professor, wrote in another Saudi daily that his young son was being taught the culture of death at school and that many teachers influence young Saudis with their extremist political agenda, a situation tolerated by the Ministry of Education.[15] After this article Dr. Muzini received death threats from Saudi fundamentalists. That shows the high degree of damage already done to the psyche of the *generation 'Y'* by initiating them into the rabid Wahabi doctrine. With that kind of commitment to radical religious teachings in madarasas, is it any wonder that hundreds of thousands of mujahideens have taken to the cult of Kalashnikov and RDX across the Islamic world, just as fish takes to water? In several countries like Palestine, Pakistan, Indonesia, India and Saudi Arabia suicide bombing has become a badge of honour or a religious statement for the youngsters, mostly those belonging to the educated and well-to-do families.

Thanks to the steep rise in the prices of petroleum in 1970s, after the Arab-Israeli war, and formation of OPEC (Organisation of Petroleum Exporting Countries) as a semi-monopolistic cartel, in recent years Saudi Arabia has become one of the richest countries in Asia or perhaps in the whole world. Every year some $6 billion leave the Arab kingdom, mostly from private charities, to build mosques and Islamic schools, feed Muslim children and deliver some life-saving drugs for Muslims from Mozambique to Mindnao. That is commendable work, but along with the money comes Saudi Arabia's second most-important export to the world: its austere and feudal 18th century brand of Islam, Wahabism.[16] At a mosque and madarasa in Zamboanga City in the southern Philippines, for example, head Imam, Jain Jali, was replaced by a Saudi trained cleric who had access to much-needed funds from benefactors in Saudi Arabia. Now, Jali's less orthodox kind of Islam is no longer preached and community women must wear head scarves and long sleeved tops.[17] Often it is hard to track where donations end up. For example, in September, 2002 Dhaka police raided a Riyadh-based international non-government organisation, al-Haramain Islamic Foundation, acting on a tip that Bangladesh branches has been recruiting madarasa students for jihad in Kashmir and Afghanistan. Al-Haramain's records showed that it had received \$2.4 million from Saudi Arabia—proof that Saudi alms aren't always used in the most benevolent manner.[18]

The stupendous growth of madarasas due to reckless funding by the Saudis during the last 30 years has made the Jihadi culture a staple religious diet of Muslims, both in Asia and Europe. It has made the younger generation of Muslims highly jingoistic by promoting bigotry and militancy among students during most impressionable years. This trend is visible in several countries of the Balkans, North Africa, the Middle East, Central Asia, the Indian sub-continent and the South East Asia. Madarasa education is largely responsible for attracting the Muslim youth to the heady mix of Quran and Kalashnikov culture. It is really tragic that while funding the establishment and growth of madarasas, the Saudis and other Islamic charities made no attempt to modernise these seminaries. No attempt has ever been made to upgrade madarasas and recondition these into centres of excellence in education and learning or broadbase their syllabi by including the modern concepts of science and technology in their curricula or make them emulate the high standards set by Christian Convents and Public Schools.

Unlike Christianity, Hinduism or Buddhism, Islam has practically little or zero tolerance for any other religion or faith. Historically there has been no worthwhile reformative movement in Islam because none was ever allowed; nor is any voice of dissent or a reformist idea tolerated. A classic instance of religious intolerance was the persecution of Baha's in Iran and the fate meted out to their spiritual leaders 'Bab' and Bahaullah. Iran, the land of the origin of Baha'i faith has been a Shia Muslim country ever since the Arab conquerors overran the Zoroastrian civilization in eighth century. It is widely believed among Shias that Hazrat Ali, the son-in-law of Prophet Muhammad, who was the last of the four caliphs of Islam (keepers of the faith in temporal matters), was succeeded to the caliphate by twelve of his descendants, referred to as 'Imams". The twelfth Imam mysteriously disappeared without leaving any heir and a legend grew among the Shias that he would one day return as the Messiah or "Mahdi". Some schools among the Shias began to teach that the Imams were some kind of a manifestation of deity, a belief which runs counter to the orthodox Islam. Therefore in difficult times occasionally some religious preacher would arise claiming to be the "Mahdi" or the hidden Imam. This became a favourite topic in the early nineteenth century Iran when the need for religious reform was being acutely felt by the masses and when according to the Shi'ite tradition a period of 1000 years was due to be completed from the year of the disappearance of the hidden Imam and his reappearance was believed to be due. At that time one Shaykh Amad-al-Ahsa, whose followers were called "Shaykhis" laid claim to being in contact with "Mahdi", the hidden Imam. He and his successor, Sayyid Kazim, were both called 'Bab' (i.e., the gate between the Hidden Imam and the mankind). They proclaimed that Mahdi would soon manifest himself. Later on when Kazim died, the sect became divided between two factions. One group believed in the spiritual leadership of Haji Karim Khan of Kirman. But a larger faction followed Sayyid Ali Muhammad of Shiraz who proclaimed in 1844 that he was the ' Bab', a manifestation of God, the long awaited "Mahdi". His followers came to be called Babis (later on they came to be known as Baha'is), while the first faction continued to be known as Shaykhis. Sayyid Ali Muhammad of Shiraz, born in 1820, claimed to be a descendant of the family of Prophet Muhammad. He was a quiet and modest man and had made a pilgrimage to the shrine of Imams in Baghdad. To convince the people of his divine mission he selected 18 "apostles" whom he started calling as the "Letters of the Living". Some Iranians eagerly accepted the "good news", but many others, including the ruling monarch, reacted with predictable hostility. The Persian ruler imprisoned the Bab. But because many Iranians were looking for the Mahdi, the deliverer, the movement spread. While in prison the Bab wrote a number of books. In the spring of 1848, while Bab was still held in prison, some Babi leaders held a conference and declared that Bab was the prophet of their new religious dispensation. Thereafter the Babis sought to take control of the province of Mazindran in Iran owing to which a series of armed conflicts with the Persian ruler ensued. The war resulted in the defeat of the Babis and finally Bab was executed in 1850. The religious writings of the Bab are called 'the Bayan' (translated as 'utterances' or "exposition"). The Bab cited the supposedly superior universal quality of his writings as proof of his divine mission, just as Muhammad had claimed superiority of his writings to the sermons in the Bible. This led to friction between the orthodox Muslims and Babis. The Bayan includes religious and social laws for the universal religious beliefs of the new age. Thus, Bab laid down the basic tenets of the Baha'i faith and these were all embracing, more humane and far more liberal than orthodox Islam.

Baha'is maintain that the Bab had taught his followers that their next leader following Bab would be greater than him and appointed Mirza Yahya Subh-i-Azal as vice regent of his movement who remained the head of the Babi community for sixteen years. Mirza Subh-i-Azal called upon his followers to give up sword and under his guidance the movement grew further. He was assisted in this effort by his older half-brother, Mirza Husayn Ali, who assumed the name "Baha" (meaning glory) and ultimately came to be known as Bahaullah, the leader of Baha'i faith. Born in 1817 in the town of Nur in Iran's Tihran province; Baha'ullah had given up all his wealth for the welfare of the poor early in life and turned to spirituality. In 1863, he declared unity of the whole world as his spiritual mission and advocated equality and justice for all. Baha'ullah enunciated three basic principles of Baha'i faith: the unity of mankind, the oneness of God who was omnipresent and omniscient and the unity of all religions. He preached the principles of equality of men and women, pursuit of scientific temper and advocated universal education for all. It was an attempt to introduce some sort of reform in the orthopraxy of Islam which was at that time the dominant religion of not only Iran but the entire Middle East. The orthodox Muslim clerics reacted sharply to the new doctrine and declared that Baha'ullah was an apostate and that his followers were heretics. Acting on the advice of clerics the Shah of Iran soon ordered a crackdown on Baha'is which led to the execution and persecution of many Baha'is and a large number of them fled to neighbouring countries. The Baha'i brothers also fled to Baghdad where Bahaullah was able to spread his spiritual movement further. But after violent clashes between Bahais and Muslims which lasted for ten years, the Ottoman rulers exiled Bahaullah and his co-religionists to Adrianpole on the extreme western border of Turkey.

It is believed that Bahaullah remained virtually imprisoned at Akka during his exile due to his reformist beliefs which were considered contrary to the basic tenets of Islam. In the entire history of Islam, Bahaullah was the only dissident who dared to challenge the Islamic orthodoxy by voicing dissidence by proclaiming that there was a common bond of love and brotherhood between all religions and preached a belief in the universality of God who could manifest Himself in different forms in different lands. The Bab and Bahaullah preached the concept of the unity of God, the unity of all religions and the unity of mankind which outraged the Islamic rulers and the clerics alike. Bahai's have been hounded for two hundred years throughout Iran and other adjoining Muslim countries and their persecution is a well-known instance of intolerance prevalent in Islamic societies. The Islamic Republic of Iran proclaims Shi'te Islam as its state religion, and recognises only Judaism, Christianity and Zoroastrianism as the other true religions. The three minority faiths are legitimised by the Constitution and accorded certain legal and political rights. The Baha'is, however, Iran's largest non-Muslim religious minority, are not mentioned in the Constitution and have the status of unprotected infidels.[19] Since the onset of the Islamic revolution in the fall of 1978, more than 200 Baha'is, mostly leaders of the community, have been put to death. Many institutions of Bahai's have been disbanded, community properties confiscated, holy places demolished, and cemetries desecrated.[20] As a rule, any intellectual interaction and informed debate or dialogue on the validity of religious concepts and practices is totally forbidden in Muslim societies. Conceding the prevalence of many social evils in Hindu society, Dr. Ambedkar asked whether at all there was any social evil which was found among the Hindus, but not found among the Muslims.[21] Even the caste system is as deeply ingrained in the Muslims of India, as indeed it is among the Hindus. There can be no doubt that the Muslim society in India is afflicted by the same social evils as afflict the Hindu society. The Muslims have all the social evils of the Hindus and something more: that is the cumpulsory system of Purdah for Muslim women.[22] The existence of these social deficits among the Muslims is distressing. But more distressing is the fact that there is no organized movement of social reform among the Muslims of India on a scale sufficient to bring about their eradication. The Hindus have their social evils. But there is a relieving feature about them. Some of them are conscious of their existence and are actively agitating for their removal.[23] Not only the lack of reform but also the absence of an urge within to reform the socio-religious system is a typical distinctive aspect of Muslim society. That is a major difference between Islam and other religions. For instance, throughout early history the original Hinduism had been a sacrificial religion with the tradition of sacrificing a he-buffalo or goat as an offering to Mother Goddess which ritual was being practised almost universally in all Hindu societies in India and Nepal. In ancient Vedic times it was customary for every Hindu (Aryan) emperor to offer sacrifice of a horse at the altar to propitiate the God on important religious functions. Every powerful king laying claim to be an all-powerful emperor or "Chakravarti" Raja used to send a sacrificial horse, accompanied by a retinue of selected warriors, to distant parts of his empire to seek a challenge from any valiant adversary showing the daring to seize and carry away the sacrificial horse after battling with his troops. And only when the sacrificial horse returned to the capital unchallenged was the Raja proclaimed as "Chakravarti" after performing the horse sacrifice. Thus offering sacrifice was an important religious ritual of the ancient Vedic civilization or Hindu society. But over the centuries, as a result of informed and scholarly debates and dialogue between religious teachers and the dissenting Hindu Dharmacharyas or religious preachers, this ritual, sort of a gory medieval practice, has been abandoned or at least substantially eliminated. Similarly the practice of untouchability, the societal bar on widow remarriage, and the weird and barbaric custom of sati (which had originated during the medieval times when invaders, mostly Muslims, used to carry away Hindu women after vanquishing the Hindu rulers or warriors), have been banished from the mainstream of the Hindu society and laws framed to ban all such antiquated rituals and customs. It may be recalled that historically the strongest opposition to most of these regressive religious practices came from within the Hindu society, although in some of the debates even western scholars, mostly British, had actively participated. Initially Buddhism itself had come up as a kind of reformatory movement against the evils of Hindu society, especially the detestable caste classification and the practice of animal sacrifice widely prevalent in the not too distant past. But Buddhism being an indigenous and liberal faith had no problem in subjecting itself to the time honoured Indian tradition of "Shastra-artha" or 'Samvad' whereby the scholars representing different religious tenets or philosophic viewpoints used to sit together and argue, debate and examine, by means of logic and reason, the different postulates of their respective faiths and the rituals and customs which appeared to have questionable validity. Consequently a strong belief in secularism and pluralism has been an integral part of the Hindu and Buddhist societies. For instance, according to an old tradition established over several thousands of years, on the death of his father or mother, only a son (if the deceased had no son, then a male child, say a nephew) was allowed to light the funeral pyre. But with the winds of reform and enlightenment sweeping across the Hindu society, this age-old custom has been given up. As a result of regular discourses and deliberations it has been accepted that there is nothing in Vedas or Upanishads that prevents female descendants from lighting the funeral pyre or performing the death-related ceremonies. Furthermore, women have inherent and equal right to study, recite, debate and preach the Vedas, the Ramayana and the Gita. According to Hindu belief, even God is genderless. Also the soul or *atma* is neither male nor female. In Pune, the centre of Maharashtrian orthodoxy, women priests (Stree Purohitas) are being trained to perform pujas and other rituals, thanks to the intiative shown in 1974 by a social reformer, Mama Thatte. The demands for the services of women Purohitas of Pune come even from Mumbai and Goa. And in Pannini Kanya Mahavidyalaya of Varanasi, the holiest town of Hindus, women Purohits and Sanskrit scholars, well-versed in samskaras, have been trained for decades. Similarly the Christian societies have had no problem in accomodating different viewpoints of their dissenting clergy and non-conformist scholars in the matter of faith through the medium of debates and discourse. That was what led to the acceptance of several religious reforms. Everyone knows that Martin Luther was a prominent dissenter of the orthodox Christian beliefs and a reformist to the core. Under his leadership Protestants broke away from the traditional Catholic Christian mores. That explains how the orthodox Christians of Serbia, Greece, Cyprus and Russia have been allowed to practise their own brand of Christianity in accordance with their beliefs and faith. Unfortunately that kind of frank and open discourse and debate cannot happen in Islam; a dissenting viewpoint in the matter of religious tenets and beliefs cannot be aired in that society. Every Muslim has to accept what is written in the holy Quran and he dare not deviate from the tenets of Sharia, Sunna and Hadith—much less question the underlying philosophy of his faith and validity of religious dogmas and practices pronounced 1400 years ago. Anyone trying to do that will be declared not only an "apostate" but additionally runs the risk of being put to death in most Islamic societies. Apparently the enforcement of this kind of over-archingly harsh clerical diktats in the matter of religion has also promoted among Muslims a general trend of not questioning the role and deeds of ruling kings, dictators and feudal warlords. History is a witness to the fact that in Muslim countries no dissenting voice about the tenets of Islam is ever tolerated or allowed to be raised, much less heard, nor can anyone dare question the authority of the kings and dictators or the propriety of what they do in the matter of public affairs. Rigid enforcement of scriptural injunctions and Sharia have acted as strong deterrents to the growth of democratic institutions in Islamic societies. Thus Islamic faith is increasingly becoming an island of isolation. Excepting Turkey where Kemal Ataturk broke the stranglehold of clerics on Muslim society with an iron hand, abolished the compulsory veil for women and introduced the concept of secularism to make Turkey a modern, tolerant and progressive State, no other Muslim country has dared to undertake any radical reform or present a modern democratic face to the world. Kemal Ataturk could do it because he had acquired a large following, had the unstinted support of the Army and was a virtual dictator. But in recent decades the shadow of the fundamentalist-Islam has returned to the centre stage in Turkey as well. The new ruling party consists of Islamist leaders, though it professes to follow a liberal pro-west policy, ostensibly with an eye on getting entry into the European Union. Turkey has a secular constitution, the women are more modern and liberated than any other Muslim country and it had its first woman Prime Minister, Tansu Ciller, from 1993 to 1995. Even so in recent years fundamentalist Islamic ideology has acquired dominance in

Turkey. But in Pakistan, the self-styled land of the pure Muslims, the degree of intolerance and hatred towards non-Muslims is astounding. Not being content with having pushed out hundreds of thousands of Hindus from Pakistan during the last five decades, now the heat has been turned on the Christians. In a soul searching write-up captioned 'It's not easy being a Pak minority', published in the *Dawn* of Karachi (and reprinted in the *Asian Age*, New Delhi) the well-known Pakistani columnist Hafizur Rahman had drawn pointed attention to the plight of minorities in Pakistan. He has recounted how Christians, Ahmediyas and Hindus were being regularly harassed. Six years ago Shantinagar, a Christian village in southern Punjab, was raided by Muslim zealots fed on false rumours set afloat by certain fanatics. They behaved like Huns and laid the village waste. The columnist had kept a tab on the matter and asserted without fear of contradiction that nothing was done by Mian Nawaz Sharif's government to either restore the confidence of the victims or bring the culprits to book. What price civilised behaviour inspired by the tenets of Islam and the much-vaunted claim about tolerance of other faiths?[24] He further wrote that the abduction of Hindu girls was going on all the time. When a hue and cry is raised, the girl is made to state in a court of law that she went away of her own accord, that she married a Muslim of her own accord and that she embraced Islam of her own accord. Then, a few years ago, there was the kidnapping of about a hundred Hindu Haris, men, women and children, in a part of the province.[25] But for the initiative taken by some minority leaders and a few good Muslims nothing would have happened in the matter nor anything heard about it. The columnist concluded that today the most privileged individual in Pakistan whom no one can touch is the Sindhi Wadhera (i.e., landlord) who was not afraid of anyone, not even God.[26] The columnist lamented that the present state of affairs has been brought about over the years by Pakistan's political and religious leaders.

One of the recent and most striking instances of intolerance typical of the militant Islamists was the destruction of the priceless Bamiyan Buddhas located in Kayan valley of Afghanistan in February 2001 by the Taliban. The two gigantic ancient Buddhas, one of them a 53 metre high statue carved into a cliff face in the central town of Bamiyan, were heritage monuments, highly prized works of Kushan era sculpture and art and admired all over the world. Historically, Afghanistan has been a melting pot of many cultures and civilizations for centuries—from Aryan and Gandhara civilizations to the Hellenic, Kushan, Mongol and Turkish cultural traditions. Northern Afghanistan was an important religious centre of Mahayana Buddhism and Kayan district where Bamiyan is located lies along the famous silk route linking Samarkand and China with India, Central Asia, Mesopotamia and Roman empire. The Bamiyan Buddhas were carved in the mould of classical features of sub-continental Buddhas, but were draped in Greek robes thereby representing a unique cross-culture fusion of the ancient Gandhara art with the refinements of Central Asian sculpture to which was added a dash of Hellenistic chic wardrobe brought to Afghanistan by the army of Alexander, the Great. According to an Islamic edict published and circulated by the Taliban-controlled Bakhtar News Agency in February 2001, Mullah Omar, Afghanistan's ruling fundamentalist leader had decreed that the statues were an insult to Islam and deserved to be destroyed forthwith so that they could never be worshipped again by kafirs. In a desparate bid to preserve these priceless heritage works of art the UNESCO (the United Nations Educational Scientific and Cultural Organisation) had made an appeal to the Taliban rulers to save the Bamiyan Buddhas, but that appeal was rejected. In an interview with the BBC's Pushto Service, Mullah Abdul Hai Mutmain, a Taliban spokesman said that *it has been the policy of the prophet and holy men of Islam from times immemorial to destroy all 'false gods'*. He said that the people worshipping the statues were enemies of the Taliban and refused to accept that Islam calls for respect for other people' faiths. He further claimed that *"Islam had defeated and cancelled out all other religions*". For several weeks the Taliban soldiers kept on placing bundles of dynamite around the Bamiyan Buddhas, while stubbing out cigarettes on the ancient statues, before they obliterated those symbols of Afghanistan's glorious heritage. It is believed that similarly several rare pieces of sculpture, including innumerable idols in some old Hindu shrines in Bakhtiar province, statues of folk dancers and calligraphic images were also destroyed by the Taliban rulers citing Quranic injunctions as the justification. It is amazing that this kind of bigotry and intolerance was allowed to go unchallenged by the civil society but what was more astounding was that not a single Muslim country, no Muslim intellectual or scholar, anywhere in the world, no member-state of the Organisation of Islamic Countries, tried to prevent the ghastly sacrilege, a wanton affront to millions of Buddhists and Hindus worldwide. The only people who openly grieved over the destruction of Bamiyan Buddhas and shared the grief of the Buddhists were the Indians who hold Lord Buddha in high esteem because he has always occupied an important place in the pantheon of Hindu deities and incarnations. And doubly tragic indeed was the studied silence of Muslim countries none of which showed even a modicum of civilizational courtesy to condemn the detestable crime of Taliban who recklessly destroyed the statues by using dynamite and resorting to artillery fire for weeks.

Islam is essentially a male-dominated and male-oriented religion and even in his 21st century, excepting Turkey, hardly any Muslim country has cared to give equal rights and a decent and deserving status to women. In Islamic countries governed by Sharia, women are covered with veil, relegated almost to obscurity and denied higher education. They are forced by the religious diktats and male family members to remain largely confined to homes. In support of the widely practised discrimination against women the obscurantist Mullahs quote several verses of Quran to assert that men are superior to women and therefore women cannot be accorded status equal to men. For instance: "Men are a degree above them (women)" (verse 2 : 228) and "Men are the protectors and maintainers of women, because they support them from their means." ....As to those women " on whose part you (man) fear disloyalty and ill conduct, admonish them, refuse to share their beds, and beat them" (4 : 34). Another point to note is that prima facie the very use of the word "you" in verse 4: 34 indicates that the Quran is mainly addressed to men and perhaps men alone. That explains the relegation of women to an inferior position in Islamic theology. Nearly all Islamic scholars maintain almost unanimously that Islam gives a Muslim male the right to divorce his wife at will, the right to take even second, third and fourth wives and command total obedience from his wife or wives. And to add insult to the injury, as illustrated above, a man can even beat his wife if she disobeys him. The clerics maintain that no woman can question these rules laid down in Sharia, because these are Allah's laws. The atrocities committed on Muslim women in Afghanistan by the Taliban, the religious police of Ayatollah Khomeini in Iran and the indignities heaped on them by the tribal warlords of Afghanistan and Pakistan are too well-known to be repeated here. Taliban's gender discrimination caused immense harm to the Afghan society; it virtually put back the clock of socio-economic progress by at least 25 years, that is by one generation. After Taliban seized Kabul they issued an edict making it compulsory for women to wear the veil (burka), disallowing them from wearing high heels and using make up. They were debarred from going out to work, except in the medical sector. Women working in the medical sector could not sit in the next seat to the driver. "No Afghan woman has the right to be transported in the same car, as foreigners," the edict continued.[27] Within three months of the capture of Kabul, the Taliban closed 63 schools in the city affecting 103,000 girls, 148,000 boys and 11,200 teachers of whom 7,800 were women.[28] They shut down Kabul University and sent home nearly 10,000 students of which 4,000 were women. By December 1998, UNICEF reported that the country's educational system was in a state of total collapse with nine in ten girls and two in three boys not enrolled in schools.[29] The Taliban's treatment of women drew enormous adverse publicity and international criticism when Emma Bonino, the European Commissioner for Humanitarian Affairs and 19 women Western journalists and aid workers were arrested and held for three hours by the Taliban religious police in Kabul on September 28, 1997. They had been touring a female hospital ward funded by European Union (EU), when journalists accompanying Bonino were arrested for taking photographs of women patients—all photography was banned by the Taliban.[30] During the Taliban regime several women activists of RAWA (Revolutionary Association of the Women of Afghanistan) underwent enormous sufferings because they continued to strive for equal status to women and secure for them social justice and human rights. RAWA was founded by a number of dedicated women intellectuals under the leadership of a gutsy lady, Meena, who was assassinated in 1987 in Quetta,Pakistan, by some fundamentalists, perhaps at the behest of Gulbudin Hekmatyar, leader of a fanatical faction of Taliban. Members of RAWA had also participated in the war of resistance against the Soviet occupation of Afghanistan in the wake of the coup of April 1978. After the overthrow of the Taliban, RAWA activists have been involved in the difficult task of restoration of women's rights and dignity in the medieval Afghan society. An instance of the atrocities committed on many innocent women in Afghanistan during the Taliban regime was depicted in a documentary made sometime ago by a newswoman from London. It depicted the heart-rending execution of three Muslim women in burka in a square in Kabul. They were shot in the back of their necks in a cold blooded manner and then the three corpses were dragged away by their feet by the sextons. The tragic details of this gory incident have been given in a touching narrative by Oriana Fallaci in her book, *The Rage and the Pride*.[31] Unfortunately in most Muslim countries women continue to be confined behind the veil and discriminated against with impunity even today, largely because of the absence of a just and fair legal framework which could accord them equal status and dignity. Even here in secular India, in matters relating to marriage, divorce, maintenance and inheritance, Muslims continue to be governed by their own religious laws, although the founding fathers of the Indian Constitution had specifically incorporated Article 44 in the chapter under the Directive Principles which laid down that "the State shall endeavour to secure for the citizens a uniform civil code throughout the territory of India." It is quite surprising that even educated and enlightened Muslims and those claiming to be intellectuals have been opposing the framing of a common Civil Code—although in matters concerning other aspects of their day-to-day living, there has never been any opposition to being governed by the Indian Penal Code, the Evidence Act, the Criminal Procedure Code, the Civil Procedure Code and hundreds of other enactments which are equally applicable to all Indian nationals, whether Hindus, Muslims or Christians. Many of these modern laws are violative of the tenets of Islamic jurisprudence enshrined in the Sharia but neither the leaders of Muslim community in India nor their clerics and ullemas nor even vocal intellectuals have ever refused to be governed by these common laws.

Unfortunately the leadership of the community is in the hands of a group of diehard fundamentalists who are determined to deny gender equality and want to perpetuate the male dominance. This is an extraordinary situation. The Supreme Court in a landmark judgment on July 25, 2003 by a three-judge bench headed by the Chief Justice V.N. Khare regretted the Government's inaction in not enacting a common civil code as stipulated in the Constitution, while striking down Section 118 of the Indian Succession Act which discriminated against the Christians. It was third time that the Supreme Court raised the issue and expressed "distress over government's failure to give effect to Article 44 of the Constitution". Earlier also there was a sharp reminder in 1985 in the famous case of Shah Bano when the then Chief Justice Y. B. Chandrachud had regretted that the state had been remiss in discharging its obligation to give effect to Article 44. Unfortunately at that time the law was turned upside down by passing the Muslim Women (Protection of Rights on Divorce) Act, just to please the fundamentalists- a retrograde legislation on every count. It led to stringent criticism of the new enactment on several counts, one of which was that it was a retrograde Act to facilitate the Muslim males marry new wives, without paying any maintenance to the former ones in utter disregard of the principles of natural justice and equality. This widely perceived impression, which is not altogether incorrect, only tends to increase the divide between the Hindus and the Muslims by signalling to the former that Muslims are getting an undue favour in the matter of application of the common laws of the land. Significantly in his recent observations the Chief Justice seems to have criticised that enactment brought forth at the behest of the then Prime Minister, Rajiv Gandhi, by observing that "it is no matter of doubt that marriage, succession and the like matters of secular character cannot be brought within the guarantee enshrined under Articles 25 and 26 of the Constitution (right to freedom of religion)." He pointed out that a common civil code will help the cause of national integration. Unfortunately this important reform had been funked by Pandit Nehru himself in 1955 when the Hindu Code Bill was brought forth. Instead of a Hindu Code Bill, Pandit Nehru's government should have brought forth a uniform Indian marriage and inheritance law, applicable to all communities and religious groups.There was no reason for the Congress government at that time not to enact an Indian Civil Code. But it was not done—could it be due to the policy of vote-bank politics? The truth is that uniform civil code is an unfinished agenda of the implementation of our Constitution and the apex court had done well to remind the government about its duty. Unfortunately many left-oriented analysts, keep on opposing the introduction of a uniform civil code. They invariably try to give it a communal slant by saying that the government wants to interfere with the rights of the Muslim minority, although they know that the matter has been brought up suo motto by the apex court, and not by the government. Their line of argument is both devious and mischievous. Basically the question of having a uniform civil code should be viewed as a step towards removing gender discrimination in Muslim society. At worst, it could be seen as a conflict of interest between Muslim women and Muslim men, in which the former deserve to be given relief in accordance with the Constitution. But somehow it has always been projected as a dispute between the Hindus and the Muslims. Since most leftists and media columnists swear by modernity, one fails to understand why don't they realise that basically a common Civil Code is also an issue of modernity versus orthodoxy. It is astounding that the Indian leftist class has reached a stage of mental decay where they can't think straight on secular issues and speak in a straightforward manner! For blocking the enactment of a uniform civil code, one of the most ridiculous arguments advanced by the leftists, and supported by some leading lawyers, is that just now the Muslim society is not prepared to accept this change and therefore the government should give more time for Muslims to accept it. By the same token, the government should not have passed the laws banning child marriage and dowry which evils have been rampant among both the Hindus and the Muslims, till the two communities were mentally prepared to accept the change. Carrying the same logic further some loony lawyers could argue that even the abolition of the abominable practice of 'sati' should have been stalled till the Hindu society was ready to accept it! This argument of interminable wait till the Muslim society becomes ready to accept a uniform code looks quite perverse. It is a classic example of *reductio ad absurdum*. To dispense justice in an equitable manner does one have to wait for the consent of the perpetrator of injustice? One simply wonders how could some eminent lawyers practising in the Supreme Court fall for such illogical logic. Frankly, if the Muslims could not be ready to accept a uniform civil code even 56 years after independence, there could be no hope of their ever agreeing to it. If that be so, how long will the Indian state continue to deny to Muslim women the right to equality enshrined in the Constitution? Can the Indian state afford to be seen as blatantly favouring the Muslim men against Muslim women? If so, how long and with what constitutional and legal justification? Interestingly, in the State of Goa a uniform civil code governing the institutions of marriage, divorce and inheritance in relation to all citizens has been in force from the times when it was ruled by Portugal. It has been accepted by the Muslims of Goa without the slightest protest, or murmur, and has remained in force without any adverse consequences now for almost fifty years. If a uniform civil code is acceptable to Muslims in Goa, why can't it be enforced throughout the country? In a democratic society no community can be allowed to deny equality and dignity to fifty per cent of its population, that is women, on the ground of religious belief. That kind of ghettoisation has to be swept aside despite opposition by the obscurantists of various communities—whether they be Hindus, Muslims or Christians. Equality is the cornerstone of democracy—you cannot deny it to someone simply because she is a woman or because she happens to be a member of a particular religious group. Despite modernisation of marriage laws in many Muslim countries, including Turkey, Tunisia and even the ever fundamentalist state of Pakistan, the leaders of Indian Muslim community have been persistently obstrtucting the passing of a common Civil Code. There seems to be no justification whatsoever for denying equality and dignity to Muslim women, under a common law. Perhaps the opposition to the uniform civil code among the Muslims of India is due to the powerful grip of Mullahs on that society but at least educated and enlightened Muslims should be able to stand up and be counted. Could their opposition be ascribed to that hackneyed belief that Huwa (i.e. the Eve) was believed to be the daughter of "Satan" and that she was responsible for seduction of Adam? Why do the Muslim men consider the option of having four wives as their inviolable right under the sharia? These are important questions concerning modernity and Islam. But no open debate is allowed in such matters by the clergy and religious scholars by invoking the shelter of the Islamic scriptures. That is the main obstacle to reform and modernisation. The repugnant practice of female circumcision, a lurid ritual, continues to be widely practised in many African countries like Egypt, Sudan, Somalia and Nigeria. But no voice is raised against that brutality towards female child. True, there are instances of brutality against women in other societies also, but those are sharply condemned and even legal provisions are made to punish the perpetrators of the crime. Interestingly there is another belief, sort of a canard, propagated by the fundamentalist Mullahs that all womenfolk are crooks, impure and unreliable. In one of her books *My Girlhood*, translated by Gopa Majumdar in English (published by Kali for Women), Taslima Nasreen, a well-known Bangladeshi writer, author of the truth-based Bengali novel *Lajja*, has poignantly raised the question of denial of equal status to women in Islamic societies by referring to what she had been taught in school. She, along with other students, was told that one of the bones in a women's neck is crooked and that was why no woman thinks straight or walks on a straight path. She questions the scriptural injunction that women were like a field for growing crops to which men were totally free to go whenever they liked, and that if a woman was disobedient the man had a right to drive her away from his bed, and if she remains disobedient, he could even beat her. She questions these scriptural injunctions and remains unconvinced. "How could Quran – a book so holy that it has to be kissed before it could be lifted or replaced—speak of such discrimination?"[32] No wonder Taslima Nasreen was hounded out of Bangladesh for holding such independent views on the status of women in Islam and for writing truth about atrocities committed by the Muslim fundamentalists on Bangladeshi Hindu women in her famous, though controversial, novel *Lajja* (i.e., "The Shame") Gender discrimination is widely practised in almost every Muslim society. For instance, there is that unjust practice of 'triple talaq', widely prevalent in India and many other Muslim countries, whereby a Muslim male can divorce his wife summarily and arbitrarily by pronouncing the word "talaq" three times in one go (i.e., by repeating three times 'I divorce thee'). And according to the Sharia, the divorce becomes instantaneously effective and the divorced lady can be immediately thrown out of the house. This malevolent formula of triple talaq hangs like the proverbial Damocles' sword over the heads of Muslim wives most of whom are otherwise, too, not allowed to go out for work because of Islam's societal taboos. It enables unscruplous husbands to blackmail their wives and maintain their dominance over womenfolk.The discriminatory treatment meted out by Muslim men to their womenfolk in Islamic societies, mainly due to 1400 years old religious edicts and the dominant role commanded by the clergy, has been acting as a drag on the social and economic progress of Muslim societies. For instance, for quite sometime past Pakistan-sponsored terrorists have been trying to enforce compulsory wearing of the veil, i.e., burka, by Kashmiri women. An edict to this effect was issued by the militant outfit Lashkar-e-Jabbar in December 2002. The militant group which hit the headlines last year for its diktat making burqas a must, in December, 2002 killed four women in Rajouri, just to prove that it meant business.[33] Posters were found pasted outside women's colleges directing women to wear burqa and in remote pockets girls were forbidden to continue education after Class 8 and wine shops were targeted leaving many liquor-sellers and buyers injured. Jabbar made its first appearance in the Valley in 2001 and created a sensation by asking women to wear burqas. An outcry followed. But none obeyed, till the militants carried out three acid attacks.[34] The burqa call given by the Lashkar-e-Jabbar has been endorsed by a women's militant outfit 'Dukhtaran-e-Millat' (Daughters of Islam), headed by Asyia Indrabi. Soon the militants' burqa call spread to Rajouri, Majakot, Thanamandi and Kotranka. The Hindu women were directed to wear 'bindis' so as to mark them out from Muslim women. In yet another attempt to curb the freedom of women in Kashmir, a newly emerged outfit known as the Shariati Nefazi Islami (SNI) has asked girls to follow a strict dress code.[35] It even warned the owners of beauty parlours in the Valley to shut shop before May 15, 2003. A local English daily *Greater Kashmir* quoted Junaid-ul-Islam, self-styled chief of Shariati Nefazi Islami, as saying that the growing waywardness and moral degradation among young girls was a matter of deep concern. Stating that jeans, transparent and short dresses were alien to Kashmiri culture, it has asked the tailors in the Valley to refuse stitching "obscene dresses".[36] The fundamentalist organisation held parents responsible for encouraging their daughters to imitate western culture and warned that strict action will be taken against the girls found wearing such dresses. Last year the women in the valley were ordered to wear burqa by another outfit, Lashkar-e-Jabbar. At that time many militant outfits had distanced themselves from the diktat. "However, at least three young girls lost their eyesight and their faces were disfigured when the Jabbar militants splashed acid on them for not adhering to the order.[37]

It may be recalled that some of the staunch Islamist terrorists who bombed the WTC and Pentagon on 9/11, too, were rabid women-haters. To begin with there was that Muhammed Attah who left two testaments. The one in which he says : "At my funeral I do not want impure beings. Meaning animals and women." Then another one where he adds: " Not even around my grave do I want impure beings. Especially the most impure: pregnant women".[38] If such is the degree of contempt towards women among Islamists, how would one expect them to treat women as equal partners in life? And remember, Muhammed Atta was no illiterate ignoramus ! How could a University-going youngman forget that he too was born from the womb of a woman? Similarly in recent years the ascendancy of Islam in Nigeria has led to a virtual reign of terror against women. A lady lawyer Hauwa Ibrahim has on her hands 15 cases of hapless women facing various forms of punishment under the harsh Sharia law that has taken roots in Nigeria's north. Her best client was Amina Lawal, the young mother sentenced to be stoned to death for having sex outside marriage.[39] It was Lawal's case that first prompted protests against Nigeria staging the Miss World contest in 2002, much to the bafflement of Lawal and her lawyer. "Amina is from a village—no roads, no TV, no radio," says Ibrahim. "She cannot read. She cannot write. She has never heard of Miss World".[40] And fat was added to the fire when a Christian woman journalist wrote that perhaps Prophet Muhammad would have approved of the Miss World contest and might have even married a contestant. The result was widespread communal violence in which more than 200 persons were killed. One of the first Sharia cases against women in Nigeria was of

Bariya Ibrahim, a teenage mother, who was sentenced to 180 lashes for having sex before marriage. Her appeal was thrown out and Bariya was flogged 100 times in January 2001. Luckily, Amina Laval was acquitted due to lack of evidence—apparently more due to the pressure of outraged public opinion. But the large number of women being prosecuted in Sharia adultery cases in northern Nigeria reflect an inherent gender bias in the way the law is applied, says lawyer Ibrahim. For a woman to be convicted of having sex outside marriage, the birth of a child is sufficient evidence. For a man to be convicted without a confession, there must be witnesses to the act of sex. That is the tragedy flowing from the rigid control of orthodox clergy over the lives of innocent people.

There are ominous signs that the fundamentalists in Pakistan are trying to make life more difficult for women. In June 2003, the newly formed Government of North Western Frontier Province announced that it will bring a slew of sharia-based legislative measures to promote Islamization of the society, according to the provincial law minister Zafar Azam. "Sharia will be the supreme law," he said. "We will preach to people to adopt good things and give up bad things."[41] Azam said that the provincial government would urge men to grow beards. Another plan was to have separate universities for women. It was feared that the next step could be to set up a version of the Department for Prevention of Vice and Promotion of Virtue—a Taliban-style body. Naturally this has caused concern to educated and enlightened women. Sherry Rehman, a member of the National Assembly of Pakistan and a former editor of the popular news magazine, *The Herald*, wrote: "Every time the spectre of a Shariat act is raised in Pakistan, women are the first to shudder." Irrespective of its content, there are widespread fears that the North West Frontier Province government's adoption of a Shariat bill could result in serious curbs on women's mobility and freedom. The first worry is that many radical clauses kept off this bill's agenda will still be pursued by self-appointed vigilantes in the streets.[42] Rehman recalls that such fears are not unfounded. "Our own history as well as the experience of other Islamicised states holds up a largely anti-women, deeply orthodox mirror to the societies they reflect. This picture threatens a large mainstream of Pakistani women today." Drawing attention to General Zia's Islamisation process that saddled Pakistan with laws such as the Hudood and Zina ordinances, she urged a quick, sobering look at the police records of the last few years. "The Hudood ordinance remains the single most commonly applied law to hold women in indefinite lock-up". According to this law, in present usage, when a woman petitions her rape she invariably becomes an accomplice instead of a victim. Needless to say, the law's axe falls mostly on poor, resource-starved women. For over three decades, Shariat-law adventurism has been a favourite ploy of rightist political forces who have been allies with the military in dominating the national agenda through the appropriation of the state's ideological discourse. She concludes that Zia's formula of "harnessing Islamist parties as a substitute for the legitimacy conferred by real democracy continues even today".[43] In such discriminatory societal environs there is no possibility of empowerment of women. They hardly have any social position or dignity. Surprisingly not many women organisations worldwide have come forward to the succour of the persecuted and beleaguered women of Islamic countries. All that one notices here and there is a loner Taslima Nasreen in Bangladesh, an activist Asma Jehangir and an outspoken journalist Sherry Rehman in Pakistan or a gutsy Meena, founder of RAWA, in Afghanistan trying to stand up to the tyranny of clerics and Muslim males. The real tragedy is that this rampant discrimination against women is carried out under the sanction of the Muslim law, of the Sharia. The singular lack of courage shown by the educated women of various countries, especially the western women's organisations, does no credit to the educated women worldwide. The specious plea that they have no locus standi to interfere in the religious matters concerning the members of another faith is hardly a valid excuse. In any case, due to exclusion of women from the mainstream of socio-economic activities, the scientific, economic and social progress of Islamic nations is not only quite poor but gravely flawed. Surely any society or religious or political group which denies to the half of its population the benefits of the vital pre-requisites of progress, e.g., education, dignity, scientific temper, basic human rights and equality of opportunity will have only slow and stunted growth.

Over the centuries, Muslim societies have evolved a typically separatist and exclusivist mindset. This negative trait is illustrated by a number of prominent examples. Red Cross has been a universally recognised well-intentioned and humanist organisation which has been accepted all over the world. But a majority of Islamic countries did not want to continue with the innocous nomenclature "Red Cross". Perhaps they thought that the word 'cross' had an unpleasant Christian odour which the faithful could not accept. So in the year 1986 in Islamic countries Red Cross had to be renamed (one dare not say 're-christened') as "Red Crescent". In sharp contrast to the Muslim attitude there has never been any objection to the nomenclature Red Cross by the Buddhist and Hindu societies. Sublimated by centuries of civility and tolerance and their belief in equal respect for all religions, 'Sarva dharma sambhava', Hindus and Buddhists do not see anything wrong or improper in the use of the nomenclàture "Cross" for serving the mankind. But Islamic nations decided to accept it as only "Red Crescent" —and could never accept its worldwide accepted nomenclature.

Again there is a well known political pressure group known as the OIC (Organisation of Islamic Countries) established in May 1971, following a meeting of the Foreign Ministers of Islamic countries in December 1970 at Karachi, in Pakistan, to promote solidarity and cooperation among Muslim nations. It is a sectarian religious forum meant solely for Islamic nations. But there is no comparable religiously denominated group of Christian or Buddhist countries. There being only one Hindu country, that is Nepal, there is no question of any religiously denominated Hindu group of countries being formed. The Hindu majority India and the Hindu-influenced Mauritius are both secular states committed to democracy and pluralism. But the OIC is quite unique in more than one way. For one thing it is the only group of nations which has a religiously denominated label and on top of it the OIC often speaks and acts in a patently partisan manner with a degree of unanimity, or near unanimity, in matters concerning the Muslims living and working anywhere in the world and not merely those living in fifty seven Islamic countries. And as a rule, where the dispute is between a Muslim group and a non-Muslim group in any country, the OIC often tends to side with the Islamic causes, as would be noticed from the position taken by it in matters concerning Bosnia, Chechenya, Palestine, Kashmir and recently in the case of Iraq. For OIC the first priority is to support an Islamic cause or movement, and not to act in a just or fair manner, nor decide any issue on merits in an impartial manner.

As a rule, in Islamic countries there is a total absence of any political space for secularism and pluralism. In Muslim countries one has to be a Muslim to be able to work and live as an honourable first grade citizen. Generally, on religious ground, the non-Muslims are relegated to the status of second class citizens and often denied equality of opportunity and the requisite dignity in socio-political matters. In fact, the term used for non-Muslims allowed to live in predominently Islamic countries or societies is "dhimmy", or Zimmy, which implies that they are allowed to exist on some kind of sufferance by submitting to the primacy of Islam. During middle ages most of the Muslim kings of India, except Akbar, had levied a tax called 'Jiziya' on Hindus for allowing the latter to practise their religious beliefs. Verse 9: 29 of Quran gives sanction for imposing 'Jizya' on 'kafirs', a sectarian tax levied on non-Muslims who do not embrace Islam but are under the protection of an Islamic regime, with willing submission and feel themselves subdued.[44] In sharp contrast to this discriminatory practice, no Hindu or Buddhist ruler had ever imposed such an unjust levy on their Muslim subjects. Even those Hindu and Sikh rulers who had waged life-and-death battles for decades with Moghuls,e.g., Rana Pratap, Shivaji, Maharaja Ranjit Singh, Peshwas, Holkars and Scindias, did not ever think of imposing any religion-based imposts on Muslims or Christians. The very thought of imposing a religion-based sectarian tax on a section of their subjects, their own people, would be an anathema to the spiritual ethos of a Hindu or Buddhist ruler. But Muslim rulers of India promptly found out a religious diktat in the Quran for imposing Jiziya on Hindus and imposed that discriminatory levy. Of course, the first victims of the imposition of 'jiziya' were the Jews of Khaibar in Medina, Arabia, on whom this poll tax was levied during the life time of Prophet Muhammad himself.

A very strange feature of most Islamic societies is their frequent recourse to senseless violence and killings, sometime in a very cruel fashion, totally out of sync with the modern societal ethos and unacceptable to the 'universal civilization'. Perhaps it springs from a number of barbaric punishments like the chopping of the hands for crime of theft, public stoning to death for adultery and rape and public beheading of the guilty, as prescribed in the Quran and the Sharia. Most of these continue to be practised in Sharia governed countries like Saudi Arabia and parts of Nigeria and were sought to be enforced in Afghanistan by the Taliban. The brutality of such inhuman punishments being awarded in Saudi Arabia and other Sharia-ruled countries is self-evident. Some fundamentalists in Pakistan also want such Islamic punishments to be instituted in their country.

Many Islamic regimes and radical organisations have a track record of wanton killings, sometime in the name of religion, sometime for sheer heck of it! One such incident of senseless killing of innocents, unprecedented in brutality and ferocity in Egyptian history, occurred at Luxor on November 17, 1997, when an Egyptian Islamist gunman, Medhar Muhamad Abdel Rahman, believed to have been trained in the Afghan guerrilla camps led five other terrorists in the mass murder of 58 foreign tourists and at least four Egyptians on the banks of the Nile barely 500 metres from the 3,400-year-old Pharaonic temple of Queen Hatsheput. The attackers, who horribly maimed about 20 more survivors, all perished in the following pursuit and gun battles with police and enraged townspeople of Luxor. The manner of the mass killings, which according to survivors and newsmen like the London *Independent* newspaper's Robert Fisk who arrived on the scene soon afterwards, recalls in some respect accounts of throat-cutting and disembowling which took place during the 1979-89 Afghan jihad-tactics which had been so rare as to be almost unknown until then in Egypt.[45] Blinded by bigotry the Islamists do not spare even their co-religionists, the Shias. One has just to recall the great tragedy which overtook thousands of Hazaras (Shia Afghans) who fled to Bamiyan when Kabul fell to Taliban in 1996. In August 1998 when the city of Mazar surrendered to Taliban, within the first few days around 6000 people, mostly Shias, were hunted and mercilessly killed by the soldiers of Sunni Talibans (Wahabi fundamentalists) who consider Shias as heretics, though not infidels. No mercy was shown even to Shia diplomats. Ten or eleven members of the Iranian consulate in Mazar were dumped into a basement and then shot dead in cold blood for no fault of theirs. A classic example of the Islamist penchant for the macabre was the brutal beheading of the *Wall Street Journal's* well-known correspondent Daniel Pearl in Karachi (Pakistan) on February 23, 2002,in front of a video camera. The jihadi captors of Pearl filmed themselves on video cutting his throat and then ritualistically severing his head from his body in an ghastly manner. "I am an American," he said on camera. "I am Jewish. My family on my father's side is Zionist", declared Daniel Pearl, before he was beheaded. The same barbaric ritualistic mode of murdering a number of hapless Hindus by beheading them or slitting their throats, has been resorted to by the terrorists in Jammu & Kashmir with impunity in a number of instances. They have been doing it to those Muslim Kashmiris, too, whom they suspect to be in league with the security forces. In fact, some Muslim women of Jammu & Kashmir, who did not obey the orders to wear the veil in accordance with the Islamic tradition, in response to the 'fatwa' issued by a fundamentalist-Islamist organisation called Lashkar-e-Jabbar, were also murdered most cruelly by slitting their throats. As far as the Pak-sponsored militancy in Kashmir is concerned the list of gory killings by the faithful Jihadi soldiers of Islam is fairly long and blood-curdling. One such instance of cold blooded killings of 24 unarmed innocent Kashmiri Pundits, including women and children, occurred at Nadimarg on March 24, 2003, which also happened to be the National Day of Pakistan. It was committed by members of Lashkar-e-Tayyeba. This ghastly crime, masterminded by Abu Mahaz, a Pakistani Commander of LeT for Pulwama area, was allegedly committed with the connivance of some of the nine armed police personnel who had been posted there to protect the Kashmiri Pandits. The role of cops came to light after the arrest of two persons who claimed that police cooperation had been sought which implied that the cops would not resist the massacre.[46] Again on the night of March 29, 2003 another brutal crime was committed by Islamists in Jammu & Kashmir, this time against Muslims whom they suspected to be collaborating with the Security forces. Militants chopped off the noses of six persons, including a woman at a village in Rajouri. Seven foreign merceneries, in combat dress, entered the Panihad village, went to the house of Mir Waiz in his absence and cut off the noses of his wife Fatima, son Mohammed Razaq and a guest Nisar Hussain. Then they went to Noor Hussein's house and chopped off his nose and that of his two sons. Yet another incident depicting the extreme brutality of the Pak-sponsored terror took place in the third week of April 2003 when "suspected militants abducted one Mushtaq Ahmed Dev from his house in Kishtwar area at gunpoint and then chopped his nose, ears and tongue off". A police spokesperson confirming the gruesome act, said that Mushtaq Dev hailed from Sigdi area of Chatroo, a remote village of Kishtwar of Doda district. According to an unconfirmed report the victim was a distant relative of the General Secretary of the All India Congress Committee (I).[47]

It may be recalled that a former President of Afghanistan, Najibullah, and his brother Shalmar Ahmadzai, had also met a very cruel and gory end in Kabul at the hands of militant Taliban in September 1996. Najibullah became President in 1985 and oversaw the withdrawal of Soviet troops from Afghanistan in 1989. He remained in power till 1992 when he was made to step down by the Mujahideen storm-troopers due to rapid growth of Islamic militancy. His family was able to escape from Afghanistan in good time, but before he could leave Kabul, the militants overran Kabul and blocked his escape. For four years Najibullah was given refuge in the compound of United Nations Mission. But in September 1996 the Taliban soldiers dragged him out of the compound of the U.N. Mission. Throughout the night they tortured Najibullah and his brother in a cruel manner, remniscent of the dark medieval ages, and then hanged their mutilated and bloated bodies outside the Presidential Palace. What followed was worse and an altogether macabre spectacle of brutality. The bodies of the ex-President and his brother were kept hanging there for public to see, while crows and vultures pecked at the corpses. And surprise of surprises, no Muslim country, no Islamic scholar, dare condemn the ghastly slaying of Najibullah and his brother and subsequent desecretion of their corpses!

One of the most heart-rending incidents of brutal killings in the name of Islam in the twentieth century has been narrated by Oriana

Fallaci to which she along with many journalists and a German photographer, was witness in Dacca, Bangladesh, after President Mujib's assassination in 1975, when the so-called twelve impure men were executed in Dacca, Bangladesh, in the stadium by stabbing them in their thorax with bayonets. Twenty thousand believers, many among them women, sitting in the tribunes of the stadium continued to pray and chant Allah-o-Akbar, Allah-o-Akbar (God is Great). After executing the impure men they killed a ten-year-old child who in order to save one of them, his brother, had thrown himself on the executioners, pleading "don't hurt him, don't hurt him". The executing soldiers crushed the child's head with the heels of their heavy boots. This ghastly incident, according to Oriana Fallaci, was reported by her as well as some German, French and British reporters—and one of them, the German, had taken photographs, too. As soon as the execution ended, these believers (many women) left the tribunes and came down to the ground. But not in a disorderly way, but in a methodical, very solemn manner. They formed a proper procession and solemnly reached the scene of the carnage, all the time chanting Allah-o-Akbar. They passed over the corpses and reduced them to a carpet of crushed bones.[48]

Isn't it shocking that out of twenty thousand spectators sitting that day in the Dacca stadium, not one stood up to protest against the atrocity? When these brutal killings took place in Dacca no contemporary Islamic scholar, no human rights activist nor any leader of the international community showed the courage to raise his voice of protest. That proud privilege of representing the sane voice of humanity fell to the lot of a ten year old boy who stood up to it and was mercilessly crushed by the jackboots of religious bigots!

And the latest call for taking recourse to the medieval Islamic practice of slitting throats of the enemies, as ordained in the name of Allah by the Prophet in Quran, came from no less than the much hyped socialist-cum-secularist favourite of India's leftist groups, Saddam Hussein, former President of Iraq. Ultimately even Saddam, the great secularist, turned out to be no more than a tin-pot fundamentalist bigot. On March 23, 2003 while applauding the

Iraqis for their so-called resistance to the U.S.-led invasion, the secular Saddam exhorted his followers to "strike them, and strike evil so that evil will be defeated". "You Iraqis are in line with what God has ordered you to do, to cut their throats," he said.[49] Interestingly, a commandment sanctioning the slitting of throats of 'kafirs' and enemies is contained in Verses 47:4, 5, 6 of Quran which lays down the treatment to be meted out to the enemy by mujahids: " So when you meet (in fight .... Jihad in Allah's Cause) those who disbelieve, smite at their necks till when you have killed and wounded many of them, then bind a bond firmly (on them, i.e. take them as captives). Thereafter (is the time) either for generosity (i.e., free them without ransom) or ransom (according to what benefits Islam) until the war lays down its burden.[50] The medieval practices like slitting of throats, though ordained by Islamic scriptures, were almost forgotten by the civil society. These have been revived, almost with a vengeance, now by the jihadis.

These recent instances of bloodletting, committed by Islamists in the name of religion, reveal a medieval mindset, wanting in humane behaviour and civilizational values. Some of these were followed in Muslim societies in the twentieth century simply because these are supported by religious scriptures. It is doubtful if the universal civilization can ever come to terms with such grotesque practices—even if these are ordained by holy scriptures – whether of Muslims, Hindus or Christians. The foregoing recent examples, just a few out of the many such instances from the recent history of Islamists, show that Samuel Huntington is not far wrong when he proclaims that "Islam's borders are bloody, and so are its innards."[51]

This peculiar aspect of deliberate and calculated recourse to raw violence is likely to occupy the quality time and space during deliberations whenever the process of conflict resolution starts—may be after twenty, thirty or fifty years from now. History of mankind is a witness to the fact that ultimately all civilizational conflicts, howsoever long and protracted they might be, have to undergo the process of conflict resolution through dialogue, debate and discourse.

A uniform feature of Islamic societies is their secessionist trait: the divisive tradition of breaking away from their parent countries to constitute themselves into exclusivist theocratic states. Wherever in any particular region Muslims constitute a majority or acquire a comfortable near-majority in numbers, as happened in Kosovo and Bosnia, they start making demands for secession and ultimately take recourse to armed struggle for breaking away from the parent country. That has been the standard Islamic tradition. In twentieth century, this trend was started with the carving out of Islamic state of Pakistan by partitioning India in 1947, when the British decided to leave the sub-continent. Since then it has caught the fancy of Muslims societies worldwide. Soon enough this very fundamentalist, religion-centric attitude was witnessed when Pakistan invaded the princely state of Jammu & Kashmir in 1947 in a bid to annexe the valley on the specious plea that it happened to be a Muslim majority area. It is really tragic that due to certain political developments, foremost among which was the presence of Lord Mountbatten as Governor General of India, Pakistan was able to capture and annex a sizable part of Kashmir valley in that war which now constitutes the Pak-Occupied Kashmir. This peculiarly Islamic trend of seeking secession and organising for them selves an exclusivist existence on the basis of religion, something like 'Dar-ul-Islam' or a Muslim theocratic state, has been the cause of many violent faultline clashes and wars in several parts of the world, e.g., Cyprus, Bosnia, Chechenya and Mindnao and Sulu islands of Philippines. Apart from the well-known examples of Cyprus and Chechenya, this aspect of a pronounced propensity for breaking away from the mother-country is best illustrated by the events of of Kosovo and Bosnia where break-up of Yugoslavia and a demographic tilt in population in favour of the Muslims brought a radical change in the mosaic of geo-political developments. Historically communal identities in Bosnia had not been strong. Serbs, Croats and Muslims lived peacefully as neighbours, intergroup marriages were common, religious identifications were weak.[52] Once the broad Yugoslav identity collapsed, however, these casual religious identities assumed new relevance and when fighting intensified they too intensified. There was a perceptible change in the attitude of both Serbs and Croats and they started identifying themselves with their own cultural groups. But change in the attitude of Muslims was even more marked and in the 1990 elections the Muslims rejected the multi-communal parties and voted overwhelmingly for the Muslim Party of Democratic Action led by Alija Izetbegovic.[53] He was the idealogue of the separate Islamic state of Bosnia—in much the same manner as Iqbal had been of Pakistan. He being a devout and radical Muslim had been imprisoned by the communist regime of Yugoslavia for his secessionist views advocating that the Muslim majority areas of Yugoslavia should break away and form a new Islamic country in Europe. Izetbegovic in a book '*The Islamic Declaration*' published in 1970 had argued about the incompatibility of Islam with non-Islamic systems. "There can be neither peace nor co-existence between the Islamic religion and non-Islamic social and political institutions." He argues that when the Islamic movement is strong enough it must seize power and create an Islamic republic. In this new state, the subjects of education and media should be in the hands of persons whose Islamic moral and intellectual authority is indisputable and absolute.[54] Bosnia is not an isolated example. It is the same story everywhere. When Muslim population reaches a near-majority status in any country, in fact even before that as soon as it exceeds 30 or 40 per cent, an Islamic struggle for secession immediately starts often resulting in organized violence. On their own admission, as candidly spelt out by Izetbegovic in recent times and by Sir Syed Ahmed more than one hundred fifteen years ago in 1888, Muslims refuse to co-exist with other religious groups on equal terms in the same country and raise the demand for a separate homeland. Evidentally the concept of Hindus and Muslims of India being two different nations was first propounded by Sir Syed Ahmed not by Jinnah and nor by Savarkar. The concept of the two-nation theory, for all practical purposes, is an integral part of Islamic theology. Muslims find it difficult to co-exist with other religious groups because Islam per se is antithetical to multicultural and multi-communal nation-states. Islam itself propounds the two-nation theory when it divides the world into two hostile camps: Dar-ul-Islam and Dar-ul-Harb, the two nations, which are in a kind of perpetual conflict with each other.

It has been widely claimed that Islam is an egalitarian faith and it assures equality and dignity to every human being. But that is only a theoretical illusion. Islam is very much a discriminatory religion. First and foremost, it is heavily loaded against all non-Muslims, howsoever, pious, truthful, meritorious and God-fearing they might be. In this respect it is far more discriminatory and unjust than any other religion. As exemplified by Dr. Ambedkar, Hinduism is said to divide people and in contrast Islam is said to bind people together. But that is only a half truth because Islam divides as inexorably as it binds. Islam is like a close corporation and the distinction that it makes between Muslims and non-Muslims is a very alienating distinction. The brotherhood of Islam is not the universal brotherhood of man. "It is a brotherhood of Muslims for Muslims only."[55] There is a fraternity the benefits of which are available only to those within its corporation. For those who are outside that religious corporation, there is nothing but contempt.[56] Islam is more discriminatory than most other religions because it has a scriptural sanction, for imposition of a poll tax called 'jiziya' on non-Muslims, which resembles protection-money. And in the time of Prophet Muhammad Jews were indeed made to pay jiziya. Similarly in India Hindus were subjected to jiziya by a number of Muslim rulers. About the treatment of non-Muslims in Islamic countries there is nothing much to write home about. According to the philosophy of Islam even the most pious and God-fearing non-Muslim is inferior to a Muslim. Maulana Mahommed Ali a close associate of Mahatma Gandhi, while presiding at the session of the Indian National Congress in 1923, had lavishly praised Gandhiji—perhaps because the Mahatma had supported the Khilafat movement whole-heartedly. But just after one year while speaking at Aligarh and Ajmer he changed tune and proclaimed that howsoever pure Mr Gandhi's character might be, from the point of view of Islamic religion he shall be deemed inferior to any Mussalman, even though the latter might be without character."[57] That statement of Mahommed Ali created a stir. Many did not believe that the Maulana, who had expressed so much respect for Gandhiji, was capable of entertaining such contemptuous sentiments about him. But later on when Mahommed Ali was speaking at a meeting held at Aminabad Park in Lucknow, he was asked whether the sentiments attributed to him were true. Mr Mahommed Ali without any hesitation replied:

> "Yes, according to my religion and creed, I do hold an adulterous and a fallen Muslim to be better than Mr Gandhi." [58]

This statement was made despite the fact that Gandhiji had given whole-hearted support to the cause of Muslims and both Mahommed Ali and Shaukat Ali were his good friends and old Congressmen. But that did not deter Mahommed Ali from according an adulterous and fallen Muslim a status better than the Mahatma.

For no apparent reason, Islam has a pronounced gender bias against women, who form fifty per cent of the humankind. Even in the matter of the treatment of the faithful, Quran does not accord equal status to everyone. There are verses which try to rationalise the centuries old practice of Muslim rulers in treating different classes of Muslims in an unequal manner on the plea that it has been so ordained by Allah. Again there are verses which state that it is Allah who decides that who should acquire the riches and who is destined to remain in poverty among Muslims. For instance, Verse 28:82 says "It is indeed Allah who enlarges the provision or restricts it to any of his servants He pleases". Again Verse 6:165 justifies inequality when it proclaims, "He (Allah) has raised you (Muslims) in ranks, some above others." But this does not mean that Islam preaches or practises a greater degree of discrimination than any other religion. Such a conclusion will be most unfair—almost a travesty of truth. Most religions are dogmatic and have a pronounced streak of discrimination, are male-centric and male-dominated. Perhaps Islam is a little more.

Eventually one has to admit that there is the problem of a mismatch between modernity and Islam. How to bridge this huge gap? Not easy, perhaps. Medieval mindset of Islamists is reflected in certain prominent traits: autocracy is one, senseless violence is another, gender discrimination yet another. To these may be added some other traits like pronounced bellicosity and an inexplicable behavioural pattern of unprovoked brutality. Islam sanctions or at least justifies, killing of innocent infidels. It berates all non-Muslims, even if they happen to be the most truthful, pious and God fearing souls on earth – even a Mahatma like Gandhiji was. The sole criterion is that unless they submit to Islam, they are no good human beings. Again Islam glorifies martyrdom in the cause of advancing the Islamic faith. That explains the spate of suicidal attacks by Palestinians, notably the Hamas and the Hizbollah, against the Israelis and similar suicide missions being carried out by the Pakistan-trained militants in Jammu and Kashmir and several parts of India, including Delhi, Mumbai, Jammu, Ahmedabad, Coimbatore and several other Indian towns and cities. These are classic examples of Islamist-jihadi fervour for martyrdom. These attacks are meticulously planned, cleverly crafted and ruthlessly executed. These are not impulsive manifestations of violence caused in response to any provocation nor are these sporadic acts of violence committed by disorderly mobs. These are all premeditated crimes against humanity which no civil society can condone. Many similar attacks have been organised by Islam's terror troops even in India against the so-called 'kafir' Hindus. The barbarism of gun-wielding militants in targetting unarmed innocent Hindu Yatris going for pilgrimage to Amarnath year after year, the two successive attacks on Raghunath temple in Jammu, the attacks on Indian Parliament in Delhi and Akshardham temple in Ahmedabad and killing of the innocent family members of army personnel, including children and infants, at Kaluchak clearly reflect a pronounced streak of sadism. It is this sadism which manifests itself in frequent homicidal and suicidal attacks by the so-called fedayeens in Jammu and Kashmir and Palestine. In recent times it appears to have been accentuated perhaps by illusions of grand entry into heaven where seventy virgin maidens are waiting for them, should they attain martyrdom! The same glory of martyrdom had perhaps fired the imagination of 19 terrorists who attacked the WTC and Pentagon on September 11, 2001. So long as the concept of paradise under the 'shade of swords' continues to rule over the minds of Muslims and they remain committed to waging holy war against all non-Muslim societies, could there be a rapprochement between the Islamic civilization and the universal civilization? That is a $ 64 million question.

The trend towards armed insurgency by Islamists in many parts of the world for bringing about regime change or achieving secession from the parent country, is on the increase. And terrorism is being used as a convenient tool to further the cause of pan-Islamic movement. During last three decades religiously motivated and jingoist groups of militant Muslims in a number of countries and diverse political regions, as far removed from each other as Bosnia and Philippines, have organised themselves into militia-like outfits to wage holy war to force secession from their parent countries on the ground of religion and carve out for themselves some sort of a Dar-ul-Islam. Most of these groups are armed with Kalashnikovs and RDX and had received organised training in Pakistan and Afghanistan (the land of strategic depth carved out through 'regime change' by the ISI and the Pakistani rulers) for waging jihad and carrying out suicidal terrorist strikes. Almost all of them were indoctrinated in Islamic seminaries, trained in the ISI run camps in Pakistan and Afghanistan and were battle-hardened in the Afghan war against Russia. Subsequently with the growth of Al Qaeda and Taliban their numbers swelled manifold and so did the quality of training and their commitment to the cause of jihad. The massive sweep of their area of operation alone is enough to convince right thinking members of the civil society about the staggering dimensions of the problem and its implications for the future of the mankind. A cursory glance around the globe will show up that a number of jihads are already in progress, say in Bosnia, Chechenya, Palestine, Egypt, Iran, Afghanistan, India, Thailand, Indonesia and Philippines. The whole of Balkans is like a tinder box which can erupt into flames of civil war any time, any day. In Europe the infection has spread to many countries, including the U.K., the Netherlands, Germany and France. The annihilation of Saddam Hussein's regime in Iraq-war has failed to stem the tide of Islamist-terror. Over a period of time it could give greater impetus to the existing groundswell of Islamic militancy which has already enveloped almost all Muslim nations and some non-Muslim countries too across at least three continents of Asia, Africa and Europe—from Britain to Morocco to the Philippines. The relief, if any, from terrorism provided by the success of the U.S. campaign in Iraq might be only marginal and temporary. In the long run, it could fuel more terrorism among the Muslim youth. There may be a lull, say for an year or two, but it should be seen as a lull before the storm. The Islamist outfits are in no great hurry and will surely strike back sooner or later—perhaps sooner than latter and with a vengeance too! There is a strong possibility of Islamist trying to form a grand alliance of the Muslim nations of Middle East and the Northern Africa through secret confabulations. A surreptitious move is already afoot for forging a joint front of Islamic nations led by Pakistan and Saudi rulers. There are unconfirmed reports of Pakistan sharing its nuclear arsenal and perhaps the technology as well with the Saudi kingdom. If their past history is any guide the terrorists groups will continue to mount attacks on their target countries like the U.S.A., India and Israel. For the time being it will be a selective, low-intensity guerrila warfare, occasionally marked by the high pitched jihadi fervour but mostly sporadic and surreptitious, full of surprises. In the second phase of this protracted civilizational conflict the Army-plus-ISI ruled state of Pakistan, General Musharraf's "fortress of Islam", might play yet another momentous role, by providing access to nuclear weapons and technology to jihadi outfits. The access to nuclear technology could also be provided to the radical Islamists by the Iranian regime which for all practical purposes is well set on the road to becoming a nuclear power. Let us admit, it is only a matter of time. After all in this technology-pervasive world how long could America alone block the flow of nuclear technology to Muslim nations. There are 57 of them, all under the OIC umbrella, most of them flush with petro-dollars. Access to nuclear know-how will herald the next campaign of radical Islam which will be far more aggressive and bloody than the one which we are witnessing presently. The next phase of Islamist jihad is likely to confront and overwhelm many more countries and regions of the world. The availability of nuclear weapons for use against "kafirs" will help in recharging the zeal of the ummah and galvanize the hordes of jihadis, embedded in many countries, and raring to go after their three arch enemies, namely the Christian, the Hindu and Jewish civilizations. The macro picture will become clearer if one adds to the long list of Muslim countries seething with anger over the fate of Afghanistan and Iraq, the huge resentment building up against the west and the growing jihadi rage noticeable among the young educated populace of Saudi Arabia, Turkey, Iraq, Iran, Pakistan and Indonesia, especially among the younger generations of educated Muslims who have been in the forefront of the Islamist campaigns. This important role of educated Muslim youths in the advancement of the radical philosophy has been highlighted by Huntington. Like most revolutionary movements, the core elements of Islamists consist of students and intellectuals. In most countries in the first phase of political Islamization the fundamentalists managed to win control of student unions and similar organizations. The first breakthrough came in the universities of Egypt, Pakistan and Afghanistan in the 1970s and then it moved on to other Muslim countries. The fundamentalist movement was particularly strong among students in technical institutes, engineering faculties and scientific departments. Later on, in 1990s the second generation Islamic indigenization started manifesting in Saudi Arabia, Algeria and elsewhere. Due to the trend of increasing proportions of university students being educated in their home-country languages they were increasingly exposed to Islamist influences. The Islamists also developed a substantial appeal to women and Turkey witnessed a clear shift in the attitudes of the older generation of secularist women and their Islamist-oriented daughters and grand-daughters. According to a study of the militant leaders of Egyptian Islamist groups it was found that they had five major characteristics, which appeared to be common with the Islamists of other countries. They were young, mostly in their twenties and thirties. Eighty per cent were graduates or university students and more than fifty per cent came from elite colleges or intellectually most demanding fields of technical specialization such as medicine and engineering. More than 70 percent were from lower middle-class with "modest, but not poor backgrounds," and were the first generation youngmen in their family to get higher education. Most of them had spent their childhood in small towns or rural areas but had become residents of large cities.[59] It was this class of educated youth who powered the new surge of Islamic militancy.

Surprisingly the general impression among the educated elite and intellectuals, both in the west as well as in Asia has been to the contrary, especially in India, where scores of intellectuals, media analysts and political leaders have been blaming the growth of militancy among Muslim youths of the sub-continent (i.e., Pakistan, India and Bangladesh) on their poverty, lack of education, ignorance and economic hardship. It is extraordinary that they refuse to understand the complex nuances of Islamist militancy which draws inspiration from the spectacular conquests of early Arab, Moghul and Turkish armies in the medieval times when they conquered large parts of Asia and Africa and battled it out with European rulers in Iberia, i.e. Spain, France, Balkans and Austria. But most important source of this inspiration to Islamists has been the mammoth growth in Muslim population across the globe. This is the theme song of a number of websites established by dozens of Muslim outfits using internet. The facts of Islam's extensive conquests are better known to educated Muslim youths, far better than the illiterate Muslim masses and for that reason the educated Muslims have been in the forefront of the movement of restoring the lost glory of Islam. Perhaps one can forgive the politicians for not stating the obvious and running away from reality because they are into the quagmire of vote-bank politics. But what could be the reason for the naivette of the educated elite, scholars and media analysts? It is difficult to believe that they are unaware of the elementary truth that in India itself the growth of Muslim separatism and the demand for a Muslim homeland by partitioning the sub-continent had been spearheaded in 1930s and 1940s by the educated elite and scholars of the Muslim society. Huntington's viewpoint is wholly corroborated by the recent research studies and empirical data. As logical as the poverty-breeds-terrorism argument may seem, study after study shows that suicide attackers and their supporters are rarely ignorant or impoverished. Nor are they crazed, cowardly, apathetic or asocial. If terrorist groups relied on such maladjusted people, "they couldn't produce effective and reliable killers," according to Todd Stewart, a retired Air Force general who directs the Ohio State University programme in international and domestic security.[60] The truth was brought out by Scott Atran when he pointed out that in the suicide bombing of a café in Tel Aviv in the last week of April 2003 which killed three bystanders, the bomber and the main accused of being his accomplice had grown up in Britain, in relatively prosperous circumstances and studied in a college. Similarly Nasra Hassan, a Pakistani relief worker, interviewed nearly 250 aspiring Palestinian suicide bombers and their recruiters in the year 2001. She found that none of them was uneducated, desparately poor, simple-minded or depressed. They all seemed to be entirely normal members of their families. Again a 2001 poll by the nonprofit Palestinian Centre for Policy and Survey Research indicated that Palestinian adults with 12 years or more of education are far more likely to support bomb attack than those who cannot read. Another report from the officials of the Army Defence Intelligence Agency who interrogated Saudi-born members of Al Qaeda being detained at Guantanamo Bay, Cuba, revealed that these fundamentalists, especially those in leadership position, are often educated above reasonable level and a surprising number have graduation degrees and come from high status families. Their motivation and commitment are evident in their willingness to sacrifice material and emotional comforts, including families, jobs and physical security to travel long distances and pay their own way.[61]

Another researcher, Alan B. Krueger, analyzed the data which the U.S. State Department collects on significant international terrorist incidents. The home-countries of the perpetrators of each event were identified. More terrorists do come from poor countries than rich ones but this is because poor countries tend to lack civil liberties.[62]

There is no substance in the oft-repeated argument that lack of education and poverty are the root causes of Islamist terrorism. Research studies and empirical observations clearly show that the educationally advanced and prosperous elite groups of Muslim community are more involved with the pan-Islamic movement and the growth of radical Islam. Historically in India, too, the well-to-do students and teachers of Aligarh Muslim University had played a very prominent role in fanning the flames of Muslim communalism and carrying forward the battle cry of jihad for creating Pakistan. The uneducated and uninformed Muslim masses became the camp followers of the elite storm-troopers of Aligarh University much later, almost a decade later. Sir Penderel Moon had expressed surprise that Pakistan came to be created so late, and with such a rush at the end, while in the beginning the idea was such a slow starter. He pointed out that as far back as 1888 Sir Syed Ahmed, the great Muslim leader of the nineteenth century, had enunciated the premise which led naturally and necessarily, to the idea of Pakistan. Sir Syed Ahmed pointed out that India was a country inhabited by two different nations and there would necessarily be a struggle for power between them, if the English were to leave India. "Is it possible", he had asked, "that under these circumstances two nations—the Mohammadan and the Hindu—could sit on the same throne and remain equal in power? Most certainly not. It is necessary that one of them should conquer the other and thrust it down." He dismissed the idea that both could remain in India on equal terms as something impossible and inconceivable.[63] There is a marked similarity in the views expressed by Sir Syed Ahmad one hundred fifteen years ago, by Iqbal in 1930 and by Alija Izetbegovic, in recent times. Three of them display the same mindset of breaking away from the parent country. And no wonder that Pakistani army brass consistently dream about the day they will be able to rule over India. After all, Sir Syed Ahmed did envision a situation in the future, after the British left, when one of the two communities, Hindus or Muslims, will overthrow the other. It was that great Muslim intellectual, a renowned poet and eminent scholar, Sir Mohammed Iqbal (better known to the average Indian as the author of the song "*Saare Jahan Se Accha Hindustan Hamara*") who had sown the seeds of India's partition along communal lines. Iqbal was the idealogue who conceptualised the theocratic Islamic state of Pakistan and for that important reason he is held in great esteem in Pakistan and is universally revered by many terrorist groups of Pakistan-Occupied Kashmir. Iqbal was an intellectual and a poet par excellence. His poetry is full of wonderful imagery and superb diction. In his magnum opus *Shikwa* (' The Lament ') Iqbal makes a passionate and soulful supplication to Allah for restoration of Islam's lost glory and grandeur and complains about the plight and marginalisation of "the faithful" all over the world. While analysing the ramifications of Islamist militancy it would be interesting to understand the import of the forceful message contained in Iqbal's *Shikwa*. He talks about the intrepid spirit and courage of Muslims in waging wars against infidels, challenging the "rich and the powerful." When he sang "*shaan aankhon mein na jachti thi jahandaron ki, kalma padhate the ham chhaon mein talwaron ki*", did he have a dream vision of the holy war against today's prosperous and powerful America? He lauds the exploits of the warriors of Islam by narrating how they had extinguished the fire of Zoroastrian temples, humbled and subjugated Khyber Pass and destroyed idols and vanquished the idol-worshippers worldwide to carry forward the banner of Islam. He praises the unique valour displayed by

Muslim horsemen in galloping across the continents from one victory to another, triumphing through deserts and oceans to spread the message of prophet Muhammad. The stirrings caused by the inspiration provided by Iqbal's *Shikwa* to the Muslims worldwide were experienced by V.S. Naipaul as early as 1979-80 in the far away Bandung in Indonesia, when he met Imaduddin, an Engineer-turned-fundamentalist instructor at the mosque of the Institute of Technology, during a three days course in 'Islamic mental training'. After recitation of some verses of Quran, Imdaduddin was called upon to read a poem. Imaduddin said, "It is by Iqbal." He explained that in the last session of the mental training course and he always ended it by reading that poem by Iqbal because it is very emotional. It was written in Urdu and translated into Arabic by Effendi and from Arabic it was translated into Indonesian by Mohammed Natsir. Iqbal was the idealogue of Pakistan. Natsir had been once the leader of the banned Muslim party of Indonesia.[64] Imaduddin explained the poem to Naipaul and then began to read and he was transformed. Giving a graphic account of the impact of the poem on Imaduddin, Naipaul observed that his social graces and his apparent humour were submerged in this new personality, not of the actor or the puppet-master, but of the mullah, the man in the mosque, reciting the Koran on some day of religious passion. Imaduddin had said the poem was emotional which became apparent because as he read his voice broke. At times he seemed about to sob as if in anguish, while talking of hell, heaven and redemption. And that was perhaps the theme of Iqbal's poem: how without the Prophet or knowldege of his mission, could the world be endured.[65] The poem in question, read by Imaduddin, the Engineer-turned-Islamist teacher was 'Shikwa'. Thus, Iqbal was not only the idealogue of Pakistan. He fathered Pakistan; Jinnah was only Qaid-e-Azam. Iqbal also played an inspirational role, truly a momentous one, in jigging the groundswell of the present day pan-Islamic movement across the globe. The truth is that long before Laden assumed leadership of the militant Islam, Iqbal's two radical poems, "Shikwa" and "Tarana", were being translated into Arabic, Indonesian and other languages and regularly used to arouse the Muslim youths across the globe for marshalling them to fight for restoring the lost glory of Islam. What Naipaul saw and experienced in Bandung, Indonesia, in 1979-

80 proves that the ideology of radical Islam had struck deep roots long before bin Laden appeared on the scene. In this respect the successive governments of Pakistan have been totally faithful to Iqbal's ideology and world vision. Naipaul was not far wrong when he said that the story of Pakistan is a terror story. It started with a poet who thought Muslims were so highly evolved that they should have a special place in India for themselves. Naipaul criticised Iqbal's wish "to sift countries of irrelevant populations as something terrible and this is what exactly happened in Pakistan".[66] Of special interest to Islamist-militants of Pakistan have been Iqbal's famous lines in another poem titled *Tarana*, in which he proclaims that "*Muslim hain ham watan hai saara jahan hamara, Chin-o-Arab hamara, Hindustan Hamara". Again "Teghon ke saye main ham pal kar jawan hue hain, Khanjar halal ka hai Qaumi nishan hamara*". Translated into English it means that "the entire world belongs to us, the Muslims; we have a claim on China and Arabia, and India too belongs to us. We Muslims have been brought up under 'the shade of swords' and for that reason the Halali dagger (butcher's knife) represents the Nation of Islam." These famous lines of Iqbal's Tarana are music to the ears of jihadis being trained in the seminaries of Pakistan and Pak-Occupied Kashmir. In this very poem there are references to the glorious history of Islam, its golden age when the valleys of Europe were overrun by Muslim warriors and Christian churches had reverbrated with the echo of "Azan" (the Muezzin's call to the faithful for prayer). And those were the glorious days when Muslim soldiers used to bivouac in the gardens of Al Andalus (Arabic name for Spain). Towards the end he goes on to assert that the Muslims were not the kind who would ever submit to the infidels and that their reckless courage has been tested hundreds of times, when he boasts: "*Batil se dabne wale aiye aasman nahin ham, sau bar kar chuka hai tu imtihan hamara*". These are not mere words, nor mere poetry; this is the truth about the vision of reviving the long lost grandeur of Islam and the raw courage sought to be breathed into young Islamists by Iqbal's philosophy taught for decades in madarasas and Islamic seminaries of Pakistan, West Asia, northern Africa and South East Asia. Some of Iqbal's soul stirring, though jingoistic, verses, including *Tarana*, are reportedly recited by the prospective Jihadis being trained in ISI sponsored

training camps in Pakistan and Pakistan-Occupied Kashmir. As mentioned in an article by Ardeshir Cowasjee, the singing of *Tarana* with gusto by students of first to fifth class has been made compulsory in all goverrnment schools of Pakistan now for the last eight years.

Again it is Islamic spirit of sacrifice and the glory of suicidal martyrdom in the cause of Allah which has kept the Palestinian cauldron on the boil for the last fifty years.This philosophy also lies at the root of senseless killings and mayhem in Chechenya, Indonesia and Philippines. This very attitude is responsible for the ongoing militancy, or "holy war" in Kashmir where ISI inspired Jihadis, volunteers from more than one score Muslim countries, are busy carrying out ethnic cleansing of the Hindus. No political analyst dare deny these facts. The ground reality of Islamic militancy and its implications for the future hits you in the eye when you look at the commitment of Islamists in the seminaries of Pakistan, the jingoistic training for jihad being imparted in madarasas of the sub-continent, the religious zeal of the volunteers joining the suicide squads of Hamas in Palestine and the ferocious comitment to jihad of the bombers of Chechenya and Kutta beach in Bali.

Bin Laden is not far wrong when he claims that all Muslims are one people, that they are one nation, and that they have joined a decisive battle against the U.S.A., the Jews and the Hindu India. Surely the turn of Europe as a soft target will come fairly soon as soon as the Balkans get fully Islamized due to the galloping growth of Muslim populations in Albania, Bosnia, Macedonia and Serbia. And France, Spain and Italy will get submerged in the overflowing stream of Muslim immigrants from Turkey, Egypt and Maghreb. The highly visible massive growth in population of the countries of the Maghreb and the Middle East will create multiple demographic divides in Europe during the next two decades leading to major religious conflicts, especially in the soft states like France, Italy and Spain, weighed down by ageing populations. Of course the Balkans have already been sucked into the vortex of centuries old faultline conflicts. That will add to the growing incidence of civilizational wars. Laden may have been killed or might die but Islamist terrorists will continue to threaten the non-militant and peace-loving Asian and European societies. And to this fact file of terror one may add a footnote that the U.S.A. too have a lurking Islamist problem in their backyard in the shape of the not-too-dormant Black Muslim movement led by that firebrand radical leader, Louis Farrakhan, who calls it "the Nation of Islam", the latter nomenclature being fully in tune with the concept of 'ummah', and the Islamic theory of a world divided into two nations. But America is too far away from Pakistan and the Middle East to be easily targeted and perhaps too powerful to be civilizationally damaged. Even then, many American scholars and military strategists especially the neo-conservatives, are worried about the future of their country. It may be recalled that the entry of Louis Farrakhan into the U.K. has been banned by the government of that country because of his rabidly racist pronouncements against the Jews. The very concept of "the nation of Islam" has a divisive connotation. It candidly proclaims that the Muslims of America are a separate nation, "the Nation of Islam", while the remaining Americans (i.e., the non-Muslims) constitute another nation—perhaps the nation of "kufr", i.e., the nation of the infidels—shades of the two nation theory propounded in India first by Sir Syed Ahmed in 1888 which was later on honed into the conceptual framework of Pakistan by Iqbal.

During the last fifty years, the militant Islam has become a force to reckon with because of three important developments. Firstly, today Muslims constitute more than one-fifth of the world population and by 2025, their proportion might grow to one-third of world population. Secondly they are highly conscious of the power of their numbers and their leaders are trying to capitalise on this huge demographic surge by propagating the cause of holy war and calling the faithful to jihad, presently being waged in more than twenty countries. By far Islam happens to be the fastest growing religion because Muslim clerics have organised an aggressive methodology for proselytisation, better than the one organised by Christian missionaries, which wins them, year after year, a growing stream of neo-converts to Islam, especially in poor countries of Africa and south Asia. This growth in numbers is further facilitated by the "fatwas" issued by Mullahs forbidding the faithful from taking to family planning on grounds of religion. The third reason is equally important. The cash flow of petro-dollars and enormous riches of the oil-rich Sheikhdoms have provided strong financial muscle to the radical Muslim groups of Pakistan, the Middle East, Bangladesh and Indonesia. This financial clout has been extensively used for establishing thousands of Islamic seminaries and madarasas in several Asian and African countries. It is well-known that in the name of imparting instructions in the tenets of orthodox Islam a whole generation of youngsters has been ideologically motivated and trained to carry forward the militant message of prophet Muhammad, wage multiple jihads in different countries and make the entire world conform to the Islamic ideal of Dar-ul-Islam.These three important developments along with the anxiety of the U.S.A. to dislodge Russians from Afghanistan in the early 1980s gave birth to Al Qaeda and provided an excellent opportunity to bin Laden to galvanize the Muslim youth for launching an aggressive pan-Islamic movement to restore the lost grandeur of Islam. These Islamists have been harking back to the middle ages and trying to make a bold bid for establishing Islam's supremacy in the realm of global politics. Though bin Laden has been called father of the resurgent Islam, which we find pitted against the rest of the world, including the mighty western powers, the truth is that it is the ISI and the successive leadership of Pakistani Army who have imparted a new fiery life to the terrorist movement by indoctrinating and training hundreds of thousands jihadi soldiers. One can notice the unmistakable footprints of Pakistani army and their relentless pursuit of the doctrine of jihad worldwide, in almost every terrorist attack during the last ten years, whether it occurred in America, or Bosnia or Chechenya or India, or in Indonesia. Osama bin Laden appeared on the horizon much later, like the typical charismatic leader at the right moment! History informs us that the threat of Islamic militancy is not something new. It has very deep societal roots, largely derived from the fiery tradition of the Arabian desert and has always been a part of Islamic theology which has a strong imprint of Bedouin legacy.

It has been argued by some scholars that Islam is a religion of peace, as is evident from the meaning of the word "Islam" itself. But that is just a theoretical statement, if not a convenient cover. In any case, this claim, often proferred by Muslim scholars mostly Indians or those of Indian origin, cannot be substantiated by any empirical evidence. The doctrine of jihad, that is permanent war in the cause of Allah is a reality, too well-known by now. Frankly, the history of Islam makes no pretence of commitment to peace, certainly not till the message of the prophet is spread worldwide and the whole world is converted into Dar-ul-Islam. Spirituality is only one aspect of Islam primarily flowing from a strong belief in monotheism and submission to a single God, that is Allah. Even a cursory reading of the Quran and Sharia reveals the militant face of Islam. According to the Quran, there is only one true religion, the "God's religion", and that is Islam. Quran does not admit the validity of any other faith as a means of salvation for human beings. Islamic thought is antithetical to the concept of pluralism. In fact, a number of Quranic verses can be cited to show that Islam is not a religion of peace; it believes in the subjugation and annihilation of all un Islamic religions and commands and its followers unleash violence against non-Muslims unless they embrace Islamic faith. For instance, Verse 59.20 of Quran proclaims. "Not equal are the companions of fire (non-Muslims) and the companions of the garden (that is Muslims): it is the Companions of the Garden that will achieve felicity (victory). Many other verses direct Muslims to fight those belonging to a different faith and kill them unless they adopt Islam. The prayer in verses 71:26-27 to Allah clearly reveals the objective of Islamic faith when it says: "O Lord, leave not of the unbelievers, a single one on earth. For if you do leave any of them, they will mislead Your devotees and they will breed none but wicked ungratefulness". If Islam were a religion of peace, it would not ordain its followers to ensure that everyone must either embrace Islam or face death at the hands of Jihadis. Prima facie this dogmatic belief in the superiority of Islam and the insistence upon its acceptance by everyone seem to be the cause of numerous faultline conflicts between Islam and other civilisations.

Unfortunately on the basis of empirical studies and the history of Islam's expansionist past, it does look true that Islamic societies are more violence-prone and have a higher percentage of faultline conflicts with non-Muslim groups. And if we eschew the temptation of resorting to the usual courtesy of taking shelter behind homilies and platitudes, the stark truth is that there are not one or two, but a multitude of frictional asymmetries between the societal values of the universal civilization and the Islamic civilization. There is a huge mismatch, an ever widening divide, which has pushed the world to the brink of the present day civilizational crisis. As against six major faultline conflicts recounted by Huntington in 1993, at present the world is facing over twenty major faultline conflicts as enumerated in Appendix-II.[67] In each one of these, Islam is at war with other religions. The Islamists have a one-point agenda of restoring the lost grandeur of Islam and converting the world into Dar-ul Islam. To this end, they want to enforce Sharia laws in all Muslim countries. Additionally they want to obtain independence for Muslim minorities of the nation-states like the Philippines, India, China, Russia and Serbia by establishing a string of new Muslim countries through jihad.They debunk democracy, modernisation and tolerance of pluralism, because these western ideas run counter to the teachings of their scriptures. As their long march succeeds, gradually over a period of time, they hope to crush all religious, ethnic and cultural minorities just as they have done in Pakistan, Bangladesh, Lebanon and several parts of the Balkans. In a bid to restore the long lost glory of Islam they have been carrying out a violent struggle to neutralize the influence of western culture in Muslim countries, including the states bordering Islamic culture, say countries like India, Russia and China. Unless there is a radical change in the Islamist mindset, there is little hope of democracy striking roots in Muslim countries. The history of democracy shows that that there are some societies and religious groups which lack the capability to develop democratic institutions, because of their societal deficits.

Huntington believes, like Dr. Ambedkar did, that Islamic societies have some inherent features which tend to inhibit them from imbibing democratic values. According to him, the conflict along the faultlines between Western and Islamic civilizations has been going on for over 1000 years and in the future, too, this military interaction between the West and Islam is unlikely to decline. For doing this plain speaking, Huntington has received flak from many Muslim scholars and secular intellectuals of many countries, including India. But there is a kernel of truth in what he has said. A classic example of the apparent incompatibility of Islamic societies and democracy is available right here, in the Indian sub-continent. Ever since the British left the sub-continent in 1947, after dividing the Indian people into two nations, India has been functioning quite well as a successful democracy. Granted that the Indian democracy has several flaws, perhaps some serious limitations. But there have been no coups nor bloodbath, quite unlike Pakistan and Bangladesh, both Muslim countries, which have been floundering in search of an effective toe-hold for moving ahead on the democratic path. In India even the imposition of Emergency in 1975 by late Mrs. Indira Gandhi, the then all powerful Prime Minister, could not suppress or supplant the democratic tradition embedded in the hearts and minds of the Indian people. It only brought her downfall and that too by the democratic mechanism of universal franchise, the cornerstone of civil society. But the kind of turmoil that has plagued Pakistan repetitively and the destabilizing events which subsequently overtook the newly born state of Bangladesh, need no comments. Ever since its birth in 1947, Pakistan has not been able to adopt and nurture democracy at all. Even after a long period of 56 years, today that country is being ruled by a blustering army General known for his shenanigans; it is a different matter that he manouvered to get himself elected as President in a sham election. But then, according to General Musharraf himself, he is still trying to evolve "a sustainable democracy" in Pakistan, whatever that might mean. The fate of Bangladesh is only marginally better-it has gone through periods of serious public disorder, coups and spells of dictatorship.

Historically and racially, Indians, Pakistanis and Bangladeshis are the same people. The difference is only one and that is of religion and the civilizational values flowing therefrom. India is a predominantly Hindu country, subscribing to the ancient ethos of "sarva dharam sama bhav", (equal respect for all religions), and wholly wedded to secularism, pluralism, tolerance, freedom and equality, the principles firmly enshrined in the Indian Constitution and more importantly in the hearts of ordinary citizens. But both Pakistan and Bangladesh are theocratic states, based on the rigid doctrinaire precepts of Islamic scriptures and perhaps there in lies the clue to the successive failures of democracy in those two countries. How is it that in those two countries democracy has not been able to survive and grow? The answer is not difficult to seek. Democracy is loathed by most Islamic rulers, and perhaps by a large majority of orthodox Muslims too. Acceptance of democracy will mean eradication of gender discrimination; it will mean equal rights to Muslims as well as "Kafirs" or non-Muslims, living in those countries which happen to be predominantly Muslim nations. And thereby hangs a tale. Democracy is bound to lead to introduction of modern ideas like freedom and equality. Who knows that introduction of democracy might break down the religious barriers between the faithful and the heathens and thus punch a big hole in the two-nation theory inherent in Islam? Who knows what consequences will flow from the emancipation and empowerment of women, once they throw away their veils? All those changes will surely lead to the development of a pluralistic and multi-ethnic society, based on equality between males and females. Will that be acceptable to the Mullahs and the chauvinistic Muslim males? For the present the answer seems to be an emphatic 'no' with a capital "N". There is hardly any Muslim country where democracy has been nurtured, allowed to strike roots and was able to blossom into an article of faith among the Muslim masses. Going by the diktats of their scriptures the Islamists will not agree to give equal rights to non-Muslims and Muslim women. Evidently there is some problem somewhere with Islamic societies, some mysterious attributes which act as deterrents to the growth of democracy, modernity and tolerance. Could it be that there is some flaw in the system of education prevalent in madarasas where during studentship Muslim children are taught to hate non-Muslims, called Kafirs, while being taught the merits of jihad. One knows for certain that at least in Pakistan, not only in madarasas but even in the government-run schools, children are taught to hate Hindus and the so-called Hindu India and taught merits of jihad, as pointed out by the well-known Pakistani columnist Ardeshir Cowasjee. Apparently similar schemes of radical Islamic instructions prevail in the madarasas of Indonesia, Bangladesh, Saudi Arabia and most other Muslim countries. After all, V.S. Naipaul did encounter similar fundamentalist conditions as early as 1979-80 in Bandung, Indonesia, during an interactive session with a group-leader of radical Islamists, one Imaduddin. As early as 1871, W.W. Hunter, in his book, *Indian Mussalman*, had impressed upon the then British-Indian Government the absurdity of the British-managed Calcutta madarasas providing an educational fare in which jihad formed a large part of the curriculum prepared for Muslim students.[68] Imagine, it was an uphill task to remove the lessons on jihad from the curriculum of government-run madarasas in the

British-ruled state of Bengal. In the free world not many governments can take the extreme step of censoring the contents of religious textbooks being taught in private schools run by non-governmental organizations nor insist on censoring their curricula. If in the garb of providing religious instructions, dogmatic concepts like jihad and ghanima continue to be taught to school children in madarasas there is little hope of peaceful co-existence between the followers of different religions in the decades ahead. When the present crop of madarasa-educated Muslim children of Pakistan, Bangladesh and Indonesia grows up, they will provide another steady supply of terrorists and suicide bombers to carry forward the holy war of Islamists. A striking example is the growing spate of bombings in Indonesia where in 1979-80 Naipaul had encountered an Engineer-turned-fundamentalist teacher during a session of "mental training" preaching radical Islam. The foundations laid then and nurtured for decades are bearing fruit now in the shape of successive bombings staged in that country. There are reasons to believe that in the madarasas of Pakistan and Bangladesh and seminaries of many Arab countries, during lessons on jihad hatred and violence against non-Muslims are regularly preached. At least in the notorious Haqqania Madarasa of Pakistan there is rampant hatred against Jews, as was evident during the interaction which Jeffrey Goldberg, a Jewish journalist, had with Maulana Haq, the Chancellor of Haqqania. It is an established fact that childhood images find a lasting place in the psyche of youngsters. Only that can explain the morbid hostility displayed by the Islamist outfits against the Crusaders, the Jews and the Hindus.

9

Travails of a Soft State

> "Nature subjects the weak to the strong."
>
> -Seneca.

We, Indians, have been known worldwide as a people who lack a sense of history, though no one doubts that we have a rich cultural heritage and enormous patience. But the world does not value the virtue of piety. It continues to give glittering prizes to those who have sharp swords and stout hearts. It will not be an exaggeration to say that as a people we have always been lacking an insight into the historical perspective which is by far the most important tool for ensuring future security of any nation. An effective survival strategy can be planned and positioned by a country, or a civilization, only by learning from its past mistakes and failures, and using those failures as stepping stones for achieving success in the years ahead.

Most of our statesmen and intellectuals often pride themselves on the fact that although the history of India is replete with instances of several invasions by foreign marauders, the Indians never attacked or invaded any country. And that self-adulating statement is further supplemented by paying tributes to the great Hindu virtue of tolerance, unlimited tolerance even at the cost of self-respect, self-preservation and freedom of the motherland, mirrored so vividly, though unfortunately, in our history of a thousand years of abject slavery. The repetitive overdoses of these two mass opiates have made the average Indian smug and easy going—living and thinking only for today and seldom caring about the tomorrow and the day after. Most Indians remain absorbed in self-centred mundane worldly affairs or seek escape in spiritual pursuits, even at the cost of ignoring important national issues and far-reaching international developments all around us. This attitude of complacency and indifference runs like a strong suicidal trait throughout the history of India. How else can one explain the phenomenon of a few thousands ruthless buccaneering soldiers successfully enslaving and keeping in subjugation such a large population and an equally large country and that too for centuries? Frankly, this misplaced and mis-applauded exaltation of the great Hindu virtue of tolerance of unremitting tyranny and slavery was responsible for the decline and downfall of the Indian civilization in the past. Unfortunately the same indifference and smugness continues to rule the minds of a great majority of Indians even now, after rebirth of the Indian nation in 1947—especially the self-styled intellectuals. The post-independence political leadership of India, too, has for the most part remained a prisoner of the creed of meek submission to senseless aggression and violence by wearing the great Hindu virtue of tolerance on its sleeves. No one can dispute that tolerance is a great quality, a good civilizational value system but only upto a point and within responsible limits. Beyond that limit, any tolerance of tyranny and aggression becomes a liability, a curse. There is very little qualitative difference between excessive tolerance and timidity—a thin line divides the two. Perhaps it is entirely due to this excessive obsession with tolerance that the Hindus have come to be considered as timid and cowardly people. Tolerance of tyranny drives iron into a man's soul and kills his conscience. It destroys the confidence, self-respect and moral fibre of the excessively tolerant people thereby making them cowards, unfit to defend themselves and their hearths and homes, when attacked by aggressive barbarians. That basic lesson from our chequered history we Indians have persistently failed to learn. The Jews, who were once upon a time equally timid and gutless, have learnt it, *albeit* the hard way, and now no one can bully them, nor pillory and pillage them. The old image of a Jew as a meek and mild, petty trader, or a submissive pen-pusher, has been replaced by a new, tough and vibrant, role model called '*Sabra*'. The word *sabra* has been adopted from a native prickly pear which grows in the desert of Israel. The fruit is called *sabra* because it is tough and prickly from outside, but tender and sweet inside. And the new image of Israeli *Sabra*, tough, prickly and ever ready to defend his faith and his holy land, has banished forever the hackneyed old image of spineless Jews poring over their scriptures, ready targets initially for the lance-wielding Romans, then for the jihadi swordsmen of Islam and ultimately for the ruthless Nazis who herded them like sheep into trains and trucks and sent them to the gas chambers of Auschwitz. That transformation of an average Jew from a despised Shylock into a gutsy Sabra was a turning point in the history of Jewish civilization. But the Indian nation still awaits that kind of change, a total transformation of the personality and mental makeup of Indians.

Let us contrast our lackadaisical attitude towards the momentous events happening within the country and across the world with that of the today's hyper power, the U.S.A. Americans are a progressive nation who pride themselves in forging ahead on all fronts for attaining greater heights in every sphere, political, economic, military and sociological, including exploration of the new frontiers of science and technology. Not only the political leadership of America, but even the average American shows far greater concern than his Indian counterpart about security of his homeland and prosperity of the future generations. It is that alert attitude, that concern about the future which has shaped America into a hyper power. The President of Brazil, Lula da Silva, was very correct when he said that if there is one thing which he admired most about the United States it was that they always first think about themselves; second about themselves; and third about themselves. And if they have anymore time, they think about themselves again. That kind of concern and commitment to motherland is missing from the Indian scene. It is impossible to imagine how the Indian civilization, both ancient and ornate, comprising a billion plus people, has allowed itself to be boxed into a corner—besieged by the Pakistani terrorists on one side, and silently invading hordes of Bangladeshi predators from the other. Unfortunately that is a reality.

Our great neighbour, China, is yet another example of what a country once dubbed as "the Sick Man of Asia" could achieve simply by learning a thing or two from its past history and promoting national pride to awaken the average citizen and make him or her work for the advancement of the Chinese nation. The difficult process of learning harsh lessons from their past history and unidimensional emphasis on national pride have been two most important factors responsible for the spectacular success of China. It is absolutely necessary for India to generate a similar feeling of national pride among its people to promote the ethos of mass participation in nation building and forging a steely resolve to defend their motherland and the Indian civilization.

And let us also look at our second next door neighbour, the eternal adversary, if not enemy, Pakistan. That nation was born in a welter of hatred for Hindus and India. The resolution demanding the creation of Pakistan as a homeland for the Muslims of the Indian sub-continent was passed in the annual session of the Muslim League in 1940. Rehmat Ali, an associate of Jinnah, formulated a statement of goals to be attained by the Muslims in general, and Pakistanis in particular, which was titled "The Millat and the Mission" statement. That mission statement of Rehmat Ali contained 'Seven Commandments of Destiny' which made an interesting reading. One of the long term objectives enunciated by Chaudhary Rehmat Ali was to convert the sub-continent of India into the continent of "Dinia" which should ultimately form a part of a bigger orbit called 'Pakasia'. He emphatically argued that Muslims "must write *finis* to the most deceptive fiction in the world that India is the sphere of Indianism".[1] Rehmat Ali visualized a stage in the near future when Pakistan will be enlarged into Pakasia— a sub-continental Islamic entity which was supposed to be the most important part of Asia in which Pakistani culture will become predominant, and Hindu India will stand decimated. Either wittingly, or unwittingly, that Millat and the Mission statement of Rehmat Ali appears to have guided the Pakistani rulers throughout the last fifty-six years. Their single-minded resolve has been to destroy India by waging a proxy war of 'a thousand cuts'. Pakistanis have not forgotten their goal, meticulously laid down in that Millat and the Mission statement, but we Indians totally forgot it or ignored it, as soon as India became independent. But why did the Indian leadership and the people forget it so soon, so easily? The simple answer is the total absence of a sense of history; we just don't want to learn from history. If Indians had developed a sense of history, and the ability to view the contemporary world events in proper historical perspective, the post-independence destiny of India could be altogether different. By learning a few lessons from our past history, we could have brought about a defining change in our response to the Pakistan sponsored terrorism and silent invasion of Bangla migrants. There could be more to it. At least India might have avoided being perceived by the world, including our adversaries, as a soft state. But that forgetfulness of the first generation of the post-independence Indian leadership is now extracting a heavy price in the shape of widespread terrorist attacks across the country with the avowed aim of bleeding and debilitating the Indian people.

It is time to recall that our hard won freedom has lasted barely fifty-six years. And once again India stands at the cross-roads of history. There are no multiple choices available any more. The times ahead are difficult and the demographic developments threaten to pull the plug on the Indian civilization and our democratic polity anytime within the next thirty to fifty years – outer limit one hundred years. The choice could be between freedom or slavery, between the survival or decimation of our ancient civilization, and between the life or death of the biggest democracy in the world. The final choice, however, is between the forces of good and evil. It is of little consequence whether or not the worldwide civil society recognizes the gravity of the situation in which India is placed. The only thing which matters at this critical juncture is whether or not, we, the people of India, wake up and become alive to the serious threat developing around us, both from Pakistan and Bangladesh – the two hostile countries covering our flanks.

The growing incidence of relentless terror attacks unleashed at the behest of our neighbour, often aided and abetted by the local ISI moles, has already taken a heavy toll of life and property during the last thirty years—perhaps fifty years. The expansive coordinates of terrorism extend from Jammu & Kashmir and Himachal Pradesh in the north to Coimbatore and Chennai in Tamil Nadu to Marad in Kerala in the south. Its east-west reach is equally massive, starting from Assam and the West Bengal at the eastern end to Mumbai, Maharashtra and Gujarat at the western end. The mayhem created by the terrorist outfits has already taken a heavy toll of life and property and considerably debilitated the system of governance and imposed heavy financial burden, both on the Central and state governments.

The audicious and horrific attack on the Indian Parliament on December 13, 2001, by a suicide squad of five terrorists was a chilling reminder of the determination of Pakistan sponsored Jihadi warriors to destroy the Indian civilization. It was a loud and clear message to the Indian people that once again the Jihadist Islam had arrived knocking at their doors. The blood-curdling episode began when a white Ambassador flashing registration number plate DL3CJ 1527 came rushing from Parliament Street and entered the grounds around the Parliament House through the Parliament Street entrance and rushed forth towards gate No.12. The Vice President had arrived just a few minutes earlier. When the driver of the terror car found his way ahead blocked near gate No. 11 by some cars which formed part of the Vice President's security entourage, he inadvertently hit one of the cars. At once the militants rushed forth firing all around. By then the policemen on duty were able to alert the watch and ward personnel inside the building who managed to close all entrance gates of the Parliament House. An officer of the Rajya Sabha Watch & Ward staff was the first to raise alarm on his walkie-talkie. He was instantaneously shot dead by the terrorists. Lady Constable Kamlesh Kumari of the Central Reserve Police Force (CRPF) became a martyr when she tried to bring the terror car to halt. The terrorists, five in all, before getting down from the car, started firing indiscriminately and rushed forth in a desperate bid to enter the Parliament House. One gutsy militant raced towards gate No.1, lobbing hand grenades and firing all the way, all over. He did reach the main entrance which had been closed by then, but could not enter the building and blew himself up on the stairs of the entrance. Meanwhile four terrorists scaled a wall near gate No. 11 and raced towards gate No. 5 through which the Prime Minster usually enters the House. Luckily the Prime Minister was yet to leave his residence. He was advised to stay back. Once the terrorists ran into the open, they came under heavy firing by the CRPF Jawans. Three terrorists were shot dead while approaching gate Nos. 8 and 9, while the fourth one was fatally hit when he attempted to reach the first floor by using a Doordarshan cable line. Thus, all five of them were killed on the spot in a gory gun battle. While trapped in the throes of death, under the hail of CRPF bullets, one of them had shouted "Pakistan Paindabad", i.e. "long live Pakistan", proclaiming his allegiance to the country whose command mission had brought him to New Delhi. The police investigations revealed that the five terrorists were members of the dreaded Pakistan sponsored outfit Jaish-e-Mohammed. They had Kalashnikov rifles slung across shoulders and were armed with 9 mm. pistols, Improvised Explosive Devices, grenades and grenade launchers. Some had grenades strapped to their bodies while others kept these in their backpacks. The fact that some even carried dry fruits in their pockets suggested that they had come ready for a long haul, perhaps a prolonged seige and a long drawn battle with the security forces. On day one, the Indian casualties were seven, but on the last count, the number rose to nine owing to the demise of two more seriously injured persons. Among the martyrs were six police officers, Sub Inspector Nanak Chand (he was part of the Vice President's security and was driving one of the cars), Assistant Sub Inspector Rampal Singh (he was driving the Vice President's car when the terror car rammed into it), Head Constable Om Prakash (another member of the Vice President's security team who was killed in the exchange of fire), Head Constable Ghanshyam Narayan (killed in action) and Lady Constable Kamlesh Kumari of the CRPF who was shot dead while trying to stop the terror car (she left behind two young daughters, 11 years and 2 years old). One more officer of Delhi Police succumbed to injuries later on in the hospital. Two members of the Parliament House Watch and Ward staff were also killed and Desh Raj, a gardener of Rajya Sabha was shot dead while working in the lawns. The number of the injured was 16, among whom were 12 security personnel and one TV cameraman. It was a long day, both for the Police as well as the Parliamentarians. When the attack took place neither the Prime Minister, nor the leader of the opposition, Sonia Gandhi, were present in the House. Among those present were the former Vice-President, late Shri Krishan Kant, the Home Minster L.K. Advani and several other Ministers including Arun Jaitley, Pramod Mahajan, George Fernandes and the former Lok Sabha Speaker, late Shri Balayogi, along with a whole lot of Members of Parliament.

Investigations by the Special Cell of the Delhi Police, headed by the Deputy Commissioner of Police, Ashok Chand, resulted in the arrest of Syed Abdul Rehman Geelani, a Delhi University Lecturer of Zakir Hussain College (Evening), on December 15, 2001. Under sustained interrogation Geelani spilled the beans which culminated in the arrest of three other accused persons, Mohammed Afzal, Shaukat Hussain Guru and his wife Afsan Guru aka Navjot Sidhu. The Police also seized from their hideouts in Delhi large quantities of explosives, electronic detonators, chemicals, maps of Delhi city and Chanakya Puri, substantial cash and incriminating documents. The investigations revealed that the conspiracy had been masterminded at the instance of notorious Ghazi Baba, a lackey of the ISI, by Mohammed Afzal, a resident of Sopore (Kashmir). Afzal had been functioning as a coordinator of the activities of Jaish-e-Mohammed in Delhi. His cousin Shaukat Hussain Guru and the latter's wife Afsan were party to the conspiracy which had the blessings of the Jaish-e-Mohammed Chief Masood Azhar and a Lashkar-e-Tayyeba leader Zaki-ur-Rehman. They had also contemplated attacks on the Indira Gandhi International Airport, Delhi State Assembly and other important buildings to disturb public order. It was further confirmed by the Director General of Police, Jammu & Kashmir, Ashok Suri, that one of the attackers on the Parliament House had been a member of the Jaish terror team which had hijacked the Indian Airlines IC-814 flight in December 1999 to secure the release of Masood Azhar, Chief of Jaish-e-Mohammed. The police investigations indicated that the ace terrorist, Mohammed, who managed to race forward to the stairs of gate No.1 where he blew himself up, was an important member of the terrorist group which had hijacked the Indian Airlines flight IC-814. He was the ruthless killer of Rupan Katyal, a youngman who along with his newly-wed bride, was on board the ill-fated flight.

The designated POTA (Prevention of Terrorism Act) court awarded death penalty to Mohammed Afzal, Shaukat Hussain and S.R. Geelani, while Afsan was sentenced to 5 years rigorous imprisonment. The accused persons went in appeal. On October 29, 2003, the Delhi High Court acquitted S.A R. Geelani and Afsan Guru for want of adequate evidence, but upheld the death sentence awarded to Afzal and Shaukat Hussain. The Delhi Police have filed an appeal in the Supreme Court against the acquittal of Geelani and Afsan Guru.

Interestingly barely three months ago, on October 1, 2001, there had been a similar dare devil attack on the Jammu and Kashmir Assembly in Srinagar. Three Pakistan sponsored terrorists in a Tata Sumo came around 1400 hours (nearabout 2 p.m.), wearing police uniforms and stopped at the gate of the Assembly. Suddenly the Sumo burst into flames along with the driver, who was one of the suicide bombers, while the other three terrorists engaged the security personnel in a fierce gun battle and raced into the Assembly building, firing indiscriminately. The toll was 38 lives lost, and scores of innocents injured.

The script-writer and director of the two blood-drenched terror episodes was Maulana Masood Azhar who had been released at Kandhar airport on December 31, 1999, after being escorted by the then Foreign Minister of India, as a part of a deal to secure the release of 155 passengers on board the hijacked flight IC-814. Masood Azhar had been under trial for a long period of five years in a number of cases and was lodged in a prison in Kot Bhalwal in Jammu.

Kashmir Valley has been the main target of jihadi terrorist groups for many decades. On November 3, 1999, around 5.30 p.m. (1730 hrs.) three heavily armed Lashkar militants had launched a major attack on an Army camp in the Badami Bagh Cantonment, located in the high security zone outside Srinagar, killing one Jawan of Border Security Force and Major P. Purushottaman, Public Relations Officer of 15 Corps, who along with seven members of his staff and a military intelligence officer was shot dead. When the attack on Badami Bagh Cantonment took place, three journalists were sitting with Major Purushottaman. Luckily for them, the Army P.R.O. had the good sense to herd them into the toilet of his office, before going out on hearing the rifle shots. The encounter lasted throughout the night and ended only around 4.00 a.m. next morning when two terrorists were killed.

All these important incidents of terrorism along with a number of similar terrorist attacks have gone unpunished thereby emboldening the terror groups and strengthening the perception about India being a soft state, ready to collapse or capitulate in the near future. In the year 2000 three Lashkar-e-Tayyeba militants had targeted the Red Fort, taking both the Delhi police and the Indian Army by surprise. In the years 1996 and 1997 there were quite a few bomb attacks in Delhi, in Lajpat Nagar Market and some other places. Similarly the Odeon Cinema in Connaught Place in the heart of New Delhi was targeted on January 31, 1994, while the Rivoli theatre was targeted next week, on February 6, 1994. Delhi has now been on the hit list of terrorists for more than ten years. According to Delhi Police sources, during the calendar year 2003 as many as 181 "red alerts" were sounded in Delhi apprehending imminent attacks by Pakistan-sponsored terror groups—the average comes to almost one red alert every alternate day. That shows the degree of strain which terrorism places on the institutions of governance.

The fate of Mumbai has been worse. On March 12 1993, a series of powerful bomb blasts had rocked Mumbai killing nearly 300 innocent civillians and injuring another 700. Property worth crores of rupees was destroyed. The subsequent investigations revealed that the bombings had been engineered at the behest of the ISI by the notorious gangster, Dawood Ibrahim, now declared an international terrorist. Although the general impression created by the media reports has been that these bomb blasts were a sort of reprisals against demolition of the disputed Babri structure in Ayodhya on December 6, 2003, the truth was somewhat different. According to police investigations and some classified intelligence reports, the landing of the consignments of explosives and weapons on the western coast around Mumbai had commenced as early as September 1992—at least three months prior to the demolition of the Babri structure. All that could be confirmed by the police investigations, however, was that Babri demolition did act as a catalyst for preponing the dastardly crime, though the Ayodhaya episode by itself was not the prime causative factor. The preparations for staging spectacular bombings in Mumbai, considered a stronghold of Shiv Sena, were already in progress long before the demolition of Babri structure. Large quantities of explosives and weapons had been provided to Dawood Ibrahim by the Pakistani establishment and these were transported to India through the motor launches of one Mustafa

Majnu, a gangster associated with Dawood Ibrahim. We Indians, especially the Hindus, have highly imaginative and inventive minds which try to rationalise through disingenious reasoning even the most irrational events. That was how even the origin of the horrific Mumbai bombings came to be blamed on the Hindus by linking it with the Babri episode. There are reasons to believe that the ISI and Dawood Ibrahim would have bombed Mumbai even if there was no demolition of the Babri structure.

It is well known that both Delhi and Mumbai and parts of Uttar Pradesh and Gujarat have been repetitively targeted by Islamist terrorists. But what is really most remarkable is that the long reach of Islamist terror has already claimed access to several parts of south India which had earlier remained unaffected by the malaise. For instance on April 14, 1995, when festivities of celebrating the Tamil New Year Day were coming to an end, a powerful bomb ripped through the newly constructed State headquarters of the Hindu Munnani in the heart of Chennai killing two members of the organization which resulted in eruption of communal riots. During investigations a circumcised body, partly blown out and mutilated by the blast, was found near the scene of crime. The suicide bomber was subsequenty identified as one Khwaja Nizamuddin who had been earlier suspected of being involved in the bombing of the RSS (Rashtriya Swayamsewak Sangh) office nearly two years ago. He was believed to have returned from Pakistan quite recently, probably after being trained and indoctrinated by the Inter Services Intelligence. Even in an hitherto communally peaceful state like Tamil Nadu quite a few fundamentalist outfits like Al Ummah, Islamic Jihad, Allah Tigers and Islamic Seva Sangh have come up during the last ten years. Earlier in Madurai, P. Rajagopalan, President of the Hindu Munnani had been brutally murdered outside his house by suspected Muslim fundamentalists. He had been in the forefront of the Hindu community's efforts to prevent conversions of Dalit Hindus to Islam by socially assimilating them into the Hindu fold, after mass conversions took place in Meenakshipuram. In February 1997 during the visit of the Union Home Minster, L.K. Advani, to Coimbatore for an election meeting, there were serial bomb blasts, seventeen in all, in Coimbatore, killing nearly sixty persons and injuring another two hundred. The serial bombings were part of a sinister plot to assassinate the Home Minister for destabilizing the country and disrupting the elections to the Tamil Nadu Assembly. These had been planned and executed allegedly by one S. A. Basha who had floated an Islamist organization called Al Ummah. Investigations into the crime led to the arrest of some Muslim youths and seizure of huge caches of explosives. It was learnt that one Zakir Hussain, a member of the radical outfit Al Ummah, had returned from Pakistan sometime ago, after being trained by the ISI in Rawalpindi. It transpired that the RDX used for bombing the RSS office and the Hindu Munnani headquarters in Chennai had been supplied by the ISI agents embedded in the state of Tamil Nadu, some of whom were arrested. It may be recalled that even the killers of Hiren Pandya, a former Home Minister of Gujarat, had been similarly trained in Pakistan. The Inter Services Intelligence of Pakistan has many faces, both overt and covert. One of the known overt faces of the outfit is a string of thousands of madarasas some of which are being funded by questionable sources. The covert face of the ISI are hundreds of moles and safe houses for sheltering the terrorists in dozens of towns and cities. Quite a few hundred ISI moles have been arrested during the last few years but many more are to be yet identified and caught. The growing incidence of terrorist attacks shows that the important Pakistani goal of undermining the institutions of governance and debilitating the vital organs of the Central and State Government is being carried forward at a steady pace in several parts of India.

Unfortunately there is little awareness in the western countries about the magnitude of the depredations of terrorists in India, and the inroads which Islamists have already made into several sensitive spheres of Indian society. Some political analysts in Europe and America continue to believe that the Indian Muslims do not subscribe to the ideology of the Al Qaeda because India is a secular democratic country which enables the Muslims to voice their grievances. Although India is a secular democracy in which the Muslims have equal rights, there are innumerable believers in the cult of radical Islam in India, too. Such platitudinous observations have the potential of doing immense harm to the coalition's resolve to fight terrorism by making the Indian masses and the government lower their guard. It is time we made it known worldwide that India has borne the brunt of the Islamist terror attacks much longer than most other countries. We have faced relentless onslaughts of terrorism now for several decades, long before the Black Tuesday. Within a short span of 8 to 9 months, i.e., between December 2002 and August 2003, there were more than half a dozen terror attacks in Mumbai alone. In Kashmir there has been, on an average, at least one terrorist attack every alternate day. There have been terrorist attacks on two Army camps—at Kaluchak in the year 2002 and Sunjwan in 2003. A number of security posts, both of the Army and the Police have been regularly attacked almost every year. In April 2003, an attempt was made to attack the building of the All India Radio Station in Srinagar (Kashmir) which was foiled by an alert CRPF contingent thereby forcing the militants to blow up the car outside the building. Sometime ago a determined attempt was made to attack the residence of the Chief Minister of Jammu and Kashmir state. Over the years there have been repetitive attacks on unarmed Hindu pilgrims going to Amarnath and Vaishnodevi. In July 2003 the Pak-sponsored terrorists had launched two successive grenade attacks on Vaishnodevi pilgrims at Banganga, barely two kilometers from Katra, in which seven devotees, including a child, were killed and 38 injured. Recently on January 2, 2004, two Muslim terrorists wearing fatigues struck at Jammu railway station. They opened fire with AK 47 assault rifles and hurled grenades on the passengers. Ostensibly the intention was to kill the Hindu pilgrims proceeding to and returning from Vaishnodevi temple. In the ensuing gun-battle one young Army officer and two Jawans of the BSF (Border Security Force) were killed and 15 persons injured. The two terrorists, suspected to be members of the Pakistan-sponsored outfit Lashkar-e-Tayyeba, were shot dead by the brave young Lieutenant, Triveni Singh, who died in the exchange of fire. This was the second attack on Jammu railway station. Earlier in a similar terrorist attack on August 7, 2001, fifteen innocent persons had been killed. Surprisingly the ISI operators have been successful in enlisting the services of scores of Indian Muslims for participating in numerous terrorist attacks within the country. They were also able to send at least quite a few hundred Indian volunteers to Pakistan and Bangladesh for training and indoctrination—perhaps the number could be in thousands, too, if calculated over a decade. This has been an ongoing process which bodes ill for the future of the country. Unfortunately the Indian government has been tight-lipped in making this truth known abroad. That could be one of the reasons for the wrong impression widely prevalent in the western world about the real situation in India.

Once again hopes of peace and amity between India and Pakistan have been rekindled following an hour-long meeting between the Indian Prime Minister, Atal Behari Vajpayee asnd Pakistan's President, General Musharraf, during the 12th summit of the South Asian Association for Regional Cooperation (SAARC) held in Islamabad. In a joint declaration issued on January 6, 2004, the two sides set aside their mutual distrust and agreed to start a composite dialogue on all outstanding issues, including Kashmir, in February 2004. Pakistan pledged to put a stop to all acts of terrorism, violence and hostility emanating from the territory under its control, while India agreed to resume the stalled dialogue on Kashmir. It is certainly a good augury because nothing could be better than peace in the sub-continent. But most political analysts, especially the knowledgeable type, continue to be skeptic about the outcome of the proposed peace process, unless Pakistan accepts the Line of Actual Control (the LOC) as the international border between the Indian Kashmir and the Pakistan-occupied Kashmir. It may be recalled that on January 2, 2004, during a media briefing about the arrangements being made for the SAARC summit, Pakistan's Information Minister, Sheikh Rashid Ahmed, stated that Kashmir problem must be resolved first because it was a question of life and death for Kashmiris. His assertion was published with banner headlines in *Ausaf*, an Urdu daily of Pakistan. Earlier on December 23, 2003, in a run up to the SAARC summit, he had declared during a press briefing that the Kashmir issue should be resolved in accordance with the wishes of the people of Kashmir. If we add to these outpourings of the official spokesman of Pakistan government, a few statements made by Syed Salahuddin, chief of the Hizb-ul-Mujahideen, it becomes crystal clear that this climbdown to a composite dialogue could be one of the usual bluff-and-bluster manouvres of Musharraf—perhaps just to mollify the international community. The clue came from the rantings of Syed Salahuddin, head of the Hizb-ul-Mujahideen, who wrote articles in two popular Urdu newspapers asserting that there could be no peace between the two neighbours unless the Kashmir issue was resolved. He also praised Musharraf very lavishly in those two write-ups for whole-heartedly supporting the struggle of the Kashmiri people. Even before drying of the ink of the joint declaration made on January 6, 2004, Syed Salahuddin announced that the jihadis would not give up their guns simply because a piece of paper had been signed. These announcements show the determination of the radical groups in Pakistan to obstruct the peace process. And barely two days after the joint declaration, on January 8, 2004, Musharraf assured a group of Kashmiri leaders that "Kashmir will be the focal point of any future talks" and that the Kashmiris from both sides will be taken into confidence to ensure a solution acceptable to them. In the circumstances, it looks certain that Pakistan is not interested in the progress of the peace process. There are, however, some down-to-earth Pakistani Economists who feel it was time that Pakistan tried to strike a deal with India because of the growing "economic asymmetry" between India and Pakistan in the realm of development. They feel that time is on the side of India whose fast growing economy could provide it a major strategic military superiority in the near future.

Going by the past experience India can scarcely trust General Musharraf. How can we forget that he was the ace plotter and director of the Kargil war? A cursory analysis of his speeches and public pronouncements during the last few years show him to be a rabid India-baiter and India-hater. Even if he has agreed to join the peace process under pressure of the U.S.A., he will try to renege on it as soon as the first opportunity comes his way. Let us not forget that in his famous speech of September 19, 2001, while agreeing to be part of the U.S.-led coalition against terrorism, he had openly indicated his ultimate intention of reneging on his commitment as soon as the circumstances turned in Pakistan's favour. He had reminded Pakistan's religious leaders "inclined towards taking emotional decisions" of the first six years of "the history of Islam" and referred to two important events. First, the signing by the Prophet of the Charter of Medinah (Meesaq-e-Medinah) to keep peace with the Jews at a time when he was busy battling with the non-believers of Mecca. Second, the signing of the treaty of Hudabiyah for keeping peace with the Makkhans (the rulers of Mecca) when the Prophet was engaged in a war with the Jews. The treaty of Hudabiyah was abrogated by the Prophet before its expiry when the opportune time came to attack Mecca. Thus, in his speech of September 19, 2001, Musharraf had clearly spelt out his intentions and revealed his opportunistic mindset. The U.S. can afford to ignore Mushrraf's penchant for deceit and doublespeak because it is located seven seas away from Pakistan. But India cannot; Pakistan is our next door neighbour. If only we care to analyse Musharraf's personality just on three counts, namely his devious role in plotting the Kargil misadventure, his extra smart, though vile, coup against his former benefactor, Nawaz Sharif, and the contents of his speech of September 19, 2001, we will realize that it will be suicidal to trust him. The Indian leadership should understand that they are dealing with a ruthless strategist and a rank turncoat devoid of any principles who loves to play high stake roulette. When he decided to oust Nawaz Sharif, the former Pakistani Prime Minister, by staging a coup, Musharraf knew that the stakes were very high for him. Yet the coup was staged by him while he was airborne! If he had failed he could be sent to the gallows. Yet he took that risk to capture a country of the size of Pakistan, inhabited by 140 million people. That shows the seamy side of his personality, peppered with reckless courage. The Indian leadership should understand from his bizarre exploits and misadventures that he is one dictator who can press the nuclear button the moment he knows that he can come out a winner in the nuclear war, or get away with it. We must also remember that Musharraf is a clever craftsman of words; he is not only media savvy but also a media charmer, and can even act as a showboy. One may deal with him, but never trust him. It will be quite foolhardy to forget his repeated threats to nuke India, announced worldwide, almost with the beat of a drum!

In December 2003, two successive attempts were made on the life of Musharraf, both within the cantonment limits – one on December 14 and another on December 25. Although the two jihadist outfits, the Jaish-e-Mohammed and Lashkar-e-Tayyeba, are suspected of conspiring to assassinate Musharraf, the complicity of some one from the Pakistani army in the plot too cannot be ruled out. But he is used to living dangerously.

While most educated Indians will agree to the idea of LOC being converted into the international border, loud voices of dissent and dissonance about the proposed peaceful settlement of the issue can be heard all over Pakistan. The jihadis will never opt for peace; their credo is the unending holy war against the infidels. For the present let us keep our fingers crossed. Only future events will tell us about the outcome of the peace process and the proposed 'composite dialogue'.

Indian polity has a surfeit of gullible doves who are ready to believe Musharraf any time and every time, despite all those humiliations which the Indian nation has gone through at the hands of jihadis, including the frightening prospect of a wholesale massacre of the people's representatives on December 13, 2001, when they visited the Indian Parliament carrying AK 47 assault rifles and grenades. Still no lessons have been learnt by our political class. No one speaks up to say that if we cannot punish the jihadi terrorists, at least let us not trust their mentors.

Due to the confusing signals from our political leadership the people of India continue to alternate between hope and despair. Amidst the recent trappings of bonhomie comes the revelation by a Pakistani political analyst, Syed Saleem Shahzad, that while the ISI was closing down its Azad Kashmir Cell (known as the Forward Section 23), it is opening a new one in Karachi to organize infiltration across the international border between Sindh and Gujarat. It is therefore futile to expect that the ceasefire along the LOC will hold for long.[2] It was further confirmed that most of the jihadi outfits operating in Jammu and Kashmir were paramilitary troops of Pakistan.[3]

But why this sudden change in Pakistan's game plan? Why does the ISI now want to relocate the focus of cross-border terrorism from Kashmir to Gujarat by shifting the headquarters of its operations from Muzaffarabad to Karachi? Is it that after opting for peace process in Kashmir, Pakistan is now thinking in terms of a repeat of the Kutch intrusion of 1965? Could it be that the jihadis now want to teach the Gujarat Chief Minister, Narendra Modi, a lesson by destabilizing his governance in Gujarat? Or is it just another red herring? This new development, if true, could also mean something more sinister than what meets the eye. In any case, the terrorist bombings and killings in the State of Jammu & Kashmir are still continuing. The new ISI focus on Gujarat border, if true, will create more security problems. The Pakistani establishment has a single point agenda : to destabilize, debilitate and balkanize India at any cost. For all that we know Musharraf's response to Prime Minister Vajpayee's peace initiative might be just a ruse to buy time—while planning to attempt a final coup de grace at an appropriate time. In any case, even if there is some kind of temporary peace between the two distant neighbours, it will be a phoney calm, perhaps a lull before the storm. Though a head on war may be avoided for now, the ultimate struggle for supremacy in the sub-continent will be joined after three decades or so, may be earlier, in the realm of demographic dominance where the Islamists appear to have an edge. That showdown could start with a clamour for vivisection and balkanization of the Indian nation by the emerging Muslim majority areas of India for secession on the ground of religion. Such a possibility cannot be ruled out in the light of the experience gained in Lebanon, Kosovo and Bosnia. Another ready example is the history of Pakistan's birth in 1947 through gross widespread violence.

Not only India but the entire world community will have to be extra vigilant to meet the growing threat of Islamist terror. In the last week of December 2003, the U.S. authorities had to raise their colour-coded security alert from yellow to orange, the second highest level, due to the increased possibility of year-end terrorist attacks. On December 22, 2003, a terse warning was issued by Tom Ridge, Secretary of the Federal Department of Homeland Security, that the danger of attacks in the "near term" was greater now than at any other time since September 11, 2001. The revised threat perception led to the increase in the level of security alert to "high" as symbolized by the colour 'orange', instead of yellow, on the five colour scale. Simultaneously Air France cancelled Christmas flights to Los Angels on Wednesday, December 24, 2003, after the U.S. security officials warned them that some extremist groups were planning "near term simultaneous attacks that would rival September 11." Much to the discomfiture of the western world a London-based Arab weekly, *Al Majalla*, revealed that Al Qaeda supremo Osama bin Laden has vowed to launch a back-breaking attack on the United States by the February 2004 which would change the order of things. The magazine further stated that the Al Qaeda leader will soon appear in a televised tape to warn the Americans that they should prepare their coffins, hospitals and graves to meet the consequences of the coming attack which will be full of surprises and historic events. Meanwhile the U.S. security officials enhanced the modalities to monitor the air for biological warfare agents in thirty cities to meet the threat of possible terrorist strikes during the current high alert status. How credible are these threats no one knows, no one can predict.

In ultimate analysis the success of the U.S. campaigns in Afghanistan and Iraq has not so far helped in curbing the depredations of Islamist terror groups. That only supports the neo-conservative view that there is a pressing need for re-ordering and remoulding the feudal Islamic societal ethos by promoting democratic institutions in the Middle East for making the world a safe place to live. But the Pentagon should also understand that during the last five decades Pakistan has been transformed into an extension of the Middle East thanks to the rapid growth of Islamist ideology. That is how it has come to be regarded as "the fortress of Islam' —perhaps a more appropriate expression would be to call it as "the fortress of jihadist Islam". To win the war against terror America will have to deploy all those severe remedial measures against Pakistan which it has been using to curb the monster of terrorism in the Middle East. Short of that there is no possibility of the Pakistani establishment giving up its commitment to the global promotion of Islamist terror.

10

Crescent and Mushroom Cloud

"Strength is life. Weakness is death"

– Swami Vivekananda

The war against terror continues both in Afghanistan and Iraq and several other countries. In spite of the widely acclaimed success achieved by the U.S. troops in capturing Saddam Hussein alive in operation 'Red Dawn', the turmoil in Iraq is not likely to die down soon. His arrest might hopefully silence for a while the critics of American campaign in Iraq. In any case, the engagement in Iraq is likely to continue as a long drawn out guerrilla warfare which could last several years. To their dismay the coalition troops have discovered that fighting the fundamentalist terror of Islam is a tough call. Afghanistan too has been witnessing a grand revival of the Taliban ideology and resistance to the Karzai regime is growing, largely due to the support of Pakistani army and the ISI to pro-Taliban outfits. In Iraq the contours of a well planned guerrilla warfare against American occupation are clearly visible. Reports from Baghdad indicate that responding to the call given in the name of 'ummah' by extremist groups, lately many young Muslim militants from a number of adjoining countries, especially Syria, Lebanon, Yemen and other West Asian countries, including some from Europe, have been flocking to Iraq to join the jihad. The intelligence officials claim that since late summer a growing stream of Muslim militants, comprising hundreds of youth from a number of countries have arrived in Iraq by crossing the Syrian or Iranian borders.[1] A senior British official, who was in Iraq in September, said most of the foreign men captured there were from West Asia-Syria, Lebanon and Yemen—or from North Africa. He described them as "young, angry men" motivated by the "anti-British, anti-American rhetoric that fills their ears every day".[2] Signs of a movement to Iraq have also been detected in Europe. Jean-Louis Bruguiere, France's top investigative judge on terror, said dozens of poor and middle-class Muslim men had left France for Iraq since the summer. He said some of them appeared to have been inspired by exhortations of Al Qaeda leaders, even if they were not trained by Al Qaeda.[3] The rising anger against America among the Muslims across the world was visible even in Berlin at a Friday prayer in Al Nur Mosque in October 2003, although political discussions were banned there. The attacks on the U.S. forces and allies are increasing. In the last week of October the average number of attacks on allied troops and international relief agencies exceeded two dozen a day, rising from twelve attacks per day in July 2003. According to a senior American intelligence official, Iraq is now a magnet for jihadists just as Afghanistan was. In an audio tape broadcast by *Al Jazeera* satellite network in October 2003, bin Laden had cited Iraq as the newest front in international jihad and called on the Muslim youth to go to Iraq to wage jihad. Presently, Iraq is mired in a war of attrition which could drag on for quite some time.

There was strong of criticism of the U.S. action against Iraq till recently which might subside now after the arrest of Saddam Hussein. While a part of the criticism appeared logical, a great deal of it was altogether uninformed. There are reasons to believe that Saddam regime had links with Al Qaeda. Moreover, the geopolitical strategy of 'Operation Iraqi Freedom' has to be viewed and analysed in the context of the pressure on the U.S.A. to move out their troops and air bases from Saudi Arabia, both because of the increased threats from terror groups and the growing disenchantment of U.S. policy makers with the role of Saudis in fanning the fire of fundamentalism globally, especially their suspect role in the events leading to Black Tuesday. Among the nineteen terrorists involved in 9/11, as many as fourteen were Saudis. One has to be an American to coolly analyse and assess the U.S. reaction to the Islamist threat. Despite being a super power, now rechristened hyper power, the Americans were targeted and bullied for as many as eight years, from 1993 to 2001, by the militant Islamist outfits. Ordinarily what should be the time frame of patience for a hyper power to swallow the shame and ignominy of being attacked and bullied by the sworn enemies of the civil society? Surely it can't be countless years and decades.

September 11 shocked the Americans like nothing ever did, not even the Pearl Harbour debacle. It was a day of great pain and shame for every U.S. citizen. No one could comprehend the how and why of the crazy attack on the twin towers and the Pentagon office by jihadis. The U.S. citizens were livid. As soon as the U.S. strategists realized that the Islamists led by Osama bin Laden were behind it, they went after him. As early as February 26, 1993, a bomb planted in an underground car park at the World Trade Center, New York, by Islamic fundamentalists had led to the killing of six persons and injuring of another one thousand. Investigations led to arrests of four Islamists, including a blind Egyptian cleric, on charges of conspiracy of bombing and killing of innocent citizens. They were convicted. The crime was believed to have been ordered by the Saudi-born terror Czar, bin Laden. Later on the mastermind of the February 1993 bombing, Ramzi Ahmed Youssef, arrested in Pakistan, was got extradited. He faced trial in the U.S.A. and was sentenced to life imprisonment plus another 240 years in jail.

The Islamist groups, operating under the banner of Al Qaeda, have been on America's trail for quite sometime, especially after the ignominous humiliation suffered by the U.S. in Somalia in 1993. In 1995 an attempt was made in Sudan to assassinate the Egyptian President Hosni Mubarak, who was regarded by the Islamists as a stooge of America. The same year saw the bombing of an American training facility in Riyadh in which five U S soldiers were killed. After taking refuge in Afghanistan, as a result of the Sudanese government yielding to American pressure, in 1996 bin Laden backed another bombing of an apartment complex in Saudi Arabia where a number of U.S. servicemen were killed. After two years, in 1998 the U.S. embassies in Kenya and Tanzania were bombed which resulted in the death of 224 persons, including 12 Americans. The FBI believed that bin Laden's terror outfit, Al Qaeda, was also responsible for the attack on *USS Cole* in Yemen in which 17 U.S.

soldiers and marines were killed. All that was tolerated by the American nation very patiently.

The arm-chair intellectuals and critics of the U.S. action against Islamists conveniently forget that a "Letter to America", purported to have been written by Osama bin Laden, was published and circulated in November 2002. It mentioned a number of crimes committed by the U.S. government and the American people. The letter had set forth the diktats of terrorists under seven headings, "what we are calling you to do, and what we want from you". Enumerated by Bernard Lewis, these were as follows:

The first important step for the U.S. is to embrace Islam; the second, to stop all acts of oppression, lies, immorality and debauchery ; the third, to admit that America is a nation without principles and manners ; fourth, to stop supporting Israel in Palestine, the Indians in Kashmir, the Russians against the Chechens and the Philippines government against the Muslims of southern islands; the fifth, the Americans should pack their bags and get out of all Muslim lands. This advice was supposedly offered for "America's own good," so that they do not have to be sent back as "cargo in coffins." The sixth, to end all support to the corrupt leaders of Muslim countries. The U.S.A. must not interfere in the political affairs of Islamic countries and their methods of education. A threat was held out that if the U.S. did not stop interfering in the affairs of Muslim countries, the terrorists would be compelled to register their presence again in New York and Washington. The seventh advice was to deal and interact with the Muslims worldwide on the basis of mutual interest and benefits rather than follow the policies of subjugation, theft and occupation.[4] The document concluded by warning the Americans that if they rejected this advice, they will be defeated like all previous crusaders and their fate will be that of the Soviets who fled from Afghanistan militarily defeated, politically broken up, ideologically destroyed and economically bankrupt. The full text of the threatening letter in both Arabic and English was widely distributed through the Internet in November 2002. Because of certain differences in the style and outlook, bin Laden's personal authorship of the letter was in doubt.[5] In addition, several threatening video tapes have been aired at frequent intervals by the *Al Jazeera* television network to intimidate the U.S.A.

Which self-respecting nation can succumb to such vile threats and intimidatory tactics? Clearly the Islamists want to have a free run all over the world to do whatever they like. Who will allow them to go on a killing spree worldwide through the motions of jihad in the name of Islam? Certainly not a hyper power like the U.S.A. For us, the Indians, the most relevant part of November 2002 letter was the reference to Kashmir which Islamists have been keen to overrun and seize. That is what Pakistan, too, has been trying to do for the last five decades. For Israelis the message was to submit to the threats of the Palestinian terrorists. Both India and Israel have been on the 'hit list' of jihadi terror groups now for several decades.

When the shock of September 11, 2001, came the Americans knew that it was the handiwork of the Islamists led by Osama bin Laden. They also knew that the real culprit was Pakistan. But due to strategic reasons, instead they chose to attack the Taliban-ruled Afghanistan from where bin Laden had been operating—albeit only after securing full support of the Pakistani establishment, especially the I.S.I. In the process the Americans made Pakistan a frontline ally in the war against terror by promising monetary offerings to revive the sagging financial fortunes of Pakistan. It was a deal, a clear buy out by America and a sell out by Musharraf. The Americans wanted to secure several high perching positions in Pakistan for maintaining a hawk-like vigil all around. Now their troops and intelligence agencies are firmly entrenched all over Pakistan, courtesy Musharraf. After attacking Afghanistan in October 2001, the U. S. strategists have not looked back. The successful attack on Iraq and the recent capture of one of the two most wanted fugitives, Saddam Hussein, has sent a strong message to the hordes of Islamists worldwide that the battle against terrorism will be followed to its logical conclusion, come what may. Osama bin Laden, however, is yet to be captured.

In this battle against terror, unwittingly the destinies of India and Israel have become intertwined with the fate of America.The radical Islam has been giving repetitive calls of jihad against both India and

Israel, the two so-called ' heathen nations', which have been on the hit list of jihadis now for several decades, long before they hit America. There is no other option available to India and Israel, except coming together for defending their people. During the recent visit of the Israeli Prime Minister, Ariel Sharon, to India in September 2003, certain partisan political groups kicked up an unseemly controversy by questioning the bonafides of the invitation extended to him. The whole thing smacked of rank prejudice and showed utter lack of elementary geo-political vision. Unfortunately there is a powerful pro-Arab lobby in India which has been hostile to Israel for no justifiable reason. They have been quite active and vocal- almost to the point of being illogical and irrational, even forgetting the timely help which Israel gave to India during the Kargil war and Israel's unstinted support to us on all major issues.

We have seen that the bond of ummah has forged a unique permanent unity among Muslims across the globe, spread in more than eighty countries, some Islamic, others non-Islamic. The Islamic ummah is almost like a corporation – the biggest and the most formidable transnational corporation across the globe. The ummah has access to astronomical funds. Apart from the massive flow of petro dollars, some of the Islamic societies also rake in huge moolah from drug trade, poppy cultivation and trading in illicit arms. No single country, not even a hyper power like America, can fight this faith-bonded global corporation, and their terror spewing ideology single-handedly. Certainly a soft state like India, cannot fight the menacing Islamists all by itself. Sheer survival instinct and the operation of the 'Tina' factor have made America, India and Israel close allies in this war against Islamist international terror. No country by itself, not even America, can fight the Islamists because ummah is a multinational corporation of more than one billion shareholders.

What should be the roadmap for future to avoid more bloody conflicts? The best alternative could be for the Islamists to listen to the voice of reason and opt for a round table conversation on civilizational issues with the leaders of non-Muslim countries, including those against whom they have any real or imaginary grievances. They must, however, be also prepared to listen to and understand the grievances of the non-Muslim societies about the injustices done to them and the atrocities committed on innocent non-Muslims during the last one hundred years or more. It has to be a multi-way dialogue, not a one-way traffic, because grievances, some genuine, some imaginary, most nations have in this wide world. Ordinarily it should be possible to resolve the conflicts through the time-tested and time-honoured method of discussion and deliberations: Indians call it *Samvad* or *Shastra Artha*. It might still be possible to arrive at some civil and peaceful solution on the pattern of what the Moghal King Akbar had tried to achieve through "Sulah-Kul" (i.e., all round reconciliation). For instance, will Islamists consider the following minimal societal agenda for discussion across the table:

a) Accept that Muslims should live peacefully in various countries along with other religious groups like Christians, Jews, Hindus, Buddhists and others on equal terms;

b) Renounce their dogmatic opposition to the concept of a secular, multi-cultural, multi-religious and pluralistic social order worldwide and grant equality before law and freedom of speech and worship to non-Muslims living in Islamic countries;

c) Grant equal rights to women and abolish gender discrimination in Muslim societies;

d) Give up their secessionist trait and penchant for breaking away from the parent country on grounds of religion and culture as soon as their numbers grow; and

e) Banish from Islamic regimes certain manifestly cruel practices like chopping of limbs, beheading, slitting of throats and awarding death penalty to women by stoning, etc.

More civilizational issues can be added to this tentative agenda when the process for reconciliation begins. Frankly, there is little hope that Islamists will ever agree to any sensible compromise on these important issues. Evidently the jihadis are a class apart. If their past and present actions could be taken as guide to their complex behavioural pattern, these warriors in the cause of Allah are virtually possessed by pronounced homicidal and suicidal tendencies. How else could anyone explain their macabre propensity for killing innocent and unarmed civillians, including women and children-and that too through suicide bombings? Unfortunately, the so-called Muslim scholars and intellectuals have no say in their community's religious affairs, nor in evolving any ethical norms to guide the wayward torch-bearers of radical Islam.

And now look at the predicament of the civil society, the universal civilization, already pushed to the wall. They cannot succumb to the wild diktats of terrorists nor can they abdicate their responsibility to protect the innocent and unarmed civilians, the peaceful gentle citizens of their countries. What should they do? Do they have really any alternative but to stand up and fight the purveyors of terror and death? Obviously none. The civil society has to meet the jihadist menace head on, fight terror in every court and alley and ultimately win the battle. Never mind the price. The battle against terror must be won. So that is what the Americans are doing; that is what the Israelis are doing. And that is what the Indians will have to do in order to survive. Hopefully when the backbone of terrorist groups is broken, they will opt for a round table discussion and come round to the philosophy of conflict resolution through 'samvad' or call it, 'Sulah Kul'. But that day might be quite far away or so it seems. The civilizational war has just begun. Many battles will have to be fought before the victory is sighted.

The problem of Islamist terror has another dimension—a foreboding one. Islamists have been desperately trying to gain access to nuclear weapons and devise a crude delivery system. As early as November 2001, the International Atomic Energy Agency (IAEA) had alerted the world to the potential threat of nuclear terrorism.[6] The IAEA felt that it was "far more likely that terrorists would target nuclear facilities, nuclear material and radioactive sources".[7] The United States immediately stepped up security at its nuclear installations. Many other countries followed suit. Some leading Pakistani nuclear scientists were arrested and interrogated on suspicion of passing on nuclear material or technology to the Taliban and Osama bin Laden. But nothing came out of that. Fears were also expressed about the safety of Pakistan's nuclear arsenal if General Musharraf was toppled. But at that time the Pakistani government had clarified that its nuclear installations were very secure. With the backdrop of two recent attempts on the life of

Musharraf in December 2003 there is, however, a possibility of his being assassinated for seizing control of Pakistan's nuclear stockpile and accessing the technological know how. It could be done by a jihadists group entrenched in the Pakistani army which is heavily Islamicised. It had been earlier pointed out by Mohamed El Baradei, IAEA Director General, in November 2001 that "the willingness of terrorists to sacrifice their lives to achieve their evil aims" of obtaining nuclear weapons could add a new dimension in the fight against terrorism.[8] Some terror groups, particularly Al Qaeda, have been desperately trying to acquire nuclear material and weapons by targeting nuclear facilities or accessing the sources of radioactive materials to make dirty bombs for causing death and destruction of civilian population and spread panic. Since 1993 there have been nearly 175 cases of trafficking in nuclear material and 201 cases of trafficking in other radioactive sources, including the medical and industrial ones. Only 18 of these cases actually concerned thefts of small amounts of highly enriched uranium or plutonium, the material needed to produce a nuclear bomb.[9]

But the fear of a nuclear strike by the terrorists will not die down easily. A Pakistani scientist was said to have approached the Iraqi President Saddam Hussein for providing nuclear weapon designs and help in procuring some components of the bomb soon after the 1990 invasion of Kuwait, according to a document found by United Nations weapons inspectors. That raised new concerns about Pakistan's role in the proliferation of nuclear technology. It followed the allegation that Islamabad had helped North Korea in developing nuclear bomb and that Pakistani nuclear scientists had met Osama bin Laden and the Taliban leader Mullah Muhammad Omar in Afghanistan. The offer by the Pakistani scientist, found in Iraqi archives, was made in October 1990 as a U.S. led coalition prepared to repel the August invasion of Kuwait. Iraq had already embarked on a crash programme to develop a nuclear bomb but told the U.N. it had not pursued the scientist's offer—a claim U.N. investigators are inclined to believe. The evidence of the contact showed that Pakistan was willing to share its technology with so-called "rogue nations."[10] Another nuclear scare statement came from Pakistan in June 2002 when Lashkar-e-Tayyeba chief, Hafiz Muhammed Saeed posted a statement on the website of his organisation, www.markaze-dawa.org. claiming that people loyal to his organisation "control two nuclear missiles". Apparently Saeed had made this statement while in the custody of Islamabad police. He had reportedly claimed that the Laskhkar will use the two missiles with warheads against the "enemies of Islam."[11] Earlier Saeed was the head of Lashkar-e-Tayyeba, now he has changed its name to Jama'at-al Dawa which aims at spreading radical Islam. In fact, Saeed's organisations, whatever be their names, have India as their principal target. Many analysts believe that he has been functioning under the direct control of the ISI. Apparently just now Saeed's groups, Lashkar-e-Tayyeba and Jama'at-al Dawa do not possess any nuclear weapons or missiles. If they had any, by now they would have surely used those deadly devices first and foremost against India. In any case, one thing is certain. Whenever jihadis manage to get any nuclear weapon or dirty bomb they will not hesitate to use it because of their pronounced homicidal and suicidal proclivity. Also they will be the first to use it because they have scant regard for human life.

The possibility of jihadi elements gaining control of nuclear weapons has been a major nightmare for the world community. Though Pakistani authorities claim to have tight control over access to their arsenal and installations, the world leaders do not feel assured on that count. In September 2003, Russia's first Deputy Foreign Minster, Vyacheslav Trubnikov, stated that Russia and the U.S. viewed with concern the threat of Pakistani nuclear weapons falling into the hands of terrorists "due to presence of large number of extremist groups in Pakistan".[12] Therefore a lurking fear of the likely threat of the terrorist groups seizing Pakistan's nuclear arsenal and installations will continue to persist.

A new twist was given to the controversy with the recent revelation of the role of Pakistan in passing on the nuclear-weapons technology to Iran, North Korea and Libya, too. Under pressure from America, in the second week of December 2003 Pakistan was forced to investigate the credentials of the father of the Pakistan nuclear bomb, Dr. Abdul Qadeer Khan and his three proteges, Farooq Mohammed, Yasin Chouhan and Saeed Ahmed. They were intensively questioned, or debriefed, as a spokesperson of Pakistan government tried to put it, for unravelling the mystery surrounding the total similarity between the uranium enrichment centrifuges of

Iran with those of Pakistan, as discovered by the international regulators of the I.A.E.A. (International Atomic Energy Agency) during inspections. Some more experts scrutinising Libya's progress in the field of nuclear weapons, after Gaddafi's recent voluntary declaration to give up nuclear ambitions, had also found similarities between Libya's programme with those of Pakistan and Iran. Though Pakistan has quickly distanced itself from the charges of nuclear proliferation by suggesting that the leaks were the handiwork of some greedy nuclear scientists, the international community is unlikely to accept that excuse. It may be recalled that in the year 2002, a U.S. satellite had detected a Pakistani plane picking up some North Korean missile components which were believed to be part of a swap for transfer of Pakistani nuclear technology to North Korea.

Thus the desperate search of Islamist terror groups and countries sympathetic to them for access to nuclear weapons and the relevant technology continues unabated. The question is how long can this access be denied to terrorist outfits and their mentors. They are operating in a number of groups across dozens of countries. Most of their ideologues are well educated and many of their group leaders are tech-savvy. Sooner or later they are bound to succeed—whether they beg, borrow or steal these weapons or technology from Pakistani establishment or from Iran which has remained engaged in furious efforts to develop nuclear weapons and is believed to have moved fairly close to nuclear capability. Making 'dirty bombs' in dozens, however, remains the easiest option.

Even the Saudi regime is reported to be looking for access to nuclear weapons. There are reasons to believe that in October 2003 Pakistan and Saudi Arabia had concluded a secret agreement on nuclear cooperation under which Pakistan will give the nuclear weapons technology to Saudis in exchange for oil. The intention was to counter what the Pakistani and Saudi leaders unofficially described as multiple regional threats—a vague expression which could include Israel and India. Pakistan has been particularly concerned about the recent arms agreement between India and Israel—the latter being seen as a long time heavy weight nuclear power having an estimated inventory of 200 to 400 nuclear weapons.

The information about the Saudi-Pakistan deal was disclosed in confidence by a ranking Pakistani officer.[13] The disclosure came at the end of a 26-hour state visit to Islamabad by Crown Prince Abdullah bin Abdulaziz, Saudi Arabia's *de facto* ruler, who came with an entourage of 200 officials. The news was denied by Mohammed Sadiq, Deputy Chief of Pakistan's Embassy in Washington. The informed Pakistani source, however, maintained that both countries will vehemently deny that there was any such deal but future events will confirm the fact.[14] The terrorists, however, could access the nuclear weapons or technology even from North Korea or any other source.

In today's science-soaked world there is nothing break-safe or fail-safe. Sometime ago there was a string of incidents stretching from Caucasus to Eastern Europe to West Africa in which gangs of criminals and smugglers were successful in stealing radiological devices and abandoned radio-active materials. For instance, in Tiblisi (Georgia), and some other nearby areas contraband radiological material has frequently surfaced in the black market as well. Such material can be used by terrorists to make a dirty bomb which is nothing more than a "radiology-dispersion device". It is not a nuclear weapon proper, but is rather a crude easy-to-make device which uses the conventional explosives or other means to spread radiation over a wide area. According to nuclear experts, such radiology-dispersion contraptions are technologically simple and could be well within the grasp of tech-savvy international Islamist groups. It may be recalled that some documents seized one or two years ago from the training camps of Jihadis in Afghanistan showed that they had been trying to manufacture a dirty bomb. If they are able to access sufficient radiological material or radio-active waste, they might still try to use it against the civil society. Logically it should be only a matter of time before the Islamists succeed in their search for nuclear secrets and shout 'Eureka'. On top of it, nuclear scientists have already made rapid strides in the field of miniaturization of nuclear weapon systems. That will make delivery of mini-nukes much easier and impart greater precision to nuclear strikes.

And come to think what would happen as and when the jihadist forces acquire the nuclear muscle? Their likely targets are three: the

U.S.A., India and Israel, the three countries against which jihad has been in progress. America is quite far away and much too powerful. Jihadis know very well that any attack on America will invite prompt ruthless retribution. So for them the second best option could be to target India and Israel—the two so-called 'heathen' civilizations on their hit list. While discussing the subject of use of nuclear weapons by Islamist terror groups let us not forget that terse boast by Ali Mazrui who wrote : "The crescent is over the mushroom cloud," and can threaten others in addition to the West. Islam could end up "playing nuclear Russian roulette with two other civilizations—with Hindusim in South Asia and with Zionism and politicalized Judaism in the Middle East."[15] That statement of Ali Mazrui should set at rest all doubts about the likely first targets of jihadi terrorists armed with nuclear capability, or when equipped with a substantial stockpile of dirty bombs. This, however, does not mean that the Islamists will not target the U.S.A. They would love to nuke America, but perhaps only after playing one round of nuclear roulette with India and Israel. If one goes solely by tactical analysis, India could easily be the first target of a surprise nuclear attack by virtue of being a very densely populated country and universally perceived as a soft state.

Thus the road ahead for the Indian civilization is not only bumpy but full of booby traps. It will require enormous strategic planning from now onwards, in addition to unwavering national resolve and steely grit to face the crescent-created nuclear threat looming large on the Asian horizon. One hopes and prays that such an eventuality does not hit India. But we must keep our plans ready and powder dry. Indians must know that there will be no runners up in the war unleashed by nuclear-armed terrorists.

Epilogue

The inspection of Iran's nuclear facility by the United Nations nuclear proliferation watchdog, International Atomic Energy Agency (IAEA), in October-November 2003, revealed Pakistan's murky role in the proliferation of nuclear weapons technology. After being cornered by the IAEA Inspectors for their inability to explain the traces of highly enriched uranium (normally used for manufacturing nuclear weapons), found on their secretly procured centrifuge machines, the Iranians blurted out the names of many Pakistani scientists who had supplied the nuclear technology, including the design of centrifuges. Most important among the names given by the Iranians was that of Dr. Abdul Qadeer Khan, father of the Pakistani bomb and a national icon, along with names of some other scientists. Under mounting pressure from the IAEA and the United States, General Musharraf was forced to order an inquiry which led to interrogation of Dr. Khan and more than twenty scientists and officials, including two retired Brigadiers said to be deputed to Dr. Khan's Laboratory and more than twenty scientists and officials, including two retired Brigadiers deputed for administrative duties. Meanwhile, some elements of nuclear technology, including centrifuge equipment and warhead designs, originating from Dr. Khan's Laboratory in Pakistan, were seized in Libya, after that country's dictator, Col. Muammar el-Qaddafi, agreed to roll back and dismantle his nuclear weapons plans while agreeing to inspection of his secret laboratories by the IAEA regulators and the United States experts. In the last week of January 2004, a box containing the design of a nuclear warhead along with loads of sensitive documents was brought from Libya to Washington by a chartered 747 aircraft which conclusively established the role of Dr. Khan and his network in peddling illicit nuclear equipment to enrich uranium for producing weapons grade nuclear fuel. Apparently the design provided to the Islamic Republic of Libya by Dr. Khan's Laboratory was of a Chinese nuclear warhead. Consequently on January 31, 2004, Dr. Khan was removed from the coveted office of the Advisor to the Prime Minister of Pakistan ostensibly under directions of Pentagon. For quite sometime Pakistani government had to impose restrictions on the movements of Dr. Khan and his close associates. Despite best efforts of the Pakistani establishment, the inquiry could not cover up the activities of Dr. Abdul Qadeer Khan and his protégés, which included nuclear scientists Mohammed Farooq, Nazir Ahmed, Yaseen Chouhan, Dr.Khan's Principal Staff Officer, Major Islam-ul Haq, and retired Brigadiers Tajawar Khan and Malik Sajawal. They were interrogated, or debriefed, as a spokesperson of Pakistan government tried to put it across, for ascertaining their role in the proliferation of nuclear technology.

Earlier on January 23, 2004, while attending a meeting of the World Economic Forum at Davos, Switzerland, Musharraf had admitted that some greedy Pakistani nuclear scientists had sold nuclear secrets abroad for personal gains. But he categorically reiterated that there had been no involvement of Pakistan government or its army in any such transaction. It may be recalled that in the year 2002, a U.S. satellite had detected a Pakistani aircraft picking up some North Korean missiles, or missile components, which were believed to be part of a swap for transfer of Pakistani nuclear technology to North Korea. On February 4, 2004, Dr. Khan admitted in a 12 page written statement that he was responsible for nuclear proliferation. The same day he filed a mercy petition seeking Presidential pardon for his dirty role in peddling nuclear technology which was referred to the National Command Authority (N.C.A.) which is responsible for overseeing Pakistan's nuclear command and control. Dr. Khan had a personal audience with President Musharraf and thereafter on February 4, 2004, made a "*mea culpa*" confession in a televised address to the people of Pakistan, saying that "I take full responsibility for my actions and seek your pardon.

I give an assurance, my dear brothers and sisters, that such activities will never take place in future/." He was granted pardon the same day by General Musharraf, after the Cabinet made a recommendation to that effect. It is difficult to believe that Pakistani Army had no knowledge about Dr. Khan's activities.

On February 5, 2004, Pakistan formally arrested five scientists and senior officials of its top nuclear facility at Kahuta on the alleged charges of tansfer/sale of nuclear technology to other countries. They included two nuclear scientists Mohammed Farooq and Nazir Ahmed, Dr. Khan's Principal Staff Officer, Major Islam-ul-Haq, and two administrators retired Brigadiers Tajawar Khan and Malik Sajawal all of whom had been interrogated earlier along with Dr Khan. Because of the growing groundwell of anger among the people, the pardon to Dr. Khan was announced by General Musharraf of February 4, 2004, itself at a news conference saying that there "is a written appeal from his side and there is a pardon written from my side." Musharraf justified the pardon on the ground that Dr. A.Q. Khan had served the country very well by developing nuclear capability for the defence of Pakistan and eulogized his services by proclaiming that Dr. Khan was his hero, too. It may be recalled that there were some protest demonstrations against the so-called public humiliation of Dr. Khan by making the former tender a public apology in a televised address, allegedly under directions of the U.S.A. These demonstrations had been organized by the Majlis-e-Muttahida Amal and some women activities, including relations and friends of the scientists under investigation. A strong current of resentment and anger against General Musharraf and America is gaining momentum among the people of Pakistan as well in the middle ranks of army. This could pose a serious threat to the life of General Musharraf and senior army officers considered close to him.

On February 5, 2004, the C.I.A. Chief, George Tenet, claimed in a speech at the Georgetown University that the activities of Dr. Khan and his associates had been uncovered largely by the U.S. and British intelligence agencies. He claimed that as result of their tireless efforts the backbone of nuclear black marketers had been broken, after arrest of several senior officers of Dr. Khan's network.

Soon thereafter, in the second week of February 2004, an alarmed American President lambasted the top Pakistani scientist, A.Q.Khan, for his clandestine sale of nuclear technology to "rouge states". Elaborating on the proliferation activities of Dr Khan and his associates, whose network, George Bush claimed, was successfully penetrated by the British and the U.S. intelligence agencies at great risk, he called for tightening the international rules governing the spread of weapons grade nuclear technology to prevent it from falling into the hands of terrorists and outlawed regimes. He warned that with deadly technology and expertise available in the market, "there is the terrible possibility that terrorist groups could obtain the ultimate weapons they desire most", and forcefully argued that such a situation must be avoided. He also proposed strengthening of the international treaties for regulating the enrichment and processing of uranium for developing nuclear power in order to prevent manufacture of nuclear weapons.

Meanwhile there are unverified reports that as a result of a deal struck between the United States and the government of Pakistan, the former has acquired some kind of supervisory control over Pakistan's nuclear weapons to ensure that Islamist terrorists, especially the Al Qaeda, are not able to gain access to that country's nuclear arsenal. According to a report broadcast by the NBC Television Network on February 6, 2004, a group of nuclear experts known as the U.S. Liaison Committee were now spending millions of dollars "to safeguard Pakistan's more than 40 nuclear weapons" in order to help Pakistan develop state-of-the-art security, including the authorization codes for their nuclear arsenal. In effect such an exercise would be tantamount to the United States taking a virtual charge of Pakistan's nuclear arsenal. It could be done only by cutting a deal with General Musharraf to enable him to draw a curtain over the murky episode through the strategem of granting pardon to Dr. A.Q. Khan, after a public apology. Incidentally, the studied silence of the Indian government and their "could-not-care-less" approach to this serious matter is also being interpreted to lend credence to the rumours about some kind of a clandestine Bush-Mush deal over Pakistan's nukes. At the same time, it is anybody's guess whether or not Dr. Khan and his accomplices have passed on nuclear secrets and the related technology to the Islamist terror groups, especially the Al Qaeda leadership who are believed to be sitting pretty, safely sheltered either in the wilderness of the Federally Administered Territorial Areas of Pakistan, or in the Gilgit and Pamir regions of Pakistan Occupied Kashmir. It is widely believed in the well informed circles that Islamist terrorists are already in possession of nuclear technology, perhaps far beyond the technological capability of manufacturing a mere dirty bomb. It is suspected that just now their immediate requirements are two. First, to select a safe haven where they could set up their nuclear facility, preferably far beyond the U.S. reach; and second to improvise or gain access to a reliable captive medium for delivery of nuclear weapons, including dirty bombs of which they might already have a stockpile. If that be the overall scenario of the fast approaching phase of nuclear terrorism, the civil society should await more action in the times.

Endnotes

Chapter - 1

1. Samuel P. Huntington, The *Clash of Civilizations and the Remaking of World Order*, ch. 2, p. 41.
2. Ibid, ch. II, p.48, footnote.
3. Samuel P. Huntington, *The Clash of Civilization and the Remaking of World Order*, 1997, p.258, ch. 10.
4. Ibid
5. Akbar S. Ahmed, *Islam Under Seige*, p. 7, Introduction.
6. Salman Rushdie, Yes, this is about Islam, *Sunday Hindustan Times*, November 4, 2001.
7. Ibid.
8. Raymond Bonner, U.S.Envoy in Indonesia Warns Americans of Future Attacks, *The New York Times*, August 13, 2003.
9. Ibid.
10. The news Item 'Bombers were trained in Pak: Indonesia', *Sunday Times of India*, New Delhi August 10 2003,p.13.
11. Joginder Singh, Intelligence: Spy versus spy, *The Pioneer*, New Delhi p.6, March 31, 2003.
12 Dileep Padgaonkar, Islam in France, *The Sunday Times of India*, New Delhi, p.14.

13. Ibid.

14. Ibid.

15. CIA's Cyclone spawned Pak madrasas, *The Pioneer*, New Delhi, March 31, 2003.

16. Ibid.

17. Ibid.

18. Ibid.

19. Phillip Shenon, White House Called Target of Plane Plot, *The New York Times*, August 9, 2003.

20. Rashmee Z. Ahmed, Britain jolted over Terror Links, *Times of India*, New Delhi, May 2, 2003, p.13.

21 Ibid.

22. 'U.S. media pins Europe as training ground for terror',*The Economic Times*, New Delhi,April 17 2003, p.2.

23. Ibid.

24. U.S. media pins Europe as training ground for terror, *The Economic Times, New Delhi*, April 17, 2003, p.2.

25. Appendix I given at the end of the book., page 385

26. Peter L Bergen, *Holy War* Inc, p.42, ch.1 (While America Slept)-Source: azzam.com/html/storieskhalladmadani. htm).

27. Peter L. Bergen, *Holy War* Inc, ch 1, p.44.

28. Bruce Crumley, *Time*, March 10, 2003.

29. *The New York Times*, news item 'A Nation at War: Briefly noted; Detainee attempts suicide', April 2, 2003.

Chapter – 2

1. Suhas Majumdar, *Jihad : the Islamic Doctrine of Permanent War*, ch.1, p.10.

2. Akbar Muhammad, Associate Professor at Binghamton University, New York, *Frontline -Muslims: major themes: Islamic beliefs, law and practice*, May 9, 2002 - www.pbs.org/wgbh/pages/frontline/shows/muslims/themes/beliefs.html.

3. Abdul Rauf, Imam, Masjid al-Farah, New York, *Frontline*: muslims: major themes: islamic beliefs, law and actices/ PBS -www.pbs.org/wgbh/pages/frontline/show/muslims/themes/beliefs.html}.

4. Ibid.

5. Ibid.

6. Ibid.

7. Simon Elegant with reporting by Zamira Loebis, *The Time*, March 10, 2003.

8. Dr. B.R. Ambedkar, *Pakistan or Partition of India*, p. 290, ch. XII.

9. Ibid, pp.289-290. ch. XII.

10. Ibid, pp.289-290.

11. Ibid, p.291, Source: *India in Transition*, p.157.

12. A news item captioned Muslim U.S. Soldier kills at own camp, *The Indian Express, New Delhi,* March 24, 2003.

13. Ibid.

14. Simon Elegant. With reporting by Zamira Loebis/Jakarta, Bullies for Islam, *Time, March 10, 2003,* p. 34.

15. Riaz Hassan, Professor of Sociology at the Flinders University of South Australia, Globalisation's Challenge to Islam, Source: *YaleGlobal Online* (www.yaleglobal.yale.edu), a publication of the Yale Centre for the Study of Globalization, reprinted in The Asian Age, New Delhi, April 27, 2003.

16. Ibid.

17. M. Hanif Lakdawala, The Four Phases of Islamic Thought, *Times of India, New Delhi*, June 17 2003, p. 14.

18. Ibid.

Chapter – 3

1. Suhas Majumdar, *Jihad, The Islamic Doctrine of Permanent War*, ch.1, p.11.

2. *Jihad in the Quran and Sunnah,* Published by Maktaba Dar-us-Salam, Publishers & Distributors, Riyadh, Saudi Arabia.

3. Ibid, Source: http://www.engr.csufresno.edu/-msa/articles/jihad.html.

4. Suhas Majumdar, *Jihad – The Islamic Doctrine of Permanent War*, p.20, ch. 2, Source: Sahih Muslim No. 4696 - Abu Hurairah was one of the most important companions of the Prophet.

5. Ibid, p.21, ch. 2, Source: Sahih Muslim, No. 4645.

6. Br. Muhammad El-Halaby, *The Role of Sheikh-ul-Islam Ibn Taymiyah in Jihad Against the Tartars*, published in 17th issue of Nid'ul Islam, Feb-March 1997.

7. Will Durant, *The Story of Civilization, Part I*. p. 465, ch. XVI.

8. *The Oxford History of India* by late Vincent A Smith, edited by Percival Spear, p. 338, book VI, ch. 3 (paperback).

9. M.J. Akbar, *The Shade of Swords*, Introduction, p. xvi.

10. Hannah Beech Shanghai, Voices of Islam, *Time Asia*, March 28, 2003.

11. Suhas Majumdar, *Jihad, The Islamic Doctrine of Permanent War*, Ch.2, pp. 21-22.

12. Ibid, Ch. 7, p.43.

13. Ibid, ch. 7, pp. 43-44.

14. Afsir Karim, Trends in International Terrorism, *India's National Security Review* 2002, p. 133 (Editor-in-Chief, Satish Kumar), India Research Press.
15. Ibid, p. 136.
16. Abdullah Azzam, *Defence of Muslim Lands* (London: Azzam Publications, 1996), pp.7-17.
17. Home Judicial Proceeding Nos 70-4, 27th September, 1865, p.1502 : cited by Y.B. Mathur *Muslims and Changing India*, p. 75.
18. Y.B. Mathur, *Muslims and Changing India*, ch. 3, p.76 : Source Home Judicial Proceedings Nos 70-4 dated September 27, 1865, p.1503, para 1.
19. Ibid, Source : *Home Judicial Proceedings* Nos 70-4 dated September 27, 1865, p. 1503, para 2.
20. Y.B. Mathur, *Muslims and Changing India*, pp. 76-77, ch. 3.
21. Ibid : *Source Home Political Secret F. No. 101 of 1936*, p.4,para 4.
22. Y.B. Mathur, *Muslims and Changing India*, ch. III, p.84 : Source: Home Political Secret F. No. 101 of 1936, p.6.
23. Dr. B. R. Ambedkar, *Pakistan or Partition of India*, ch. VII, P. 153.
24. M. Mujeeb, *The Indian Muslims*, p. 400, ch. XVIII.
25. Ibid, pp. 400-401, Source: *India in 1920*, Superintendent, Govt. Printing, Calcutta, 1921. pp.51-3.
26. Ibid.
29. Gopal Das Khosla, Stern Reckoning, *The Partition Omnibus*, publishers Oxford University Press,2002, p.49.
28. Ibid.
29. Gopal Das Khosla, Stern Reckoning, *The Partition Omnibus,* Oxford University Press, pp. 51-52.
30. Ibid, pp. 58-59.
31. Ibid, p. 65.

32. Lane Pool, *Medieval India*, p.153.
33. Dr. B.R. Ambedkar, *Pakistan or Partition of India*, p.37.
34. Dr. Titus, *Indian Islam*, p.10.
35. Ibid, quoted by Titus.
36. Suhas Majumdar, *Jihad, the Islamic Doctrine of Permanent War*, p.28, ch.3,Source: This rendering is by Abdul Hamid Siddiqi, a Pakistani scholar.
37. Ibid, p.29, ch.3.
38. Ibid, p.29, ch.3.
39. Ibid, ch.1, p.14.
40. Suhas Majumdar, *Jihad The Islamic Doctrine of Permanent War*, Appendix-II, p.83.
41. Lane Pool, *Medieval India*, p. 104.
42. Suhas Majumdar, *Jihad, the Islamic Doctrine of Permanent War*, Appendix-II, p.84.
43. M.J. Akbar, *The Shade of Swords*, p.24, ch.1.
44. Ibid.

Chapter – 4

1. Suhas Majumdar, *Jihad: The Islamic Doctrine of Permanent War*, ch. 8, p.46.
2. Suhas Majumdar, *Jihad : The Islamic Doctrine of Permanent War*, Appendix-I, p.76, Source: Hadith No.4364 of Sahih Muslim.
3. Ibid, Source: Hadith No. 4366.
4. Will Durant, *The Story of Civilization*, Part I, ch. XIII, p. 378, Source: Rawlinson, iii, p.235.
5. Ibid.
6. V.S. Naipaul, *Among the Believers*, An Islamic Journey part 2, ch. 4, p. 125.
7. Ibid, p.126.

8. Source:http://members.tripod.com/- INDIA RESOURCE/ sindh.html
9. Dr. B. R. Ambedkar, *Pakistan or Partition of India*, ch. IV, p. 39.
10. Source: http://members.tripod.com/ -INDIA RESOURCE/ sindh.htm.
11. Dr B. R. Ambedkar, *Pakistan or Partition of India*, ch. IV p.37.
12. M. Guizot and Mme Guizot De Witt, *A History of France (New York, 1869),* 6:16.
13. V. S. Naipaul, *Among the Believers, an Islamic Journey* part 2, ch. IV, p. 126.
14. Ibid.
15. Source: Compiled from *Militant Islam* by Godfrey Jansen, Harper & Row, 1979.
16. Yossef Bodansky, *Bin Laden - The Man who Declared War on America*, Introduction: Inevitable Struggle, p. x.
17. Ibid.
18. Ibid.
19. Penderel Moon, *Divide & Quit*, ch. I, page 11.
20. V.S. Naipaul, *Among the Believers, An Islamic Journey*, p.344, part IV, ch.6.
21. Yossef Bodansky, *Bin Laden - The Man who Declared War on America*, p. 8, ch. I
22. Ibid, p.25, ch. 1.
23. Ibid.
24 Peter L. Bergen, *Holy War Inc,* ch. II, p. 59
25. Mark Urban, *War in Afghanistan*, (London: Macmillan 1988, p.244).
26. Peter Bergen, *Holy War Inc,* ch.2, p.602.
27. B. Raman, You Shall Reap What You Sow, *The Hindustan Times*, Sept. 23, 2003.

28. Ibid.

29. G. Parthasarthy, Accident-prone road to peace, *The Pioneer, New Delhi*, June 19, 2003.

30. G. Parthasarthy, Pakistani Army : Loot at sight, *The Pioneer, New Delhi*, August 14, 2003.

31. Pramod Kumar Singh, Pak nurses three, not one designs on India, *The Pioneer, New Delhi*, August 28, 2003.

32. Ibid.

Chapter – 5

1. Dr. B. R. Ambedkar, *Pakistan or Partition of India*, Thacker & Company Ltd., Bombay, 1945, p.326.

2. B.L. Kak, *The Fall of Gilgit: The Untold Story of Indo-Pak Affairs from Jinnah to Bhutto*, pp. 21-22.

3. Ibid, pp.22-23.

4. Ibid, p.23}

5. B.L. Kak, *The Fall of Gilgit: The Untold Story of Indo-Pak Affairs from Jinnah to Bhutto*, p.53.

6. Ibid, pp. 53-54.

7. Ibid, p. 54.

8. Ibid, p.54.

9. Ibid, p.54.

10. Ibid, p.54.

11. Ibid, p. 51.

12. Ibid, p. 51.

13. Mohammed Amir Rana, CIA' s Cyclone spawned Pak madrasas (excerpted from *Jihad-e-Kashmir and Afghanistan), The Pioneer*, New Delhi, March 31.

14. James Risen and David Johnston, 'Report on 9/11 suggests a role by Saudi spies, *The New York Times*, August 2, 2003.

15. News Item 'Pandya murder plan was hatched on the Net', *The Times of India, New Delhi*, September 15, 2003, p. 8.
16. Bernard Lewis, *The Crisis of Islam – Holy War and Unholy Terror*, p.15, published by Weldenfeld & Nicolson, London.
17. Ibid, p.16.
18. Ibid, p. 25.
19. Ibid, p.125.
20. James Adams, *The Next World War*, part One, p.71.
21. Ibid, p.72.
22. Chidanand Rajghatta, The Times News Network, *The Times of India, New Delhi*, October 15, 2001.
23. Susan Sachs, A Muslim Missionary Group Draws New Scrutiny in U.S., *The New York Times*, July 14, 2003.
24. Ibid.
25. Ibid, Susan Sachs.
26. *India's National Security Review* 2002, Editor-in-Chief, Satish Kumar, p.494, Source: http://www.forisb.org/CEO1 06.html
27. *India's National Security Review* 2002, Editor-in-Chief: Satish Kumar, p.494, Source: http://www.forisb.org/CE01 _06.html
28. Ibid, p.495.
29. Ibid, p.496.
30. Ibid, p.497.
31. Appendix-II, p.395
32. News item 'Pak attacked for 9/11 connection', *The Economic Times*, August 2, 2003.
33. Ibid.
34. Ibid.
35. *South Asian Intelligence Review*, Jammu & Kashmir Backgrounder, April 29, 2003.

36. Audit of Terror (editorial), *Times of India*, May 2, 2003.

37. Ibid.

38. Yossef Bodansky, *Bin Laden- The Man who declared war on America*, p.17.

39. Ibid.

40. Ibid.

41. John K Cooley, *Unholy Wars, Afghanistan, America and International Terrorism*, p.64.

42. Yossef Bodansky, *Bin Laden - The Man who declared War on America*, p.108.

43. Ibid, p. 218.

44. Ibid, p. 218.

45. Ibid, p. 218.

46. Bullet Rules Kashmir (Foray) by Dina Nath Mishra, *The Pioneer*, *New Delhi*, March 30, 2003.

47. Ibid.

48. G. Parthasarthy, Pakistan: Under Indian Eyes, *Daily Pioneer, New Delhi*, March 13, 2003.

49. Ibid.

50. Ibid.

Chapter – 6

1. Source: *www.cqnet.com.au/-user dancasey/population_ control.html.*

2. Pendrel Moon, *Divide and Quit*, p.11.

3. A P Joshi, M D Srinivas and J K Bajaj, *Religious Demography of India*, Preface, p.xxii.

4. Ibid.

5. Samuel P. Huntington, *The Clash of Civilizations and the Remaking of World Order*, p. 260.

6. Susan Woodward, Balkan Tragedy: Chaos and Dissolution after the Cold War (Washington D C, Brookings Institution, 1995), pp. 32-35, cited by Samnel Huntington in *The Clash of Civilizations and the Remaking of the World Order*, p.260.
7. Samuel P. Huntington, *The Clash of Civilizations and the Remaking of World Order*, p.260.
8. Ibid.
9. Jonas Widgren, Overview of topical refugee and migration issues in South East Europe's, presented on September 14-15, 2000, at the Council of Europe Parliamentary Assembly Conference in Struga (Macedonia), Source: *www.icmpd.org*.
10. Jonas Widgren, the Statement made at the Stability Pact Regional Meeting on Co-operation in South Eastern Europe to Stabilize Population Movement, Tirana, December 12-13, 2002, Source: www.icmpd.org.
11. Scott L. Wheeler, @2002 News World Communications Inc., Blonde, blue eyed Muslim terrorists? Security expert Bodansky says Bosnians put 'new face' on jihadist stereotype, World Net Daily, December 5, 2002.
12. Ibid.
13. Ibid.
14. Ibid.
15. Ibid.
16. Ibid.
17. Source: A.P. Joshi, M D Srinivas and J K Bajaj, *Religious Demography of India*, Religious Profile of West Asia, table D-33e, p.319.
18. Priyadarsi Dutta, Choose the Civilization, *The Pioneer*, New Delhi, May 2, 2003.
19. Samuel P. Huntington, *The Clash of Civilization and the Remaking of World Order*, p.264.

20. Ibid.

21. Richard H. Curtiss, *Demographics: Year-End Population Statistics Gloss over Israel's Biggest Problem*, Source: http://222.washington report.org/backissues/ 0397/ 9703040.htm.

22. Ibid.

23. Ibid.

24. News item by Reuters 'Israel to Keep Building Barrier Despite U N Censure, *The New York Times*, October 22, 2003.

25. Ibid.

26. Samuel P. Huntington, *The Clash of Civilizations and the Remaking of World Order*, p.65.

27. Ibid.

28. Kenneth R. Timmerman, The World's Most Wanted Man, *Reader's Digest (Indian Edition)*, October 2001, p. 140}.

29. Samuel P. Huntington, *The Clash of Civilizations and the Remaking of World Order*, pp. 65-66.

30. John K Cooley, *Unholy Wars, Afghanistan America and International Terrorism*, p.83.

31. Ibid.

32. Compiled from *CIA Factbook* updated till July 2003, with population inputs, wherever necessary, from http://www.infoplease.com).

33. Ibid.

34. Samuel P. Huntington, *The Clash of the Civlizations and the Remaking of World Order*, p. 260.

35. Ibid. Source: *New York Times* 15 January 1993, p.A9, Henry Clement Moore, Images of Development: Egyptian Engineers in Search of Industry (Cambridge Press: MIT Press, 1980, pp.227-228.

36. Russian Cross: Do-it-yourself-genocide, February 21, 2001, *www.1h1a.org.world/ dsp_article.cfm.*

37. Ibid.
38. Ibid
39. Fred Weir, Mother Russia is barren, *The Sunday Hindustan Times*, New Delhi, September 14, 2003.
40. Ibid.
41. Fred Weir, *Christian Science Monitor*, April 18, 2002, Source: http://www.csmonitor.com/2002/0418/p06s02-woeu.html.
42. Ibid.
43. Ibid.
44. The Russian Cross - Do-it-yourself-genocide, February 21, 2001, Source: *http://www.1hla.org/world/dsparticle.cfm var=14.*
45. Source: Dr A P Joshi, M D Srinivas and J K Bajaj, *Religious Demography of India*, p. 335, table D-35b South Europe.
46. Oriana Fallaci, The Rage, the Pride and the Doubt. Thoughts on the eve of battle in Iraq, *WSJ.com Opinion Journal*, March 29, 2003.
47. Rashmee Z. Ahmed, 'Europe expectantly longs for a demographic bulge', *The Times of India*, New Delhi, p.15, October 5, 2003.
48. Ibid.
49. Richard Bernstein, Ageing Europe Finds Its Pension Is Running Out, *The New York Times*, June 29, 2003.
50. Ibid.
51. Ibid.
52. Ibid.
53. Ibid
54. *The Asian Age*, June 28, 2003, 'U.K. booklet on threat of Islamists may whip passions', p.3.

55. Ibid.
56. *The New York Times*, November 2, 1997.
57. Source: Australian Population Facts, www.cqnet.com.au/ —user/ dancasey/ Population_control.html].
58. Ibid.
59. *Sunday Mail*, Sydney, November 21, 1999.
60. Australian Population Facts, *www.cqnet.au/—user/dancasey/ Population control.html.*
61. Dr A. P. Joshi, M D Srinivas and J.K. Bajaj, *Religious Demography of India*, pp.8-9.
62. Ibid, p. 21, table 2.2.
63. Ibid, p.27, table 2.7a.
64. Ibid, p.31, table 2.11.
65. Ibid, p.32.
66. Source: Ibid, p.31, Table 2.11.
67, Ibid, pp.32-33.
68. Ahtesham Qureshi, *The Hindustan Times*, New Delhi, July 9, 1995.
69. Source: http://www.cqnet.com.au/-user/dancasey/ Population control.html.
70. Source: *http://www.suntimes.com/output/news/mus02.html.*
71. Steven A Camarota, 'The Muslim Wave: Dealing with Immigration from the Middle East', *National Review*, Issue: Sept 16, 2002.
72. Ibid.
73. Ibid.
74. Source: A.P. Joshi, M.D. Srinivas and J.K. Bajaj, *Religious Demography of India*, (Religious Demography of the World), p. 340, table D-36:North America.
75. Rachel L. Swarns, '13,000 Arabs & Muslims in U.S. face deportation', New York Times Service - Source: *The Asian Age*, June 9, 2003.

76. Ibid.
77. Ibid.
78. *Pentagon Files* - Population Control as a Military Issue, Source: *http://www.africa2000.com/INDX/pentagon.htm.*
79. Ibid.
80. Ibid.
81. Ibid.
82. Ibid.
83. Demographics of Investments, *The Business Standard*, New Delhi, May 22, 2003.
84. Ibid.
85. Source: Dr. A.P. Joshi, M.D. Srinivas and J.K. Bajaj, *Religious Demography of India*, p.328, table D-34e West Africa.
86. Source: Dr. A.P. Joshi, M.D. Srinivas and J.K. Bajaj, *Religious Demography of India*, p.328, table D-34e West Africa.
87. Yashwant Singh, At $1.5 trillion, terrorism is the world's largest private business, *The Hindustan Times*, New Delhi, November 23, 2003.

Chapter – 7

1. A.P. Joshi, M D Srinivas and J.K. Bajaj, *Religious Demography of India*, p.21, Source, table 2.2 : Religious Composition of India (Percentage Distribution,1881-1941.
2. Ibid, p.22, Source, Table 2.3: Rates of Growth of Different Religious Communities, 1881-1941.
3. Ibid, p.25, Source: Table: 2.6: Religious Composition of Indian Union, 1991-1941, in thousands.
4. Ibid, p. 27, Source: table 2.7a: Religious Composition of Indian Union, 1951-1991 (for the total estimated population, in thousands).

5. Ibid, pp.27-28.
6. Ibid, p.35.
7. Ibid.
8. Ibid, p.199, Source: table: D-9.
9. Dr. A. P. Joshi, M.D. Srinivas and J.K. Bajaj, *Religious Demography of India*, p. 96.
10. Ibid.
11. Ibid, p.95.
12. Sandhya Jain, Political lesson of demography, *The Pioneer, New Delhi*, August 26, 2003.
13. Ibid.
14. Ibid.
15. Ibid.
16. Hiranmay Karlekar, Deal carefully with Dhaka, *The Pioneer, New Delhi* May 16, 2003.
17. Source: A.P. Joshi, M D Srinivas and J.K. Bajaj, Religious *Demography of India*, p.319, table 33e: West Asia.
18. Ibid, Source: p.313, table: D-33b: Southeast Asia.
19. Ibid, p.328, Source: table D-34c : West Africa.
20. Akbar S. Ahmed, *Islam Under Siege* (Published in 2003 by Blackwell Publishing Ltd., U.K., and Vistaar Publications, New Delhi, in India), p.7, Introduction.
21. Ibid.
22. Samuel P. Huntington, *The Clash of Civilizations and the Remaking of World Order*, p.126.
23. Ibid.
24. Ibid.
25. Balbir K. Punj, Right remedy wrong diagnosis, *The Asian Age*, New Delhi, June 10, 2003.
26. Ibid.

27. Y.B. Mathur, *Muslims and Changing India*, p.1, footnote.
28. Ibid, p.2, Source: Government of India's Note dated 6.10.1893. Home Political Proceeding Nos. 169-89 dated November 1893.
29. Ibid, pp. 3-4.
30. Dr. B. R. Ambedkar, *Pakistan or Partition of India*, p. 154.
31. Ibid, p. 155
32. Bibhuti Bhusan Nandy, Space Invaders, *The Hindustan Times*, New Delhi, February 14, 2003}.
33. Ibid.
34. Bhadra Sinha, 'Can't deport Bangladeshi immigrants', *The Times of India*, New Delhi, September 25, 2003.
35. Ibid.
36. Reeta Sharma, Fernandes confirms Bangla infiltration, *The Pioneer*, New Delhi, September 29, 2003.
37. A news item captioned 'Bangla migrant issue alarming says CPM finally', *The Economic Times, New Delhi*, July 15, 2002.
38. Bibhuti Bhusan Nandy, Space invaders, *The Hindustan Times*, New Delhi, February 14, 2003.
39. Ibid.
40. News Item titled 'Sangma: Laden is financing Bangla madaris', *The Asian Age*, New Delhi, September 20, 2003.
41. Bibhuti Bhusan Nandy, Space invaders, *The Hindustan Times*, New Delhi, February 14, 2003.
42. PTI news item captioned 'Ayodhya on terror hit list', *The Pioneer*, New Delhi, September 15, 2003.
43. Balbir K. Punj, 'The Secular Trojan Horse, *The Asian Age*, New Delhi, September 30, 2003.
44. Ibid.

45. Ibid.

46. Ibid.

47. Mahatma Gandhi, *To the Protagonist of Pakistan*, p.204 (Gandhi Series, Vol. V), edited and published by Anand T Hingorani, Karachi. January 26, 1947 : Sole Distributors Rupa & Co., Calcutta, Ahmedabad.

48. Times News Network, 'Israeli guns to guard Tirupati deity', *Times of India*, New Delhi, p.8, August 20, 2003.

49. Dr. B.R. Ambedkar, *Pakistan or Partition of India*, p.44, Source: Dr. Titus, Medieval India, p.24.

50. Ibid, p. 44.

51. Prafulla Goradia, A war graver than any other, *The Pioneer*, New Delhi, September 30, 2003, Source: Dhananjay Keer's Ambedkar, pp. 399, as referred to in the *Free Press Journal*, November 28, 1947.

52. Ibid.

53. Will Durant, *The Story of Civilization*, Part I, p.459.

54. Francois Gautier, Learning from History, *The Pioneer, New Delhi*, September 3, 2003.

55. Ibid.

56. G. Parthasarthy, 'Pakistan's guns and poses', *The Pioneer*, New Delhi, September 11, 2003.

57. Rizwan Salim, Heritage – What the invaders really did, *The Hindustan Times, December 28, 1997.*

58. Ibid.

59. Ibid.

60. Will Durant, *The Story of Civilization*, part I, p. 480, Source: Watters, i.340.

61. Ibid, p. 441.

62. Ibid.

63. Ibid.

64. Ibid.
65. Ibid, p. 528.
66. Ibid, p. 528, Source: Monier Williams, 183-4.
67. Rizwan Salim, Heritage - What the invaders really did, *Hindustan Times*, New Delhi, December 28, 1997.
68. Ibid.
69. Ibid.
70. Will Durant, *The Story of Civilization*, part I, p.462.
71. 'Population Control - it is killing us !' The reality behind the overpopulation myth: Source: *http://www.cqnet.com.au/ -user/dancasey/Population_control.html*
72. Ibid.
73. Ibid.
74. Ibid, Source: Catholic Family & Human Rights Institute, March 13, 2002.
75. A.P., Bric by bric - How the world will change, The *Business Standard*, New Delhi, October 16, 2003, p.7.
76. Ibid.
77. Ibid.
78. Bernard Lewis, *The Crisis of Islam, Holy War and Unholy Terror*, p. 85.
79. Ibid.
80. Jonas Widgren, the statement made at the Stability Pact Regional meeting on Co-operation in South Eastern Europe to Stabilize Population Movement, Tirana, December 12-13, 2002 (source: www.icmpd.org)

Chapter – 8

1. TAKE 2, *The Economic Times*, New Delhi, April 24, 2003.
2. Dr. B.R. Ambedkar, *Pakistan or Partition of India*, p. 285.

3. Ibid, p. 287.
4. Ibid.
5. Jeffrey Goldberg, Pakistan's Jehad Machines, *Readers Digest*, February 2002, p. 148.
6. Ibid.
7. Ibid.
8. Dr. Y.B. Mathur, *Muslims and Changing India*, p.59: Source, Sharp H., Progress of Education in India, 1907-12, para 601, Calcutta, 1912.
9. Ardeshir Cowasjee, First Teach your Class V Students, General, *The Asian Age, New Delhi*, June 16, 2003, published by arrangements with Dawn.
10. Mushirul Haq, *Islam and Secular India*, p.32.
11. Terror Tentacles, editorial in *The Pioneer, New Delhi,* October 15, 2002.
12. Ibid.
13. Amir Taheri, Guest Column, The Saudi's Islamist Frankstein, *Hindustan Times*, November 16, 2003, p.10.
14. Sulaiman Al- Hattlan, 'Homegrown Fanatics', *The New York Times*, May 15, 2003].
15. Ibid.
16. Brian Bennet/Bombay, with reporting by Nelli Sindyan/ Zamboanga City and Amzad Hussain/ Dacca, Wahabism-Money Trail, TIME, March 10, 2003, p.27.
17. TIME, March 10, 2003, p.27.
18. TIME, March 10, 2003.
19. Firuz Kazemzadeh, *The Baha'is in Iran : Twenty Years of Repression* (non-Muslim religious minority), *Social Research*, Issue: Summer, 2000 (source: www.FindArticles.com).
20. Ibid.

21 Dr. B. R. Ambedkar, *Pakistan or Partition of India*, p.215.

22. Ibid, p. 220.

23. Ibid, p, 223.

24. Haifzur Rahman, It's not easy being a Pak minority, View from Pakistan, *The Asian Age, New Delhi,* July 9, 2003 – by arrangement with the Dawn.

25. Ibid.

26. Ibid.

27. Ahmed Rashid, *Taliban, Islam Oil and the New Great Game in Central Asia,* p.106.

28. UNOCHA statement, October 1996.

29. UNICEF statement, December 11, 1998.

30. Ahmed Rashid, *Taliban, Islam Oil ad the New Great Game in Central Asia,* p. 65.

31. Oriana Fallaci, *The Rage and the Pride*, pp. 107-110.

32. Poornima Joshi, *The Sunday Hindustan Times*, Nov. 4, 2001.

33. M. Saleem Pandit, *Veil of Fear Back in J&K, The Times of India*, New Delhi, December 26, 2002.

34. Ibid.

35. The Times News Service, *Times of India, New Delhi*, p.10, April 24, 2003.

36. Ibid.

37. Times News Service, *Times of India*, New Delhi, p.10, April 24, 2003.

38. Oriana Fallaci, *The Rage And The Pride*, p.64.

39. Michael Peel, 'Counsel for the Condemned', Lunch with Hauwa Ibrahim, *The Business Standard, June 2, 2003*, p. 6 (reproduced from The Financial Times).

40. Ibid.

41. 'Pak province goes the Taliban way', a news item in *Times of India,* June 4, 2003, p.15.

42. Sherry Rehman, Under the Shariat axe, *The Indian Express*, June 9, 2003.

43. Ibid.

44. *Jihad in the Qur'an and Sunnah* by Sheikh Abdullah Bin Muhammad Bin Humaid (ex-Chief Justice of Saudi Arabia, (source: website http://www.engr.csufresno.edu/^msa/articles/jihad.html).

45. John K. Cooley, *Unholy Wars: Afghanistan, America and International Terrorism,* p.185.

46. *The Pioneer*, New Delhi, March 30, 2003.

47. A news item, Militants cut off Doda man's ears, nose and tongue - *The Asian Age*, New Delhi, April 19, 2003.

48. Oriana Fallaci, *The Rage and the Pride*, pp. 101-102.

49. The Pioneer March 25, 2003.

50. *Jihad in the Quran and Sunnah* by Sheikh Abdullah Bin Muhammad Bin Humaid, ex-Chief Justice of Saudi Arabia.

51. Samuel P. Huntington *The Clash of Civilizations and the Remaking of World* Order, p.258.

52. Ibid, p.269.

53. Ibid.

54. Alija Izetbegovic, *The Islamic Declaration* (1991), pp. 23, 33.

55. Dr. B. R. Ambedkar, *Pakistan or Partition of India*, p.325.

56. Ibid.

57. Dr. B.R. Ambedkar, *Pakistan or Partition of India*, pp. 295-296, Source: 'Through Indian Eyes', Times of India, March 11, 1924.

58. Ibid, p. 296.

59. Samuel P. Huntington, *The Clash of Civilizations and Remaking of the World Order*, pp.112-113.

60. Scot Atran, Who Wants to Be a Martyr?, *New York Times*, May 5, 2003.

61. Ibid.

62. Alan B Krueger, Poverty Doesn't Create Terrorists, *The New York Times*, June 13, 2003.

63. Pendrel Moon, *Divide and Quit*, p.11.

64. V.S. Naipaul, *Among the Believers, An Islamic Journey*, p.344, part IV.

65. Ibid.

66. A news item 'Naipaul spits fire on Pak', *The Economic Times*, New Delhi, October 5, 2001.

67. Appendix - II, p.395

68. Suhas Majumdar, *Jihad, The Islamic Doctrine of Permanent War*, p.74.

Chapter – 9

1. Gopal Das Khosla, *Stern Reckoning*, Appendix-I, p. 303, *The Partition Omnibus*, Oxford University Press, New Delhi, published in 2002.

2. P.N. Khera, Will the ceasefire hold? *The Pioneer*, New Delhi, December 12, 2003, Source: Asia Times Online.

3. Ibid.

Chapter – 10

1. Don Van Natta Jr. and Desmond Butler, Jihadi hunters flock to Iraq, *The Sunday Hindustan Times*, New Delhi, November 2, 2003, p.11.

2. Ibid.

3. Ibid.

4. Bernard Lewis, *Holy War and Unholy Terror*, p. 122.

5. Ibid.

6. A news item ‘Fusion Terrorism A Reality, Warns IAEA’, *The Economic Times*, New Delhi, November 2, 2001.
7. Ibid.
8. Ibid.
9. Ibid.
10. A news item, Pak scientist offered Saddam nuclear designs, The Indian Express, New Delhi, source: http:// www.expressindia.com/fullstory.php.
11. Manoj Joshi, Lashkar chief claims to have Nuclear weapons, *Times of India*, New Delhi, June 7, 2003.
12. News item by PTI, U.S., Russia fear Pak nukes may fall into terrorists hands, *The Asian Age*, New Delhi, September 18, 2003.
13. Arnaud de Borchgrave, Pakistan, Saudi Arabia in secret nuke pact, *The Washington Times*, October 22, 2003.
14. Ibid.
15. Ali Al-Amin Mazrui, *Cultural Forces in World Politics* (London: J. Currey, 1990), pp.220, 224.

Appendix - I

Terrorist/Extremist Outfits of Radical Islam across the Globe

(Note : Terrorist organizations banned by the Government of India have (*) asterisk placed before their names, while those banned by the U.S. Government have (#) hash placed before their names)

Afghanistan

\# 1. Al-Qaeda (Osama bin Laden's global terrorist organisation)

2. Hizb-e-Islami (Gulbudin Hekmatyar's terrorist outfit - terrorist outfit)

3. Taliban (Splinter groups and remnants of Taliban left in Afghanistan)

Algeria

\# 4. Armed Islamic Group (GIA) : The Algerian Armed Islamic Group is known by its French initials GIA. This outfit has a French nomenclature. It is a well known transnational Algerian terrorist group - had robbed some banks in Belgium, set up their branches/cells in the U.K., tried to bomb the Los Angeles airport and their volunteers fought in Bosnia and Afghanistan

5. Islamic Salvation Front (FIS)

6. National Liberation Army (FLN)

Bangladesh

7. Harkat-ul-Jihad-al Islami (HUJI, an ISI sponsored militant outfit)
8. Hizb–ut Tawhid (a radical group which aims at establishing a fundamentalist Islamic regime in Bangladesh through terrorism and insurgency)
9. Islami Chhatra Shibir (a militant anti-Hindu outfit of Muslim student)
10. Islamic Shasantantra Andolan (a radical outfit affiliated to the Bangladesh's four party ruling alliance government under Khalida Zia)
11. Shahadat-e-al-Hikima (of Syed Kawsar Hussain who on Feb. 6, 2003 laid claim to W. Bengal saying the it should be part of the Islamic state of Bangladesh)

Note: According to an intelligence report by now Bangladesh has about 50 small, but active militant groups boasting a membership of one lakh. {Source: a news item 'Bangla cracks down on terror groups, *The Asian Age*, New Delhi, October 6, 2003, p.5}

Egypt

\# 12. Gama' al-Islamiyya (The Islamic Group, IG)
13. Al-Takfir wa'l Hijra (Withdrawal and Flight - after attacking)
\# 14. All Jihad Group.
15. Muslim Brotherhood (presently less active)
16. The Jihadi Movement Bureau set up by Al Zawahiri in 1980 to upgrade foreign liaison, supply of weapons and financial assistance to various ongoing jihads in various countries)

India

* 17. Al-Umar Mujahideen
18. Adam Sena (an ISI sponsored North-East based militant Islamist group)
19. Ahle-e-Hadees

20. Al Badr (A Pakistan-based outfit which operates in Jammu &Kashmir also)

21. Al Jihad Force (Pakistan based group which combines Muslim Janbaz Force and Kashmir Jihad Force both of which operate in J&K)

22. Al Mansurian - A terrorist outfit active in Kashmir, responsible for trying to attack Mufti Mohd. Sayeed's residence - an offshoot of Lashkar-e Tayyeba. One Abu Shakir, a spokesman of the group claimed that their target on October 17,2003 was the Chief Minister's residence, but the two gunmen stormed the wrong building.

23. Al Nasirin - A terrorist group operating in J&K - associated with LeT of Pakistan.

24. Al Ummah - A Tamil Nadu-based outfit responsible for 1997 Coimbatore blasts (formed in 1993 by S.A. Basha)

25. All Parties Hurriyat Conference (It appears to have intimate contacts with Pakistan and perhaps with the ISI)

26. Allah Tigers (A Tamil Nadu-based outfit)

* 27. Deendar Anjuman (a South-India based radical Islamist group)

28. Dukhtran-e-Millat (a radical Islamist outfit of Muslim women functioning in accordance with the diktats of Pak-sponsored terrorists groups operating in J&K)

29. Farzandan–e-Millat - A radical group of Islamists, active in J&K, closely associated with Jaish-e-Mohammed and Lashkar-e-Tayyeba.

30. Gujarat Revenge Force (Supposed to be set up by one Nissar in Mumbai in Sept. 2002 - responsible for many Mumbai bomb blasts-Nisar shuttles between Dubai & India)

31. Harkat–ul-Jihad (another ISI sponsored radical Islamist outfit functioning in north–east and operating in tandem with radical Islamist Bangladeshi groups)

32. Harkat-ul-Jihad-e-Islami (A Pakistan based outfit operating in J&K)

33. Harkat–ul-Jihad (Huj - a North-East based ISI sponsored outfit functioning in tandem with radical Islamist groups of Bangladesh)

* 34. Harkat-ul-Mujahideen / Harkat-ul-Ansar / Harkat-ul-Jihad-e-Islami

* 35. Hizb-ul-Mujahideen (A Kashmir based terrorist outfit supported by Pakistan)

36. Islamic Liberation Army of Assam (An Assam-based pro-Bangladeshi outfit)

* 37. Jaish-e-Mohammed/Tehrik-e-Furgan (now Markaz-ul-Dawa Irshad, a Pakistan based outfit of Maulana Masood Azhar which operates in Jammu & Kashmir as well as in India)

* 38. Jammu & Kashmir Islamic Front

39. Lashkar-e-Jabbar (A Pakistan-based outfit which operates in J&K)

40. Lashkar-e-Omar (A Kashmir-based terror group supported by the ISI)

* 41. Lashkar-e-Tayyeba (A dangerous Pakistan-based outfit operating in India & Jammu & Kashmir which is also known as Pasban-e-Ahle Hadis)

42. Mahaz-e-Azadi (Pakistan-based group operating in J&K)

43. Muslim Defence Force (A radical Islamist outfit)

44. Muslim Security Force (An Assam-based radical outfit)

45. Muslim Tiger Force (A North-East-based pro-Bangladeshi outfit)

46. Muslim United Liberation Front (A North-East-based militant Islamist group)

* 47. Students Islamic Movement of India (SIMI). (It aims at establishing an Islamic socio-political order in India. It has been named in many cases of terrorism).

48. Tablighi Jamaat (A radical proselytizing Islamic group having international contacts with terrorist outfits).

49. Tamil Islamic Pervai (A Tamil Nadu based radical group)
50. Tehrik-e-Qisas (A newly formed terrorist group operating in Maharashtra and Gujarat)
51. United Muslim Liberation Front of Assam (UMLFA, a radical Islamist group of Assam)

Indonesia

52. Jemmah Islamya - An associate outfit of Al Qaeda.
53. Laskar Jihad - Was responsible for killing thousands of Christians of Sulawesi Island.

Lebanon

\# 54. Asbat al-Ansar (a hardliner Sunni extremist group)
55. Fatah Revolutionary Council (Abu Nidal's Organisation)
\# 56. Hizbollah (The Party of God)

Pakistan

57. Ahl-e-Hadith
58. Al Badr
59. Al Baraq
60. Al Jihad
61. Al Jihad Force (Combines Muslim Janbaz Force & Kashmir Jihad Force)
62. Al Mujahid Force
63. Al Mustafa Liberation Fighters
64. Al Qaeda (originally set up in Peshawar - now it has branches wordwide)
65. Al Umar Mujahideen
66. Al-Rashid Trust (A notorious financial group supporting Islamist terrorist groups in many countries)
67. Brigade 313 - A new radical group suspected of complicity in the recent attacks on Musharraf.

68. Harkat-ul-Ansar (presently known as Harkat-ul Mujahideen)
69. Harkat-ul-Jihad-I-Islami
70. Harkat-ul-Mujahideen or HUM (previously known as Harkat-ul-Ansar)
71. Hizb-ul-Mujahideen / Hizb-ul-Mujahideen Pir Panjal Regiment
72. Ikhwan-ul-Mujahideen
73. Islami Inquilabi Mahaz
74. Islamic Jihad of Pakistan (of Qazi Hussain Ahmed)
75. Islamic Students League
76. Islami-Jamaat-e-Tulba
77. Jaish-e-Mohammed Mujahideen-e-Tanzeem/Tehrik-e Furqan (Maulana Masood Azhar's dangerous outfit)
78. Jamait-ul-Majahideen
79. Jamiat-e-Ulema-e-Islam (a radical outfit led by Maulana Fazlur–Rahman)
80. Jammu & Kashmir National Liberation Army
81. Jammu & Kashmir Student Liberation Front
82. Kashmir Jihad Force
83. Khuddam-ul- Islam (It is probably a new name for the banned Jaish-e-Muhammad)
84. Lashkar-e-Jabbar
85. Lashkar-e-Jhangvi (a radical sunni outfit trageting Shias)
86. Lashkar-e-Omar
87. Lashkar-e-Tayyeba / Pasban-e-Ahle Hadees (now renamed Markaz-ul Dawa Irshad)
88. Mahaz-e-Azadi
89. Millat-e-Islamia
90. Muslim Janbaz Force
91. Muslim Mujahideen
92. Muttahida Jihad Council (MJC)

93. Rabita Trust (a pan-Islamic financial support group based in Saudi Arabia)
94. Sipah-e-Muhammad Pakistan (SMP)
95. Sipah-e-Sahiba Pakistan (a radical Sunni outfit operating against Shias)
96. Tehirk-e-Jafria Pakistan (a radical Shia group earlier known as Fiqah-e-Jafria)
97. Tehrik-e-Hurriyat-e-Kashmir
98. Tehrik-e-Islami Pakistan
99. Tehrik-e-Jihad-e-Islami
100. Tehrik-e-Nafaz-e-Shariat-e-Mohammed
101. Tehrik-e-Nifaz-Fiqar Jafaria
102. Tehrik-ul-Mujahideen
103. Ummah Tamir-e-Nau

Also there are two mutually warring groups of Mohajirs, both Karachi-based, namely MQM (Altaf Hussain) and MQM Haqiqi. The latter is a pro-government splinter group.

Palestine

#104. Abu Nidal Organization (A.N.O.)
#105. Al Aqsa Martyrs Brigade
106. Democratic Front for Liberation of Palestine
107. Fatah Tanzeem
108. Force 17
#109. Hamas (An ultra radical outfit - also known as Islamic Resistance Movement)
#110. Hizbullah (An associate group of the Lebanon-based radical group Hizbollah)
111. Palestine Liberation Organisation (P.L.O. of Yasser Arafat)
#112. Palestinian Islamic Jihad (P.I.J. of Fathi Shkaki)
#113. Popular Front for Liberation of Palestine (PFLP)
#114. PFLP - General Command (PFLP – GC)

Philippines

#115. Abu Sayyaf Group (An outfit led by Abu Sayyaf of Peshawar in Pakistan which had fought against Russians in Afghanistan, now fighting in the Philippines)

116. Moro Islamic Liberation Front (MILF) - trying to secede from the Philippines.

United Kingdom

117. Al Muhajiroun - A London-based radical outfit of migrant Muslims formed by Omar Bakri - has been trying to glorify the attackers of 9/11.

118. Hizb-ut-Tihrir - A London-based radical Islamist group - in touch with many radical groups operating from other countries.

Uzbekistan

119. Hizb-ut-Tahrir (An Islamist group trying to promote radicalism in Uzbekistan).

#120. Islamic Movement of Uzbekistan.

Other Countries

121. Al Waqf-al-Islami Foundation. It is a radical group based in Netherlands which has been very active in training and indoctrinating Islamic militants in the Al-Furqan mosque in Eindhovan (Netherlands). Some of the attackers of September 11, 2001, had attended the lectures in Al-Furqan mosque.

122. Armed Islamic Movement (of Afghan Arabs)

123. Asbat al-Ansar

124. Committee for the Defence of Legitimate Rights (based in Switzerland)

125. Eritertean Islamic Jihad (Eriterea)

126. Geneva-based Al Jihad

127. International Legion (Brigade of Islam)

128. International Muslim Brotherhood of Adrian Sadedine
129. IRGS (Pasdran of Iran)
130. Islamic Liberation Party of Somalia
131. Malay Kumpulan Mujahideen of Malayasia
132. Al Nahadha of Tunisia
133. Popular International Organisation of Sudan (Turabi led PIO)
134. The Islamic Change Movement (Jihadi Wing of Arabian Peninsula)
135. Gerakan Mjuahideen Islam Pattani (G.M.I.P.) of Thailand - A dangerous radical group, which attacked a Battalion Headquarter of Thai army on Jauary 4, 2004, and killed four soldiers. Is active in Narathiwat province of southern Thailand and has close ties with groups of Malaysian Mujahideen.

Appendix - II

Jihads being waged by Islamic Terrorist/Outfits Across the Globe

1	Algeria	The radical groups like GIA (the Armed Islamic Movement), the Islamic Front led by Ali Belhaj and Al Takfir-Wal-Hijrah have been mounting sporadic attacks on governmental institutions and military posts and government officers. For sometime the GIA was able to push the country into a virtual civil war in which approximately 60,000 or more lives were lost. Even now the terrorists hold sway in several rural pockets. The terror groups have been pushing for establishing a fundamentalist Islamic government in Algeria.
2.	Azerbaijan and Armenia	There have been faultline conflicts between the Muslim dominated state of Azerbaijan and the neighbouring Christian Armenia. The tension between the two neighbours continues and there are frequent conflicts.
3.	The Balkans	Religion-based faultline conflicts between the Serbs and the Bosnian and Albanian Muslims have been going on. Secession of Bosnia and Kosovo from Serbia led to a civil war. Macedonia which has seen a quantum jump

	in Muslim population, now at 30 percent with Christians down from 90 percent to 67 percent, is likely to face major conflicts.
4. Chechenya (Russia)	On Sept. 6, 1991, Chechen militants declared the establishment of the Chechen Republic of Ichkeria, independent of Russia. Since then the Chechen Muslims have been involved in guerrilla warfare and terror attacks on the Russian troops and civilians even in Moscow, now for almost 15 years. Some Chechens call this jihad as 'ghazwah' (a jihad led by the Prophet).
5. Dagestan (former USSR)	Attempts are being made by militant Islamist outfits to turn Dagestan into a fundamentalist Sharia-based Islamic country.
6. East Timor & Indonesia	The conflict between the Christian state of East Timor and the Muslim dominated Indonesia continues to erupt every now and then.
7. Egypt	Egypt has been the breeding ground of militant Islamists for the last 30 years. Several radical outfits like *Al-Gama'ah al-Islamiyyah,* Muslim Brotherhood, Egyptian Muslim Jihad and *Tala'i al-Fateh* (Vanguard of the Conquest) have been working for the establishment of a fundamentalist regime in Egypt. The Egyptian jihadis were responsible for setting up many training camps in Pakistan and Afghanistan with the help of Pakistani establishment, especially the ISI. They have been in the forefront of planning and execution of terrorist attacks, including the bombing of World Trade Center in New York in the year 1993. One of the top associates of Bin Laden is Dr. Ayman al Zawahiri, an Egyptian Islamist. A prominent terror attack carried out by 'Al-Gama' Ah

		al-Islamiyyah was the attempt made in 1995 to assassinate Hosni Mubarak during his visit to Ethiopia. Al Qaida has a fairly large number of Egyptian militants.
8.	Ethiopia and Eritrea	Clashes between the Christian Ethiopia and Muslim Eritrea have been breaking out often. The hostilities between the two neighbouring countries, one Christian and the other a Muslim, have been going on for some time now.
9.	India	Pakistan-sponsored Islamic militancy for the annexation of Kashmir has been there for a long time now. A jihad has been going on since October 1947. India is now being regularly targeted by terrorist groups like Jaish-e-Mohammed, Lashkar-e-Tayyeba and Students Islamic Movement of India. There have been a series of bomb blasts in Mumbai, New Delhi, Coimbatore, Ahmedabad and many other cities. There were many terrorist attacks, including the one on the Indian Parliament on Dec. 13, 2001; prior to that on Oct. 1, 2001, there was an attack on the Jammu & Kashmir Assembly. There were attacks on Raghunathji and Akshardham temples and Hindu pilgrims going to Amarnath and Vaishnodevi have been regularly targeted and many killed. Also there have been a number of bombings in Mumbai, Delhi and Jammu.
10.	Indonesia	A number of Islamist terrorists, especially Jemmah-e Islamiya and Laskar Jihad have been taking recourse to suicide bombings and multiple attacks on western tourists. In October 2002 an attack was made on Kuta Beach, and on August 2003 an attack was made at Hotel J.W. Marriott in Jakarta. The

		radical Islamic movement is on upswing now. Hostility towards the Chinese and other minorities often leads to violence.
11.	Iraq (West Asia)	Jihad was declared against the U.S.- led coalition forces by Islamic militants groups. Since then, suicide bombings and guerrilla warfare is going on.
12.	Nigeria Sokoto Jihad Vs Christians of Southern Nigeria	The religion-based faultline conflicts between the Muslim dominated northern states and the Christian dominated South are rapidly increasing. There have been many clashes between the two communities. Sometime ago there were riots over organising the Miss World contest sponsored by a privately-run commercial organisation. Now with Muslim numbers touching fifty per cent of Nigeria's total population the faultline conflicts between the two hostile religious groups seem to be escalating.
13.	Palestine (West Asia)	It is a 55-year old religion-based conflict between Israel and terror groups like HAMAS, Palestinian Islamic Jihad and Martyrs of Al Aqsa, etc. (a jihad against Jews has been going on).
14.	The Philippines	The Jihad against the Christian regime by the Moro Islamic Liberation Front and the Abu Sayyaf-led extremist outfit for secession from the Philippines and for establishing an independent Islamic Moro country.
15.	Sudan & Ethiopia	There are growing conflicts between the Islamic Sudan and Christian dominated Ethiopia. It is an old faultline conflict which refuses to die down.
16.	Tajikistan	Growing Sunni radical groups will continue to disturb peace in this area. There are likely be many faultline conflicts between the moderates and the extremists in Tajikistan.

17.	Tunisia	A number of Tunisian fundamentalists trained in Pakistan and Afghanistan for waging a jihad against Russians in Afghanistan returned to Tunisia after victory in Afghan jihad. They formed a terrorist outfit called '*Al Nahdha*' and tried to overthrow the liberal Tunisian regime to set up an Islamic government - based on Sharia. In May 1992 an attempt was made to shoot down the aeroplane carrying the Tunisian President, Ben Ali. Many Terrorist groups have been banned and their leaders arrested. The head of Al–Nahdha, Rashid Ghannushi and many prominent terrorist leaders have fled abroad.
18.	Turkey	The hostility between Turkey and Greece, especially in relation to the Cyprus continues. Even otherwise the Islamist influence is growing fast and Turkey could face faultline conflicts. Recent examples of a double bomb hit at two synagogues on November 15, 2003, and bombing of British consulate and Hongkong & Shanghai Bank on November 20, 2003, show the growth of terrorism in Turkey.
19.	Uzbekistan	Radical Islam has been gaining ground in Uzbekistan also. A militant organization by the name Hizb-ut Tehrir has been trying to overthrow the present pro-Russia liberal dictatorial regime.
20.	Xinjiang region of China	The faultline conflicts between the Uighur Muslim militants of Xingiang and the Chinese government continue to surface now and then. This ethnic and religion-based militancy still continues in Western China.

Note : Apart from the jihads at present being waged in the above mentioned 20 countries the Islamists are also waging jihad against the present regimes in Saudi Arabia, Jordan, Yemen, Morocco and Turkmenistan. Attempts to speed up the process of Islamization in Bangladesh, Malaysia and Indonesia by stepping up terror activities are also afoot. With an attack on a Brigade headquarters of Thai army on January 4, 2004, a new wave of Islamist terror in Southern Thailand is feared.

Index